· · · **WAY OUT THERE** · · ·

EDITED BY JAMES LITTLE

WAY OUT THERE
THE BEST OF explore

GREYSTONE BOOKS

Douglas & McIntyre Publishing Group

Vancouver / Toronto / Berkeley

06 07 08 09 10   5 4 3 2 1

Greystone Books
A division of Douglas & McIntyre Ltd.
2323 Quebec Street, Suite 201
Vancouver, British Columbia
Canada V5T 4S7
www.greystonebooks.com

Library and Archives Canada Cataloguing in Publication
Way out there : the best of Explore / James Little and the editors of Explore.

ISBN-13:978-1-55365-164-2 · ISBN-10: 1-55365-164-2

1. Voyages and travels. 2. Outdoor recreation. 3. Outdoor life.
4. Natural history. I. Little, James, 1959–
GV191.2.E962 2006   910.4   C2005-907466-3

Cover design by Jessica Sullivan & Naomi MacDougall
Cover photographs: top: © S. Kotoh/zefa/CORBIS;
bottom: © Michael DeYoung/CORBIS
Text design by Peter Cocking
Printed and bound in Canada by Friesens
Printed on acid-free paper that is forest friendly
(100% post-consumer recycled paper)
and has been processed chlorine free.
Distributed in the U.S. by Publishers Group West

The publishers gratefully acknowledge the financial support
of the Canada Council for the Arts, the British Columbia Arts Council,
and the Government of Canada through the Book Publishing Industry
Development Program (BPIDP) for our publishing activities.

explore magazine is published six times a year and is available on newsstands
across Canada. For more information, visit www.explore-mag.com.

CONTENTS

INTRODUCTION

DURING MY TENURE as editor of *explore* magazine, I've had writers approach me with some pretty unusual story ideas. One of the strangest came from Mike Randolph, the magazine's intrepid editor-at-large. A number of years ago, Mike asked whether I'd be interested in a feature on eels. More specifically, a piece about him going to New Zealand to swim with giant eels—apparently toothy and aggressive creatures—so that he might then catch one and eat it. I have to admit that at first, I wasn't too keen. I worried that our readers might find a story about eating a giant eel a bit, shall we say, distasteful. Hell, I worried that even *I* might find such a story distasteful. But Mike felt strongly that his eel quest would make for an interesting and entertaining tale, and the resulting story—"In Search of the Giant Eel," included in this collection— is that and more. Strange yes, but also fascinating, and written with a healthy sense of both humour and adventure. It's the kind of piece that once read cannot be forgotten.

The same can be said of many of the stories *explore* has published over the years. Partly this is because of our subject matter. We like to describe ourselves as a magazine dedicated to outdoor adventure, and we tend to interpret that mission rather broadly. In recent years, our writers have travelled to the front lines of Sudan's long-running civil war, to the snowy backcountry of the Rocky Mountains and to the remotest islands of the South Pacific. They've reported on human-powered speed competitions in a desolate corner of the Nevada desert, marathon swimming in the potentially heart-stopping cold of a Quebec lake and the experience of sailing through a hurricane in the North Atlantic. And they've searched for a supposedly extinct dog breed, the oldest rock in the world, a mysterious mountaintop monolith and even the Holy Grail itself.

Intriguing subjects all, but what really makes these stories memorable is the writing. We at *explore* have been fortunate to attract many of Canada's finest magazine writers to our pages. Between 2001 and 2004 alone, these correspondents earned 57 National Magazine Award nominations and picked up seven Gold awards and eight Silvers. It's largely thanks to our writers that the Canadian Society of Magazine Editors named *explore* the Best Magazine of the Year in 2002, 2003 and 2005.

One of the few frustrations of editing this magazine is knowing that the extraordinary stories our writers have worked so hard to create will more or less disappear once an issue is no longer on the newsstands. Which is why we wanted to preserve some of these pieces in the more permanent pages of a book. The occasion of the magazine's 25th anniversary in 2006 gave us just the excuse we needed.

A lot of people deserve thanks for making this book possible, not least the magazine's current owner and publisher, Al Zikovitz. Al's passion for adventure and for magazine excellence continues to inspire all of those connected with *explore*. Thanks also to Peter Thompson, the British expat who founded the magazine back in 1981, and who—together with long-time editor Marion Harrison—established *explore* as an award-winning publication.

In recent years, some extremely talented editors have helped to bring out the very best in our writers. Special thanks to David Leach and to Don Obe, Mike Randolph, Mark Schatzker and Kate Barker. Wendela Roberts, Terry Sellwood and Linda Cooper have provided much-valued advice. And art directors Gary Davidson, Susan Meingast and Jackie Shipley, along with their army of photographers and illustrators, have continued to give the magazine a fresh, distinctive look in keeping with its contents.

I'm also grateful to Greystone Books publisher Rob Sanders, who enthusiastically embraced the idea of this anthology on first hearing of it. Editor Jan Walter helped me in many ways, especially with the difficult task of story selection. Jackie Davis, Leigh Doyle, Rochelle Lloyd, Susan Rana and Ruth Wilson all played important roles in the production of the book you're holding.

Finally, I thank our writers, who continue to make every issue of *explore* a truly excellent adventure, and our readers, who share our passion for interesting outdoor stories well told. Even stories about giant eels.

JAMES LITTLE

||||||||||||

27 FUNERALS
AND A WEDDING

··· **GEOFF POWTER** ···

OCTOBER/NOVEMBER 2003

NO LONGER REALLY remember my first kiss. Like so many other rites of adolescent passage—the first time I drove a car, my first drink, the first furtive hit of a joint—my first taste of a woman has blurred over time, so that I no longer remember where or when it happened. Even though these other rites all occurred at roughly the same time in my life, it is only the memory of my first blood that is inviolate, written as clearly inside me as it is written in the scar on my right arm, where I first hit rock.

A close, humid, eastern summer morning, barely two months after we'd started climbing. The sun was already brazing the air and the mosquitoes were swarming as we geared up for the longest, hardest route we'd yet tried. I was terrified and I should have been; we were really just kids, book-taught because no one else climbed, with gear chosen out of poverty rather than common sense, and an attitude that far exceeded our abilities. We were pushing harder and harder, way past our limits, cowboys every time we went out that first summer.

I shook and clattered and grunted my way up the first half of the first pitch that day, quickly coming to the realization that I was playing in the wrong league. I just barely kept my head together, but that only got me deeper into trouble, because it let me pause briefly behind a small tree before seeking salvation out to the right, where I suddenly found myself completely off route, lost in a maze of brittle, loose granite shards scabbed with rusty lichen.

Everything I touched moved, sending little skitters of dust down the rock and into my eyes. I sweated and held my breath and prayed, while miles below my hungover partner started to bellow some inane song. I shook, I cursed, I tried to find God, I screamed, then my arms melted and I pitched. Every single piece of discount gear pinged out or broke; only the tree held. I landed upside down, 90 feet below, my head barely bobbing above the ground.

Once my partner realized that no matter how bad I felt, I hadn't broken anything, he sagely advised that the only thing to do was get back in the saddle again. "Go back up," he insisted, "or you'll never climb again." "Good," I said, pulling a blood-soaked sleeve out of a gouge in my arm. "Why would I ever want to do that again? Oh, and fuck you. You were sitting on your ass down *here*." "No, I mean it," he said. "Go back up, before you get too scared."

It was madness, but he was absolutely right. By the end of the day, I could hardly move for the bruises and scrapes, but we'd done the climb and our marrow-deep exuberance outweighed any pain I felt. Joy had blood in it, and that understanding made me *different*. As though I suddenly had charge of my life. No kiss ever offered half that much.

OF ALL the questions that climbers, backcountry skiers and other outdoor athletes are asked, it's the toughest one: "Why?" Why do what you do, when you know the consequences? When you've even *seen* the consequences? Why in the world would you get back up and do it again? What is wrong with you people?

It's certainly not as though we don't know there might be blood involved. Outdoor literature drips with the stuff; death and maiming and pain flow through adventure tales with the power of stigmata and the predictability of war. And yet we play anyway—climbing, skiing, paragliding, paddling, diving—while average, sensible people shake their heads and ask, again, "Why?" You know the risks, but you ride it anyway. The weather man says storm, but you keep packing. That hole could be a keeper, but you line it up. Half your group gets swallowed by an avalanche, but you head out and ski the next day.

There are a million individual reasons for what we do, reasons that run far deeper than Mallory's koan "Because it's there" will ever reveal. The reasons change as we age and gain experience, but for most of us, they begin at the same place: that great hubris of adolescence. Death? It might happen to somebody else, but not to *me*.

A SHORT month after my fall, I was press-ganged into helping out in a rescue in the Shawangunks, the climbers' mecca in New York State. Some guy had cartwheeled off the top of a 300-foot cliff, and the local climbing ranger loaded six of us into the back of his pickup truck. Ten minutes later, we unloaded the Stokes litter, scrambled up slippery brush to the foot of the hot white wall, and set up just below a ledge. The ranger was giving orders to ready the stretcher, but I wasn't listening, because my eyes were following the course of a crimson stream slowly making its way down the rock from the ledge. The stream started in what I sickeningly realized was a cave in a man's skull at the edge of the ledge. The body suddenly went into seizure, the ranger climbed up to hold the man down, and one of the rescuers threw up.

The fool—that's what everyone called him later, an act of distancing ourselves from the event after the two hellish hours of getting this broken, delirious man to an ambulance—the fool had bought a couple of hundred bucks of brand new gear, tied into a terrible little piece of protection, right beside an enormous oak, and stepped off the top for his first rappel. He was gone before he reached the hospital. And we all said, "Christ, what a fucking idiot! I'd *never* do something that stupid."

AFTER A time, we convinced ourselves that our skills, our experience, were the real magic we needed to survive. We didn't need superstition or luck, because we had knowledge and understanding that we could use like an amulet to get us out of epics. Even help us avoid them entirely. "I know what this weather's going to do," we started to hear ourselves say. Or "I can *make* this safe" or "If you know *this* move, you can get through that trouble on the river."

And at some point, with experience and skills and lessons learned, we'd moved past most of the fear, and the point of the game changed. The beauty of things revealed suddenly made the risk make sense: beauty of place, the pure, graceful joy of movement, the pleasure of friendships built in shared challenge—and the victory of doing what everyone said we couldn't.

Those things all became the *real* reason to be out there; we loved what we saw and how we felt. The fear was just a hurdle on the way to some place new and remarkable.

In the face of what we thought of as our great knowledge, the blood seemed less a threat—all we had to do was blind ourselves to the fact that people with much greater skills and knowledge were dying around us. By my tenth year of climbing, I'd been to 15 funerals. At one, I'd watched a mother bury her only two children; at another, I said goodbye to a lover. Twenty years later, I look back and realize that was the lowest number of funerals I'd go to in any subsequent decade. My older brother has been to five funerals his entire life.

IN 1988, I was given the chance I'd dreamed of all my life: to go to the Himalaya, to perhaps the most beautiful mountain in the world, with friends. Blood wasn't in the picture, not even in my worst dreams. Beauty can obscure clouds on the horizon, and for three weeks on Ama Dablam, beauty was what we had. Incredible weather, climbing in T-shirts on perfect, dry, crystal-studded granite. But then two days from the top, a storm hit us as suddenly as an avalanche, and a friend slipped off the end of a rope shredded by the wind and fell into the clouds.

It was impossible to think of not going to look for him, though I knew right away it was going to be the back of the ranger's truck all over again—this time alone. How ironic: we had nearly a mile of rope with us, thoughtfully strung out all over the mountain to guarantee our safety, but not one spare foot in the camp where Charlie fell. So I climbed down into the rising dark, unroped, calling his name, afraid of what I knew I would find. In the end, though, it wasn't really Charlie that I sat beside in the fading light, just the flesh and bone that used to hold him back. We made a funeral pyre and left the mountain, and in Namche, Tom proposed to

Susan. In the shadow of the mountain, perhaps with Charlie watching, we gathered for one of the richest, happiest weddings I've ever seen. We left for Thailand and I didn't climb again for quite a while.

JOHN. RON and David. Catherine. Wilma. Simon. Nicci. Alex. Bugs. Dion. Mugs. Mark. Rooney. John. Guy. Jim. Dan. Karl. Chris. George. Dan. Ian. Lauren. Lawrence. Charlie. We're not alone as a community in the numbers of our lost friends—firefighters, cops, the gay community and soldiers everywhere put our own losses in chilling perspective—but as a group, we adventurers may be unique in the way we consecrate the activities that kill us as great and noble pursuits. Of course, not all agree with the consecration. I've stood on one side of the fence when I buried friends, but I've also stood on the other, when I counselled the people left behind. Grieving widows, angry children, angrier parents, friends whose hearts hurt. It's the part we don't talk about too much. In adventure, you're never supposed to leave your partner behind.

EVOLUTIONARY BIOLOGISTS have an answer to the puzzling "Why?" They argue that we have been sculpted by our distant, collective experience in ways that we're not the least aware of—in fact, in ways that we try to deny, in the hopes of being greater than what runs in our blood. We forget that for the vast majority of our time on Earth, our survival was completely determined by our capacity to stare down death. But instead of celebrating this power, we declare art, faith, love and community as our salvations, and decry risk as the enemy, as though our successes in the gentle realms are not entirely contingent upon our ability to kill or to face fear. Somewhere, deep down in the bones, there may be a need as resolute as survival, an instinct to prove that we live as a result of personal agency, and not because someone else lets us live.

FOUR YEARS after Ama Dablam, I returned to the Himalaya, in the way that one returns to a lover who has betrayed you—hesitant, not wanting to discover that the perfect love, violated once, was bound to hurt me again. It didn't. It was an iconic trip—a summit, a great team, a magnificent mountain—and I climbed my heart out.

And yet as we left the mountain, swathed in our bliss, another climber whom we'd just met watched his friend and then his fiancée slip away down the sun-burnished wall. He stumbled down alone in a storm. Our mountain was not the same as his.

THE PAST year, my thirtieth in the mountains, was unlike any other, summing up all the good and the bad, the grand and the tragic, and framing risk against the bigger picture in a way I'd never experienced. There was real world blood: my mother died—supposedly a blessing, because she had been painfully sick. Unlike any other death I'd experienced before, she was able to say, "It's time." My wife fell seriously ill and angrily decided it was *not* time; she bounced right back into the saddle. There were climbing deaths—two young, bright lights avalanched off a mountain in Alaska—and there were the two skiing avalanches in B.C. that the press and the public dissected, bringing into luminescent relief just how different our community seems to be at times. And then there were losses that combined the mountain and real worlds: climbers taken by illness rather than rockfall.

Blood was back on the surface of things—*everything*, it seemed—and I was given the chance to question the differences in all these losses. Which made more sense? Which hurt more? Which seemed a tragedy while the other was simply *life*?

And finally, my own blood came full circle. Last year, it was my turn to do something "I'd never be stupid enough to do." I rappelled off the end of a rope. I screwed up. Plain and simple. From 30 feet, I hit the ground and bounced so high that my partner thought I'd died. Once again, the lesson was in getting back in the saddle. Committing to a faith that it would make sense in the end. I put it off for a while, then went to a favourite crag, chalked up and climbed. Why? Because it was worth it.

DON'T CRY FOR US, ARGENTINA

··· **DAVID ZIMMER** ···

JULY/AUGUST 2004

FIRST THERE WAS "travel." And then somebody invented "adventure travel," the difference being, I think, the amount of suffering
you endure getting from one place to another. In my mind, the best
way to suffer while travelling is simply to fly through the TWA hub in
St. Louis, that dank-smelling maze of human degradation, bad hairdos
and heat-lamped cheese nachos south of the border.

But Keely, my travelling co-conspirator, had grander ambitions. She
wanted real adventure travel, having cut her teeth on hiking, diving and
paddling, in places other than St. Louis. Her plan was that we should head
to Nepal, for some hardcore altitude sickness and the life-affirming tsunami of lactic acid that would be ours after a few weeks trekking the high
mountain passes. This sounded like work to me, but I must admit Keely's
off-the-beaten-path doctrine of "pack light and carry a big map" did
appeal. "Fly by the seat of your pants." "Make hay while the sun shines."
These are bromides my partner uses every day. So we did all the legwork,
picking our routes with care.

Then, just days before investing in airfare, I checked the weather and
discovered that in January and February—the time we would be travelling—the mountain passes of the Annapurna Circuit would be buried in

40 feet of snow and experiencing blockheater-in-Nunavut temperatures. Faced with these conditions, even the hardiest Sherpas simply hunker down, rheumy-eyed, to soak their feet in basins of hot water for the duration. Well, boy, did we feel stupid.

Fortunately, fate smiled on us in the form of a friend, an Air Canada employee, who would sell us a pair of fly-anywhere-in-this-hemisphere "friends and family" passes at rock-bottom prices. What a break! But where to go? It had to be somewhere less travelled, with mountains (for her) and plenty of grilled meat (for me). The trick, we agreed, was not to plan too far ahead—it would ruin the spirit of the whole enterprise. And so, at the last minute, we settled on Argentina. When friends asked, "Why Argentina?" I just waggled my chunky *Lonely Planet* and said, "Look how thick this book is!"

We had heard that when flying on Air Canada passes, your chances of being bumped up from steerage were exponentially increased if you dressed up a little. But when we arrived at the airport shouldering purple 80-litre packs, me with a ridiculous tie cinched over a uniform of quick-dry and Keely quite dazzling in a skirt and stylish sandals, we weren't even allowed on the plane. Turns out that a Brazilian visa is required for standby passengers routed through São Paulo, which is something that you don't learn when you buy your tickets from an avionics technician instead of an accredited travel agent. Apparently, the Brazilians had their balls in a knot over some cattle-related impasse and we were going to suffer for it. Well, boy, did we feel stupid. Fortunately, the next day, the lady at the Brazilian consulate in downtown Toronto was both friendly and expeditious, and after we handed over $150 each for the privilege of visiting Guarulhos International Airport for two hours, we were again on our way.

BUENOS AIRES is a beautiful city, a bit crumbly and soot-stained these days, but still a majestic and vibrant place with a stunning architectural heritage—they don't call it the Paris of South America for nothing. It also has nightlife to beat the band, inexpensive wine, beautiful women (it's a world capital for unnecessary cosmetic surgery), and more varieties of charcoal-grilled meat than anyone has a right to experience. That was the good news. The bad news was that our national carrier had somehow managed to lose our luggage. All of it. After four days of negotiating with the embittered woman at the Air Canada office, a taut-faced harridan with painted-on facial features and supply-teacher glasses, they discovered our bags had been there all along. And somehow, she made it clear, it was all our own fault.

Our plan was to strike west across Argentina, then south through the Andes to the Patagonian cordillera and Torres del Paine National Park, then ever southward to Tierra del Fuego. The very tip of the South American continent! We would trek mountain trails, we would ascend glaciers, we would camp and maybe even fish for trout. Argentinian friends had suggested we use aircraft to get around their country, but we wanted to really get a feel for the place, if only to visit the activity-rich towns the guidebook assured us were there. And so we would do it all by car. This was adventure! This was travel! This, as it turned out, was a big mistake.

Driving in Argentina, especially in Buenos Aires, takes a special kind of person, namely a person who is desperate and suicidal. The country has one of the world's highest rates of traffic fatalities with good reason. I routinely saw packs of six yellow-and-black taxicabs madly accelerating down a four-lane avenue, bumping quarter panels like monstrous bees in a NASCAR race. Why use the brakes when you can use the horn? More than once, crowded city buses came careening around corners in the heart of the city. Rather than stop at the red lights, the bus drivers accelerated, laid on the horn and drove directly through the melee of madly braking and swerving vehicles that scattered in their path. In Buenos Aires, this is normal. And the buses run on time.

Out of the city, you begin to appreciate how much Argentinians worship Juan-Manuel Fangio, the country's legendary Formula One driver who posted 24 Grand Prix wins and five world championships, and who some fans say is the greatest racing driver who ever lived. At the state-run YPF gas stations, the brand name for premium 98.5-octane fuel is Fangio XXI. When I learned that Fangio won his first race in 1940 driving a Ford taxicab, it all became clear. To survive in Argentina, you must drive like Fangio, and we did our best, pushing our little red Hyundai Atos to a foot-to-the-firewall top speed of 150 kilometres per hour across the lush, humid pampas, passing trucks with just inches to spare and generally violating every defensive-driving technique taught at Young Drivers of Canada. The Atos is a box-shaped subcompact with 12-inch rims and a 900cc engine. We named ours The Shopping Cart. And we made it scream. For 10 hours at a stretch. Even so, we were often the slowest car on the road, as BMWs and Peugeots blew our doors off, rocketing by on a road that stretched to the horizon.

AFTER MAKING it through an electrical storm that flooded the highway with rain and a couple of microbursts that came close to flicking The Shopping Cart off the road, we made it to Mendoza, a lovely college town in the heart of Argentinian wine country, nestled in the foothills of the Andes. Mendoza is a classy place, with plenty of fine restaurants, but after a few days in the car, we both craved tube steak and skipped the haute cuisine for a little place called "Salchicha Mr. Dog." Not a good idea, as it turned out. We hadn't made it halfway back to the room before I was doubled up with a pain that felt like Mr. Dog was running off-leash in my gastrointestinal tract. Keely offered her usual line of sympathy—"Buck up, camper!"—but faster than you can yell, "Honeykins, we're out of toilet paper!" she, too, was pounding at the bathroom door.

We began to worry that we were taking too long to get to the ends of the earth, so we pushed south, hard, reasoning that the best stuff was at the end of the rainbow. Keely is an excellent high-speed driver. (In fact, on a couple of occasions, she has had to explain to the folks at the Ministry of Transportation why she should be allowed to keep her licence. One lady at the ministry, after examining Keely's record, calmly noted that she must be a very good driver, having not killed herself already.) Once, in the process of passing two trucks around a blind curve on a double yellow line, we had to screech to a stop to avoid killing the machine-gun-toting police officer conducting a vehicle inspection. Keely instructed me to not reveal her fluency in Spanish and, after we played dumb *turistas* for a while, he let us go. Ten minutes later, she was pulled over driving the wrong way on a one-way street while I was buying some pastries. The officer suggested, in very polite Spanish, that Keely take a driving lesson before she killed someone.

CLIMBING INTO the Andes, we made a couple of new discoveries. One was that just because the map says "primary road" doesn't mean it's a paved four-lane highway. The other was that in the mountains, it takes a lot longer to cover a few inches of space on the map than you might expect; on the accordion surface of the Andes, there's more up and down than forward. Once, it took us an entire day to travel about 100 kilometres as the crow flies. At some points in the highest passes, the road just disappeared into a track of broken rock and tumbled boulders. The only way you could tell it was a road was by the tanker trailers bearing down from the other direction, horns blaring, spitting rocks in all directions.

We pushed on, stopping in a number of picturesque mountain towns. Outside St. Martin de los Andes, we did manage to hike Cerro Malo, at just over 6,500 feet a stubby hill by Andean standards. The L.P. said the hike would be a six-hour return trip, but we knowingly discounted this figure. After all, the trail signs in Algonquin Park are usually way off the mark; if they say six hours, you can usually count on three if you get the lead out. On Cerro Malo, I think we must have chosen the wrong trail, because even at a breakneck pace, we barely made it back down in daylight. We also neglected to bring any food and our water ran out halfway up the ascent. At the top, we paused for a quick photo, hugging the ground to avoid being blown off the mountain by the ceaseless winds that actually reversed the direction of a small glacial stream we encountered. We literally ran back down in semi-darkness and spent the remainder of the evening gulping sangria to ease the spasmodic twitching of our calves and quads. Total hiking time: six and a half hours. Boy, did we feel stupid.

DOWN ON the Patagonian cordillera, The Shopping Cart was not faring well: after four punctured tires (cheaply fixed at local tire shops called *gomerias*) and a shattered windshield, The Cart was beginning to make ominous sounds. And so were we. Morale was low, and every detour we took to find adventure just led us further away from our final destination and ended in disappointment. It seemed *The Lying Planet*, as we now called our guidebook, was loath to omit any town from its recommendation. When we asked one man about the promised scenic hikes, he simply waved his hands at the endless panorama of the cordillera as if to say, "Sure, walk anywhere you like."

We now drove 12 to 14 hours a day, the accelerator flat to the floor, as the rugged beauty of the endless Patagonian landscape began to wear. We'd cover hundreds of kilometres without so much as a curve on the road, with only an endless string of sheep fencing disturbing the emptiness. For one entire day, we didn't even see a single ewe. The landscape was so vast and featureless that if it were not for the red-lined scream of The Cart's engine, we'd have sworn we were standing still.

By now, we were subsisting on a diet of crackers and peanut butter, supplemented by the cold beer we stashed in the empty spare-tire well. Radio reception outside of small towns was non-existent, and we did everything possible to keep from cracking up. We played 200 Questions, I impersonated each and every character from *The Hilarious House of Frightenstein*, and as the giddiness set in, we sang endless rounds of "Girls on Cheese," a bastard version of Duran Duran's "Girls on Film" with all-cheese lyrics, that soon had manic tears of insane laughter coursing down our cheeks. Sing along if you know the words! ("Girls on cheese... big slice of Münster... girls on cheese.") Things were getting out of hand.

Reality struck when we understood that our vacation time was slipping away. There was no way in hell we'd make it to Tierra del Fuego and still be able to drive back to Buenos Aires to return The Cart. Even Rio Gallegos, the town our Argentinian friends had wisely suggested we fly to, was way out of range. Admitting total defeat, we struck east across the cordillera towards the Atlantic coast. When we got there, we'd turn north again and maybe pick up some beach hours on our way back to Buenos Aires.

BY THE time we reached the ocean, things were getting even uglier. The interior of The Cart smelled like the inside of a hockey bag. Keely and I were half-crazed, and after a constant diet of car food—supplemented by a pizza or a two-pound steak Milanese for lunch—we were both getting fat. My bones ached, and we were developing bedsores from too much car time and very little exercise. After a trek around Península Valdés, a spectacular nature reserve brimming with elephant seals, penguins and guanacos, and a prime whale-watching spot, we headed for Las Grutas, a beach town described by some friendly locals as very quiet and *muy preciosa*. Just the ticket, we thought, but a glimpse over the seawall revealed a mass of sunbaked humanity packed tighter than the seals on Valdés. Other beaches were even more congested. Beachgoing, we learned, was a national pastime. For most of the summer there is even a national TV channel with a direct feed from the human-stained sand.

Our mad dash back to Buenos Aires is but a blurry memory. It didn't really matter anyway, because, by this point, the travel atmosphere had become so poisonous that nothing short of euthanasia could have cheered us up. We even managed to join every resident of the city returning from a beach holiday, in a seven-hour bumper-to-bumper crawl through the outskirts of town that Fangio himself couldn't have defeated. Bloated and aching, we slouched into the car rental office as the attendant—a friendly guy—surveyed the damage. Four repaired tires, a broken windshield, a dent on the roof (I have no idea) and upholstery that would need steam cleaning. As for the grinding noise from the front axle, I steadfastly maintained that the car had been that way when we got it. After noting the 6,000-kilometre odometer reading, he asked where we had gone.

We told him.

"*¿Eres tu loco?*" he laughed, shovelling refuse out of the back seat. "Why didn't you fly?"

I resisted the urge to jump up and down and yell, "Because we are complete fucking idiots!" Nor did I break down into a shuddering fit of bitter weeping. Instead, as we wearily shouldered our packs, I gently explained that in our country, we do this all the time. We call it adventure travel.

|||||||||||||

SO THIS IS WHAT IT'S LIKE TO SAIL THROUGH A HURRICANE

· · · **ADAM KILLICK** · · ·

OCTOBER/NOVEMBER 2003

IN MY LIFE, there have been only a handful of times when I have been well and truly humbled at the hands of Mother Nature. In Alaska, I was once dragged by my foot across the (thankfully frozen) Yukon River by an out-of-control sled-dog team. When I first tried surfing, on the west coast of Vancouver Island, I was smacked underwater by a wave and spun by the furious undertow until I didn't know which way was up.

None of that, however, approached the feeling of insignificance that came over me as I lay on the deck of the EDS *Atlantic Challenge,* the 67-foot vessel that was meant to be my initiation into the world of trans-Atlantic sailing. We'd ridden through the eye of a hurricane seven days before and had assumed the worst of our three-week voyage was over. But now a gale had ambushed us mid-ocean, 1,900 kilometres from the nearest point of land.

Every few seconds, a cold wave would crash over the side of the boat, lift me up and then body-slam me back down again. To keep from panicking, I tried to concentrate on the tiny grey stippled dots that made the surface of the deck—in dry weather, at least—non-slip. Another wave. Up I went. Down I came... on the bum knee that had convinced me to trade in hockey and soccer for the "safer" sport of sailing.

Eventually, I managed to stagger to my feet and wipe the sting from my eyes with one hand while I held on with another. I was standing on the "low" side of the deck as the sailboat leaned into the heaving seas. To get back to the cockpit, I had to scramble up the sloping deck to its high side. In my haste, I unclipped my safety line from one cable but didn't clip it back into the next cable properly. Without knowing it, I was now walking along the slick deck of a sailboat pitching in 50-foot waves—completely untethered.

I heard a Welsh accent warped by the wind and saw the captain gesturing at the flailing end of my tether: "Are you *mad*, man?"

I was beginning to wonder.

MY SURNAME, Killick, would suggest that I come from a seafaring family. In mariner's jargon, a *killick* is a leading seaman in both the Canadian and British navies. In Newfoundland, it's a rudimentary anchor constructed by strapping several slats of wood around a large rock and attaching a sturdy rope.

I have ancestors who spent more time on water than land—one was the captain of a *Cutty Sark*–era tea clipper—and even my father used to race homemade sailboats in the English Channel. But while I was born on the southeast coast of England, just steps from the sea, I grew up breathing the landlocked air of southern Ontario.

Then one day, not so long ago, while laid up with a soccer injury and reading tales of maritime adventure, I hatched a brilliant plan: I would learn to sail and cross the Atlantic, just as my forefathers had done. I would step off a salt-stained deck onto the land of my birth, swaggering with a newfound maritime savvy. I would shape myself into a true Killick.

First I bought a 13-foot dinghy, practised sailing on the lake at my in-laws' cottage, and participated in a couple of races on Lake Ontario. A little while later, I read about the dramatic finish of the BT Global Challenge, a round-the-world race sailed against prevailing winds and currents, and crewed by amateur sailors. After travelling more than 55,000 kilometres, two of the boats had been minutes apart from each other as they crossed the English Channel to the finish in Southampton. The race was organized by a British company called the Challenge Business, founded by maritime legend Sir Chay Blyth, the first person to sail non-stop around the world against the prevailing winds. Every four years, his Challenge Business mounts a round-the-world race crewed by volunteers who raise money to cover the cost of their berth, on a fleet of some 35 boats identical to the EDS *Atlantic Challenge*. They were looking for volunteers—no sailing experience required—to form part of a training crew.

How could I not sign up?

"LARRY WAS saying something about throwing coins into the water. This seems an appropriate time."

Jon Jeffreys, the Welsh skipper of the EDS *Atlantic Challenge*, stood at the steering wheel. It was a pleasant October afternoon, barely a whisper of wind as the sun glinted off the wavelets in Boston Harbor. The receding mix of glass skyscrapers and older architecture framed the captain as we motored away from the dock. We were about to turn the motor off. The propeller would not spin again for 5,000 kilometres.

Larry Deshler, a quiet retiree, explained his maritime ritual. "In the two ocean crossings I've done," he said, "we've thrown coins in the water and said a silent prayer for a safe journey." As I rifled through my pockets for spare change, several of the other crew members tossed various types of currency overboard and made their wishes to the sea gods.

This trip was designed as a training run to prepare the crew for what might be encountered in the Southern Ocean off Cape Horn during the 2004 Global Challenge. Our course would take us northeastward, south of Nova Scotia, just kissing the Grand Banks, before crossing 3,700 kilometres of open sea to land at Plymouth, England. The North Atlantic is not considered one of the world's more relaxing cruising areas. It's notorious for being stormy and cold. Indeed, it's far more pleasant to sail across to the Azores, off the coast of Portugal, and visit southern Europe instead. If you are determined to follow the northerly route, then October is possibly the worst month to go: summer hurricanes are still pounding North America, and on the far side of the Atlantic, the winter gales are beginning to flex their muscles.

We were told that we would likely be the only vessel under sail out there at this time of year. The passage was expected to take three weeks, although we were reminded to tell loved ones not to worry if we were a little late. On the boat's single-sideband radio, the skipper would call in daily position updates, which would be placed on the company Web site. My wife would be able to follow our progress on the Internet: a tiny red dot inching over a borderless blue space.

"Anybody got a coin I can use?" I asked.

About five hours out, I took the chance to climb the mast. From 93 feet up, the view was breathtaking, even if the bosun's chair—a sailboat's version of a climber's harness—proved pinchingly uncomfortable. From my vantage, I got a good sense of the layout of the boat, which looked far too narrow and tippy to be carrying sails this big.

The Challenge boats are designed for racing, not comfort. There would be no sherry and brie served below; blazers were not on the list of required equipment. As far as modern marine technology goes, the boats are relatively poorly equipped. While there is a GPS system, there are no computerized course plotters. Navigation is done with a pencil on a paper chart. The sails don't furl, and there are no hydraulic winches to raise and lower them. If you want to change the heavy Dacron sails—which we would do 45 times—you lean over the bow pulpit in the spray (or worse) and haul them up and down by hand. The largest foresail weighs several hundred pounds. Most important, there is no autopilot on the Challenge boats: somebody must be steering 24 hours a day, whatever the weather.

There were nine of us onboard to sail a boat that under normal conditions carried a crew of 14. Along with Jon and Larry, the crew included a Dutch first mate, the former captain of an Irish rugby team, a retired U.S. Marine, a software company executive, a Brit who worked for a Boston chemical-measurement company, and an English surveyor nicknamed "Rocky" who bore a striking resemblance to Captain Highliner. Six nationalities were represented among the nine of us. I was the sole Canadian.

The watch schedule was simple to follow: two six-hour watches beginning at eight AM, then three four-hour watches, starting at eight PM. One watch on, one off, for three weeks. As the sun set, we had our first wildlife encounter. A shark's dorsal fin made slow circles in the water on the starboard side of the boat. After dark, we sat in the deep cockpit and admired the clear view of the cosmos that comes only from escaping the artificial incandescence of land. Every few minutes, a shooting star spritzed across the sky. I could get used to this, I thought, as the dew began to glisten on the deck.

DAWN BROKE exceedingly grey, and fog rolled lazily across the sea in dense chunks. The wind had picked up, to about 12 knots, and choppy waves punctuated the slow, undulating swell of the Gulf of Maine. The boat skipped along the water, casting back a misty spray.

By lunchtime, the wind speed had jumped to 16 knots, and the seas had gone from choppy to rough. Pointing as high as it could against the wind, the boat took the 12- to 16-foot waves on the bow. Below, where I was trying to sleep, they made a horrible crashing sound against the hull. My bunk was jammed up against the inside of that hull. Less than an inch of steel separated me and the cold North Atlantic.

The motion of the sea soon claimed its first victim: Larry, cleaning below, suddenly stuck his head out the companionway and deposited his breakfast across the deck. The surging waves quickly washed the evidence away.

Seasickness was something that terrified me. In my limited time on boats, I had never been sick, but the experience looked excruciating. Maritime veterans say there are two types of sailors: those who get seasick, and those who haven't been seasick yet. I was trying a drug called scopolamine, which was supposed to be released over two days through a dime-sized disc I had attached behind my ear. It washed off after less than a day when a wave smacked me in the back of the head. Still, I'd survived so far with my stomach contents intact.

Every day, someone dropped out of the regular watch routine to go on 24-hour "mother watch." From midnight to midnight, they did all the cooking and the cleaning on the boat. Although it was a reprieve from the usual duties of helming and changing sails, mother watch was spent almost entirely below decks, without a view of the horizon, where the pitching and tossing of the boat was felt most acutely. As they took their turns at mother watch, several other crew members succumbed to seasickness. Soon that would be the least of our worries.

Less than 300 kilometres southeast of us, a tropical storm was spinning along on a northward course towards Nova Scotia. A U.S. Air Force Reserve "hurricane hunter" plane flew across its breadth to take wind speed and pressure readings. As we made tea on the EDS *Atlantic Challenge,* Tropical Storm Karen received a promotion. It was now Hurricane Karen, generating wind speeds in excess of 120 kilometres per hour. Marine forecasts came over the boat's radio in strings of fax tones, which a laptop computer interpreted into a weather map. Due south of Halifax and slightly southeast of Boston was the telltale sign: a quotation mark and a comma joined at the dot, surrounded by tight concentric circles with three Xs lined up underneath. *Hurcn Karen,* it read, with an arrow pointing up, east of Nova Scotia, towards Newfoundland, suggesting its course.

Our captain decided to turn southward to let the hurricane pass by in front of us. Shortly after we turned southeast, however, the computer or the radio or something at the navigation station that usually made a comforting beeping noise went on the blink, and the weather faxes stopped coming. Not to worry, Jon said, saying the course on which we were headed—towards Africa—should keep us clear of the hurricane's path. So we had no idea that instead of carrying on northeast towards Newfoundland, the hurricane had actually turned northwest, setting her sights on the south shore of Nova Scotia. And us.

By four PM, the barometric pressure had dropped from 1,011 millibars to 1,002 millibars, and was still going down. A dropping barometer, I learned, indicates that you're sailing into a storm. When the barometer drops 10 millibars in three hours, however, you're not just heading into *any* storm. You're heading into hell.

As night came on, it became difficult to tell what was the sea and what was the rain, which had gone from a drizzle several hours ago to a horizontal onslaught of needles. Only when it got in my eyes could I tell the difference: the salt water stung a little more. The ocean seemed to have closed around the boat in a frothy tunnel of phosphorescent green. Whenever waves crashed over the side decks that protected the cockpit— which they were doing with alarming frequency—tiny glow-in-the-dark green algae would blink briefly on my arms and legs. Moving around the boat was a matter of crawling along the deck commando-style, held fast to the boat by the three-foot-long umbilical cord of webbing that clipped from the front of our life vests to safety cables that ran along the deck. Staying hitched meant staying alive.

By midnight, the winds were gusting to nearly 70 knots—130 kilometres per hour—and sustained a good 60 to 65: force 12 on the Beaufort Scale. (There is no force 13.) We were officially caught in a hurricane, although nobody seemed keen to discuss it. The screaming wind made conversation impossible anyway.

We took 20-minute turns at the helm. Holding the wheel while balancing on a deck tilted at 40 degrees felt like dancing with a 400-pound partner who objects to you leading—as someone else dumps frigid, salty water over your head every few seconds. On the helm, I could feel each gargantuan wave lift the bow of the boat up, up, up, and then release the boat to surf down its face.

Because a sailboat ends in a point at its bow, it presents a curved shape in the water. As the wind exerts pressure on the sails to one side or the other—even when sailing downwind—the boat's natural inclination is to turn into that wind, especially when surfing down a wave with speed. To compensate and keep the boat on course, I had to lean into the wheel and force the rudder against the weight of the wave. With every wave, there was a brief sensation that the boat was escaping control. Then, as a knifing pain seared my shoulders, the boat would slowly come around and get back on course—just in time for the battle with the next wave. After 15 minutes of struggle, I was too exhausted to concentrate on the lighted instruments that, only six feet in front of the helm, were nearly impossible to read in the rain and spray.

Then came the awkward changeover: the next helmsman (or woman) would clip into the eyelet in the cockpit and crawl in front of me, while I held the wheel. When the new helmsman was in position, we'd yell "Okay!" to each other above the din, and I could let go, crawl into the back of the cockpit and hunker down against the relentless spray.

I finally knew why we Killicks had eventually become landlubbers.

As I prepared to end this shift, a strange thing happened. In the space of several heartbeats, the wind dropped from 60 knots to six. The wind direction indicator started spinning madly, and we lost nearly all of the boat's speed. The waves fell to a confused chop, and the rain stopped. After the cacophony, the quiet seemed eerie, with only the gentle sounds of the waves lapping at the hull.

Finally, we could hear each other speak—except we were speechless. After several minutes, it dawned on us where we were. Those who have travelled into the eye of a hurricane (and lived to tell about it) say you can look straight up and see clear sky. Unfortunately, it occurred to none of us to do so. We were too stunned.

Within half an hour, the wind began to pick up again, this time coming from the other direction. I was off watch and collapsed, wet, into my bunk and strapped myself down. The back half of the hurricane proved to be less intense than its front, however, and the sun rose the next day to clear skies and calmer seas. By noon we had the mainsail back up. That night, as we picked up the Gulf Stream and prepared to turn northeast off the tail of the Grand Banks, the mood was buoyant, and we held an impromptu limerick competition. Rocky's muse struck first:

There once was a hurricane called Karen.
Who thought, right, that's it, I'll have 'em.
So she screwed to the west,
Stripped bare to her chest,
But all she caught was young Adam.

My rebuttal, I'm afraid, is unprintable. We were sailors, after all.

WE PASSED our watch hours playing 20 Questions, solving moral conundrums and sharing the kind of personal information we are often only comfortable giving to strangers. We each found our favourite places on the boat: One crew member stood on the stern rail, watching the dolphins that rode alongside nearly every day. Another leaned on the roof of the companionway, fiddling with a lock whose combination had been lost. And still another sat opposite the chart table, composing poetry. I liked to sit on the quarterdeck, my feet resting on the rail while I scanned the sea and sky for wildlife.

One day, a sperm whale breached off the port bow. Another time, a fin whale, longer than the boat, drew alongside to give us the eye. Flying fish launched themselves through the air, pursued by hungry tuna. A 10-foot sailfish burst from the water, its spiny dorsal fin glinting green in the light of the setting sun.

I began to appreciate the cold beauty of the sea. When a wave crashes over the bow, it takes about a second to travel from the stainless steel pulpit, the most forward part of the boat, to the cockpit, some 60 feet back. In that second, it undergoes a sublime transformation. A frothy turquoise wall of water wells up, and as it passes the mast, it stretches apart into numerous watery blobs. Passing the entrance to the area below decks, these blobs shatter into thousands of bubbly missiles that dance in the light before striking your face. Even then, as you wipe the sting away, the wave isn't finished with you. It slithers down the back of your coat and comes to rest between your shoulder blades. Off the stern, the part of the wave that didn't end up in your underwear joins the boat's wake, a deep, glacier-blue pattern of fractured slabs bordered by millions of tiny bubbles. Then the next wave hits.

More than a week out, at around 30 degrees west longitude, I looked at our largest-scale chart of the Atlantic. If we had turned south, we wouldn't have reached land until we hit Antarctica. Northward, we would have run into polar pack ice east of Greenland. We were truly in the middle of the ocean. And that's when the weather started to turn ugly again.

The weather fax had begun working as soon as we passed through the hurricane and now showed a succession of low pressure systems that stretched from just east of Newfoundland clear across the ocean. They were producing gales that, while not the same strength as a hurricane, still packed a good punch. There were three gales on the map, and we seemed to be right beneath the middle one.

While the hurricane had hit us when we were still on the North American continental shelf, this gale now had about 1,500 kilometres of very deep water to work with, with no land masses to get in its way. The result was extraordinarily high waves, the likes of which our captain, who has sailed much of the world's oceans, had never seen before. They were like fluid, black mountain ranges, topped with snowcaps of spray. As they built from astern, it took several seconds of looking up before I could see the foaming crest against the sky. The waves seemed higher than the mast. Allowing for the skewed perspective, the skipper calculated they were probably pushing 50 feet.

Which is how I came to find myself lying on the deck, contemplating its dimpled surface and my own fragile mortality. I was supposed to be holding down the trysail while Jon and another crew member struggled to haul down the main. The trysail was a smaller replacement used when the weather conditions were too hairy for the main. We had "heaved to," an attempt to remain stationary in the water by setting the sails so that they counteracted each other. All hands were on deck. The urgency of the circumstance, and weight of the wet sails, needed the full attention of the entire crew.

Between waves, the wind tried to toss the loosely folded trysail overboard, and me with it. Eventually, the main was down and lashed. Jon was ready for the trysail, and I got up to retreat to the cockpit. That's when I forgot to properly clip my tether back into the safety wire. And when Jon noticed my mistake—I guess that's why he was the captain— and screamed at me to clip back in.

Although it was never discussed, we understood that if anyone fell overboard in conditions like these, it would be nearly impossible to retrieve him. Even finding someone among the towering waves would be a miracle. Still, the procedure was drilled into us: as soon as someone went over, one person dropped a danbuoy while another dove down the companionway and hit a red button on the GPS marked M.O.B., which recorded the exact position, give or take the 300 or 400 feet the boat had travelled in the time that it took to reach the button.

Before the day was over, the wind had shredded one sail, and the mainsail was coming apart, too. But we all managed to stay on the boat. Later that night, strapped tight in my bunk, I woke to the sound of pots and pans crashing in the galley. Instead of lying parallel to the floor, I seemed to be against the hull. My long underwear and fleece sweater, which I'd hung on a hook on the wall, were now parallel to the floor and dangling their wet cuffs in my face. The situation lasted only a few seconds before my topsy-turvy world righted itself again in one violent rocking motion.

Up top, the situation was more chaotic. Peter, the Irish rugby captain, had been on the helm when a huge wave crashed over the corner of the stern. The force sent the boat reeling until the mast lay horizontal in the water. Peter was swept off his feet and was about to bob overboard when another crew member managed to grab his tether and pull all 280 pounds of him back into the boat.

After that, conditions remained rough, but we carried on without incident. Out of the storm-tossed sea, I witnessed a trio of dolphins sprout forth, 10 feet above my head, chattering and enjoying the ride of their lives. One mammal's fear is another's fantasy.

SEVERAL HOURS before dawn we first saw the arcing glow of the lighthouse on Fastnet Rock, the steep-sided sentinel that guards the southern tip of Ireland and the western border of the Celtic Sea. It had taken us exactly two weeks to get to this spot. We were nearly a week ahead of schedule, so we decided to stop over in Ireland and celebrate our survival with a few pints of Guinness.

Three days later, we finally arrived at Queen Anne's Battery in Plymouth, England. We pulled in moments before last call at the marina's pub and collected some beer, wine and bubbly to celebrate our trip. During that night of revelry, we probably did more damage to the boat than the gale, thousands of towering waves and Hurricane Karen combined.

Back in Canada, a true Killick at last, I was going through my dirty laundry, when I found a coin in the shorts I'd worn on the first day of the trip—the only time the weather was suitable for them. It was a large, Irish 50-pence piece I'd been given in Boston Harbor when we were tossing currency to Neptune. For some reason, I hadn't thrown it overboard.

I guess it still brought me luck.

||||||||||||||

HAIL TO THE CHIEF

··· **J.B. MacKINNON** ···

SEPTEMBER/OCTOBER 2001

FOR **JIM BALDWIN**, the centre of the universe is, for the moment, a single piton hammered into a crack in a rockface. The piton is connected to a carabiner, and the carabiner is connected to a harness, and the harness is connected to the hipbone, and the hipbone is connected to the thighbone, and so on through the gamut of frail human anatomy. And the anatomy of Mr. Jim Baldwin is, at this instant, dead tired.

The previous night he had shared a ledge with a rat and a cloud of mosquitoes. Today, it's so hot that the stone is hard to touch. He has forgotten his last meal and is so dehydrated that he will later claim to have licked groundwater out of tiny seams in the rock. He *sucked moss*, for God's sake. But it will all be over with one small effort. For the millionth time, he steps up; his feet, too, are suspended from the piton, because below his boots there is nothing but 1,700 feet of air and then, finally, the canopy of a West Coast rainforest. And now one hand reaches for a shrub sticking out from the summit of the cliff, and at this exact moment the piton pops noiselessly out of its crack.

Stop the clock. Here, at this deadpoint in time, we will remember the great question asked of so many rock and mountain climbers: *why do you do this to yourself?* Rarely mentioned is the fact that so many climbers ask themselves this exact same question. They ask it at moments like the one in which Jim Baldwin became the first person in history to climb the Grand Wall of the Chief in Squamish, British Columbia, 40 years ago this summer.

It was June 1961, and yes, just as his last piton cast its vote with gravity, Baldwin caught a fistful of greenery and hauled himself up. How he feels about it now, no one can say. Having completed the first "big wall" rock climb in Canada, Baldwin took to the high, sheer lines of Yosemite National Park, California, where he died in a climbing accident three years later.

DRIVING THE 60 kilometres up Howe Sound from Vancouver, you don't see the Chief until it's looming large. If you're a 16-year-old climbing fanatic who thinks he's hot stuff on the kindergarten crags of his small-town home, you will want very badly to swear out loud, except that your mother is driving. You will suddenly understand, with the kind of clarity that's rare at that age, that you will not be climbing the Chief on this trip, or the next, *ad infinitum*.

Then the Chief disappears behind trees, only to reappear even larger and more menacing. From this aspect, some people claim to see features that form the face of a devil: deep-set eyes, sharp nose, goatee. The 16-year-old is one of these people. Further along, at a tourist pullout, he meets the Chief full-frontal. The *Baldwin-Cooper Route*, now known loosely as the Grand Wall, is stomach-churning. It beetles up a chalkboard slab until, in the middle of space, it reaches the world's loneliest cedar. There, a shallow corner rises plumb-line straight. This is the Split Pillar. Above it arches an overhanging scythe of stone: the Sword. These are capped by a glowering eyebrow, a canted roof of bone granite—the pitch known as *Perry's Lieback*. A few strata higher is Bellygood Ledge, an escape route off the face. To reach the summit, however, there is still a third of the cliff to go.

The pullout is always crowded for the same reason that ratings are high for any TV program that shows men being struck in the crotch. We love to watch. As that 16-year-old grew up, he never did get used to the sight of the Grand. He would stand in the parking lot and pick out the little white, blue, yellow or red speck of a climber. The tiny figure would eke upward a little, a barely perceptible movement. Then it would stop. And then the speck would suddenly be much, much further down.

A fall. A big one.

I've been there again and again, staring at the wall with my innards tied in a monkey-fist knot. For me, the burning question wasn't, "Why climb?" It was, "Why not?" The Grand Wall has been climbed by grandmothers and pre-teens and drunks. Why, after 15 years of on-again-off-again climbing, had I still not gotten up it? Every few years, I would once again find myself romancing the stone, ticking off classic routes like *Crescent Crack* and the *Squamish Buttress* that are the harbingers of Grand Wall readiness. Then, preparing for the real thing, I would turn on myself. This climbing thing—it's nothing more than a selfish game. Pointless. Undignified. Out in the real world, far from the shadow of the Chief, people were finding true love, solving the pressing problems of humanity, earning spectacular golf endorsements. I would convince myself to drift away.

It was a cycle of passion and drama, all of it pointing to a personal truth. I was scared silly.

JIM BALDWIN'S partner on the Chief, Ed Cooper, is now a retired photographer in Sonoma, California. Cooper remembers one overwhelming emotion as he pulled onto the summit: "It was a relief."

The two men had run up and down the Chief for 40 days, had hand-drilled 136 bolts into the white granodiorite. On the wall, they were tested by the climbing, and off it by the rubberneckers that gathered so thick that Cooper can still hear the echoes of police bullhorns resounding on the stone. "The highway up to Squamish was *jammed*," he says. "I mean, you wouldn't believe it." One weekend, the gridlock held 12,000 cars.

I'd heard Baldwin and Cooper referred to, in jest, as "the first fully sponsored climbing team." Cooper laughs—and agrees. Squamish, then a lumberjack village lost in the black jungle that begins wherever Vancouver ends, became the largest base camp rock climbing has ever known. Today, the truce between Gore-Tex and mackinaw jackets is uneasy; then, it was Squamish's chance to debut to the young nation, and the climbers enjoyed free meals and lodging, while local blacksmith Ross Barr crafted custom pitons. Jim Sinclair, a veteran climber and unofficial keeper of Grand Wall lore, remembers seeing the two men cast their old boots aside when a delegation from town appeared with new pairs. It was then that he realized the climb was making history. "I picked up the boots, and I carried them into the woods, and I stashed them under a big rock," Sinclair recalls. Fourteen years later, a local museum curator was wishing aloud that the boots had been saved. Sinclair hiked into the forest and hauled them out of memory; they're in the museum today—still pale green from their years under moss.

The hospitality came with an unspoken agreement. Cooper and Baldwin did their best to keep the media happy and were up on the wall each weekend when the tourist trade would boom. The climb descended, Cooper says, into a "circus" and a "spectacle," and when I ask if they'd have succeeded on the route without such a push from below, he is unequivocal. "We still would have done it," he says. "We were committed."

As Cooper predicted, the route soon became a rite of passage that could be done in a matter of days. As standards changed, the climb attracted critics, too. To some, it was "the hundred bolt error," a climb too much, too soon. But if mistakes were made, they are long forgotten. In early July, over 200 people gathered to cheer the climb's 40th anniversary, sending Ed Cooper home with a plaque under his arm. But the route and its pioneers had already achieved the True North equivalent of sainthood: the Grand Wall has been featured on a Kokanee beer can, and Baldwin & Cooper Best Bitter is on tap in a Squamish pub.

ON A late June evening, I once again find myself in the lot below the big wall. Two climbers come stumbling in, hung all over with gear and tinkling like twin human wind chimes. One cuts straight for the outhouse; the other pops the trunk of a car, squeezes some kind of nutrient gel into his mouth, and immediately starts to retch. When the heaving subsides, I approach.

"What did you climb?"

"Grand Wall," he replies, eyes set on the middle distance.

"I'm climbing the Grand tomorrow," I admit. "How was it?"

He paces off again, hacking and spitting, then turns back on me with unnaturally wide eyes. "Crazy," he says, staccato voice. "It was fucking crazy up there." Long pause. "Holy shit." Another pause. "I mean, it is pretty fucking full-on."

He walks away, staring into space like a man who's seen the devil.

TO CLIMB well, you must collect courage. Experience. Grossly overpriced gadgets. Above all else, you must collect "beta." The term was coined by an American, Jack Mileski, to refer to the hints, trade secrets and Yoda-like insight that help a climber get from bottom to top. The definition is constantly expanding, so there is now beta on pubs, on campsites, on the best approach to an eligible bachelor. I made it my mission to collect Grand Wall beta, on the theory that forewarned is forearmed. Unfortunately, I overdosed.

My friend and partner for the day, Colly Blenkinsop, pulls into the parking lot at seven AM and immediately notes the symptoms. "If I didn't know that you don't drink coffee," he says, "I'd have guessed that you'd had four cups."

I titter. Yes, I *am* having a spot of trouble with my fine motor skills this morning. Beta, it turns out, cuts both ways. On the one hand, I knew to hold out for a good backstep edge 15 feet up the Split Pillar. On the other, I knew that falling below the backstep could result in matching casts. In between yin and yang, I was finding, is some pretty fierce kung fu.

Colly and I sort gear, strip off every ounce of unnecessary weight, and then drink water until even shifting weight makes us seasick. A Swainson's thrush sings a poignant tune. It's time to go.

The trail to the base of the Grand is haunted. Baldwin and Cooper cut it with machete and axe when they were still innocents, before their climb had gone all Barnum & Bailey. Since then, the path has been packed hard by every great North American rock climber you'd care to name. Just inside the close of the trailhead, a boulder features a carving of a nude climber; it's the handiwork of Squamish stoneworker Jack Richardson, who took inspiration on a day when there was a climber on every rope-length of the wall. His stone figure is a reminder that if you feel sick with fear on the walk up to the Grand, you are in the best possible company.

At the base of the climb, we get down to the business of clipping carabiners and tying knots. Here's the beta: it won't do any good to stand there with your jaw wagging like Scooby-Doo. What you see is plain enough. Picture the North Atlantic Ocean under cloud—great grey swells, each undulation scalloped with scoops and divots carved by the wind. Turn this scene on its end, and you have the Grand Wall. At the horizon, throw in the curl of a distant tsunami.

A final gut check. We will bring only one rope, making escape impossible before Bellygood Ledge. The weather is cool and clear and I'm feeling fit, but again, I remember the beta: motivation beats preparation. Greg Foweraker, a Vancouver climber who has been up the Grand over 40 times, faced a much bleaker situation at the base on Easter break, 1979. The sky that day was a black eye, but nothing could stop three teenagers still buzzing from Jethro Tull, live in concert. By nightfall the party was on a high ledge, soaked to the skin by sleet. "We rolled ourselves up in foamies and tied ropes around ourselves, trying to keep it all together," he recalls. In the night he awoke; something weird was going on. He shook his nearest buddy. "Do you smell hair burning?" In the darkness, they struggled over to the final member of the trio—so cold he was trying to dry his hair over a candle.

I begin leading the first ropelength, or pitch, placing wedges into cracks and clipping the rope to them for protection. The potential fall is always twice the distance to the last wedge; that is, if I climb five feet past a wedge, I'm looking at a 10-foot drop. That's assuming the wedge stays stuck in the rock, and that Colly is not sound asleep. Colly is "on belay," meaning he must pay out rope to the leader, or, in the case of a fall, hold it tight with the help of a friction device.

The *Baldwin-Cooper Route* is now forgotten, remembered instead as three separate climbs: the *Flake*, the *Grand Wall* to Bellygood Ledge, and the *Roman Chimneys* to the top. I have started up the *Flake*, which is unusual. Most climbers scramble up a side trail to a ledge two pitches above me, or cruise up a beautiful thin crack dubbed *Apron Strings*. They do this because the *Flake* is a miserable slog. Within a minute I'm crammed, back to the wall, in a slot barely deeper than my chest, yesterday's rainwater running down my right shoulder and algae staining my new white jersey. Twisting to face the rock, I lean back onto my arms, my feet skating on damp crystals. In this manner, I creep upward while slowly losing my mind.

Colly follows once I've reached the first perch. He appears, his moves long and simian where mine are nervous, like a weasel's. His eyes are lost in that strange climber's limbo between clarity and panic.

"How're you doing?" I ask, too cheerfully.

"Trying to remember that I like this," he mutters, more to himself than to me.

Baldwin and Cooper were direct aid climbers, meaning they placed their faith in their equipment. To move upward, they would pound a piton or a bolt into the stone, clip into it, pull up, and hope that it held. Today, most of the Grand Wall is "free," meaning you place your faith in your hands and feet. You grab a hold, pull up, and hope you have the strength to hang on. The second pitch of the *Flake* is one of the only places where Baldwin and Cooper climbed free.

The pitch is a wide chimney choked with broken rock, and today's free line runs straight to its top. This alone can be enough for some people; the first major ledge is called the Flake Escape. Baldwin and Cooper didn't go there, however. Instead, they broke away midway up the chimney, driving in dozens of bolts in a right-leaning ladder. They missed the easy climbing off the top of the *Flake* that might have taken them higher, faster. They didn't even consider the line of seams and edges that is now *Cruel Shoes,* a line climbed free 20 years later by Perry Beckham. Today, Beckham calls the rusting bolt ladder "a sign of Baldwin and Cooper's mental state when they did the climb." The two men were feeling the blinding gravitational pull of the Split Pillar.

Climbers still do. Under the Yosemite Decimal grading system, the Pillar rings in at 5.10b. For any committed weekend warrior, that's an achievable goal. But the Pillar remains notorious.

"I defy the 5.13 indoor climbers to get their asses up there," says Tami Knight, the climbing community's ornery cartoonist. "They'd be filling their trousers pretty quick, no doubt about it."

To get to the Pillar today, most climbers start up a pink basalt dyke, *Merci Me,* then cut right on the next pitch, running across granite below an overhang that frowns like a giant stepfather. Colly and I swap leads as the moves grow steadily more delicate, the holds progressively smaller. After a creative traverse, Colly humps up a short bolt ladder—some of the few aid moves remaining on the climb—and I follow, joining him at that lone tree that looks so otherworldly from the ground. This is Passing Ledge.

They call it Passing Ledge because you pass it when you fall off the Split Pillar.

All the beta in the world didn't prepare me for the Pillar. It's what they call a "splitter"—a perfect crack in an open-book corner between feature-less walls. It's vertical, but seems to arch outward, hanging your bacon over the forest. "It's one of the absolute best on the planet," says Knight of the Pillar pitch. "For position, setting—the only thing that's missing is spectacular alpine views." She laughs. "And most people say it's the hard-est 'job they've ever climbed."

It doesn't help these struggling climbers that the Pillar is detached. A single crack runs up one side, across the top, and down the other. The rock, roughly the shape of an enormous coffin, is balanced or stuck on who-knows-what. After rain, the Pillar pitch dries quickly, *because the wind blows right through it.* When a 6.8 magnitude earthquake in Seattle shook B.C.'s south coast in February, an on-line post promptly reported that the Pillar had fallen. Climbers in Squamish fielded panicked calls from friends taken in by the hoax.

The Pillar is the most storied pitch on the most storied rock climb in Canada. The guides at Outward Bound in nearby Pemberton have an informal "Split Pillar Fall Club" with a tightly limited membership—the fall must be 40 feet or more. Colly is a member. If the Fall Club were open to all and any climbers, and collected dues, it would be able to finance universal psychotherapy for the complete Squamish climbing commu-nity. In other words, falls are regular, and because moving upward is eas-ier than stopping to place special cams for protection, the air miles add up quickly. Those who pass Passing Ledge do all right; those who hit it on the way down go home with broken ankles or worse. Important beta: no one has ever died while climbing the Grand Wall.

Still, the potential withers the soul. "I've seen people up there in tears, their arms all bloodied, and they just don't know what to do. It's a sorry sight," says Squamish climbing guide Kris Wild, smiling broadly. "I love it, because I get to go up and get the cams they leave behind." A good camming unit might cost $100, and all abandoned gear is considered fair game. "The majority of people come down humbled," says Wild. "They climb the Split Pillar and they figure, 'If that's 5.10, I can't keep going.'"

NOW IT'S my turn. I plug in a cam, grab the edge of the crack, lean back on my arms, and walk my feet up the wall—the gorilla move known as liebacking. Fifteen feet later, I reach that backstep edge; popping here would mean a 30-foot fall. Another cam. Above it, I start jamming: wedging my own hands and feet into the crack as my only means of support. The jams are solid at first, but the crack slowly widens and I start to feel my feet rattling, the skin on the back of my hands slipping. It's hard to stop for more than a few seconds, so I tinker in a final piece of protection below the crux bulge and cut loose, liebacking 10 feet, then 15, and suddenly I'm about to become a pledge for the Fall Club fraternity. My forearms swell like soaked blood sausage, and I remember that I was warned not to lieback too soon. But just beyond the bulge, I know, are the Thank God holds, and I strike for one with a long reach. My right knee does a kind of James Brown thing, and then I'm on the T.G.s, white-knuckling to my feet and a no-hands rest. Some people are so drained by this point that they wedge their head in the crack for good measure.

A little squeeze in a chimney, and I'm on the top. "The spiritual home of Squamish climbers": that's how local veteran John Howe describes the cap of the Pillar. It's a rock triangle, just large enough for two people to practise extreme square dancing. In the aid-climbing days, parties would camp here for the night. Later, in the "hard core" years of the 1970s, it was a place to go "to debauch," says Perry Beckham. "We'd sit up there and wait until we were sober enough to climb."

The best measure of the place, though, might be found in the following images. The first: there is, rumour has it, a Split Pillar version of the Mile-High Club. The second: more than one person has climbed onto the Pillar's cap only to find it caked with blood from some serious business on the pitches above. The spark of life, and something near death, all bound up in the middle of nowhere.

THE STORY of the Grand Wall is a history of liberation. From the first ascent forward, milestones were marked by the effort to smooth out the aid climbing and "free" every possible move. Today, when people are picking over boulders for the best remaining lines of untried holds, it's hard to imagine what it must have been like to cast into the unknown on the premier Squamish big wall in, say, 1975. That year, Eric Weinstein freed the Pillar.

Weinstein is a legend, a man who died of cancer too young but left behind a string of visionary routes. That few people remember the details of his Pillar ascent is testament to Weinstein's skill; it was *assumed* he would succeed. In that era, the Pillar was undergraded at 5.9; one year later, Weinstein climbed Squamish's *Sentry Box*, then one of the hardest pitches on the planet. Today, *Sentry Box* makes the guidebooks at 5.12a.

"Eric was intense—very intense," says Dave Nicol, a Vancouver lawyer and climber who was one of Weinstein's best friends. "You weren't allowed to talk while he was climbing. He always did a warm-up, and stretching. It was like he was on a mission. It was almost as if it wasn't something he did for fun."

So we can picture Weinstein, starting up the Pillar in absolute silence—maybe. On belay was Daryl Hatten, a member of the 1970s Squamish hard core, vulgarians who mixed fierce climbing with even fiercer boozing. It is hard to believe Hatten would be Weinstein's ideal Zen belayer; more likely, Hatten was on the team because he had the guts to catch a potentially godawful fall.

Consider the bleeding and crying and jesusing still associated with the Pillar, and then consider this: Weinstein climbed the route in hard-rubber shoes and a Whillans harness that could neuter a man in even a short fall. Worse, he would have protected the route with hexentrics—huge aluminum wedges. (Today, the route is almost always led using camming devices designed to hold in the parallel-sided crack.) Worst of all, if Weinstein fell off up high—becoming the founding member of the Fall Club—then Hatten, his belayer, would have to hold the line with just his bare hands and the rope round his hips. In the days before the advent of friction belay devices, the belayer needed nerve almost equal to the leader.

The beta: a moment of silence for Eric Weinstein before climbing the Pillar is almost certain to improve your courage.

At the top of the Pillar, I pay silent dues—to Colly, who will take the next dead-vertical lead, this one threatened by a flake of rock that hangs overhead like its namesake, the Sword of Damocles. This dangling guillotine almost scared Baldwin and Cooper off the wall when Cooper tapped it with a hammer and set it humming like hell's dinner gong.

We are entering Peter Croft country. There are dozens of powerful Squamish climbers, but only one that has transcended into the iconic. In the 1980s, climbers worldwide were opening long free climbs on big walls. Croft caught the bug, moving from his hometown of Nanaimo to come of age as a hardman on Squamish granite. Each climber imprints a climb with personality, and Croft's routes tend to be beautiful loners, the kinds of eccentrics that are at once appealing and unsettling. But that's not where the Croft myth begins. Instead, it has its roots in images like the one that hung in the original Squamish climbing shop, now a forgotten wood hut at the side of the highway. In it, Croft is climbing "free solo"—ropeless—halfway up a grim test piece known as *Hot Cherry Bendover*. You try to remember where you've seen eyes like that before—wide, immediate eyes, with the faintest hint of mischief. Then you remember: Peter Pan.

Croft is a master of many games—speed climbs, endless peak-to-peak link-ups, first-attempt leads of 5.13 cracks—but it always comes back to that image of man and mountain and nothing in between. Peter Croft, ropeless, the speck above the void. Croft, with no safety net, rampaging through 110 hard pitches in a single day in Australia. Croft, free solo in the death zone on a Yosemite big wall, and oh lord, pity his poor mother.

He kept the rope tied tight, however, when he began freeing the line above the Pillar in the early 1980s. Working with Foweraker, Knight and the unheralded Hamish Fraser, Croft freed eight of the final nine pitches of the *Baldwin-Cooper Route*.

"In some rock climbing areas there's a bunch of routes that all have some kind of status, but in Squamish, the *Grand Wall* was *it*," he says now. "It was kind of like picking the best fruit from the tree."

Those who struggle on the Sword, take heart. Croft, a climber described by Foweraker as "an unstoppable force," did his fair share of wheezing up there. "At the time we weren't climbing much harder than 5.11," Croft says (the pitch is graded 5.11a). "It felt pretty full-on. We would be up there and, I mean, look where we *are*." The Sword features the climb's most exposed move, a long, blind step from a corner into a face crack with an unobstructed view of ground zero. "We were holding on twice as hard as we had to, and there was always that question of, 'Is this even possible?'"

Apparently so. By July 1986, on the 25th anniversary of the Baldwin-Cooper climb, Croft and Perry Beckham were able to climb the entire route in under three hours. Even today, an average party will take three times as long.

There is still a bolt ladder above the Sword, the last long stretch of direct aid still used by most climbers. Then comes *Perry's Lieback*, a pitch first freed by Beckham after a twist of fate that secured, at least for now, the opportunity for climbers like myself to get up the Grand.

Perry's Lieback angles sharply to the right beneath a looming overlap. The only "hold" is what is known as an off-width crack. No part of the human body fits neatly in an off-width, so a climber must either lieback off its outside edge, or jam a combination of bent arms and torqued knees into the bowels of the stone. *Perry's Lieback* was the final pitch of the standard route to go free, and around kitchen tables and at bar stools circa 1982, it was the Squamish climbers' equivalent of religion and politics. There was the liebacking camp and the jamming camp. There was the camp that supported bolts for protection, and the camp that rooted for "tube chocks" (aluminum cylinders cut to wedge into wide gaps). There was, Beckham remembers, "speculation and discussion."

Finally, Beckham says, he convinced himself that jamming the crack and placing chocks was the better way to go. Not that he was the one to do it, however. He headed up the wall with wide-crack maestro Greg Cameron, a bold climber out of California. "Greg conveniently dropped the tube chocks from the top of the Split Pillar," Beckham recalls. In this inglorious manner did the dream of the tube-chocked off-width nightmare fade from collective memory.

Instead, Beckham bolted the route and liebacked it. "It's always an option that the bolts could be removed and climbers will continue to climb it using today's big cams," he says. "The only problem with that is that it would obligate everyone who does the climb to drag up $300 to $400 worth of gear that you wouldn't need to use on almost any other climb."

The fact is, the shiny, solid bolts are downright popular, particularly with those who, like me, fall off on this pitch.

In the days leading up to the climb, my dreams had been troubled by falls. I would turn a double helix in the air, or spin upside down, or slap a ledge. I would see myself weeping, or watching pieces of protection spit out of the wall like watermelon seeds. But in the end, back in the pinch-me world, I didn't even merit my Fall Club badge. My grip faded and my hands slipped and I was suddenly off the wall, turning a half-pirouette, like Trudeau behind the queen. Then the rope went tight, held fast by a bolt. I rested, then pulled past the sloping holds that had stopped me— imagine holding two volleyballs full of sand, palms down—and then I came to this most amazing place.

I'll call it "The Headstone," since no one seems to have settled on any other nickname. Liebacking hard off the wall, feet plastered flat, you suddenly notice a tablet of rock poking down behind you. So you lean out until you can prop your head against it, and then your shoulders, and you discover you can wedge yourself in there pretty well. In fact, yes, you can let go with one hand. And then the other. And then you're just kind of standing there, hands at your sides, as though you're waiting for a bus to drive up the middle of the Chief. When you turn to look, you look straight down for 900 feet.

THINGS GO weird high up on the wall. Beyond *Perry's Lieback* are the Flats, from which retreat is no longer an option. It is here, on the final three pitches to Bellygood Ledge, that people are suddenly dive-bombed by bats, or swarmed by biting flies. They're struck from above by frogs, or by the severed head of a songbird that's fallen prey to a peregrine falcon. Maybe they're hit by human feces rolling off Bellygood, or lose two teeth to rockfall, or they see a homemade zeppelin drift by, burning like a mini-Hindenberg. They might watch a body fall past, horribly, only to see the parachute open a few moments later. There is the spectacle of a rescue worker suspended from a chopper with a very lucky Rottweiler clutched in his arms. There are UFO sightings. It is possible that the dehydrated see hallucinations, but these are never any worse than reality.

And so, at Bellygood Ledge, most people shuffle across the wildly exposed traverse—or make the namesake crawl—and head for bed, the bar, the comforting arms of their loved ones. That night, behind their eyes, they will see the words of hardman and guidebook author Kevin McLane, with emphasis added: "Those who are old or weary, thirsty or plain knackered, can traverse off... Everyone else should do the next route. *The Grand Wall is not complete without it.*"

The "next route" is the *Roman Chimneys,* and Colly and I know it is out of our league—four more pitches of 5.10 and 5.11, and already my forearms feel like Popeye's in the middle of a spinach crop failure. The chimneys are for another day. But we aren't about to traverse off, either. We want the summit, and we've chosen an alternate line called the *Upper Black Dyke.*

We start up on the rough basalt, probing for holds under toques of moss. We have achieved that odd inner cool that comes after hours of climbing. Exposure has lost its meaning, and the idea of falling into so much air feels almost welcome. We hit a rhythm. Hand, foot, hand, foot, forever through a devious, wandering, vertical path, bolts appearing like afterthoughts. Above us, the clouds are beginning to close, and we have long ago finished our one litre of water. For the first time, I feel like a Grand Wall climber.

I find myself thinking about a single tiger lily I had seen on Bellygood Ledge, its impossibly golden petals nodding out into the ether. It brings to mind all the climbers I had talked to and their strongest memories. Only rarely would it be the big fall or the badass lieback. More often, it was the early evening light. For Greg Foweraker, it was watching the seasons change in the wall's tenacious, scrubby trees; for Anders Ourom, president of the Squamish Access Society, it was the falcons with their chicks; for Perry Beckham, it was the misery of being stuck on the wall at night while he could see and hear his friends at an epic party in the Grand Wall climbers' campground; and for Peter Croft, it was watching his friend Hamish Fraser lose his footing in the *Roman Chimneys,* only to recover with a one arm pull-up, "smooth as silk, from a dead hang." This is the private history of the Grand Wall, handed down in mild nose-stretchers, out-and-out fish stories and as often as not, the Scout's-honour truth. It's the ultimate beta, and its message is this: none of us climbs alone.

The official history, too, continues to be written. Only last year, Scott Cosgrove of Joshua Tree, California, became the first person ever to free climb every inch of the Grand, from the base to the top of the *Roman Chimneys*. Climbing a vague ramp to bypass the bolt ladder between the Sword and *Perry's Lieback*, Cosgrove graded his new pitch a fierce 5.13b. Some people shrugged. It would take the average climber an inhuman effort to repeat the moves across that 40 feet of cut gemstone. Why bother?

"I've travelled all over the world and I've never seen a line like that on such a blank wall," says Cosgrove. "It's amazing—it's like you're walking on the edge."

But the meaning of that final free pitch is more personal than that, reaching back through the history of Squamish rock. Cosgrove's father grew up in Britannia, just south of Squamish, and worked there in the copper mine. His parents remember clearly the time they first heard that two lunatic climbers were making tracks up the centre of that incredible face. They remember it like they remember the first man on the moon.

WHEN I pull over the top of the Black Dyke into the shaded forest of the summit plateau, there is still one more bit of unfinished business. Every day from thaw to freeze-up, dozens of people hike the Chief up a back-side trail. At the high point, they take in the kind of view that affects us at the level of genetics, dark chocolate and God. I'd been up the trail any number of times, but had never taken in the view. Each time, I stopped well below the peak. It was a personal declaration: I would get there the hard way or not at all.

Colly and I shuffle over to the last granite dome and jam a final, easy pitch, *Talking Crack*. For years, I had wondered what it would feel like to reach that point where there's nothing left to climb. Some days, I saw myself slapping high-fives with Japanese tourists. In other visions, I was wrapped in a sacred silence, as though I'd attended my own funeral and now had the honour of casting my own ashes into the wind. But somewhere en route to the stratosphere, the conquering hero had faded. As the self-help books warn, it isn't always about *you*. Sometimes it's about time and timelessness on one of the world's finest granite monoliths. It's about the great, po-faced stone itself.

Colly and I shake hands. I take a deep breath, and look out with a view I might never have seen.

||||||||||||||

THE HAPPY, TORMENTED LIFE OF A MOUNTAIN LEGEND

GEOFF POWTER

SEPTEMBER/OCTOBER 2002

YEARS BEFORE HE became *the* Blanchard, a mountaineer so revered that aspiring alpinists pin his photo in their high-school lockers... long before he earned the nickname Bubba Blanch, crazy party boy, best friend to every climber on the planet... way before he lived large as *Bah*-rry, mountain guide to the movie stars, 80-foot-high hero of Imax *Extreme*... ages before he descended into the underworld of Blanchard *agonistes*, explorer of the dark terrain of the climber's soul... years before he returned as the Warrior Blanchard, born-again Metis mountain man... before all that, he was just the chubby kid in the milkman's uniform.

Back then, we rock jocks gathered to preen and pose on the climbing puzzles carved into the brick walls of the University of Calgary. Every so often the milk truck would pull up, and the kid in the white polyester shirt with "Barry" embroidered over the pocket would hop out the sliding door, all smiles and bubbling energy. He'd try a few of the problems, always fall flat on his ass, and cackle one of those great laughs of his. Get us all laughing. "Nice kid," we thought. "Can't climb worth a damn, but a nice kid." Then we'd stare as he'd load a pack with rocks and start traversing the wall, a hundred feet back and forth, back and forth, till his forearms flamed and his calves set to burst. Then he'd do it again. And again. The most boring thing in the universe, we thought.

The rest of us never really got that much better, though, working those 10-foot-high "hardest climbs in the world." But the chubby kid in the milkman's uniform, grinding his way across the wall, he would become *Blanchard* within a year.

NEARLY 25 years later, Barry Blanchard leans back in his Canmore condo and launches into an assessment of the world of climbing, and his position within it. As he pontificates—one of his friends laughingly describes him as "the Pope" of alpine climbing—I take a measure of the distance he has travelled. Blanchard has lost the milkman's baby chub, but he still doesn't fit the wiry, long-limbed-spider mould of the typical mountain star. Instead, he's a barrel of a man; two huge lungs on a pair of tree-trunk thighs, with the hands of a longshoreman. He's grown his hair out, and it falls down to the middle of his back in a proud salt-and-pepper mane. He sports a telling tattoo—a heart speared by an ice axe. His face reflects the complexities in the man: skin worked by years outside but framed by youthful sideburns; almond eyes in deep folds that shape-shift from basset hound mournful to twinklingly mischievous. He releases deep whistles through his teeth when he's serious and pensive, and sudden bellyful chuckles when, more often, he's not. He tells just-got-into-port stories that would make a Marine blush, but melts when talking about his love for his mountains, for his climbing partners and for his wife, Catherine.

At 43, Blanchard is still as hooked on the mountains as he was as a kid, and it shows in the climbs he continues to do. The accomplishments of his forties are as significant as the climbs of his twenties. But it's a measure of the man—and his game—that he's still relatively anonymous outside the cloisters of the climbing world. Climbing has gained a greater profile since Blanchard started out in the late 1970s; these days there are *Into Thin Air*-heads in every café, climbing gyms in prairie backwaters and ads that use rock climbers to shill arthritis medicine. But for the most part, *real* top-end, high-risk climbing, the kind that Blanchard excels at, remains invisible except to other climbers.

If his game were a more public one—or if he lived in Europe, where top climbers receive the national press of hockey stars—Blanchard would have the profile of a Gretzky or a Tiger Woods, a grandmaster who sets the standards by which his game is judged. But as with many outdoor sports, there's no objective means of comparing climbs or climbers, which leads to odd people making a name for themselves. Fame certainly isn't the best measure of skill in the climbing world: it's one thing to get up Mount Everest; it's another to climb it well. But that distinction is based on nuances of style that lull Joe Public to sleep. If you stood on top of the mountain, who cares *how* you got there?

Blanchard cares. Sitting forward in his chair and furrowing his brow, he is adamant that there *is* a way that climbing should be played. There *are* rules that make the sport the best it can be. There have been great mentors whose paths *need* to be followed because they understood what climbing is about: no hype, no sponsors, no media. Just climb hard, climb clean and climb all the time. But to live by that philosophy, he allows, the alpinist must take a journey that's often more lonely, more complex—and more risky—than the average glory-hunter is willing to follow.

THERE AREN'T many places in Calgary that qualify as "inner-city" living, but the neighbourhood where Blanchard grew up, hard by the railway tracks and shadowed by the overpasses of Crowchild Trail, comes closest. His Metis mother had Blanchard when she was 19 and then moved to Calgary to escape a hard-luck future in rural Saskatchewan. "I got the adventure gene from my mother," he muses. "Coming to the big city, leaving behind all of her family, living on welfare and raising five kids pretty much on her own—man, that's a bigger adventure than *I've* ever had."

Throughout Blanchard's early life, forces were pulling him in opposite directions—native and white, rich and poor (his school straddled the poorest and one of the wealthiest parts of the city), good and bad—and he bounced between these worlds. "I had these straitlaced friends who were kids of accountants and lawyers," explains Blanchard. "Meanwhile the police brought me home many, many times." He insists that even then he was just out for adventure—"the life of Huck Finn," he calls his early hobby of shoplifting and B&Es.

One day between heists, 12-year-old Blanchard took a Greyhound back to Saskatchewan. The woman next to him was reading *The White Spider*, an account of climbing the Eiger by Heinrich Harrer, the German mountaineer who would become best known for *Seven Years in Tibet*. Blanchard asked what the book was about, and the woman passed it to him for the rest of the ride. That was that. "I just knew it, first time I saw that book, that was what I wanted to do." He started to devour the mountain classics, like Hermann Buhl's *Nanga Parbat Pilgrimage* and Walter Bonatti's *The Great Days*. "I'd probably be illiterate if it wasn't for those books," he laughs.

Through them, he pieced together, awkwardly, how to do the climbing thing, rappelling out of the second-storey window of the family townhouse on a clothesline tied to a bed. ("I'd have to add my brother as extra weight so the bed wouldn't come flying out the window after me," he recalls.) He mastered the finer details of rappelling at cadet camp—until he got kicked out for running a cigarette-selling ring. ("Made good money," he shrugs.) Then he discovered a more utilitarian value in climbing, and used the first equipment he bought to rappel off warehouse roofs for what he wryly describes as "extra-curricular gain." ("Made good money at *that*, too.")

Blanchard stops short of saying that climbing *saved* him. Instead he remembers that the sound of a steel door shutting behind him on a visit to a B&E buddy in prison was enough to scare him straight, whether he ever climbed again or not.

The problem for a mountain-mad kid wanting to escape downtown life in the late 1970s, even in Calgary, was that the peaks seemed a million miles away. There weren't any climbing schools, and guides were expensive; no one even seemed to know about the sport. That's when the 19-year-old Blanchard, the milkman now, stumbled into Kevin Doyle, whose sister was dating Blanchard's roommate. Doyle was the first person Blanchard had met who actually called himself a climber. "The day we met, we circled each other like bighorns in rut," recalls Blanchard.

"'Oh you *climb*, do you?' 'Yeah, what have *you* climbed?' Truth was, neither of us had climbed shit."

So they figured out how to do it themselves. "Right from the beginning," Doyle explains, "we knew that we didn't want to do the easy stuff. We wanted to push ourselves." In the pairing, Doyle brought remarkable natural skill and a head for fear, while Blanchard added an unwavering commitment. "Barry may not have been the best climber on the hill," says Doyle, "but more than anyone I've ever met in the mountains, he just loves being out there. We wouldn't have done half of the things we did without that."

What they did was form one of the strongest partnerships in the history of Canadian mountaineering. Between 1979 and 1982, Blanchard and Doyle climbed nearly 1,000 days together, racking up mileage that most climbers take a lifetime to amass. They had more than their share of crazy, bumbling moments—stranded overnight on ledges, using up several lives in huge falls. ("That was me," laughs Doyle. "Barry was always the cautious one—I never saw him take a big fall.") But they also started gaining talent faster than seemed possible, firing up ice, rock and mountain routes in the Canadian Rockies that no one else seemed willing to tackle. Then they tested their limits on the bigger peaks in Alaska and the Alps, where the two men were thrilled to discover they measured up. Their performance on these international stages drew new partners to them, big-leaguers who helped mature their craft and stretch their sense of what was possible in the mountains.

PICTURE THOSE perfect mountaineering images: a cobalt-blue sky, a brilliant sun, a gentle wave of snow, a line of footprints snaking its way along a crest to a windless summit. Happy brown faces waiting for you at camp with hot tea.

Blanchard's climbs have as much in common with those mountain clichés as bubblegum has with heroin. Block the sun—hell, exile it to the other side of the mountain. Add showers of spindrift and a 65-pound pack. Replace the pristine snow with shattered black rock, glued together with a veneer of rotten ice ready to melt and let loose a deadly fusillade of rocks.

Risk is the thread that connects all of Blanchard's climbs. But it's not the kind of risk that you've read about in *Into Thin Air*. There's no sitting down in the snow and freezing to death because you fall asleep, no stumbling around in a storm because you haven't been short-roped to your high-priced guide. On Blanchard's climbs, death wins when you don't execute the perfectly controlled movement at exactly the right time: Shift a finger, you die. Swing an ice axe too hard, you die. Grab that loose rock, you die.

Blanchard's mountains are steep, 50- to 90-degree faces—whereas the most familiar mountaineering routes are on 20- to 30-degree slopes—that connect vague dots of ice runnels, snowfields and crack systems on otherwise barren, enormous walls. His lines follow ephemeral features: frozen water streaks that evaporate or disintegrate within days of the ascent and don't reappear for years; cracks that fill up with snow and have to be excavated to be climbed; routes that would never form if they saw sun.

These are climbs that, in Blanchard's eyes, demand a certain style. Forget fixed ropes and bolts; forget tents and satellite phones, porters and backup teams of spare climbers. That's not the way his hero Walter Bonatti did it. In the 1940s and 1950s, during the era of massive military-scale sieges of Himalayan peaks, the Italian master quietly set a different standard of climbing with his ascents of massive faces in the Alps. Bonatti and his rare peers did their climbs with a minimum of equipment and a purity of intent, and Blanchard's approach to the mountains follows their lead: reduce the advantage that technology offers; rely only on yourself and your fortitude; find the straightest line and climb from the bottom to the top; embrace rather than avoid the obstacles in the way.

"I want to live up to the standards set by these great climbers, with climbs that are more about the *inner* journey than the outer route, about *how* you do the climb rather than *what* climb you do. So we go at the peaks with small teams, never more than four people and preferably two. And we go via the challenging route. We take two ropes, an ice rack and a rock rack. We don't take bolts, ever, and if all that's not enough to get us up the mountain, then we come down."

What Blanchard's talking about is the distinction, perhaps arcane to the outsider, between the *alpinist* (Blanchard's game) and the *mountaineer* (the game played by most everyone else). Mountaineering is about getting to the summit, about the aesthetics of the experience. Alpinism is about those, too, but it's more so about fighting the mountain on its own terms. "If you throw enough money and technology at a mountain, you can beat it into submission," he says. "What we're doing is trying to absolutely minimize what we're taking up there. At every point we choose *less*, so the mountain still has huge power."

BLANCHARD SOARED through the ranks of world climbing in the 1980s, like no Canadian before or since. He put together a string of groundbreaking ascents in the Rockies, the Alps, the Andes and the Alaska Range. By mid-decade, he pushed into the Himalaya; in 1984, with Doyle and David Cheesmond (one of the Rockies' finest climbers and a mentor to Blanchard), he summitted Rakaposhi, a mountain with huge relief and complicated terrain. Their six-day ascent remains one of the high points in Canada's climbing history—though little known by an Everest-fixated public.

Not that Blanchard was immune to the lure of the big mountain. By the mid-1980s, he was well into the difficult process of becoming a mountain guide, and summitting Everest would be both a wise personal and career achievement. His reputation secured his place on a Canadian team that went to the mountain in 1986, organized as a response to the massive expedition that had put the first two Canadians on the summit four years earlier. Everest Light '86 was a smaller, closer-knit team trying a hard, unclimbed route on the more difficult north side of the hill.

The strength of the team proved necessary. That spring, ferocious winds whipped the mountain, making travel nearly impossible. After more than a month, the team had stretched their resources to place a camp below the top, and Blanchard felt he was one of the few climbers still fit enough to have a go at the summit. But he was asked to step aside, to be on the B-team, while Sharon Wood and Dwayne Congdon made their successful climbs of the peak. After their ascents, the trip leader pulled the plug on the expedition, deciding a second summit would be too dangerous.

Blanchard describes Everest Light as a personal failure because he betrayed his alpine ideals by committing to a large-scale project that seemed to prize the summit over style. But the expedition helped clarify, once again, how he wanted to climb. "I realized that I didn't want to go with 13 other climbers and fix 15,000 feet of rope," he says. "The political decision was made to have me turn around far before I was finished with my climb. Rather than me deciding to come down, I was *told* to come down, and that's not what climbing should be about."

Blanchard had his chance to climb without the politics when he returned to the Himalaya two years later. Blanchard, Doyle, unsung Canadian climber Ward Robinson and the fine American alpinist Mark Twight launched an ultralight attempt of the Rupal Face of Pakistan's Nanga Parbat, the world's highest face on the most dangerous of the 8,000-metre peaks. No fixed ropes, no support, no tents. Just a single-push, bottom-to-top ascent. Nanga Parbat was a trial by fire of Blanchard's minimalist philosophy. The climbers were brutalized by the mountain, and all four came close to dying in an avalanche. After losing their food and their descent ropes, they made it back down the peak only after stumbling upon a cache of gear left behind by a previous team who'd perished on the mountain four years earlier. Blanchard later described the experience as "like having sex with death."

If the climb had succeeded, it would have been one of Canada's landmark ascents in the high mountains, no contest. Still, as Canadian alpine historian Chic Scott notes, even if he hadn't reached his "ultimate summit," Blanchard had "gained the respect of mountaineers worldwide." He was on fire.

AS HE climbed his way through the 1980s, the rest of Blanchard's life was rumbling in the background. He was immersed in the humbling process of becoming a mountain guide; already one of the world's best climbers, he still had to prove he could tie basic knots and trudge up snow slogs. He'd married his high-school sweetheart in 1985 and was struggling to keep that relationship alive through the strains of back-to-back expeditions to lethal mountains and the temptations that went along with his growing fame in the climbing community. He was also doing his best to be big brother to his siblings, some struggling with addictions, some with the law.

Once again Blanchard had his feet in two worlds. In the one, he played the part of a stable, professional, married man with family responsibilities; in the other, he was "Bubba," a larger-than-life alpine hero, living life broad under the big top and partying like he climbed: hard, often and to the limit.

Throughout the 1980s, Blanchard also witnessed firsthand the terrible price that a serious commitment to the mountains meant, losing friend after friend, and most painfully, two guided clients in an accident in the Rockies. Every one of these deaths—especially the clients'—sent the naturally self-critical Blanchard into a tailspin of doubt. Several times he swore off climbing, only to decide he couldn't live without it.

In the fall of 1991, Blanchard was back in Nepal. On the surface at least, things seemed to be going better: He was feeling strong, climbing well and had just finished a dream gig of guiding clients in the Himalaya. That outward success, though, concealed an inner turmoil. After seeing his charges on their way home, Blanchard set off up Kusum Kangguru—one of the most ambitious climbs of his life—alone.

"I'd hurt my wife with infidelity and the lying that surrounded it, and I couldn't live with that," he admits. "I went up to that climb and wrote out a will—the only time I've ever done that. I approached that climb as a test of whether the universe deemed me worthy of being in it, or whether I should be out of it."

Blanchard launched up the unclimbed wall of the 21,000-foot peak despite suffering symptoms of a cold. By the first night, he was hacking up finger-sized chunks of bloody phlegm and realized he had developed pulmonary edema, an altitude-induced swelling of the lungs that can drown climbers if they don't descend. He faced the classic dilemma of the alpine purist: he'd carried so little gear with him that despite his condition it would be easier to climb the rest of the route than go back down—in fact, it was impossible to retreat.

On his first bivouac, Blanchard was huddled in a snow cave barely large enough to curl up in, heating water, when he noticed feathers mixed in with the snowflakes that swirled around the cave. It took several minutes before he realized his down jacket was burning on the stove.

"I thought I wasn't going to get off the mountain," he admits. He climbed through a delirious nightmare, digging shelters with his helmet, wading through terrible snow, relying on pure mountain instinct to impel him over the peak. Two days later, he stumbled into camp, where his Sherpa guide was burning juniper and chanting death blessings for him. "I cried when I saw him," recalls Blanchard. "Someone still cared about me."

He may have survived the universe's test on Kusum Kangguru, but Blanchard's ordeals were far from over. When he got back to Canada, his marriage collapsed, the taxman came hunting for him, his brothers and sisters' lives were capsizing. Even within the climbing community, things had changed. His early partner Kevin Doyle had moved on from climbing to focus on his carpentry business; other partners had turned to marriage and children. And despite Blanchard's remarkable solo in Nepal, the deaths of friends—especially his mentor, Cheesmond—ate away at his commitment to hard climbing. "I just didn't think it was worth it anymore. I didn't want to do the same thing to people around me. I'd already done enough hurting."

Blanchard journeyed through a hell of emotions—over his marriage and his family, over his future and his past. He did depression like he climbed, as though the path to self-knowledge involved crossing an avalanche slope just to see if it will hold. He moved into what he jokingly calls The Cell, a blacked-out room in the aptly named Dead Man Flats outside of Canmore, and spent a couple of years sorting through his angst. "I wore black clothes, listened to black music, read black books," he says. "There was an attraction—maybe even a need—in me to go as low as I could go, to get to the bottom. I don't know if I ever did get there, but I sure tried."

Blanchard insists, however, that despite all the chaos in his life, climbing was a stabilizing force, that he never risked beyond the edge of his abilities during this period of darkness—even on Kusum Kangguru. "Climbing was the surfboard that kept me on *top* of the waves," he insists. "Mountains are such good arbiters of honesty. They'll sort out your reasons for climbing them pretty quick, and they won't let you stay long if you're there for the wrong reasons."

LIKE MANY people in the Canadian climbing community, I was surprised when Barry came out of his exile a few years later as an "Indian." We'd never heard him mention his Metis heritage, and suddenly he appeared wearing buckskin jackets and native jewellery, and burning sweetgrass.

"Growing up in the 1960s, I experienced prejudice being a 'half-breed'," explains Blanchard. "Even into my late twenties, going into a store with a white girl on my arm, I just felt the disapproval. So I was embarrassed and tried to hide it. For a long time I tried to be a blue-eyed, blond-haired guy to try and fit in." Then, when Blanchard found himself at his lowest emotional ebb, a couple of his aunts encouraged him and his family to reconnect with their Metis roots. "I started to grow my hair long, spend a lot of time in Saskatchewan and be proud. Proud that I am where I am, with a foot in the native world and the white world, because that's what my people have always done—lived between those two worlds. In the end I was a lot more settled and—what's the big word?" He pauses. "Oh yeah, *healed!*" And he releases that great guttural chortle of his.

Blanchard had clawed his way out of The Cell through a lot of hard work: reading, writing, therapy, spending time with his family, finding comfort in his growing reputation as a guide—and climbing. In the Rockies, he paralleled a classic ice-climbing route called *Whiteman Falls* with a new, much harder line that he named, aptly, *Red Man Soars*.

"The ride has smoothed out now," he says. "The depressions don't last anywhere near as long and they're not nearly so intense. Likewise, I don't get the euphoria so much. But I don't miss either one, really. I kind of like the even ebb and flow these days."

Blanchard hasn't exactly mellowed with age, though. Into his forties, he has continued to push the edge, with world-class ascents in Alaska and the Himalaya, and especially at home in the Rockies, where he's the undisputed master of the region's steep dark walls. In Canmore, there's a group of young guys who've taken up the torch of alpine climbing just as Blanchard and Doyle did 25 years ago: work just to climb, live just to climb. Rob Owens, a superbly talented 26-year-old at the heart of the self-described House of Youth, expresses Blanchard's importance to these climbers: "His style has influenced the values of every one of us. Every time I take my climbing to a new level, I'm following in Barry's footsteps."

Still following? "Oh yeah," Owens insists. "He's gone through four generations of climbers, and look at him: who's climbing harder than Barry?"

But there have been changes. Blanchard's gone a bit grey and gotten himself a dog and a mortgage. He's settled into his career, establishing himself as one of the great guides in the history of the Rockies. He's
honed his writing skills and earned a reputation for his literary explorations of his alpine motivations, fears and accomplishments. He has also
started a lucrative new gig as a mountain-safety consultant on the sets
of movies such as *K2*, *Cliffhanger* and *Vertical Limit*. "It's like high school—
too much fun," says Blanchard of his experience babysitting Hollywood
stars in the high country. "But the headaches on these projects are *cosmic*
for a simple mountain guide who's used to being God." (Still, he insists I
check out the "Making of" section on the *Vertical Limit* DVD, in which an
exotic starlet purrs, "*Bah*-rry was my idol…")

The biggest change for him has been settling down again with a
woman for longer than the brief intermissions between expeditions.
Blanchard met Catherine Mulvihill on a return trip to Everest, this time
to attempt the massive Kangshung Face in 1994. (The trip was organized
by alpine socialite Sandy Hill Pittman of *Into Thin Air* infamy, and the
sponsor she secured resulted in the climb being known, painfully, as the
"Vaseline Research Expedition.") Blanchard coos at his wife and describes
their meeting as "love at first sight on the high plains of Tibet." A fiery
courtship, another failed trip up Everest, and then Blanchard returned
home with his new bride-to-be.

Catherine can be as much of a fireball as Barry, but in her, he seems
to have found a muse who challenges him as much as he challenges himself. The mad love between them is as tangible as the floor in the room,
but it comes at a price. "When you're with an alpinist," Mulvihill explains,
"there's a beautiful part to your life because you're so aware of the fragile
risk. You don't take anything for granted. But that doesn't mean it doesn't
feel like there's a hot knife crossing your soul when he doesn't come
home on time."

A FEW weeks after I first sat down with him, Blanchard is packing his
bags again, back to the big top, back to practise what he calls his "lethal

art" on one of the great prizes of the Himalaya, the South Pillar of Nuptse, Everest's "little" sister. It's a perfect Blanchard climb: a monstrous jumble of shattered granite pillars threaded together by the faintest hints of ice, a wall that has killed some of the very best players in the game—a real test of his mettle.

I have dinner with him and Catherine the night before he leaves. Listening to his ruminations about the climb, it occurs to me that there's a better than good chance this might be the last time I ever see him, that this story might turn out to be his obituary. But then he starts riffing— about how cool the climb's going to be, how great it will be to be back in Nepal—and despite all the contradictions, the trip does seem to make sense. We say our goodbyes and he assures me he'll see me soon—saying it as though he truly believes he has control over that.

In the end, Nuptse turns out to be yet another twist in Blanchard's road. The next time I see him, breakfast turns into one of the parties that spontaneously erupt when you hang with Bubba. Ten, 15 climbers straggle into the café, and everyone's coming up to give him a welcome-home hug and get the word on the trip. Barry's chuckling out the story: how terrible the weather was, but how great the climbing route was; how the political situation in Nepal was insane ("Man, I had to drag Catherine under the bed in the middle of the night when the soldiers started firing off their guns in Namche!"); how he and the boys had "so much fun," and how that made it perfectly okay that they had to give up the climb just a thousand feet below the summit.

And then he explains, again and again, how he's just tired of climbing at high altitudes, what he describes as that "getting-run-over-by-a-truck-every-day" feeling. "It's way too much work at my age," he admits. "I'm just going to stick around *here* and climb."

No more Himalaya?

So what. Blanchard laughs and starts to talk about all the great plans he has for the Canadian Rockies. He describes some of those monster walls he's been staring at for years, convinced there is a way up those forbidding black faces, certain he'll be able to find one of *his* routes to the top. Suddenly, he seems as happy as I've ever seen him.

¿POR FAVOR, SEÑOR, DONDÉ ESTA EL SINGLETRACK?

DAVID LEACH

JUNE 2004

THE ROAD TO Machu Picchu is paved with good intentions. In the dusty lot of a gas station, we exchange high-fives with our padded gloves and then wheel onto the shoulder in a tight, proud line: five bikes towing five trailers with five yellow duffels couched in each. The wild heart of Peru lies before our handlebars. A local constable salutes our departure and promises to alert his fellow officers to our bold passage through his nation. In the receding distance, a cement plant hunches like a great grey mantis, grinding rock into dust—the two fundamental elements of this steep and monochrome and near-lunar landscape.

The ride begins well, in the big chain ring, as we shake ourselves loose of the town's limits and our own. Then the highway steepens, and we settle into our bikes' middle rings. It steepens more, and I give in to the rising grade and shift down into the small ring. And down again—*click, click, click-ick-ick*—until I bottom out against my lowest gear, the mechanical wall that cyclists know and fear as The Granny. Our two-week trip has only started, and already our tight formation of bikes has drifted apart into an irregular line of private struggles, muttered curses, slowing cadences. We're still on asphalt, have yet to veer onto the 4×4 tracks that will carry us over the mountains. I twist my shifter, wishing for another gear—a *great*-granny gear, a thin-air gear, one that might let me spin on the spot until I catch my all-too-ragged breath.

I'm not helped, of course, by the nearly 50 pounds of stove fuel and breakfast cereal I tug behind my bike on a single-wheeled rig that goes by the brand name of BOB. On these steeps, I can feel BOB's weight—I imagine him as a middle-aged sofa slug with a ratty comb-over who insists, loudly, on double-riding over my back tire—though he's not as much of an anchor as I first feared. When the grade finally relaxes, BOB tracks behind me virtually unnoticed. I could haul a house over these level stretches. But on the abrupt descents, I feel the force of so much food and fuel tied to my tail, all this BOBness urging me on. When I lift my butt off the seat, which I learn not to do, the bike's aluminum frame flexes between my thighs, like toffee torquing on a spinner. It's not a welcome sensation.

So I'm relieved when the road rises again to meet the mountains, and once more I'm coaxing BOB up the incline rather than holding back his urge to run. I'm alone now except for the transport trucks and buses that brush past my left shoulder, bobble-headed saints jiving on the stage of their dashboards. Every driver greets me with a pneumatic bleat, but I can't figure out if it translates most precisely as "Atta be, boys! Don't let the mountains grind you down!" or "Get off our frickin' road, *loco gringos!*"

This I do know: if any one of these horn-happy motorheads rear-ends my gassed-up trailer, BOB and I will likely be blasted into the next valley on a comet's tail of burnt oatmeal. I'm already wondering if that might not be our best hope of getting over the Andes.

LIKE ALL great expeditions, our trip began with a map and a dream. The dream belongs to Shane Jolley, a bike-shop owner from Owen Sound, Ontario. So does the map. Last fall, he spread both before me, and I did my best to read the one in the creases of the other. On a Rorschach blot of Peru, Shane had worked a highlighter through a maze of roads that the legend suggested were navigable by four-wheel drive—and, he presumed, by mountain bike. He had stitched together a route that started just north of Arequipa, the country's second-largest city, and wriggled

across the vast *altiplano,* a mountain-hugged plateau over which generations of cartographers have simply scribbled *Here be llamas.* Our final destination—the mile-high ruins of Machu Picchu.

In 1911, another dreamer headed for the same hills. Hiram Bingham III
may have been saddled with the most machismo-deficient name in the
annals of adventure, but that didn't deter the ambitious Yale professor as
he crisscrossed the country's southern interior. He returned from Peru
with photographic evidence of a mysterious city high in the Andes. It was
a find on the scale of King Tut's tomb, one of the defining feats of modern
exploration. Ninety years later, baby Binghams continue to trek through
a landscape still rich with mystery. In 1995, archaeologists dug out a trio
of ice-shrouded sacrificial mummies on a peak not far from our proposed
route. A month before we left, relic hunters with infrared sensors detected
yet another Inca outpost hidden near Machu Picchu.

The trail that now leads to the Lost City of the Incas has become a
must-do on the trek list of adventure nomads, but we would be leaving
this Inca Interstate to the tourists. We would get to Machu Picchu the
hard way, travelling by bike, for 10 days and nearly 500 kilometres, without a support van, ferrying all our supplies in the BOBS, over corrugated
demi-roads and some of the most remote mountains in the world. Five of
us would undertake the scouting mission. After we returned to Canada,
Shane hoped to market the expedition as a guided adventure.

In the weeks prior to take-off, my training consisted mostly of letting
the romantic notion of the trip percolate in my imagination. "I'd love to
go for lunch that week," I'd casually inform friends, "but I'll be mountain
biking in Peru." Only after we'd been spit from the plane into the bumper-
car arena of Lima did reality set in: we were going to bike over the Andes.

Not only that, we still barely knew each other. Shane I'd met previously at least. He'd grown up fixing bikes in his father's shop—tire rubber,
he says, is "the smell of home"—and then mountain biked competitively
for five years. He might seem intimidating at first, with his death-row
brush cut and Boris Karloff physique, if it weren't for the "perma-grin,"
the way his heavy jaw drops like a drawbridge and welcomes one and all
into the travelling circus that is Jolley Land. Shane's perma-grin clicks
open whenever he's remembering some memorable ride, or is deep in the

moment on a roller coaster of singletrack, or is anticipating the pleasures of some as-yet-uncycled trail—which is to say, *all the bloody time.*

We're joined by Ian, a mechanic from Shane's shop with the Roadrunner legs of a former BMX racer and the quiet competence of a good guide. "Shane and I belong to the same fellowship," Ian tells me, as he unholsters a bible from his day bag. They don't look like hobbits, so I have to assume they're Christians. Their only zealotry, though, seems a rock-solid faith that real salvation begins by first lubing your bike chain. Shane has also brought along an old buddy named Pat, a Rasta-haired pagan with a fondness for firearms and the gastrointestinal etiquette of a barnyard animal. By day two, I've excused myself from ever sharing his tent. He's also a rock climber and an emergency medical technician who likes to disappear into the middle of nowhere (a.k.a. northeastern Manitoba) for months at a stretch, to live off the woods and his wiles. If the *mierda* hits the fan where the only medevac is a burro's back, Pat will be our man with the plan.

Finally, I convinced Shane to invite Patrice Halley, an adventure photographer who has tramped through the world's wildest nooks and can haggle or sweet-talk in several official languages. Like the Brits who broke for tea in the middle of a Zulu raid or the conquistadors who erected opera houses along the Amazon, Patrice also knows to save room in his pack for one luxury item on every expedition. This trip, he lords over a sack of gourmet coffee as if it were the Shroud of Turin.

A roll call, then: two born-again velophiliacs, a flatulent Wiccan, an over-caffeinated Frenchman and me—a downtown desk jockey with delusions of grandeur. *Now* it was beginning to feel like a proper expedition.

All that remained was to christen our team. Before arriving in Lima, we'd transited through Miami. As we re-checked our bags for the connecting flight to Arequipa, many were still flagged in big block letters: MIA.

"That's what we should be called," I joked. "Expedition MIA."

I really must be more careful what I wish for.

THE MORNING after our first ride, I wake up wasted at 12,500 feet: I've climbed too high, too fast. While I've avoided alcohol, sucked water like a sponge, popped *Gingko biloba* and now altitude pills to ward off mountain sickness, my head still feels like a migraine wrapped in a tumour bottled with the bends. Pat feels woozy, too, and Patrice has cultivated a rib-rattling cough. Whatever. I feel *worse*. I moan and mutter and generally make myself useless. After breakfast, Shane and Ian pedal off towards the hills that snuff the horizon—to scout the 4×4 trail, they insist, though I know they really want to leave me here to die.

After cycling seven klicks, they return; the so-called jeep track has the tire-sucking consistency of Cavendish Beach, and the climb into the foothills soon forced them off their bikes, even without the weight of the BOBS. More troubling, we're at the tail end of the dry season, and there's no telling if the staccatos of blue on our map hold more than just the promise of water. Shane weighs options. "Okay, I've got a new plan," he announces. It won't be the last time he says this.

He uses the satellite phone to call for another bus shuttle. We'll get ferried over the 15,830-foot Pata Pampa pass and then drop nearly 4,000 feet to Chivay. The town sits near the bottom of the Colca Canyon, a mammoth crack in the earth as wide as the Grand Canyon and twice as deep. Its walls are so sheer in its western reaches that the lines on our topo fuse like rings in a drought-struck tree. The detour will cut out the sketchy approach to the Colca over the desiccated pseudo-roads. It means more driving, less riding, but we all agree it's the safest call.

Waiting for the lift, we filter water into our bike bottles. A lone Quechua man shuffles up to the well, his skin as finely creased as a 10-*soles* bank note. He explains, in Spanish, that a puma has killed 15 of his cattle. He has come down from his high-country pastures to sell his remaining stock and earn enough, he hopes, to see him through the next winter. "There are spirits in the mountains," he warns, "and not all of them are happy."

ON THE final few switchbacks down to Chivay, it feels as though we're falling from the sky, and the symptoms of my altitude ennui slowly improve. With our bikes roped to its roof, the bus wheels past the colonial façades of the town's main square and through the narrow avenues of the busy market, bemused vendors glancing up from their stalls. We skirt the hot springs on the edge of town, stop beside the Colca River and negotiate with a farmer to pitch our tents in his field.

That night's sleep is a hallucinatory triple feature, backed by the Surround Sound of Patrice's breath rattle, the canyon hounds baying at the moon and the slow decompression of my own eggshell skull. My first few shut-eyes in the wild always uncork my id like a bottle of Baby Duck. Back home, I can rarely rewind this dream life, but cocooned in a tent and sleeping bag, the REM'd up plots seem as vivid as a summer blockbuster. It's refreshing, this rush release of psychic studio time, and the next morning I rise to consciousness through the credits of the final feature feeling better, ready to kick-start the expedition.

"Hey, dudes, the bikes are gone."

We scramble up to the higher terrace and join Ian beside the stone wall against which we squirrelled the bikes last night. The locked cable has been sliced cleanly, with bolt cutters, it appears. Three of the bikes are AWOL. I feel a warm rush of relief topped by guilt: *my* bike is still there. And then a moment of pique: wasn't it good enough to swipe? The thieves have ridden off with Ian's, Pat's and Patrice's bikes and then punctured the tires on the other two, as well as the BOBs.

The floppy-eared farm dog that greeted us yesterday joins our huddle around the crime scene. (*Peru*, amateur linguists may be interested to learn, seems to derive from an old native word for "Land of the Terminally Cute Puppies.") There was a reason beyond mere moon madness for the relentless yawping we all heard last night. His liquid eyes stare up at us, as if to say, *Well, I tried.*

"If we don't find the bikes," Shane admits at last, "this expedition is screwed." It is the one moment of pure doubt he will voice the entire trip.

"Don't say *screwed*," suggests Patrice, "say *seriously jeopardized*."

Shane, Patrice and Ian hike into Chivay to report the thefts. Pat and I are left to mind what remains of our gear. It seems a safe assignment. It isn't. As I head down to the river for *agua*, I discover that descending a steep, rocky slope in bike shoes is like ballroom dancing on stilts: "doable," as corporate boosters are fond of saying, but ugly to watch and prone to disaster. Halfway to the water, my pedal cleats skitter over loose rock, and I execute the trip's first official "endover"—a dry-land belly flop. I've just fallen down the deepest canyon in the world—print that on a T-shirt and sell it—though, fortunately, only the last 10 feet. (Then again, those are the ones that usually hurt the most.) I nearly dropped both water filters down a hole, too, which would not have made me popular.

It doesn't take long for my left hand to swell like a catcher's mitt and a huge brown hickey to half-moon below my ribs, as though I've been gummed by a Great White. We haven't cycled kilometre one of our off-road itinerary, and already I've enlisted in the walking wounded. The others... well, until we find their bikes, they're just *the walking*.

BACK FROM a session with the tourist police, Shane shuts down the SAT phone and amps up his perma-grin for the first time in hours. He's down-loaded a message from the heavens and the word is good. "I spoke to my wife," he says, "and our entire church is praying for us to find the bikes."

A day later, we get a spiritual second opinion. We've regrouped in a hostel in Chivay, where we learn of a fortune-teller who might be able to offer clues about the bikes' whereabouts. If her clairvoyant CSI work doesn't pan out, we'll have to find replacements. I don't know what I'm expecting at the house of the psychic: a beadwork sanctuary perhaps, with sandalwood candles and noodling panpipes. Instead, Fabiana ush-ers us into a tiny chamber, and we crowd around the corner of her small cot. An old TV squats atop a cabinet; beside her bed, a pack of smokes. Flies buzzsaw the shadows. It's as though the Oracle at Delphi operated out of her college dorm.

In a rainbow shawl and the wide-banded hat of the canyon women, Fabiana at least looks the part of the wizened soothsayer. She takes five one-*sol* coins, blows on them and drops the change into my bandanna, already filled with coca leaves. Coca may be the huff-and-snort scourge of *Norteamérica*, but for centuries throughout the Andes, the leaf has been a fundamental ingredient in rituals sacred and banal—the mildest of morning pick-me-ups and, to an eye like Fabiana's, a window into the spirit world. (We've already taken to chewing a few leaves over breakfast, a habit that's supposed to put the boot to mountain sickness, too. "Are you getting a buzz from that?" Patrice asks later. Ian and I just shrug, a *pichu* of chaw bulging our cheeks. "Coca is like religion," says our philo-sophical Frenchman. "It only works if you believe in it.")

In her bedroom, Fabiana shakes the bandanna, leans over the leaves and interprets their new constellation. "Your bikes are still around here," she says. "But they are hidden, and the thieves are watching what you are doing." Construction workers have been trucked up from Lima to build a school. "It's most likely the workers," insists Fabiana. Her suspicions could be sour grapes: the citizens of Chivay have been prickly ever since the jobs went to outsiders rather than locals. But her charge carries a certain logic, too: if anyone has ready access to bolt cutters, it's the builders.

"Should we ask her about the success of our expedition?" I wonder, as the meter on our fortune runs low.

"No," insists Patrice. "I don't want to know the truth."

"OKAY, I'VE got a new plan..."

We don't have much time for any more detective work. If Shane hopes to salvage the scouting mission, we need to locate some guide-able riding, here in the Colca Canyon. We're not going to make it to Machu Picchu, it's clear. Perhaps we never would have. We're disappointed, of course. But it helps that we reach this decision over plates of fruit salad, river trout and rice pudding at our hostel.

The rough edges have already flaked off the expedition. Our original plan was to be the ultimate DIY trip and it suffered, we now understand, from a naiveté of colonial proportions: we would just grunt our way over the Andes, tugging our homes behind us, local knowledge be damned. "Now, the trip's going to be about mountain biking and *culture*," says Shane, rallying the troops. "We bring people up here. We stay in hostels rather than tents. We eat at restaurants—which are cheaper than freeze-dried food. We let them see the real Peru, and we introduce them to some wicked bike trails."

We arrange three rental rides that *look* like genuine mountain bikes but turn out to be of cut-rate provenance. It's little wonder someone might want to pinch our bikes, if these are typical Peruvian wheels. Our three guides fall upon the wobbly knock-offs like E.R. surgeons in a trauma ward. I can only stand back and hand them fresh tubes and multitools. Then we hitch up the BOBs with lighter loads and pedal 27 kilometres to Maca, a soporific farm town that was nearly erased from the topo by an earthquake a dozen years ago. It will be our base camp for the next three days.

The road out of Chivay starts at 12,000 feet, follows the high bank of the river west and snakes us into the steeper-walled mid-section of the Colca. Here, the canyon lifts its broad shoulders in a series of terraces, cut into the slopes and hemmed in by stonework fences, the most extensive remains of such agricultural architecture in all of Peru. (The canyon itself takes its name from the many *collcas*, or stone granaries, still found here.) Ever since a pair of gobsmacked aviators from the Geographic Society of New York buzzed the canyon in 1931, the Colca has been pitched to visitors as the Lost Valley of the Incas—like so much else in modern Peru, riding the cultural cachet of the sun-worshipping technocrats whose brief dynasty was shattered by the Spanish Conquest. But the irrigated terraces date back more than a millennium, well before the Incas ruled. Everywhere around us rise picturesque mesas and these cultivated steps, like a giant's StairMaster to heaven. Mario Vargas Llosa, Peru's most famous author and presidential also-ran, called the Colca the "valley of wonders." It's like Utah without the Mormons, Arizona without the Denny's.

Not everyone is impressed. Pat's lead-weight rental bike fares poorly, and as he struggles to keep pace, its spineless seatpost begins to wilt. We wait for him at a turn-off and spot him tramping through the dust, pushing the bike by its bars. The seat has bent backwards to a cartoon angle. Pat doesn't find it nearly as funny as we do. He unleashes a hailstorm of profanity—none of which I can repeat, some of which I suspect is new to the English language.

"That's it—I'm done," he announces later, after we arrange cabins in Maca. "I can't do this. I hate this sand. I hate this bike. I hate this country. I don't care if I have to go back to pumping gas for six bucks an hour. I'm *done*." His tirade must invoke the curse of Tupac Amaru, the last of the Inca emperors, because for the next 48 hours, his expedition really is over, except for bilious sprints between his bed and the *baños*.

The following day, the rest of us decide to explore the far flank of the valley. During the rainy season, the Rio Colca unleashes a furious riptide of whitewater, class V and worse, the most dangerous river in the world that's commercially rafted. Almost 25 years ago, a band of Polish paddlers needed 33 days and 24 portages to run the 75-kilometre gorge for the first time. The expedition's shaken leader dubbed it the "Mount Everest of rivers." A few years later, another team's head guide vanished entirely into the Colca's inhuman hydraulics.

Today, only a slow, cold wash rolls over the exposed boulders of its bed. A set of ladders has been plopped across this flow as a dry-season bridge. We hike-a-bike over the Colca and up its switchbacking north shoulder. The route we've just climbed would be a perfect descent: a hardpacked couloir of dead-man's curves that would deposit you and your bike, should you manage to stay together, at the gates of a hot spring with a riverside view.

But we're still in scouting mode, so we push on to locate a possible day-loop back to the cabins. Such is the sweaty self-denial of our mission—we are bike-humping pioneers who must suffer so that those who follow (and pay) won't have to. Yesterday, from the far side of the valley, Shane spotted an S-drop of singletrack that he hopes will prove the missing link, but we discover it's too scrabbly to ride. We descend instead down an unremarkable road, ford the Colca without a ladder and carry our bikes up the far side. There's not a hot spring in sight.

My bike's frame has worn a groove into my shoulder. My tires have barely spun, yet somehow both are pierced by cactus spines. This has to be my worst day ever on a bike.

IT'S FOLLOWED by one of the best.

Even with our early reveille, the sun beats us out of bed and springs over the horizon as though from a catapult. We need a quick start today to ride 20 kilometres and 1,500 vertical feet up to Cruz del Condor, the lookout from which the famous Andean vultures, as huge as sport-utes but far more scarce, can be seen gliding on the morning thermals. It's the Kodak Moment of the Colca Canyon, and as we grind towards the photo-op, we're overtaken by a steady convoy of day-tripping tourist buses. "You're all going to die of hemorrhoids!" Patrice shouts as they kick dust in our faces. Near noon, the wind tunnels down the canyon until it sweeps the warmth from the thin alpine air. I can understand why the Incas prayed to such a fickle sun. I tuck into a village for hot soup and coca tea and promise to meet the others back in Maca.

After lunch, I ride alone up the winding road. The valley drops away on these steeper slopes, with little room to carve even the tiniest terrace. Twenty editions ago, the *Guinness Book of Records* put the Colca on its cover and declared the 10,470-foot drop from peak to river near here the deepest in the world. Since then, the Cotahuaxi, a valley to the north that allegedly stands 500 feet taller, has staked a counter-claim to the title of Big Canyon on Campus. Such tape-measure bickering seems moot as I ride beside a precipice as unfathomable as this one.

The Grand Canyon, however mammoth, at least has a human order to it that turns every point-and-clicker into an instant Ansel Adams—aim your camera off its edge, and the plateaus and pinnacles fall into place. But the Colca turns its cheek on easy vistas. I look down, and it simply drops and drops and, just when I think it must touch bottom, it drops some more. Out of this void, a crenellated wall of rock soars like a mock-up of Mordor left from the director's cut of the *Rings* cycle, too unbelievable even for Orc fans. The scale of these raggedy Andes is, well, right off the scale.

I reach Cruz del Condor late in the afternoon, still hoping to see the last of the carrion birds that roost on the sheer slopes. Instead I find a picnic of Aussies. They're a package tour of young bus travellers on a soft trip through a hard land. Several of the 20-something women ask where I've ridden from. "Well, we've been biking over the Andes…" I begin in my best Indiana Jones drawl. But I can't go on. I tell them instead about big plans laid low, bikes stolen, fortunes bought and sold, and how this grandest of canyons looks while you're wheezing up its raw slope. It's not so epic, but it's true. They seem impressed enough as it is.

Besides, an adventure is forged as much in its telling as its doing, and sometimes you don't know what you've done till you're gone. After he uncovered Machu Picchu, Hiram Bingham III opened Peru to a century of amateur explorers, but he had gone to the Andes for an ulterior purpose and considered his own trip a disappointment. His real goal was to be the first to stand atop Mount Coropuna, estimated to be South America's highest peak, and to scoop this glory from the Joan of Arc League, whose suffragette summiteers wanted to plant a banner demanding "Votes for Women." In the end, the feminist-alpinists climbed the wrong mountain, while Bingham (a conservative Republican) mistakenly topped out on the shorter, second summit of Coropuna. Both teams later learned they were still a thousand feet shy of the continent's *real* high mark, Mount Aconcagua in Argentina.

Months before this alpine anticlimax, Bingham had been led to a ridgetop ruin by a native guide. At the time, his imagination had still been fixed on claiming South America's mountain crown; only several years of reflection and two return visits convinced this accidental explorer just how significant this find was. When he finally published the account of his expedition, he flipped the chronology so that his story might end in the mists of Machu Picchu rather than on the bogus summit of a mismeasured peak. The rest is history. Nearly a century later, I won't get to see his Lost-and-Found City, but already I appreciate our own fortunate stop in this Valley of Wonders.

The day leans low, so I hop on my bike and let the canyon spill me back towards the river. The wind sings between my spokes. The condor in flight, I've been told, is the most near-perfect design to come off nature's drafting board; its only rival in the pure translation of effort into motion is a man on a bicycle.

Maybe not this man. Maybe not this bicycle.

As soon as I lock eyes upon the one rock that mars the road's smooth surface, I know I'm sure to hit it. And I do. My front tire goes gunshot flat and the bike bucks and tries to throw me free and nearly does. I chatter to a stop at the edge of another lookout. Minutes later, the bus rushes past and then slows, pretty blond faces pressed to tinted glass, but I wave them along. I have a pump and a patch, and that's all I need to keep the freedom of the hills beneath my treads. I just want to sit here for a moment and let my legs dangle off the countertop of eternity, if that's okay.

That's okay.

BACK IN Chivay, Shane has heard rumours of a riverside route that's begging to be biked, so the next afternoon I join him and Ian to scout it while the others recoup. Bending eastward towards the town of Sibayo, the canyon shucks its shadowy depths and takes on a new incarnation. It's less steep and yet somehow more wild. Framed by blunt-topped projections of bald rock and emptied of life aside from a few troutmen casting nets, these wide braids of the Colca River could be wending through some remote corner of Nunavut—except for a trail that's been groomed by Inca runners, alpaca herders and now a couple of thrill-shepherding bike guides.

After a bus drop, we cross the bridge in Sibayo and begin to cycle the 30 kilometres back to Chivay. We're seriously off-road, on the wrong side of a big river from the sissy route back to town. My head has been steeped for too long in bogeyman books about expeditions gone awry, of perfect storms streaking out of the clear blue, of "turnaround times" ignored by luckless amateurs. When the trail disappears off the edge of a ravine, I crank my whine to dental-drill intensity: *Do we know where we are? Shouldn't we turn back? Haven't either of you seen or read* Alive?

Yesterday, I tamed the Colca as Johnny Adventure. Today, Little Mister Pissy Pants has signed on instead.

Shane just looks at me: "Try to remember the name of the magazine you're working for."

The honourable member from *explore* declines to comment. There's nothing I *can* say to that.

We find the trail again, of course, and cycle past herds of skittish llamas and down precarious stone paths and, guess what, we don't have to chow down on each other after all. It is, by any measure, a fantastic ride. But I'm too ashamed to admit it.

So, on our last day in the canyon, I lead Patrice and Pat back to my breaking point, while Shane and Ian test-ride another route. Rewinding yesterday's trail, I get a sense of what it will be like for them to guide future trips, the anxious joys of discovery papered over by the more subtle pleasures of rediscovery, of sharing a backroad once travelled with someone experiencing it for the first time. Here is the detour around the ravine, I say. Here is where the farmer's dog tried to tear a chunk from my bike shorts. Here, we ride with the llamas.

Later, we'll listen to Shane and Ian describe their own 25K depth charge off the canyon's south rim, riding 5,000 vertical feet from the high plateau of Pata Pampa all the way down to the riverbank, with only one portage through a field of sheep dip. Later, we'll leave a ring around the local hot springs and look across to the terrace on which we camped just eight days ago, where we lost our bikes and found our adventure. And later, for a solid (or rather, not-so-solid) week after I get home, the ghosts of Inca kings will whisper to me, too: *dude, you should have so not had that sandwich at the bus station.*

For now, though, we're in no hurry to be anywhere but here. We lie back for lunch with our bikes at our feet and admire the slow grind of a wild river as it etches its signature deeper into this fragile earth. Anyone who stumbled upon us, frozen in time on the slopes of the Andes, would need more than just bolt cutters to pry free our perma-grins.

||||||||||||

THE RIDE OF HIS LIFE

MIKE RANDOLPH

JUNE/JULY 2003

HE NEWS CAUGHT me off guard. I was sitting on the patio of a restaurant, talking with Steve Bauer, the Canadian cyclist who once finished fourth in the Tour de France. "Have you heard about him?" Bauer asked me, after I mentioned Thierry's name. "He committed suicide."

A warm, early summer afternoon suddenly took on a different feeling. I did not know Thierry Claveyrolat personally. I had never even spoken to him. Thierry, a Frenchman from a small Alpine village called Vizelle—I still remembered the name—raced in the Tour de France during Bauer's era. I had wanted to meet Thierry one day. He was not a superstar like Bernard Hinault or Miguel Indurain or Laurent Fignon—all of whom I had met—but I once took a photo of Thierry that meant something to me. And I thought it might mean something to him, too.

In the late 1980s and early 1990s, when Bauer was famous in Europe but barely on the radar of Canadian sports fans, I was a cycling journalist in Canada, which is to say I was an adoring fan of professional European road racing, willing to accept financial ruin in order to be close to the sport I loved. Thierry was what the cycling world calls a climber. Climbers are feeble sprinters, and generally don't make for very good time-trialists either, so Thierry never had a good shot at winning the

Tour, because to win the Tour you have to be good at all three. But cycling fans reserve a special respect for pure climbers. When climbers attack on the infamously steep mountain roads of the Alps and Pyrenees, dropping some of the fittest men in the world, the fans, especially the French fans, melt like butter. Probably, the French admire climbers because they try so hard. The French say that the difference between a good climber and a great climber is not always physical. They say a great climber just knows how to suffer more.

Thierry Claveyrolat was once the best climber in the Tour de France. In 1990, he rode into Paris not with the winner's yellow jersey, but with the polka-dot jersey of the King of the Mountains. On paper, it was his grandest prize, but the French don't pick their heroes on paper. Winning is not enough; the fans want something more. The day Thierry gave it to them was July 24, 1991. I happened to be right beside him at the time.

IT WAS the 18th stage, from Bourg d'Oisans to Morzine, the toughest of the 1991 Tour. Actually, at 255 kilometres long, with seven major climbs, including two rated beyond classification, it was one of the toughest mountain stages for a long time. That stage had more climbing than two ordinary mountain stages have now.

The day before, I had witnessed a part of the battle up the famous L'Alpe d'Huez between Miguel Indurain, wearing the race leader's yellow jersey, and Gianni Bugno, the champion of Italy and Indurain's main threat. I had situated myself about three-quarters of the way up the climb, in the hopes I might be able to get a shot of some decisive attack by one of them. But I didn't. The irony of being a photojournalist in the Tour is that you rarely get to see the really important moments because they always seem to happen somewhere else. Some photographers ride on the backs of motorcycles, dodging in and out of the action, but that's no guarantee either. The narrow mountain roads are crowded with hundreds of thousands of fans pressing in so close there's barely enough room for the riders, let alone dozens of cars and motorcycles. Only the video cameraman gets to see it all—and, by extension, the hundreds of millions of people around the world who watch the Tour on TV.

It was eight in the morning and already the sun had a bite to it. Scanning the map of the 18th stage, I figured I could catch the action in two places. The roads that the Tour uses are closed to traffic, but with my press pass, I could drive on the route either in front of or behind the riders. I decided I'd get a shot as the peloton—the main pack of riders—wheeled through a town about 30 kilometres from the start of the stage; then, I'd take the highway north towards Geneva to get in front of them again and place myself near the top of the day's last climb, the brutal switchbacks of the Col de la Croix de Fer, only a few kilometres before the finish.

With the road closed, it took me only 10 minutes to reach the small town where I planned to photograph the peloton. The main square was packed with people anticipating the arrival of the race. There was a castle on the west side, and I thought I'd get a good shot of the pack whipping by in front of it. The town's name was Vizelle.

There was an unusually festive atmosphere in the main square. A buzz in the air; you could feel it. Colourful streamers decorated the square, and along a bridge on the route, flags of every nation snapped in the wind. Film loaded, exposure checked and re-checked, I staked out my turf on the inside corner of the square, beside some old men who had left the bar behind me with their glasses of Chartreuse in hand. The gendarmes kept the crowd out of the road. There was a raised platform with loudspeakers and a few TV screens set up. An announcer called the play-by-play, but I ignored him, partly because my French wasn't that good and partly because the town was only 30 kilometres from the start. Nothing important ever happens that early in a mountain stage.

But I caught something the announcer said. A breakaway by a lone rider. *What?* I thought. A breakaway so early on such a long, hard stage has no hope, which is why it's never attempted. Then I caught the name. Thierry Claveyrolat. That's when the crowd erupted into cheers.

The Eagle of Vizelle, they called him. The nickname was cribbed from another climber, the Eagle of Toledo, Spaniard Federico Bahamontes, who won the Tour once but wore the polka-dot jersey into Paris five times. Legend has it that Bahamontes once broke away on a climb in the Alps and left the entire field behind him. When he reached the top, having racked up what he really wanted—points for the polka-dot jersey—he stopped. While he waited for the rest of the riders to catch up, he sat down and enjoyed an ice-cream cone.

Claveyrolat was no Bahamontes, though. He had only finished the Tour in the top 20 once, and most of his other wins were in minor races. But he was a local hero nonetheless. He was one of them. And the Tour, for the people of Vizelle and other towns like it, is the only sporting event worth watching. It is more than just a race. For 23 days in July, it's a grand, beautiful, uncertain struggle. A metaphor for life.

Thierry was near Vizelle now. That one of Vizelle's own sons was even in the Tour was cause for celebration. That he was going to ride through town with the race was even better. But with a lead of almost three minutes, the hero was not only going to pass through his hometown with the Tour de France, he was going to lead it in.

Crouched on the inside corner, I jostled with the fans as they pressed in closer, the excitement growing. The announcer was in a lather, the cheers rose to a deafening level and then all of a sudden there he was, the golden boy, alone, mashing the pedals around the corner and into view. When he finally entered the square, the crowd chanted, "Thier-ry! Thier-ry! Thier-ry!"

The hero let off the pace, straightened up and rode no-hands, smiling and waving to his friends and neighbours. He stopped pedalling, gliding more slowly now, feeling the glow of the moment. He made his way to the corner of the square across from me, and to my amazement, came to a full stop.

Grabbing my camera bag and flashing my pass at the gendarme beside me, I ran across the road, dodging team cars and police motorbikes. I switched lenses while running, putting on my wide angle, figuring I could get in close and get my shot without anybody getting in front of me.

Thierry's wife and two children were waiting for him. It had been his plan all along. Thierry leaned over to his wife and kissed her. Images of the kiss flashed on the TV screens and the crowd loved it. He took his young boy in his arms and held him up, smiling and kissing him. What luck, I thought. For once, at the right spot at the right time. When the motorbike photographers arrived, the crowd around Thierry was too thick for them to penetrate. With Vizelle in the background, his wife by his side and their boy in his arms, I snapped shot after shot. Everyone was so happy. Even the gendarmes couldn't help but look over and smile. I kept waiting for Thierry to jump back on his bike, but he was in no rush to leave. Minutes later, the racers rolled into town—more cheers from the fans—and when every last rider had come and gone, Thierry gave his wife one last kiss, got back on his bike and casually rode after them, now the last man. The crowd chanted his name again, "Thier-ry! Thier-ry!" and he saluted them before sprinting away.

I threw my gear in the passenger seat of my van and drove north towards Geneva. An hour later I turned off the highway, hoping that I'd gone far enough to get in front of the riders. I had no idea where they were. Traffic was horrible and I sped like a maniac along the secondary roads, making my way back into the mountains. I finally reached the road where the race would pass, and after clearing a path in the spectators, I motioned to a gendarme. He examined my pass suspiciously. He asked me something I couldn't understand, so I just pointed at the accreditation on my windshield and insisted, "C'est official, c'est official." He decided to let me in and dragged open the metal barrier. Relieved I'd made it, I sat back to enjoy the ride. With the road closed for the race, I could cruise through the route, going right through stop signs and red lights, and driving past throngs and throngs of fans along tree-lined boulevards.

It took another hour to reach the base of the Col de la Croix de Fer. There were people on the whole route, but here they were packed deep on both sides. I was forced to drive in first and occasionally second gear—the climb is 30 kilometres long at an average gradient of over five per cent, and just goes up and up and up—and so the van's clutch soon began to burn; I could smell it even inside. But the drive was beautiful. Roadside cliffs gave way to steep flower-covered meadows, and above them, the immense shining peaks of the central Alps. The higher I got the more people there were. I sailed through a sea of people, thousands upon thousands of them, a non-stop tunnel of humanity all the way up the mountain. Excited about the imminent arrival of the Tour, they cheered anything that moved, including me. The roads were covered with graffiti, painted with the names of Tour heroes. People in shorts and tank tops waved flags and cardboard signs. The kids were wearing the hats of their favourite teams, jumping up and down, shrieking and waving as I drove by and honked the horn.

After a long time, I sensed I was nearing the top so I pulled over. Just in time, too. The van was not smelling good at all. Even driving a car up these climbs, you get an idea of how tough it must be to race a bicycle up.

Wearing shorts and a T-shirt, I soon grew cold in the brisk air. Clouds were moving in. By the time the riders were near, it had begun to rain, but by then no one seemed to care. The big moment was almost upon us. The 1991 Tour de France would be decided here, stage 18, the last hard mountain leg. If Gianni Bugno had managed to drop Indurain, Bugno would be in yellow. It was his last chance. It was everybody's last chance. Anything could happen.

Team cars started zooming into view, blaring their horns in a desperate plea to part the crowd. I set up on an outside corner with a telephoto to catch the riders as they rounded a switchback below. Soon a parade of police motorbikes appeared and then the red car of the race official, signalling riders were right behind.

Through the big lens, I recognized him instantly, his R.M.O. team cap pulled down in his distinctive way. But it took a moment to sink in—there he was, the Eagle of Vizelle, rocking back and forth on the last brutal kilometres of the Croix du Fer. Soaked and looking tired but determined, Thierry ate up the final stretch of climb with a vengeance, a sneer of pain and effort etched on his face. No one was behind him. When the crowds recognized him, they screamed his name. *"Allez, Thierry, allez!"*

I hoped desperately that nobody would catch him. One minute later, the rest of the leaders came into view, including Indurain and his shadow, Gianni Bugno. The field was strung out, an indication of how hard the day had been. I remained in my spot and got shots of Steve Bauer as he put on a rain jacket, and Greg LeMond, who was struggling badly.

When all the riders had passed, I drove to the finish line in Morzine, unsure whether Thierry managed to hang on during the descent. By the time I got there, the downtown was alive with a carnival of lighted merry-go-rounds and a Ferris wheel, and the rain had stopped. I went straight to the media truck and grabbed a freshly photocopied sheet of race results. Thierry Claveyrolat, winner in 7 hours, 26 minutes, 47 seconds.

Clutching the paper, I walked into the centre of Morzine, smiling. A street vendor was making crêpes suzettes. I was hungry and they looked good, so I got in line and bought a plateful. I sat down to eat with some locals on a wooden bench. We talked about Thierry, of course. The only thing better than a winner, said an old man wearing a beret, is a stylish winner. And everyone agreed, Thierry had won with *panache*. I watched as the square filled up with people. Everybody was in such a good mood. The local boy had had the day of his life, and a little of the magic had rubbed off on the rest of us.

AFTER SOME searching, I found a cold, five-line report on Thierry's death in a British cycling magazine. Thierry Claveyrolat, it read, had been driving his car when he caused an accident in which two people were grievously injured. Devastated, he felt he couldn't live with the guilt. Three weeks later he ended his life. That was all it said.

At first I wanted to find out more. What were the circumstances of the accident? My thoughts flirted with the inevitable questions. Had he been drinking? Did he fall asleep at the wheel? Or was it, as I had somehow hoped, just bad luck, at the wrong place at the wrong time? After a while, however, I felt I didn't want to know the answers to those questions because I didn't like where they led. Nothing would lessen the tragedy. And I did not want to judge him. I had never even met him. It's just that I wished I still could.

There is a bar in Vizelle dedicated to Thierry Claveyrolat. One day I plan to visit, during July, when I can join the locals and watch the Tour de France on TV, over a glass of Chartreuse. I'll take along my photo of the Eagle of Vizelle. Maybe they could find a spot for it on the wall.

WHAT HAS TWO LEGS,
122 TEETH AND
GOES 80 MILES AN HOUR?

ROSS CROCKFORD

MARCH/APRIL 2002

AS THE SUN sets behind the dusty Nevada hills, the wind dies and the low whistle of the shivering transmission lines falls silent. The desert is hushed, anticipating. Just like our small congregation, standing amid the sagebrush alongside a flat, empty stretch of two-lane highway.

Off to the side of the road sits a hulking old diesel bus, on loan from a chapter of the Assembly of God. A sign over the driver's window indicates our ultimate destination: *heaven*. I'm not particularly religious, but the Christian sentiment fits. We are gathered in the desert this evening to witness a miracle.

"Here he comes."

Everyone turns and looks down the highway to the south. About a mile away, a tiny red object appears on the road, the waning October sunlight glinting off its polished body. It's getting closer. It looks like a space capsule, silently hovering over the asphalt. Closer. I can see it now, the smooth bulbous shape of the craft, and in the windshield, the face of a young man, nearly pressed against the glass, gasping for oxygen—then there's a thunderous WHOOOM as it blasts by us, fanning a penumbra of noisy air, and just as suddenly it's gone, disappearing down the highway.

The congregation is jubilant. We're cheering, whistling, laughing with disbelief. We're still trying to comprehend it: the vehicle that just rocketed past at more than 70 miles per hour was a *bicycle*.

Brothers and Sisters, I give you the Fastest Man on Earth. That guy in the windscreen is Sam Whittingham, a 29-year-old racing cyclist from Victoria, B.C. A year ago on this same stretch of blacktop, Sam pedalled a similar human-powered vehicle or HPV—essentially a recumbent bicycle encased inside an aerodynamic shell—to 72.75 miles per hour, becoming the first human being to ever travel more than 70 miles per hour entirely under his own steam. Now he's back in Battle Mountain, Nevada, defending his title at the World Human Powered Speed Challenge, a six-day race for the most innovative bicycles on the planet.

It's day four of the competition. Every few minutes more weird machines roar past us, and the congregation cheers them on, like floats in a supersonic parade—one resembles the tip of an airplane wing standing upright, another looks like the fuselage of a WWII bomber. By the time we get down to the finish line a half-hour later, Sam's secret weapon, the Varna Diablo, is tucked in the bed of a pickup truck to keep it out of the dust. Right away, I can tell Sam knows he's done something big. Leaning against the tailgate, waiting for the official results, he can barely conceal his smile.

"I think that was probably my quickest run," Sam says. He's already topped last year's record: three days ago, he did 76.61 miles per hour. But it isn't official yet. According to the rules, he needs another run nearly as fast to validate it.

Sean Costin, the race organizer, calls everyone milling about the parking lot to gather around. "Now for the moment you have all been waiting for," he says. "History has been made. The Varna Diablo, over a distance of 200 metres, hit a speed of 77.03 miles per hour—a new world record!"

Everyone's applauding, and clapping Sam on the back. George Georgiev, the designer of the Diablo, comes over and gives Sam a fatherly hug. Sam's been racing George's bikes for 10 years. "Can we retire now?" Sam asks, laughing.

George smiles, stands back and puts up a finger of warning. "Now we got to do 80!"

SAM WHITTINGHAM and George Georgiev have been preparing for this moment for a long time. They first met in British Columbia in 1989 when Sam was a theatre student at the University of Victoria and George was establishing his home on Gabriola Island. George had built several streamlined HPVs, but he needed a rider, and a friend introduced him to Sam. They set their first land-speed record together in 1993, and they've never looked back.

Many sports marry athletic skills with ingenious technology, and Sam and George know enough about each to form an unbeatable team. Sam is one of Canada's best amateur cyclists—he won two silver medals at the 2001 National Track Championships in Edmonton—and he's only 5′7″, so he can fit into vehicles with a small aerodynamic profile. George is a sculptor. Born in Varna, Bulgaria, he studied in the art centres of Europe before he emigrated to Toronto in 1972. (One of his famous works, a male torso made of limestone, stands in front of Joso's, a restaurant in Toronto's Yorkville district.) Now he applies his artistic skills to HPVs. "Sculpting involves many professions," points out George, who's 59. "Welding, carpentry, working with the fibreglass—you have to know them well if you're going to put a monument in the middle of town and it's not going to crush people."

George has always been playing around with experimental machines—when he was a kid, he designed a piece of farm machinery that could be powered by a house cat—but he didn't start making them seriously until he read about competitions for human-powered vehicles in *Popular Science* magazine. He decided to enter the contests, and in 1984, thanks to his artistic flair, one of his HPVs won "best-looking machine." Then one of his friends, Jocelyn Lovell, the Canadian cyclist who won three gold medals at the 1978 Commonwealth Games, was hit by a truck and paralyzed. That tragedy inspired George to start designing and building hand-cranked tricycles and quadricycles for people who'd lost the use of their legs, and he discovered there was considerable demand for such machines. ("Every disabled person should have a chance to cycle like any normal person," says George. "A wheelchair is good for domestic use, but not on the roads.") So when he moved to B.C., he made them his full-time business. He now sells about 100 of his custom handcycles every year, mainly in Europe, at around $2,000 apiece, and they hold many of the speed records for hand-powered vehicles.

"It's not the speed, it's what the human being can achieve that interests me," says George. As he points out, HPVS now go as fast as most automobiles, even though a car engine generates 100 times the horsepower of a cyclist. "So this is about pushing the limit, from one side the technology, from the other side the human body, and through the right combination, we can show to people that cycling is not a dead issue. If we can work it from here and there, maybe we can improve it a mile or two per hour for the average person, which is tremendous."

On the wall of George's workshop, overlooking a clutter of drills, lathes, air compressors, acetylene torches and boxes of bicycle parts, there's a poster of Albert Einstein, with one of the physicist's epigrams: "I want to know God's thoughts. The rest are details." With his wiggy hair and gently stilted English, George comes off as a bit of an eccentric genius himself—when I first meet him, he's got two pairs of eyeglasses perched on his forehead, to help focus his farsighted vision on the detailed components of his bikes.

Today, after decades of tinkering, George produces machines that are as much works of art as they are marvels of engineering. His latest masterpiece, the Varna Diablo, is proof: its Kevlar shell is as streamlined as a dolphin, and its mechanics are as compact and precise as a Swiss watch. Unlike other HPVS that use huge 100-tooth chain rings, the Diablo employs a snug "double-reduction" gear system; the pedals drive one gear-and-chain combination, which transfers power to a second connected to the front wheel, its rotary speed multiplied by every stroke. Like George's earlier record-setting bikes, the Diablo's lightweight frame is built from hand-welded tubing and aircraft parts from the Boeing plant in Seattle. But the Diablo is simpler, and smaller. Sam has to hunch his shoulders to squeeze inside the Diablo; he's had to shave material off his shoes to clear the walls when he pedals.

Piloting and powering this rocket ship also requires specific training. The Nevada course is five miles, start to finish: there's a four-mile run-up for racers to build their momentum, and then they hit a series of timing areas, the shortest (and most likely to record the fastest speed)

200 metres long. "There's not really an event on the track that's the same," Sam says. The run-up requires terrific aerobic endurance, which he's got from regular bicycle racing. But turning it on for the 200-metre sprint demands an extraordinary anaerobic capacity—he can't possibly get enough oxygen into his lungs, especially inside a tight-fitting HPV, so his legs must draw entirely on their own stored energy until they cramp with lactic acid. Weeks before an HPV race, Sam starts doing sprints on a stationary bike, repeating them again and again, building his lactic tolerance. "It's teaching your body to deal with no oxygen—which is painful," Sam says. "But the longer you can go at maximum effort, the faster you go in the end."

Sam and George haven't been training and refining the Diablo merely to improve upon their record, however. This year, they're also facing a formidable challenger: Jason Queally, the British cyclist who won gold in the 1,000-metre time trial at the Sydney Olympics. An Internet broadband company is backing Queally's bid and has put up over $350,000 to have a new bike built for him by Reynard Motorsports, a U.K. firm that designs Formula One race cars. (The Diablo cost George about $5,000.) Sam and George may be seasoned HPV veterans, but the prospect of going up against an Olympic hero with a Grand Prix machine has forced them to get serious. As Sam told me before we headed to Nevada: "It'll be David versus Goliath."

DAY FIVE. I'm standing on the road, shielding Sam from the sun so he doesn't overheat while he gets sealed into the Diablo. Neil Carson, a UVic engineering student and Sam's right-hand man, runs tape around the seam holding the two halves of the Diablo's shell together. From above, Sam looks like he's in one of those cryogenic tubes the astronauts used for the trip to Jupiter in *2001: A Space Odyssey*. Then I remember: those guys relied on clever technology, and they wound up dead.

Neil rolls the Diablo out of its braces. "Ready, Sam?" Sam nods. "Let's do it." Neil pushes the Diablo down the road, launching it like a bobsled. Sam's on his way. We run to the chase truck and peel off after him.

It doesn't take Sam long to get up to cruising speed: at 3.5 miles from the timing traps, he's already up to 50 miles per hour. We follow

200 metres behind, far enough that the bow wake of air compressed in front of our truck won't give him an extra push, but close enough to help if he gets into trouble. He could blow a flat, or worse. HPV pilots have blacked out after sucking up all the oxygen inside their vehicles' airtight shells, and the consequences at highway speeds could be ugly. If Sam dumps the bike and it slides across the asphalt, the friction will turn the walls of the Diablo hot enough to scorch him inside. If the shell cracks apart, he'll be smeared across the road like a sausage pizza.

Two and a half miles from the traps, Sam's approaching 60 miles per hour. At two miles, he's nearing 70. I can't help feeling a tug of emotion, watching this tiny, fragile spacecraft hurtling through the moonscape. Silence all around, and him trapped in there, pedalling furiously, the gears and wheels screaming like buzz saws between his legs.

A mile before the traps, Sam starts pulling away, accelerating past 70 and approaching 75. "There he goes," Neil says, and he lays on the horn to warn the photographers on the road. It takes Sam less than six seconds to cover the distance of two football fields, and then he's through the traps and nearing the finish line. "He was *movin',*" says Neil.

We cross the line, park the truck, and Neil runs to help Sam out of the Diablo. A few minutes later, the British team pulls in. Sam's guess about David and Goliath was right: like many Internet ventures, the British bike is turning out to be an expensive, over-hyped disaster. It was still in the shop on the first two nights of the race; when it finally got on the road the third night, it did 44.29 miles an hour. Last night, when Sam hit 77.03, Jason Queally barely cracked 60. Queally is 6′2″ and his machine is half a foot taller and wider than the Diablo, and now the Brits are learning the hard way that bulk can be murder on aerodynamic efficiency.

The English have a thing for land-speed records—in October 1997 a Royal Air Force pilot drove a turbojet car to 766 miles per hour in Nevada's Black Rock Desert—and reporters from BBC television and radio and two London dailies have travelled all the way here, hoping to document another success. Instead, they have disappointing news to beam back home. "I still feel very positive about it. We've competed with the fastest riders on the planet," Queally tells them, graciously. "The bike was built around me. My width of shoulders and my dimensions, that's the design they came up with. It's down to my size—you look at something like Sam's vehicle, I couldn't even put my backside in it."

It's too early for Sam to celebrate though. Another bike arrives, a huge grey cruise missile driven by Matt Weaver. A tall, toothy mechanical engineer from California, Weaver entered the contest this evening, and he's had a phenomenal first run—the handlers on his chase truck are whooping like cowboys. Rumours are buzzing around the parking lot: Weaver may have hit 80. And Sam is chafed. "If anybody is, Matt's the wild card," he admits.

Weaver is also a triple threat. A *cum laude* scholar and middle-distance runner, he's one of the few who designs and builds his own HPVs, and then pedals them to top speeds. Two years ago, HPV racers were having difficulty finding a straight, level section of high-altitude highway for their competitions; Weaver found this one near Battle Mountain himself, after driving around Nevada for a month with a laptop computer connected to a series of altimeters and barometric pressure gauges. Then he put his bike on the road for a test run—and, he claims, hit 85 miles per hour. But few believed him, especially when he did only 69 in last year's race. He's had something to prove ever since.

I wander over to check out Weaver's bike, the Kyle Edge. The thing looks like a shark on wheels, and it's just as blind: Incredibly, there's no windshield. As Weaver explains, catching his breath, his aim is to achieve the Holy Grail of aerodynamics, an extensive "laminar flow" around the shell, allowing it to slide effortlessly through the atmosphere. "That means there can't be any cracks, seams, bumps, any imperfections on the surface, all the way back to about three-quarters along the body. Soon as you put a windshield in, you mess that up." Instead, the whole bike slides in the back of a sealed nose cone. Weaver breathes through a gas mask running from a high-pressure zone at the back of the bike, and navigates by watching video monitors connected to two cameras in the tailfin. His only problem is forgetting to stop. "There's something about watching a video screen that makes you forget this is reality. I almost crashed on my first ride 'cause I thought I was playing a video game."

Crazy. But it works. The results are announced. Sam has upped his speed to 77.59. The Brits did 63.05. And Weaver has hit 77.40. Not only is he the second person on Earth to do better than 70, he's only a few pedal strokes shy of Sam's record. The doubters have been proven wrong.

"I imagine they're a little humbled right now, thinking, 'Wow, he wasn't kidding, was he?'" says Weaver, smiling at the scare he's put into the Canadians. "I will be targeting for 80 miles an hour tomorrow."

Sam is stunned. "The big stress is that this was his first run. So he could improve on that for sure."

One of the helpers on Weaver's team sees George Georgiev and calls out: "You're going to have to wax 'er up tonight, George!"

"It's going to be a tense 24 hours," mutters Sam.

EVER SINCE bicycles were first developed, people have wanted to see how fast they could ride them. In 1816 Karl von Drais, the "father of the bicycle," created a two-wheeled "swift-walker," and within a year he was bragging to German newspapers that it only took him an hour to get between towns that took four in a horse-drawn wagon.

With every innovation developed during the 19th century—pedals, chain drives, pneumatic tires, hub gears—bicycles and the people who raced them got faster. Designers experimented with the shapes of the machines as well, but by the start of the 20th century, nearly all manufacturers were exclusively making "safety" bicycles, the upright, diamond-framed vehicles most people ride versions of today, and they became the racing standard. Although a few were tinkering with long-wheelbase recumbent bikes, cycling purists thought recumbents far too heavy to win races.

All that changed in July 1933, when a little-known French racer named François Fauré set a new world hour record (45.055 kilometres) on a recumbent. A few months later Fauré rode a recumbent against Henri Lemoine, a famous track-bike champion, and humiliated him in a pursuit race at the Winter Velodrome in Paris. The low profile of the recumbent gave Fauré a tremendous aerodynamic edge, and the purists were outraged. On April 1, 1934, the Union Cycliste Internationale, the governing body that continues to oversee bicycle racing, banned recumbents from competition forever.

From then on, recumbent bicycles seemed doomed to be a mere curiosity, forever associated with tweedy eccentrics and sufferers of enlarged prostates. But the energy crisis of the early 1970s inspired a California engineering professor named Chester Kyle to start experimenting with recumbents, and in 1975 he and a few colleagues organized the first speed championships in which HPVs of any design could compete. Inventors started showing up with all sorts of weird machines: hand-rowed tricycles, tandem bikes with the riders sitting back-to-back, three-man units with the riders facedown in a row. That first year, the top speed was 44 miles per hour. "We had no rules, except the things had to be human-powered," says Kyle. "Other than that, you're free to do anything you want—and look at what they've done."

Today such events are sanctioned by the International Human Powered Vehicle Association, an organization with chapters in more than a dozen countries. The IHPVA oversees a dizzying array of records and contests for all sorts of vehicles, including submarines, hydrofoils and airplanes, all employing the basic gear-and-chain mechanics of the bicycle. (No one has yet been able to claim the $20,000 prize for the first human-powered helicopter.) As IHPVA people see it, they're not just continuing the tradition of bicycle innovation, they're expanding the human imagination. "We're a fraternity of speed," says Carole Leone, a past president of the IHPVA. "We're basically building the world's most efficient transportation vehicles."

Sadly, these noble pursuits rarely get the respect they deserve. The cycling establishment still turns its nose up at HPVs (a bit of a joke, since the UCI now permits all sorts of aerodynamic advances, like streamlined handlebars and teardrop-shaped helmets). IHPVA events don't have big corporate sponsors, and they have difficulty finding venues. Velodromes aren't designed for bikes that do more than 50 miles per hour, HPV riders rarely have the cash to book auto-racing tracks, and many towns aren't willing to shut down a highway every night for a week. That's why the Speed Challenge has ended up in Battle Mountain, Nevada—"the armpit of America," the *Washington Post* recently called it—a dying mining outpost studded with born-again churches and rusting trailer parks.

Battle Mountain seems like the last place on Earth you'd expect to find futuristic bicycles. Though brochures claim there's hiking and bird watching in the barren surrounding hills, its most visible forms of recreation—playing nickel slots at the Owl Club, firing Colt revolvers at the pistol range, leg-wrestling with the $100/hour girls at Donna's Ranch—are straight out of the Old Wild West. But perched at an elevation of 4,600 feet, Battle Mountain is blessed with thin, dry air that provides little aerodynamic drag, and its rarely used secondary road (State Highway 305) is flatter than a tortilla. Desperate for tourists, the town has embraced the Speed Challenge, treating the racers like visiting royalty and throwing a huge banquet featuring the steak-and-potatoes cuisine of the Basque immigrants who settled in northern Nevada in the 1850s. HPVs have found their Promised Land.

The race organizers are giddy. Between 1993 and 2000, the speed record remained stuck at 68 miles per hour. Now, a year later, two racers are poised to hit 80—a leap so quantum it's as if a runner suddenly woke up one morning and did a three-minute mile. But how much faster can these bikes go? Just before Saturday night's final race, I sit down at a Mexican restaurant with a couple of IHPVA officials and veteran designers, and soon they're talking drag coefficients and ground-effect turbulence. (Most sports aren't rocket science. HPV racing is.)

As Chris Broome, the IHPVA president explains to me, on any bike going over 10 miles an hour, nearly all a cyclist's energy goes towards overcoming air resistance. Even an Olympic athlete can generate a peak output of only one horsepower, "and that's not much to play with," he says. "That's why the designers do everything to lower the frontal area of their bikes, and pay more attention to aerodynamic detail. Just applying pure power is not going to make a bike that much faster."

What fascinates them is that designers with two completely different approaches have come up with equally fast bikes. Matt Weaver has proven that it doesn't necessarily matter how big the machine is if the aerodynamic math checks out. "When Matt says something, it means he's calculated it," says Sean Costin. "He's going to be making some people eat their words when he hits 85 miles an hour." George Georgiev, on the other hand, has proven the importance of experience, mechanical simplicity and artistic intuition. "George is just a miracle the way he sculpts his bikes," says Broome. "He doesn't do aerodynamic testing, he builds them so they look right. And they *are* right."

But when the bikes are finished, power is the only variable you've got, and that's where the athleticism of HPV racing comes in. The aerodynamic drag on a bike goes up exponentially with an increase in its speed. If anybody's going to top 80 tonight, it'll require a superhuman effort. As George Leone, an engineer from California who's been watching HPV racing for over 20 years, tells me, "We've never had a competition like this before. This is epic. This one is going to be talked about for a long, long time."

THE SENSE of historic importance is palpable around the starting area. There's no easy laughter tonight. The teams fine-tune their machines with grim determination. As Sam and Matt warm up on their stationary bikes, facing into the setting sun, they don't even glance at each other.

Time to go. The roadblocks are up. I drive down to the finish line: if someone breaks 80 tonight, I want to make sure I'm there when it's announced.

It's a perfect night. The races are held at sunset because that's when the wind drops. I get out of my car at the other end of the course, and there's no breeze at all. In fact, the air is utterly still—it's tense, almost nervous, the way it gets in 40-below cold, when you can hear someone cough a mile away.

A voice crackles over a walkie-talkie: "Varna Diablo has been launched."

We watch, and wait. Then a cheer goes up from the timing area. Less than a minute later, the Diablo is pulling up to the finish line; it slows down, and the handlers gently catch it like a newborn child. They rip at the tape sealing the upper half of the shell, and lift it off. Sam is gasping, wheezing, and he groans as he's lifted out of the bike. He's a 5′7″ body cramp, his muscles flooded with lactic acid.

Just before the race, he and George sealed all the drafts on the Diablo to give it a little more speed. There was almost no air coming in, and Sam went flat out two miles before the timing traps. "I couldn't have done that all week," Sam gasps, as he hobbles around the parking lot. "I had nothing left—my eyes were starting to go *whoop whoop*—I had tunnel vision through the traps. That's the best I can do, the best the bike can do and the best the weather can do."

Matt Weaver pulls in a few minutes later. Sam and Matt are fierce competitors, but they've been doing this for too many years to hold grudges. When they see each other, they hug like exhausted boxers. "Before we even know," Sam says, "I just want to say I'm glad you're here, I'm glad we're doing this and I'm glad we're going so goddamn fast. I couldn't have done it without you."

"I know, you psyched me up, too," Matt tells him.

The bus pulls in from the timing area. Now there are a hundred people in the parking lot, Battle Mountain families out for a Saturday night. George walks over; every other night this week he's been at the finish line, catching bikes, but tonight he decided to see them as they ran the timing traps. He was so amazed by the sight, he tells me, that he forgot to push the record button on his video camera.

George puts his arm around Matt's shoulder. For years, they've been corresponding by letter and by e-mail, exchanging design ideas. "Matt, I told you many years ago that you're going to be the future, and now it's here. Do you remember that?"

"I remember it to this day," Matt says. It was in California in 1988, at his first speed championships, before he started building his own HPVs. "I saw this one bike, the details in the machine work, and I said, 'Wow, this is beautiful!' I walked away from that event, and all I could talk about was George's bikes. There's a certain mastery and elegance in his craftsmanship that just jumps out at me."

Then Sean Costin calls everyone together for the final results. "It took a great challenge to bring out the best in a champion," he says, bathed in the lights of TV cameras. "There was an incredible milestone reached tonight. One rider reached a speed in excess of 80 miles an hour—"

Even before Costin names the winner, everyone's hooting and hollering. Together, the fraternity of speed has crossed a threshold. And then Costin makes the announcement:

"Sam Whittingham."

The cheers are deafening. Sam hit 80.55. Weaver did 78.02. The British bike reached 64.34, making it the fifth-fastest vehicle in HPV history.

"Thank God!" Sam exclaims, laughing, and we're all laughing along with him. It's been an extraordinary week.

A few hours later, after a wrap-up barbecue, I run into Sam and Matt again, talking on the steps of the motel. They still can't quite believe what they've done, and how much their strange sport has evolved.

"Before, I used to see the signs, people on the side of the road," Sam recalls. "Now I don't see anything."

"I know! It's like *brrrrr*—" Matt says, mimicking the shaking handlebars, the world whipping past his video screens, "—and then *whish, whish, whish!*"

"The amazing thing is that these bikes *cruise* at 65 miles an hour."

"This is a whole new level," Matt agrees. "We're not talking speeds that people drive every day in their cars. We're beyond that now."

The coordinator for the British team stops by. It's been a disappointing week for them, but he's confident the sponsors will finance another run next year. "You're the fastest man in the world," he says, congratulating Sam. "You're very marketable, you know."

"I wish," Sam replies, knowing how slow Canadians can be to celebrate the accomplishments of their countrymen.

Meanwhile, up in his room, George is resting—and thinking about his next bike. He fell ill while working on the Diablo, and the shell warped slightly in its mould. "That bike is crooked in my eyes," he tells me. "I built it, and I know what is not yet perfect." He figures he can trim another 20 square inches off the nose. Build a ventilation system to give Sam more air. Seal the wheels inside their own wells. All these could add another couple of miles to Sam's speed and further advance the HPV fraternity's ongoing experiment in applied science. "We are finding these things out slowly," George says. "With each race, we learn more."

Then we hear a pop and a bang from outside. I go to the balcony. Someone is setting off fireworks. A small congregation of revellers stands in the parking lot, marvelling at the rockets as they soar into the darkening sky and loudly illuminate it with flashes of brilliance.

BEHIND THE
GRASS CURTAIN

J.B. MacKINNON

SEPTEMBER/OCTOBER 2002

THE DRIVER SPEAKS into the air with the manners of a tour guide. "We have just left Uganda and are now in no man's land. If you take a bullet here, no one will even come to get you." Then he laughs lightly, as though laughing too hard could make the joke real.

A United Nations fieldworker from Kenya, the driver has agreed to take us on board his Land Cruiser, provided this fact does not get back to his bosses. The wheels hum on the laterite road, smooth red dirt running down to the Kaya River. Just like Prince Edward Island, I think to myself. Strips of bright mud between the fair and green.

Everything seems to change at the river. On the far side of the bridge, the wheels of the four-by-four drop off an edge and begin to heave over shattered tarmac. Uganda's border lookout was a cluster of mud-and-grass huts, or *tukuls,* but here at the frontier of southern Sudan, the watch-posts are old plaster buildings, every corner serrated with bullet scars.

Now a teenager is at the window of the jeep, a tiny puff of fabric keeping road dust out of the barrel of his AK-47. *Get out,* he gestures. I obey, followed by Jason Payne, a photographer from Vancouver. The teen guerrilla leads us to a checkpoint officer, who is sitting beneath a declaration barring the use of child soldiers. He doesn't care to see our passports.

Here, all that matters is the rebel army pass, a blue paper card handed to us four days earlier by a silent man in a room the colour of an old lampshade. The checkpoint officer takes down every detail—nothing is so bureaucratic as revolution. Finally, he lifts his head. "Make yourself at home," he says.

Which is hard to do in a corner of Africa known as War Zone One. The tribes are watching us: the Kakwa on the sly; the Nuer directly; the Luwo with interest; the Dinka—tall and black as wet stone—with just a hint of arrogance. *Who are these* kawija? They carry cameras and microphones, like journalists, but travel on the ground, like aid workers or the CIA. There is only one reasonable answer: the two men are evangelists.

We sit through this deconstruction because we're waiting for a spy. The rebel army won't let us past this border village without a representative from the Military Intelligence division, which sounds Orwellian until he appears, on foot, armed only with a bedroll. His name is Sgt.-Maj. Albino Ulau, a 30-year-old with a smile so broad that it changes the shape of his head. "We will be friends," he says, in the voice of a soldier who is weary of killing.

The kids with the machine guns wave us on and we roll past the ruins of a Russian-made tank. At a trucking compound on the outskirts of town we wait again, this time for the UN World Food Program convoy that we'll follow into the civil-war zone. Our driver enjoys the downtime—on his last Sudan tour, government forces had attacked the village where the aid was to be unloaded. He remembers watching, wondering, as a helicopter gunship swung its weapons towards the arriving convoy. The government army and the UN don't always get along.

Hours later, the sunset flares against the horizon and catches a billow of rufous dust on the hill above town—the first convoy trucks are finally heading out. Men stub out cigarettes and drink last swallows of warm beer. Our driver stands up from the bumper of the Land Cruiser just as the radio crackles to life in the cab.

"Location?" asks a voice in heavily accented English. "Location? Location?"

The UN driver smiles warily, adjusts the battered World Food Program cap that he had to buy with his own wages. He slips into the truck's cab.

"Location?"

He picks up the handset. "Who is calling?" he says.

"Location?"

"Who is calling?"

"Location? Location?" The question has now turned into a demand.

The driver says nothing and hangs up the handset. Then he motions that it is time to sit in, get going. "It's the GOS," he says, meaning the government of Sudan, whose border we have just illegally crossed. "They want to know where we are."

A WEEK before we left for Sudan, Jason and I had met with a world-weary journalist in an attempt to convince ourselves that we were off on more than a peculiar lark. The theory was this: that Canadians can no longer ignore the planet's outposts of misery. That ours is a global nation, and sometimes the Maple Leaf flies over some shady terrain. That there are pockets of the world, a small but growing list, where a Canadian can get a sense of what it must be like to be American—to be the running-dog imperialist pig for a day. Southern Sudan would test the theory. It is a place where the survivors of war could remember Canada for all the wrong reasons. We spread a map across a darkwood bar and traced the roads we would travel, from here to here to here. The world-weary journalist finally seized the map and flipped it over to its unprinted backside. He stabbed a finger at the middle of the nothingness. "Here," he said with finality. "Here is where you are going."

Southern Sudan—what the locals optimistically call "New Sudan"—has been in civil war against its government, based in Khartoum, for 19 years. In reality, though, the dispute runs back to 1955, the year of the Anya-Nya ("Snake Venom") mutiny of southern Sudanese within the government army. No matter where you start the apocalyptic clock, the conflict is arguably the longest-running war on Earth. It is also among the least well known; military historian Edgar O'Ballance called it "the secret war," fought behind "a grass curtain of silence." In the West, people have had time to learn there is a great war going on in Sudan, and then to forget; to relearn and then to forget again. Meanwhile, just beyond the elephant grass, two million people now lie dead.

Wars need reasons, and in Sudan, the shorthand excuse is this: the largely Arab Muslim North wants to rule the largely black animist and Christian South. The latest round of warfare began in 1983, when the Khartoum government tried to impose Islam's no-nonsense shariah law on the South; instead, they inspired the rise of the Sudan People's Liberation Army (SPLA). You can also look for roots 50 years ago, when Britain abandoned the South to northern rule, as Sudan became the first African country to gain independence after World War II. Just as fruitfully, you can begin in the seventh century AD, when Arabs first began raiding the South for slaves. The country remains one of the few where the slave trade has never been utterly abolished.

It takes international cooperation to let a war drag on for half a century. For years, world leaders turned their backs, failing to drop by for photo-ops with Commander-in-Chief John Garang (South) and General Omar Hassan Ahmad Al-Bashir (North). That finally began to change after September 11, 2001, when Khartoum ended up in America's gunsight—the North was home to Osama bin Laden from 1991 to 1996. In danger of becoming the next war-on-terror target, Sudan turned over its files on al-Qaeda and began to talk peace. Observers now hope for a ceasefire in southern Sudan by the end of the year.

It will be, at best, a fragile truce. The SPLA now controls most of the lower third of the country; the North controls the rest, including Sudan's airspace, which it uses to drop bombs on civilians. For most of its history, the conflict had been a war of the poor against the poor, as slow and sad as a fistfight between drunks. But in what may be remembered as the war's final chapter, that changed for the worse—and the reasons include a distant nation called Canada.

In 1998, a consortium of oil interests began to build a pipeline from disputed areas in south-central Sudan to a port on the Red Sea. You might expect to find Texas CEOs pulling the levers, but no—the U.S. had slapped the country with sanctions. Instead, the Greater Nile Petroleum Operating Company is a partnership between the state oil companies of Sudan, China and Malaysia, along with one independent. The odd-duck partner, holding a 25 per cent stake and paying royalties to Khartoum that totalled $250 million last year, is Talisman Energy Inc., of Calgary, Alberta.

The problem, of course, is that giving money and support to a government at war helps pay the bills for the bloodshed. Under pressure from a small but committed corps of activists, Talisman has said for years that it would sell its holdings in Sudan—the current potential buyer is the government of India. But the damage is already done. Talisman backstopped the rise of the northern government as an oil power, and no divestment can turn back time. Flush with petroleum dollars, government forces take to the killing fields with bigger, better toys: artillery cannons, tanks, helicopter gunships, jet fighters.

Which is why, without newspapers, television or Radio Canada International, most southern Sudanese can tell you at least two things about the True North Strong and Free.

Number one: it sends food aid to their families.

Number two: it helps buy bombs for their enemies.

OUR UN driver sits on the roof of the Land Cruiser and begins a lecture on America, which he visited last year. Men there have only one wife, he explains, but that is not the strangest thing. Even San Francisco is not the strangest thing. No, the strangest thing in America, he says, is a rural attraction somewhere in California.

"I saw a place—a park—where there was a very rough road," he says, then leans closer, his eyebrows tight with emphasis. "People were *paying* to drive on this road." He pauses to let the enormity of this weirdness sink in. "I could not believe it."

The driver is a UN monitor, which means he spends his life in a Land Cruiser, keeping tabs on the flat tires and breakdowns that plague the movement of food to the hungry. Today, our convoy of 22 aid trucks covered 250 kilometres. It took 14 hours. There was, shall we say, a very rough road.

In North America, we talk about "road-tripping" or "car-camping," words that subtly admit that the scale of adventure will be limited to, say, epic drinking at the 20th Annual Testicle Festival in Clinton, Montana. In Africa, the term is "overlanding," which sounds very cool, very Hemingway. Often it's a sham, a mobile Club Med with stops for Zulu dancing, gorillas in the mist and ganja on the banks of the Nile. Off the beaten path, however, there remain many routes where the local police can only wish you luck and the single rule is BYOB: build your own bridges. It's worth noting that when Ugandan truckers head into Sudan, they say they are "going on safari." There will be no phones, no gas stations, no ambulances, no traffic, though every few days there might be a light bulb running on a diesel generator.

A typical day: it's morning. I return from watching children try to kill a small and presumably venomous snake by throwing rocks from a distance of 10 feet, only to find Jason on the receiving end of a comparable attack. A group of Dinka herders are in his face, spouting vitriol and waving sticks. I piece together the clues. We were sleeping in a cowshed. The Dinka have come to town with cows. There is a dark stain on the wall of the shed, a mark familiar to any male. Either the Dinka have seen the stain and taken offence, or, worse, have caught Jason in the act of despoiling a shed full of cowshit with his own foreign urine.

It takes our rebel chaperone to calm the situation. Albino speaks eloquently, negotiating with the universal body language that says, clearly, *Forgive these men, they are idiots.* We nod eagerly and look contrite.

Later, on the road, we look back on the moment and try to unwind. Remember when? We were fools, no? But those Dinka—so angry! Hey Albino, do you think that they've calmed down by now?

"It will go to court," he deadpans. We have a good laugh at that, until we realize Albino isn't laughing at all.

We have changed drivers, our original man called to a solo mission, and we follow the convoy east to Mabia, a point that fails to appear on any map. Now we ride with Biga Nasur, a burly Ugandan, and his sidekick Marino Sule "Ismail" Ismail, a southern Sudanese. They sit in the front, in charge of the UN radio and a cassette that plays Congolese pop on an endless loop.

The first hour is always the worst. Jason, Albino and I are packed in the back, each of us making constant strategic shifts to gain legroom. Almost immediately, temperatures punch into the mid-30s. Every day, we start out believing that finally, for god's sake, the roads are bound to be a little better. And every day, within two minutes, we are all clinging to some handle or windowsill as the lurching and pummelling begins anew.

Going overland in Sudan beats you first into submission, and finally into unconsciousness. Most nights you don't sleep until midnight, and then only on a tarp unrolled under a tree, or perhaps on the patio of a bombed-out building. At the first wink of light, the ubiquitous rooster calls the reveille. And so, by mid-morning, you find yourself stealing miraculous catnaps, your head snapping in time to the ruts while a hand maintains a death-grip on the Land Cruiser's frame.

Here is what you see when you open your eyes: a woman with a full, wood-frame bed balanced on her head. A man, slam-dunk tall and naked but for a long, grey beard and a fishing spear. Six people on a single bicycle. A mother walking, two huge teak leaves pinched in a perfect fold to shade her baby's head from the sun. A soldier with two guns but no shoes. A troop of olive baboons. A mongoose. One other thing, also. Everywhere there are people at the side of the road who, as you pass, offer up whatever they can spare, for sale or trade. A woman presents a gourd and a jar of kerosene; a man has two cigarettes and a jerry can with no lid. Alone, a tiny boy cups a single egg in an out-stretched hand.

For hours at a time, no one speaks, and then suddenly, a single word. "Africa." After a pause to let today's topic take weight, Biga continues. "Very, *very* dangerous."

And then they're off. Biga tells us about a plant with leaves that burn your flesh in the wet season and cut it open in the dry, and then about the time his legs were swarmed by the flies that can cause river blind-ness. (He wept.) Albino mentions a scorpion whose sting burns for a day with a crippling pain that you never adjust to. Ismail discusses sleeping sickness and the tsetse fly, then points out that the black mamba, a snake as aggressive as it is poisonous, can rear its head high enough to strike through an open jeep window. In Sudan, no one seems to shrug off dan-ger; instead, they cling to it like a talisman. If you pull off the road to get around a broken-down truck, you say, "I hope there are no land mines." If you step out of the jeep in the night, you say, "I hope there are no snakes." And if, in that jungle darkness, you say out loud that hyenas are normally harmless animals, easily frightened, someone will reply, "A hyena is only a coward when it's full."

By the time you've heard about a kind of banana that can cause internal bleeding (bananas—very, *very* dangerous), the odds of survival seem alarmingly long. At about the same time, a remarkable cool sets in. It is a trickle-down lesson, as true as it is trite: everybody dies. It might be a leopard, or AIDS, or blood poisoning from a shaving cut. When it's your turn, try to be gracious.

If you miss the lesson by day, the drills continue at night over plates of bushrat stew, the knuckles of meat suggesting an animal the size of a beaver. In the darkness, I can only see the shine of sweat on Obitre "Musa" Musa, a convoy trucker so tough he has long ago forgotten to act that way. "I am a guerrilla fighter," he declares. "I fight with food."

The metaphor is close to the reality. Sometimes, Musa says, the aid drivers will hear a strange buzzing. "We think at first it is the engine," he says. Then comes the flash of recognition: it is an Antonov, one of the Russian cargo planes the Sudanese government uses as bombers. The drivers pull the trucks under the trees and cover the windows with blankets so the glass won't reflect in the sky. Next, they run like hell. "Sometimes, there is no time. We are running only," he says.

Another trucker squats beside us in the dark. I ask if he has seen the Antonovs.

"Yeah, I have seen," he says.

Have you seen them drop bombs?

"So many people are dying if they drop. That's why we are fearing."

You are fearing when you drive?

"Yeah."

But this trip should be safe, right? This trip to Mabia?

"I cannot tell you lies," the truck driver says. "I don't know. Today, we are here alive. I don't know of tomorrow."

ALMOST 20 years ago, my older brother took a small shoulder bag on the obligatory young-man's-trip-to-Europe. Before he left, he decorated the bag to guarantee a bond of trust with strangers, who would then open their doors to him and introduce their daughters. The bag, now in my possession, is not having this effect on a man named Rizik Zakariah, however. He is eyeing the two small Maple Leafs, one on each strap. "You are Canadian," Rizik says respectfully, but his expression is a gentle warning. *The flags? Not necessarily a good idea.*

We're sitting on a woodpile at the end of the road. In the clearing in front of us, men and women climb the convoy trucks and unload bag after bag of wheat and pulses, tin after tin of cooking oil. This is Mabia; we knew we were getting close when we passed through a final grove of mango trees. It is high season for mangoes, and along the way, the fallen fruit had carpeted the road. In this last grove, however, the trees had been stripped bare, the fruit eaten long ago, green and sour.

People around here are hungry.

Not long after we stopped, Rizik appeared and introduced himself as the local secretary for the Sudan Relief and Rehabilitation Association (the humanitarian wing of the SPLA). A story about Mabia cannot begin in Mabia, he said. Instead, it has to begin in Raga, a town far to the north, in south-central Sudan. In June, 2001, the SPLA captured Raga and its surrounding county from the government of Sudan. It was the largest town the rebel army had ever taken, but the government struck back just two months later. "They utilized all of their financial and military capacities," said Rizik. "They came with very huge ground forces, with heavy artillery, and they also used jet fighters, plus an Antonov high-altitude bomber, plus a gunship."

Like sensible people anywhere, Raga's civilians fled to outlying areas. A World Food Program airdrop brought them together, and they officially became what the UN calls "internally displaced persons"—refugees within their own country. On the banks of the Sopo River, the SRRA offered a plan. Raga could resettle in a largely abandoned village, Mabia. The only catch: Mabia was 700 kilometres away.

They walked it, 21,000 people moving through the bush on forest paths and old roads. It took the strongest more than a month. Ninety-seven people died en route, and 26 children were born.

As Rizik spoke, I took notes, nodded, and acted like a person who has heard it all before. But in my head, a logic was forming. What Rizik was describing is the world's current nightmare—that somewhere, out behind some grass curtain, terrible things are happening to innocent people. Worse, that those people could decide—for reasons you aren't even aware of—that you, your people, your country are to blame. Worse still, that they might find a way to lash out. The more important story is that usually they don't. Usually, people forgive us our ignorance and ask, almost too politely, that we be just a little more vigilant. They notice our Maple-Leaf iron-ons and, though they know that Canada refuses to sanction the regime that made them refugees, they only laugh softly and say, as Rizik does now, "I hope the government of Canada will be holding a point of making peace with the New Sudan people."

He waves away further questions, and instead leads me into the mayhem of food-aid delivery day. I chat with Martin Mogadingari, who walked the 700 kilometres with his five-year-old son. Two of his brothers were "blown to bits" in Raga, and he had to leave behind a successful blacksmith shop. Today, he doesn't even own shoes.

Then there is Rita Khamis, who remembers international observers taking photos of her pregnant sister, killed in the shelling. Jason shakes hands with a man with leprosy. I meet Antoni Valentino, who took 75 days to walk to Mabia, and now stands guard in the tiny souk, or market, where people trade handfuls of peanuts for snuffs of corn flour. And here is Fashir Kamun, a former banker still in his workaday slacks and V-neck sweater: "Antonovs and gunships and jet fighters, they used to come and bomb everywhere, randomly. You might move for one hour to get food and so on, then you go again into your hole. That's how we were living in Raga."

As the sun begins to set, the drumming begins. We wander from celebration to celebration—the Dinkas' big feet beating clouds from the earth, Albino joining his Chat tribe as they dance to sticks scraped over tin rattles. The crowds drag us in, leaping, hooting, and in the mosh of bodies I feel a first trace of fear. One lean young man, more than a head taller than me and with arms like oiled rope, lurches close several times, his face queer with an ecstatic rage. Others pull him away, but he reels back into my orbit, again and again.

Returning to the convoy camp in thin twilight, we pass a man who appears to be sitting at the side of the road, both hands upturned in a traditional greeting. We make the same gesture, which is when the magnitude of the Raga exodus strikes me in the gut. I had heard, without flinching, that the epic journey had been made by children, the elderly, the blind and the sick. Now this man appears at the roadside, his legs erased by a land mine or some other disaster. On what remains of his lap sit the wooden hand-pegs he uses for locomotion, and upon which he had travelled more than the distance from Toronto to Montreal.

A few minutes earlier, I had asked the commissioner of Mabia camp, Maurice Baptist Peter, if he had any message that he would like me to take home. He nodded, and cleared his throat to make a statement. "Our situation is good," he declared. "Not any matter."

They say that Allah laughed when he created the Sudan. They also say that Allah wept. Truth is, Allah doesn't know whether to laugh or cry.

WE SPEND our last few days in Yei, where even the chickens know how to take cover. I learn this almost immediately from a teenager, with whom I share a glass of *kedkede,* a tea made with a sweet, cinnamon-scented flower. He explains that he is visiting his home from his school in Uganda. He doubts he will ever again live in Sudan. "Yei is beautiful," he says, "but there are the ravages of war."

Yei is almost synonymous with bombing by Antonovs, and though the skies have been quiet for weeks, a gas mask is provided in my rented tukul. I measure the distance from my bedside to the nearest bomb shelter. Thirty-one paces.

We are here to negotiate a trip to the front line of the war, a place called Mile 40 (named for the distance from Juba, the capital-in-waiting of New Sudan and one of the northern government's few strongholds in the South). Our breakthrough comes when a Ugandan trucking company agrees to lend a driver and a Land Cruiser truck for a day. There is no public transport in southern Sudan, and even the army has only a handful of jeeps.

The next morning, the SPLA issues Albino an AK-47; he'll stand watch from the bed of the pickup. We leave immediately, slowly climbing through elephant grass so lush that we can barely see the barrels of Yei's anti-aircraft guns. The road is the worst yet; the rains are coming now, and potholes the size of the truck are everywhere. Still, Bosco—a driver from Idi Amin's old hometown in Uganda—refuses to waste gas in four-wheel drive. He steers with the precision of a cat walking a windowsill.

The trip takes hours, but the empty landscape is the most beautiful yet. The forest is in groves and glades, and here and there great domes of blue-black granite press to the sky. Wind draws across them, and the air is almost cool. From the high passes, we can see monsoon clouds blurring the horizon. Closer to hand, the road is lined with flights of white butterflies and the burned-out wrecks of tanks and troop-carriers.

At a checkpoint, a few more rebels join Albino in the back of the pickup. The road worsens, and in one trench of tumblestones, it takes all of us, lifting and pushing, to get through. At the next series of potholes, Bosco swings the wheels wide into the grass. From behind the cab come shouts of "*Simas! Simas!*"—land mines. Then we roll into an open expanse, and see a few men gathered in the shade beneath a tree. Among them is Alternate Cdr. Elias Lino Jada, the soldier in charge of Brigade 23 at Mile 40.

Commander Jada is a wild man with a salt-and-pepper Afro and yellow-fever eyes. He was once a lieutenant-colonel in the northern army, but was jailed and nearly executed as an SPLA sympathizer. He escaped to the bush, then to Eritrea, and today has the air of a man who knows that life is short. There is none of the caution of the SPLA bureaucracy. You want to go to the front? Why wait? He leaps into the pickup bed, where he stands, legs splayed, directing Bosco with a black pointer that he wields like Patton's horsewhip. "Faster! Faster!" he shouts, and Bosco responds by driving exactly as fast as he damn well pleases.

At a cluster of tukuls, Jada signals to stop. Young men appear out of the huts and forest, approaching with their odd salute of clicking and lifting their heels, like Dorothy in Oz.

"This is Jebel Iraq!" Jada declares. "The hill of the Iraqians! Here, we killed so many of them."

He stalks off, with us in pursuit. He leads us past trenches and gun positions, stopping to place his large hands on favourite soldiers. I peer out towards Juba, and notice the open meadow is eerily uniform. A minefield maybe? But it seems more familiar than that.

"Is this a cornfield?" I ask.

"Yes, we have this, what do you call it—sorghum!"

"You're producing food up here?"

"Well, we are strugglers," he explains. "Everyone is cultivating for himself, to support his family, because we are not getting any support from anywhere." He leans over and mimes the motions of digging a seed row. "You see, you take your gun, here, and then you cultivate like this…" Sudan is ready, it seems, to beat its swords into ploughshares.

Now he's off up the hill, beads of sweat beginning to spatter at his feet. The hill was taken in 1997, he explains, when SPLA soldiers fought government forces all the way up the road from Yei. The last stand was against a battalion of hardened fighters, Islamic fundamentalists from Iraq who held their ground. And here, says Jada, is a pile of their bones.

I stop cold. The skeleton is at my feet, exactly like that of a deer on a forest trail back home. But with a difference. "These are the bones of—"

"Iraqians!" shouts Jada in triumph.

It is a hill of human bones, clusters of them all over, and always in little heaps, the way a skeleton falls to the ground when a cartoon character is zapped with a cartoon ray gun. There was once a hand-painted sign here that declared that 2,300 Iraqis had died in this battle, but in reality, nobody was keeping score. No one really knows.

A question suddenly strikes me. "Standing where we are, where is the enemy right now?"

"You see they are up there," he says, pointing. "That jebel, there. You see there are some things, very white, you see?"

I see. Two specks, 800 yards away.

"Enemy forces," he says.

We retreat then, to the jeep. As we prepare to drive back to the commander's shady tree, I take a moment to inspect Brigade 23. These are the unpaid fighters of the world's poorest war. Some have pilfered uniforms, but most wear whatever the aid trucks bring: brown slacks, brogues, caps that read "Marlboro" and "Cobourg, Ontario." This is a flip-flop army, and at least one soldier still carries a spear—he's the guy in the "I Support Ronald McDonald House" T-shirt. As we pull away, they clamour for anything we can give: a couple sheets of paper and a few cigarettes. One soldier walks away, delighted, with an empty water bottle. This is an army, really, with nothing to lose.

Back at the tree, the commander sits us down. He has a message to deliver to Canada.

"What we are after is our rights as human beings in this world," he begins. "This land has been given to us from God as our father's land, and grandfather's land. We don't have any objection if the Arabs want to stay with us as brothers and sisters. But we have an objection if they want to stay to *control* us. If we be under their mercy."

Oil money changed the face of the war, he says, convincing the North that it need never surrender. It made the government of Sudan, once one of the most isolated in the world, a force to be reckoned with in negotiations. Like so many southerners, the commander hopes for peace but doubts that what the North agrees to on paper will play out in the field. He is suspicious of the new trust between Khartoum and the international community.

Jada talks on, slowly tapping into his own sense of outrage. At some point, he stops talking about oil and Canada and Talisman Energy. Suddenly, he's getting personal.

"Without peace, how can you exploit somebody's resources? Who can accept that?" he demands, as though we might make an on-the-spot policy shift on behalf of our country. "You, as human beings—support us! Yes! Why should you support a government that is against even Christians? Why? Is it because of money? What is money, after all?"

His anger crests and he calms and grows quiet. Once again, it is late afternoon and we'll be driving in the dark. Jada stands to shake our hands, and everyone thanks everyone else and makes goodbye promises that no one can keep. We move through the groups of soldiers, all of them chattering in Arabic and Bari—some kind words, I think, and some less generous. I round the front of the jeep, heading for the far door, and a soldier, perhaps 20 years old, blocks my path. He has the ubiquitous machine gun strapped across a Chicago Cubs T-shirt. His face is clouded, and he has clearly been preparing a few choice words in English.

"Canada," he spits. "A Christian country. Why this hypocrisy?" He seems uncertain what he wants to do next, and then steps back to let me pass.

THE DRIVE back to Yei is the longest of my life. The war front was quiet, but also eerie and intense. And then there is this road, doubly frightening in the dark. A thunderstorm is exploding to the north, and if it closes on us, the dirt track will become shifting mud, and every pothole a plunge into the unknown. Minutes later, a second storm begins to the south. Flashbulb lightning pops on either side. We are racing the sky at 20 klicks an hour, and none of us is sure what it would mean to lose. Albino slumps over his weapon in the truckbed. No one says a word.

I am thinking about what it means to be hated. I am imagining people washing dishes in Chicoutimi, or checking e-mail in Prince Rupert, or putting children to bed in Summerside. They are dreaming of new jobs, the lottery, true love, and not one of them knows about a place called Mile 40. But not knowing doesn't make the place less real. It doesn't stop a Sudanese kid in a Cubs jersey from dreaming that he could, just once, stick a fist in the face of some smug *kawija* from the land of plenty.

My thoughts are cut short when I notice, in the faint yellow light of the CB radio, that there is something stuck to the sleeve of my shirt. I can just make it out, but it's there, an object the size of a deck of cards. It appears to be alive. I run down the list of possibilities, in rough order of preference: a lizard, a bat, a spider or a giant mystery bug.

Africa. Dangerous.

I try to come up with a cool-headed strategy. First, get a better look in the next flash of lightning. All I can see, though, is that the creature is now on the move, slowly crawling up my sleeve towards my naked throat. It's time for action. I stick my arm towards the window and, with artificial calm, ask Jason to please brush off whatever's clinging to my sleeve. Just as casually, Jason sweeps with his hand.

In the blackness we hear his palm hit something of substance, which lets out an ungodly squeal and ricochets off the window frame. We panic, pawing the air without shame, even Bosco struggling to keep the wheels on the road. When we are just calm enough to ask the obvious question—*What the hell was that?*—we hear a sound in some loose papers at our feet.

"I think it is still here," says Bosco.

In the compressed universe of the truck cab, we are three men from two cultures united by fear. We hear crinkling noises again at our feet, and then under the seat. Silence. Finally, we pick up the sound of something inching its way across the dash. Jason digs out his penlight.

"Shine it from outside the window," I say, "in case it goes for the light." Bosco tightens his grip on the wheel, and Jason twists the torch on. There in the jostling spotlight is a very large, very, *very* harmless cockroach.

We start to laugh. We laugh because we were scared of a miserable insect. We laugh because we've just spent a day among angry young men with loaded guns, and because we are hungry and thirsty and tired. We laugh because there are a million ways to die, and because in this instant we are gloriously alive. We laugh because, for the moment, we are a tiny vessel shooting the tube between storms in the forgotten Sudan, and because, in the end, we will get to go home.

POSTSCRIPT: Talisman Energy sold its interests in Sudan in March 2003, and the civil war has since ended. A final peace agreement between the southern rebels and the government of Sudan was signed in January 2005. In 2003, however, a new crisis began unfolding in Sudan—the conflict and genocide in the western region of Darfur.

SEARCHING
FOR BIG MAN MAGIK

CHARLES MONTGOMERY

MARCH 2004

SILA GIBOTO WAS a real charmer. She had the warmest smile and the mildest grandmother eyes. She spoke with a gentle hum, so that when she described the way her great-grandfather had cooked children ("Off with the head, then a slice down the belly, then into the oven with the pigs"), it was as though she was singing a lullaby to the urchins who clung to her ankles.

Sila led my friend Peter and me away from the shore of the lagoon and the glare of the equatorial sunlight, and into the forest. The tree trunks were rocket ships, their roots splayed out like great fins. The air was heavy with the scent of rotting leaves and coconut husks. Steam issued from the earth. It was dark there.

Sila stopped by a heap of fractured coral rock arranged in a rough square. She pulled aside a slab to reveal a pile of bones and skulls. The skulls were caked with lichen. Some had teeth. Others did not. Sila wiped her hands on her frock and gingerly picked one up.

"Here is my great-grandfather, Tamtame," she said.

Tamtame was a very great chief, Sila explained, a very respected and accomplished raider. One of the best. He would paddle away with his men each year and return with his canoe loaded with the heads of his enemies. Sila petted the skull as she spoke, the way a child might stroke a kitten.

Something amid the heap of bleached remains caught my eye. I reached between what might have been a couple of femurs and rescued an English smoking pipe from the shadows. It was as white as chalk.

"Yes, that belonged to a white man," Sila said, now beaming with pride. "Two missionaries came in a boat to bring the gospel to Tamtame, but he cut their heads off before they could change him. Oh, he was so powerful! He collected hundreds and hundreds of heads."

"But why? Why did he want all these heads?" I said.

She frowned for the first time, and lowered her voice to a whisper.

"You must understand that my great-grandfather was a servant of Satan. He offered all those heads to his devils, and they used their magic to make him stronger."

"Tell me about the magic," I said.

"You forget about magic. We do not follow Satan here anymore."

I was not going to forget about the magic. It was magic that had brought me to Marovo Lagoon in the first place. But Sila didn't want to talk anymore. She was shuffling back to her shack, and Peter was pulling me away towards our waiting kayaks and the lagoon, which shone like a vast tin roof in the afternoon light.

SOLOMON ISLANDERS will tell you that the Marovo is the world's largest lagoon. It might be. The calm water stretches like a giant moat around the extinct volcanic peaks of New Georgia, Vangunu and Nggatokae islands, protected by 100 kilometres of barrier islands and reefs. Its bathtub-warm waters hold such a spectacular concentration of marine life—Gorgonian fans, giant clams, sea turtles, barracuda, sharks—that UNESCO has considered listing the area as a World Heritage Site. In anticipation, villagers built thatched guesthouses and prepared for the arrival of the eco-touring hordes, but then, in 2000, the Solomons fell into a civil war. The government tried to pass off the bloodletting as "ethnic tension," but tourists stayed away.

It was history that brought me to Marovo. That, I suppose, and a dash of romantic primitivism. My great-grandfather was a missionary bishop. He sailed through the South Pacific in 1892, intent on rescuing the heathens from the spirits and ghosts that bound them, in his opinion, to lives of violence, fear, nakedness and promiscuity.

The old man's diaries were thick with tales of murder and martyrdom beneath the palms. A dozen of his predecessors had been drowned, shot or clubbed to death. The survivors had nevertheless convinced thousands of islanders to trade their sacrifices and bloody rituals for hymns and cricket.

But it was the bishop's description of traditional island religion that fascinated me. His converts told of a world where supernatural power flowed through objects, people—the very atmosphere of life. They called that power *mana*. Like the Force in *Star Wars, mana* could be concentrated and directed for good or evil. You could use it to bring rain for your crops or to convince a shark to eat your enemy. Everyone had a little *mana* in them. In Marovo, islanders had concluded that it was concentrated in people's heads. That explained the stacks of skulls I had seen. It was a gruesome harvest but quite logical, if you thought about it: a storehouse of heads was *mana* in the bank.

The bishop and his peers turned the central Solomon Islands into an Anglican stronghold, but they stopped a day's sail short of the Marovo Lagoon. I suppose they chickened out. When the bishop stepped off his mission ship at a nearby island, he found the locals living in utter fear of their headhunting neighbours in Marovo. They were so terrified that they'd abandoned the coast and taken shelter from the raiders in tree houses and mountaintop forts.

After years of dreaming of the islands, I could resist no longer. In 2002, I travelled south to judge the missionaries' South Pacific legacy for myself. I told my friends that my interest was academic, positioning myself as a sort of curious but detached adventurer. But as I moved from shore to shore over the months, I was seduced by fireside tales of miracles and magic. The islanders were all believers. Could a man turn himself into a bat and fly to another island for dinner? Yup. Could a priest stop a bullet with his walking stick? No problem. Could a sorcerer still convince a shark to eat his enemy? Hell, yes!

Problem was, while the islanders were big on magic talk, they were short on the walk. I wanted to believe. All I needed was a little proof. That's why I came to Marovo. Once there had been no islanders as fierce and feared as the lagoon people, and no *mana* as kick-ass as lagoon *mana*. Surely some of that metaphysical mojo still lingered among the reefs and jungled shadows.

I FLEW in to a WWII airstrip—tall grass, wide puddles, bad landing—at the village of Seghe, on New Georgia Island at the west end of the lagoon. From there I took a speedboat a half-hour north to Uepi Island, where a pair of Australians ran a tiny dive resort. The Australians served the only cold beer for a hundred miles around. That was a temptation. But they also had kayaks and employed a local man who was set on leading me away from said temptation. Peter Mara was the quintessential Marovan: his skin was as dark as crude oil, his teeth were regularly stained crimson from chewing betel nuts, and he was unwaveringly, evangelically Christian. Peter promised that if I followed him away from the comfort of Uepi he could lead me to the lagoon's last pagans. At least, that's what I thought he said. In fact he was using the singular.

"And magic?" I asked as we pushed our kayaks down through the sand. "We'll find magic?"

"Magic is a lie," said Peter, lighting a cigarette he had rolled using a page of my notebook. "No magic compares to the magic of the Big Man."

Actually, what Peter had said was: *Magik, hem i bulsit. No ani magik wea hemi strong ovam magik blong Big Man,* using the pidgin that was born in the days of explorers and traders, and which had become a de facto common tongue for Solomon Islanders, despite the fact they were now educated in English. I was a fan of pidgin. It was a language of metaphor and poetic directness. For example, a *pijin blong solwota* was a seagull. A *glas blong diver* was a mask and snorkel. A *rubba blong fakfak* was, of course, a condom.

And the *Big Man?* That was God.

We paddled away from the palms and the Australian bar, heading south towards Marovo Island, which sat tucked into the volcanic folds of Vangunu Island.

The lagoon was two worlds. They were close to each other, and they communicated through light, shadow, rhythm and vibration. The world beneath the surface terrified and fascinated me. In the shallow water off Uepi, it looked like abstract art seen through stained glass, a collage of glowing pink, gold and indigo. There were mustard broccoli heads, leafless bushes with purple tips and orange anemones waving like animated shag carpet. There was the gaping mouth of a giant clam, its green lips speckled with blue spots and puckered into a metre-wide kiss. It all seemed miles away, but when I plunged a hand into the water the coral tore the skin off my fingertips, and a flurry of tiny fish the colour of Bunsen-burner flames rose to chase the trail of my blood. The coral plateau ended in an abrupt precipice, which fell through the electric blue towards a vastness of shadows.

The other world, the one above the surface, was heavy and humid. My skin grew crusty with salt as I pulled through Peter's wake. The sun was an engine and the ocean was its fuel. I could feel the water around me being sucked up into the atmosphere.

The first storm was a surprise. One minute the sky was brilliant, the sun searing. The next an immense wall of cloud had risen above the peaks of Vangunu, and tentacles of vapour were racing across the sky. The clouds did not dampen the heat of the day. They were like coals pulled from a fire. They pressed down, blowing a hot wind before them. A nasty chop rose on the lagoon, which at this point was more than 10 kilometres wide. The rain came in thick sheets and seemed to turn to steam as soon as it hit the lagoon.

In the fury of the storm I realized that Peter had fallen behind. I looked back to see him waving. I waved back, but he wasn't even facing me. He was waving at the sky: both arms in the air, motioning back and forth like those guys who help park jumbo jets. I shouted but he could not hear me in the roar. I gritted my teeth and paddled hard through the headwind. The storm passed as quickly as it had come.

Our itinerary was ruled by religion. Half the villages in Marovo were Seventh-Day Adventist. The other half were Methodist. The Adventists were forbidden to work from sundown on Friday until sundown on Saturday. The Methodists were forbidden to work on Sundays. The lagoon people took their prohibitions seriously. Which is why Sila had cut short our visit so suddenly. She was an Adventist, and it was late Friday afternoon when we reached her skull garden in the village of Olovotu. Afterwards, we pushed east along the coast of Marovo Island, which was not at all inviting. Its slopes were tangled with thick jungle and creeping vines.

"We are going to find the heathens, right?" I asked.

Peter wasn't a big talker.

"The heathen's name is Frank," he said.

We paddled hard as the sky turned purple, and pulled ashore at a rough pier made from hunks of coral stone. Night was falling. The shore was lined with dugout canoes. Oil lamps flickered among the trees.

"Chea Village," said Peter. "Adventist."

A young man lurched onto the pier.

"You are a tourist! Ah, I have built you a hotel," the man said, peering back over his shoulder. A church bell rang in the distance. "Hurry! Quicktime!"

The "hotel" consisted of an outhouse-sized thatched hut built on stilts above the water. This was evidently not one of the UNESCO-inspired ecolodges.

"Your Sabbath has begun," I said. "You cannot do business with me now."

"Ah, friend *blong* me, no worries! This is a private operation."

The man had the glassy eyes of a drunk. His breath was devastating. I looked at Peter. He shrugged. I told the drunk we would sleep in his hut if he promised to leave us alone. He yelped a sort of agreement, accepted a few dollars and then stumbled off into the night. A clutch of villagers had gathered around us.

"That poor boy has been corrupted by beer," said an old man with a sarong wrapped around his withered midsection. "It's all the doing of the heathen."

"Frank?"

"Yes. Frank is destroying Marovo with his beer."

"So where is this Frank?"

He lifted a bony finger and pointed out towards the darkened lagoon.

We ate with the old men of the village: papaya and fish soup, prepared over a fire before sundown, of course. I asked about magic.

"It's a terrible problem," said an old codger with Q-tip hair. "The young people are learning how to use it again. They do bad spells."

"Such as?"

He described a magic called sweet-mouth, which involved using prepared ginger as a charm to attract love. I told him it didn't sound particularly evil to me.

"Some magic is much, much worse than sweet-mouth," said another of the men. "Like pela."

"Mmmm, pela," they all said, shaking their heads.

"The pela man is a wicked man. He can shoot you in the head with an invisible arrow. Then a boil will grow on your head, and you will die," said the codger.

"I might like to meet one of these pela men," I said.

"Not possible. The pela man works in secret. And he uses the special gingerroot to make himself invisible to everyone but his victims. If he wants to get you, you will see him at night. His eyes will seem as big as the moon. Then he will come in your sleep, cut open your stomach and fill your guts with sticks and leaves."

"And then he will sew your mouth up so you can't tell anyone his name," said another.

"My mother once saw a pela woman eating another woman's belly," said another.

"So how do you stop this witchcraft?"

"You can pray to God. But sometimes there is no hope. If a man has been pela'd, we give him special ginger so that he can break the spell on his mouth and tell us, on his last breath, who killed him."

Pity the enemies of a dying man, I thought. I pulled out a notebook and began to scribble. The men panicked.

"Oh no! No writing! No work! It's the Sabbath," said the codger.

"You can't do that until Saturday night," said another.

And that was that. The oil lamp was soon extinguished. When Peter and I were alone, he said very solemnly: "Ginger's bullshit. Only prayer can stop pela. Only true Christians are immune from it."

We set off again early in the morning, skirting the coast of Marovo and Vangunu. We hit the Methodists on Saturday and the Adventists on Sunday. Chumbikope, Peter's home village, was mediaeval in its layout: hundreds of thatched-roof huts clung to the water's edge beneath an imposing twin-gabled church. We waited out a storm while Peter's mother smashed nuts with a rock on the dirt floor of her kitchen. We napped for hours. In my dreams the heathen was chasing me through the forest with an axe.

We set out again in the silver light of late afternoon. The lagoon was busy. Men threw nets from dugout canoes. Fibreglass longboats buzzed past, loaded with fat women and rainbow umbrellas.

In Marovo a storm always seemed to be in process: either building in the west, thundering down on you or exhausting itself into mist to make room for the next front. Now it was beginning again. The sun was racing, losing ground to a breaking wave of hot black cloud. The lagoon lost its glow. The sky bubbled. And just as he had done the previous day, Peter raised his arms and started gesturing to the heavens, now like a mime teasing strands of imaginary wool from the air. He stopped when I paddled closer. Curtains of rain swept across the lagoon to our east.

In each village we sought out *olgeta olman blong stori*—the old storytellers, who fused history and myth so artfully it was hard, at the time, to tell which was which.

James Worakana, a man with a voice like a door creaking in the wind, told me that the lagoon was created by the giant Langiti, whose wife on Marovo Island was kept awake at night by the sound of crashing surf. Langiti took the seashore and pushed it far away so she could sleep. That's how the barrier islands were formed. Oh, and the site of the first Christian church on Marovo Island was decided by a rock that floated out of the sea.

The curiously named John Wayne (whose splendid lodge in Telina had not seen tourists in months) told me that Christianity came to Marovo like a light from the east. His great-grandfather, the gun-slinging warrior Kanijama, went on a headhunting foray to newly converted Isabel Island, but the mission failed because the Christian God was stronger than the Marovan's ancestor spirits. He tried to transfer all his old spirits to his son. "You obey me or I will kill you!" Kanijama said, but his son refused—he wanted to take up the new religion. Kanijama fasted for seven days. His ancestors wouldn't let him sleep; they banged on the wall of his house at night, begging him not to abandon them, but Kanijama realized he was no longer fierce enough to kill anyone, let alone his own son. He changed his name to Jorovo—the shy one. He was finished as a warrior after that.

THERE WAS more to the conversion of Marovo than the clash of supernatural forces. Britain claimed the Solomon Islands as a protectorate in 1893. The British resident commissioner sold or leased vast tracts of waterfront to coconut plantation owners. The British needed peace in order to make money. By the turn of the century, the colonial government was answering every headhunting raid with a punitive expedition of its own. Villages were burned to the ground. Skull collections were smashed. Suspected murderers were lynched along with their families. By 1908 the navy had made Marovo, in the words of resident commissioner Charles Woodford, "safe for the white man." It was becoming abundantly clear to the lagoon people that their *mana* wasn't up to snuff.

Something very strange happened when headhunting and raiding were abolished: the population in the lagoon began to decline. This was attributed partly to the introduction of European diseases. But the anthropologist W.H.R. Rivers suggested that in fact the demise of headhunting was to blame. He pointed out that the yearly raids had been a crucial component of religion and social life in the lagoon. Headhunting was part of what made life meaningful and, well, fun. The lagoon people were dying out, he said, from sheer boredom. Rivers insisted they needed a new religion to fuel their passions if they were to survive. He hoped the Church of England would fit the bill, but the Adventists and Methodists had already beaten the Anglicans to Marovo.

A century later the lagoon is full of babies and everyone seems quite content. That is, everyone except Frank the heathen.

We found him on our fourth day. He lived on the island of Varata, a pincushion of sand and palms in the middle of the lagoon. We pulled our boats ashore and poked through a ramshackle collection of oil drums, beer crates and huts. The heathen was a trader. One of his huts was built in Polynesian style, with palm-thatch eves hanging low to the ground. There was an enormous old woman sitting in the shade. She had the brow of a Polynesian warrior and a belly crisscrossed with geometric tattoos. I could see those tattoos because the woman wore no shirt, which was unheard of in these parts. She was the heathen's wife.

The heathen was a fearful sight: a towering, weathered rhinoceros of a man with a nose so long, so hooked and sunburned it could never be native. He marched across the yard, kicked a chicken, barked at some men who had come to trade sea slugs for beer, and then asked me my business. He huffed when he spoke, as though he was preparing to sneeze. I told him I was following in the footsteps of my great-grandfather, the missionary. That was a mistake.

"Them's the trouble, ah," he said. "Those bastards robbed these people of their fire, their warrior spirit. Ah! Look at 'em now," he said, gesturing to Peter, who had ordered a beer from Frank's larder. "Weak! Lazy! Ah."

Peter chuckled and then rolled himself a cigarette.

"They used to be capable of great things, ah. They paddled hundreds of miles to other islands."

"To kill people," Peter interjected quietly. Frank ignored him.

"The missionaries told people their ancestors were stupid. They took away their custom and gave them fairy tales in return. Like the one about Jesus walking on water! Ha!"

It turned out the heathen—his full name was Frank Mulvey—was a descendant of Seghe's first European plantation boss. Frank's grandmother was from Polynesia. That's where Frank had his first run-in with missionaries, who had convinced the local government to ban tattooing. The conflict ended in a brawl between Frank's band of war-painted traditionalists and the Anglicans in their Sunday best.

"We won," he said, "and I've been fighting the Christians ever since."

"So you really are the last heathen in Marovo," I said. "What is it that you believe in?"

"I believe in my own spirit," he said, pounding his leathery chest.

"Yes," I said. "It's good to believe in yourself."

"No! I'm talking about my Polynesian ancestor spirit. He was a warrior. When I have a fight on my hands, I call on him. I feel him inside me, giving me the power to whup these boys if I have to," he said, looking again at Peter, who stared right back at him.

"No magic to that," said Peter.

"Listen, ah," said Frank, who was vibrating with intensity now. "I told a man on Ontong Java that if he didn't behave, he would die in three days. Guess what? Three days later he fell over dead. Ah! My spirit gives me power, ah. And the only time I feel weak, the only time I feel it draining, is when I go near a church. Ah? Ah! Ahhh."

The air was sticky. The lagoon was dead calm. As we pulled the two boats back into the water, Peter looked at me and said without smiling: "Frank is lucky. If we were not Christian, if we were still heathen, we would have cut his head off a long time ago."

We decided to camp on one of the uninhabited barrier islands on the northern horizon. The mountains, jungle, villages, fishermen and dugout canoes faded into the haze behind us. We were alone with our paddle strokes. Peter sang me hymns. I told him about the northern lights. The water grew shallower and so clear that it was as though we were drifting above a surreal blue desert. It glowed like the sky. Here and there coral colonies rose beneath us like giant yellow muffins or cumulonimbus clouds. Sometimes they stood like castles. Parrot fish swirled around their ramparts like flocks of birds.

From a distance the barrier islands resembled sections of a crumbling rock wall, but as we approached they seemed like ships foundering in the surf. Each island trailed a whorl of creamy white sand. The shallow passages between them seethed with blacktip reef sharks, whose fins sliced the surface and darted away at our approach. We drifted through a channel, then over what looked like a field of sunken caribou antlers. Their points were flecked with violet.

Now another storm was rising like a great black curtain behind us. It swallowed all the volcanoes and sent shadows across the lagoon. Peter balanced his paddle on the deck of his kayak, and then once again raised his arms in the air. This time, he reached out, embraced the air, tugged at it and pushed it towards the east. I paddled up to ask what he was doing.

"We will not have rain tonight," he said quietly.

"Why not?"

"No good for camping," he said, and winked at me.

"You think you can move the storm away from us?"

"Not me," he said. "The Big Man."

THE SOLOMONS changed my great-grandfather. His peers in the evangelical biz considered him a fairly level-headed guy, but by the time he left the islands, he was convinced that sorcerers could kill men by shaking handfuls of cobwebs at them, that black magic existed but could be defeated with prayer, and that a holy light sometimes shone out from the thatched cathedrals his followers erected. Like the others here—the folks who once hoarded skulls for their *mana*, Frank the heathen and now, apparently, my friend Peter—my great-grandfather believed that supernatural power was indeed flowing through the material world. Being Christian didn't mean giving up that belief in magic. It just meant a change in allegiance. This would never have washed with my Sunday school teachers back home.

As it turned out, the storm did barrel over those mountains, and the lagoon did shiver as though it was preparing for impact. But then, even as the rain curtains dragged across the reefs to our east and the wind pulled whitecaps from distant waves, the front seemed to falter slightly, and collapse a little, and then it ruptured. The clouds split apart. We were left untouched.

Now, you could witness this kind of thing and declare it a work of magic, which seemed a bit of a stretch. You could dismiss it outright, which hardly seemed fair to Peter. Or you could make peace with it, place it among an afternoon of wonders and allow it to live on as a possibility. Yes, that's it. We paddled on as the last light drained from the day and the palms turned into spiky silhouettes. We paddled on, trusting in the power of *mana* and the benevolence of the sky above us.

THE MYSTERY
OF THE MONOLITH

ANDREW STRUTHERS

APRIL/MAY 2004

WE'RE IN A floatplane, hanging a thousand feet in the air above Clayoquot Sound, when the sun comes up, sharpening the shadows till you could almost cut your thumb. For miles around, shattered islands bristle up through a gunmetal sea. Ahead of us lies the green expanse of Flores Island. Somewhere in all that green lies a mystery.

Where I live, on the west coast of Vancouver Island, the line between the time of legend and the time of day sometimes gets blurred. Last winter we had a spate of Bigfoot sightings near the Long Beach reserve. There are still stories told of giant Clayoquot sturgeon, although these creatures don't officially exist. And floatplane pilots occasionally glimpse a mysterious 100-foot monolith, apparently carved with curious designs, high in the mountains of Flores Island.

For years I'd dismissed the tales of the monolith. Then John Armstrong, a doctor friend who lives nearby in Tofino, snapped a blurry photo of something very odd on his weekly flight over Flores. The photo showed a column of yellow rock towering high among the trees near a mountain ridge. Real live monolith.

Which made no sense. The Nuu-Chah-Nulth people have been living in Clayoquot Sound for 5,000 years. They have an epic tale about every boulder. There's a pool on Flores Island where ancient whalers once retreated to pray before the hunt. It's only a few yards across, but the elders have sung about it for millennia. Yet there are no native legends about the monolith. How could they miss a 100-foot spire? Real live mystery.

One night, a handful of us sat around Armstrong's kitchen table poring over a crude survey map. Using it and his photo, we marked the monolith's location on a handheld GPS and fleshed out a plan of attack: we'd charter a floatplane to Flores and then hike straight into the mountains using the GPS location like a homing beacon. Simple.

AS OUR plane banshees over the island's cathedral treetops, I'm already having second thoughts. Hiking through this kind of megaflora is exhausting work. And we'll have to make our way through miles and miles of it.

Doctor John rides shotgun, a dog-eared survey map on his knees. He's a long way from Ontario, where the trees are so small they stack them on the logging trucks sideways. Fifteen years ago, he took a break from med school, camped at Long Beach and out of curiosity followed the string of H signs to the hospital in Tofino. It was a trap. He never escaped.

Wedged into the seat beside me, photographer Adrian Dorst cranes for a shot. He prefers to fly with the plane door open. Heights don't bother him. For years, he worked as a steeplejack in the construction industry, and he could do a day's work in two hours because he didn't use a safety harness. Then one day he watched a man fall 90 feet—*thwack!* The foreman ran to the body and strapped a safety harness on it before WCB showed up, and Dorst began to rethink his career. After Pacific Rim National Park opened near Tofino in 1972, he landed a gig cataloguing birds for the Canadian Wildlife Service. He's also never escaped.

The plane throttles back and we drop like a rock into Matilda Inlet on Flores's southeastern tip. At the end of Matilda Inlet lies the Nuu-Chah-Nulth village of Ahousat. Ahousat has a thousand souls, but the roads are still gravel and weed. There was no electricity here until 1972, when CBS filmed *I Heard the Owl Call My Name* and left a generator behind. We pick our way past rusting satellite dishes, unpainted houses and salmonberry bushes that peel back weathered siding. It's not a pretty sight. But if you close your eyes and just listen, it's beautiful. Quiet as a drowned man's whisper. A stark contrast with nearby Tofino, which is coyote ugly to the ears. Every room is haunted by the drone of the 60-hertz bagpiper, every street by the roar of infernal combustion.

My first visit to Ahousat many years ago was pretty hairy. I was canoeing past Flores when a storm drove me onto the sand spit at the edge of town. The first guy who saw me invited me home. His house was warm and dry and chock full of couches. The walls were papered with photos of his nieces and nephews. I thanked him for his kindness. He pointed at a painting of a very gentile-looking Jesus on the wall. "That's my master."

An hour later, gentile Jesus had fallen behind a couch, five guys were duking it out on the deck, and my host was impersonating a water cooler with a Texas mickey of vodka. He jabbed at a string of purple marks on his neck. "My girlfriend did that. She got passionate. Now she's gonna have a baby."

I checked out the love bites. "Looks like twins."

He laughed and punched me hard on the head. But as the party raged he wouldn't let anyone else hit me, which probably saved my life, and every time the door opened, he told the new arrivals what I'd said. There's nothing the Nuu-Chah-Nulth like better than a joke. "They will give a wrong meaning intentionally to a word," one ethnographer noted back in 1864, "and afterwards, if you use it, they will laugh at you."

We've come to Ahousat to pick up the fourth member of our team, Jimmy Swan. Swan is a descendant of the Manhousaht nation, a branch of the Nuu-Chah-Nulth. Two hundred years ago, the Manhousahts' territory included most of Flores, Sydney Inlet and the coast up as far as Hesquiat. But warfare and smallpox whittled the Manhousaht people down to a very few families—including the Swans.

Jimmy Swan's *ah-hoolthie*—the region where he holds seigneury over salmon and other resources—includes the mountain where the monolith stands. If we seek the monolith, Swan must be with us. At least, that's the plan. But Swan hasn't been answering his phone. The grapevine says he's busy hosting an anthropologist from the University of Victoria. When we reach his porch it's quiet. Too quiet.

After we knock for a couple of minutes, Jimmy appears at the door, the tousled blond head of the anthropologist behind him. He's surprised to learn we were serious about trekking to the monolith. He's still half asleep when we shoehorn him into the Cessna.

As we take off, I watch our riveted pontoons skim Matilda Inlet, which ebb tide has turned into 10 acres of mud spiked with fish boat ribs. Once we're in the air, I can see several Zodiacs below leaving white scars down the surface of the water. Each carries a dozen tourists in bright red survival suits, like football teams from hell.

BY THE time we drag our gear onto shore in a small unnamed cove, the sun's already high. We have to find the monolith and make it back here by an hour after sunset. Any later and we're on our own. Floatplanes don't fly after dark because there are no runway lights, and a dark blue kayak makes a hell of a speed bump. So we head up an abandoned logging road at a trot.

Logging roads depress me. Don't get me wrong—like most B.C. boys I've had my share of Mac&Blo jobs and thrilled to tales of Eight-Day Wilson and Bull Sling Bill, early loggers who could fell these giants and boom them down to Alberni single-handed. The gold standard in those days was a 60′ × 3′ × 3′ beam of Douglas fir called a B.C. Toothpick. Nine filled a flatbed train.

But there's nothing romantic about what's left of the area near the cove. The forest was clear-cut in the early 1980s, and now it looks like the valley where the dinosaurs went extinct, great bleached stumps twisting into the sky. The rest of Flores might have ended up the same way, if the Friends of Clayoquot Sound hadn't moved in to protest what was going on in 1988. Having logged myself, I was loath to blockade. But I didn't want to turn a blind eye, so I went as an observer. On my first day, I observed that an area that had been recently clear-cut looked like Woodstock after the music stopped. By day two, I was hiding in the trees so the loggers couldn't work. At dawn on day three, six cops in a Zodiac came whizzing up to our coastal camp at Sulphur Pass. Still groggy from sleep, I ran into the nearby bush wearing only my underpants.

I had imagined the scene of my arrest quite differently—something with lots of cameras, and the Friends of Clayoquot singing "This Land Is Your Land" in the background. The uncool truth: Pierre the local cop ran me down half-naked and alone. He dragged me back to camp and began reading a court injunction the size of a phone book. It took him forever to plow through all that legal mumbo-jumbo with his Trois-Rivières brogue, and all the while, the black flies were biting. In desperation, I began to help with some of the bigger words.

After my arraignment we had coffee and watched the sun light up the island. "Those bastards gonna destroy the whole 'ting," Pierre said. He was wrong. Today the clear-cut area stops right where the old protest camp stood. The forest beyond is untouched.

FIVE KILOMETRES of crushed rock later, we're poised on the edge of the forest like surfers at the break. Armstrong, Swan and I watch Dorst repack his camera gear. I can't believe he brought a tripod.

The foliage near the road is almost impassable; whenever the canopy relents in the B.C. rainforest, wild raspberry and salal bushes crowd towards the light like paparazzi. It's part of a system. The bushes fix the soil against the endless rain. Alders take root, and their broad leaves filter sunlight so that young cedar and hemlock shoot straight up in search of sky. This yields tall, straight trees that eventually kill the alders with their shade, but the cycle takes a century. To speed things up after clear-cutting, logging companies slash and burn the alders, which is why second-growth timber is often bent and wiry and will never become majestic old growth.

The only way through this prickly mess is a network of bear trails. (Don't try this at home.) It's reasonably safe in late summer because the bruins have followed ripening berries up the mountain. That's the theory anyway. After a gruelling, spiky slog, the canopy closes overhead and the undergrowth abates. But now we have to deal with the trees themselves.

It's impossible to grasp the true magnitude of British Columbia's rainforest until you have to traverse it. The apartment towers in Vancouver's West End are smaller on average than the Douglas firs they replaced, which sometimes broke the 300-foot mark. No one knows how big these trees can get, although one felled in Lynn Valley north of Vancouver around

1890 was reported to be more than 400 feet tall. When these behemoths fall, they form small hills. Where two lie across each other, you end up feeling just like an ant, as if you're finding your way through a giant game of pick-up sticks.

My usual method for dealing with such terrain is to strip naked, drop to the needles and slither. There's always 10 inches of crawlspace above the forest floor, so you can go anywhere. It sounds crazy but it works. You can reach the wildest places this way.

A few years ago, four of us were bushcrawling on Vargas, the next big island to the south of Flores, when we stumbled (or slithered) upon the site of an ancient native settlement. The place was uncanny. You could sense the silent passage of years. The longhouses were long gone, leaving a meadow of smooth green grass that rose into strange, steep mounds 10 feet high, like an ocean frozen in mid-swell. The contours may well have been caused by the curves of whale bones buried in the soil.

But bushcrawling won't get us to the monolith. It doesn't work if you bring gear or clothing. So I have to deal with the trees head on, and for the next hour I can see only inches in front of me. At one point I have to laugh. I'm tangled in a knot of tree limbs, dangling over a pit filled with dead cedar branches. Those things are sharp. Fall on them from this height and they have the same effect as a Bengal tiger trap.

I avoid the fall by crawling down into the pit. Below the bone-white cedar spikes lies a sandy creek bed, dry from summer and speckled with wolf, deer and raccoon tracks. It's a critter causeway. We follow it for a hundred yards until it disappears under another giant cedar.

Two hours into this giant land, Swan and I glare up at a mountainous nurse log and scratch our heads. This is ridiculous. We're sweating like fat bayou sheriffs, and we haven't even started the real climb. No way will we make the monolith at this pace. Doctor John sits on top of the nurse log, huffing. His pants are shredded and his GPS doesn't work at all. It can't find the satellites for the trees. "I think I see something," he says.

It's a ravine. At the bottom, a river sweeps smoothly over black and blue rocks. It feels as if no one has passed this way for years. But a smile flicks on Swan's face, like he had this place on the tip of his tongue. When we climb down into it, the vault of the forest stretches twice as high. It seems to enclose the ravine like a longhouse. The far side of the chasm is one big overhanging root. At the top, the forest suddenly opens up. A contour line on Doctor John's tattered map leads us onto a saddle between two mountains. We skirt a lake through knee-deep sphagnum. Through the canopy at the far shore we glimpse two mountains, but it's hard to tell which one has the monolith on top. We choose the slope closest to the ocean. If we're wrong, there will be no time for a second sally.

AT TIMES during our ascent, we can see far down below to the coast, where tourists in Zodiacs are watching for humpbacks. Since logging stopped here, whales have become the lynchpin of the local economy, as they were in ancient times.

For the Nuu-Chah-Nulth, whaling was serious business. When the summer wind blew steadily from the west, Swan's kin moved from the capital Opnit—near what is now called Hot Springs Cove—down to summer villages along the coast. The chief, celibate for six months, retreated into the mountains to a shrine. For two weeks he fasted, prayed and abraded himself with twigs. When he came down again, he and seven other men would shove a great cedar dugout into the surf. Each man in the canoe inherited his position and was part of a hierarchy more rigid than the English navy's. At the prow stood the chief. He held a yew-wood harpoon with a detachable mussel shell tip.

Back at the summer village, the chief's wife, also celibate, prayed for a whale's soul to enter her body. When she caught one, she lay still as a corpse in her ceremonial bed. If she flinched, the whale would move, too, smashing her husband's canoe or dragging the whalers out to the open ocean. If she lay perfectly still, the whale would move slowly enough for the chief to fire his harpoon into the creature's flank. The tip would detach, leaving a medicine bag lodged under the whale's thick skin. A cedar bark rope connected the tip to two floats made from inflated seal skins, which prevented the whale from diving while the contents of the medicine bag either killed the whale or knocked it unconscious. If the whale died, the men had to stop it from filling with water and sinking.

One of them would jump into the water and sew up its mouth, breathing through a bull kelp tube. If they subdued it alive, they would trim its flippers so it couldn't steer and drive it towards shore, canoe in tow.

After the hunt, the whalers retreated to their winter village in Sydney Inlet. King George's men saw them wandering with the seasons and classified them itinerant, which is a fancy word for drifter. As drifters, their claim to the land was compromised. Confined to reserves, their ancient round was broken.

THREE HOURS later, a thousand feet higher, my legs are a mass of bleeding cuts. But the trees have thinned out, and the forest floor is a carpet of moss and golden needles. We know we've gained some real altitude when we see some Douglas firs. These sun-loving trees thrive at drier, cooler heights cleared by forest fires, which keeps them from wandering too low, out of their ecological niche. Fir is so rare on the wet coast, in fact, that when settlers built their fish boats they had to salvage their fir keels from landslides. The dearth of these trees put the kibosh on early logging plans in the area, and that's why Clayoquot's forests still stand. Their hemlock, cedar and spruce were not worth the cost of transportation. Until recently.

Commotion ahead. Dorst and Swan have found a grove of cedars whose trunks are oddly fluted, like cathedral columns. Straight lines do exist in nature—sunbeams, the horizon, the line of holes left by a woodpecker—but this is different. These trees have been altered by human hands—in academic lingo, "culturally modified." To an anthropologist, culturally modified trees are a culture's fingerprint. A swath of blackened stumps, for example, indicates the presence of Europeans. Nuu-Cha-Nulth leave more subtle prints. The yellow cedars in this grove have had their bark peeled away in strips. According to Swan, it was probably done by women, who used the bark to weave blankets, hats and whaling ropes. They came all the way up here because the bark doesn't have salt in it and can be pounded soft as butter without falling apart.

Unless we're on the wrong mountain, we must be a stone's throw from the monolith. So it seems reasonable that if Swan's forebears came all this way for hats, they must have known about the giant stone column nearby. I think of their traditional whaling shrines, where the chief would come beforehand to purify and strengthen himself. Could the monolith have been such a place?

The depth of the checks left in the cedar trunks suggest the women entered this grove maybe two centuries ago. And perhaps this holds a clue to the absence of legends about the monolith. Two hundred years ago, while the Manhousahts controlled most of Flores and the surrounding islands, another tribe called the Ahousahts lived farther to the south. The Ahousahts had fallen upon hard times; their tribe was so small they used the same word for "brother" and "cousin." Their territory was all open coast, with no salmon rivers. To get rights to a salmon river, they married into the Manhousahts, but the newlyweds quarrelled. Relatives were drawn into the dispute. Finally, the Manhousahts castrated the Ahousaht chief and sat him on a yew stake. The Ahousahts retaliated en masse and killed 80 braves. The counterattack was botched when the Manhousahts got lost in the giant trees on the south end of Flores. They retreated to Opnit, the capital near Hot Springs.

Opnit was too heavily fortified for open attack, so the Ahousahts made a deal with a family who was visiting the Manhousahts. One summer morning, the guests rose early and slew their hosts while they slept. By breakfast, only two fragments of the once-mighty Manhousaht nation survived: the Swans, who were farther north in Sydney Inlet at the time, and two of the chief's sons, who escaped to Neah Bay in Washington State and became part of the Makah nation. So there's a possibility that the knowledge of the secret monolith may have perished that bloody morning at Opnit.

A HUNDRED feet higher, the ground breaks into mossy chunks. Doctor John and I work along a ridge, gripping the springy limbs of dwarf trees that might be a century old but have grown no bigger than children. While the forests of the Himalaya and Ruwenzori and Clayoquot each have their own bouquet, a mountain ridge always smells the same, the cauldron sky stirred by jagged rock and sharp with ions. If you climb enough mountains, the smell becomes as distinctive as brine.

Up ahead we hear a cry. Ten minutes later, we find Dorst and Swan sitting with their backs to the base of a gigantic column of rock. Real live monolith.

After a breather and a drink, Doctor John pulls out a huge tape measure and starts measuring. It's an impressive column that has been formed from volcanic basalt, like the cliffs at the top of Lone Cone on Meares Island. What makes the Flores monolith unique is that the surrounding basalt likely cooled more rapidly, forming weaker rock that crumbled away into soil, leaving this one pillar to jut like a stone thumb. Exposed to the sun, the hexagon of rock became a living thing, yellow with lichen.

Two blocks of stone lie tumbled against the monolith's back like giant dice. Dorst scrambles on top of them to get a group shot. He finds a narrow ledge that slants further up the sheer rock. Soon we're all edging along it. Halfway up there's a gap in the ledge. We can see promising handholds on the far side, but Dorst turns back, steeplejack skills notwithstanding. So does Doctor John. A shattered shinbone up here would be inconvenient. Swan glances at the drop, then at me, then he lunges across the gap and disappears round the side. I follow. I figure it's not every day you get to climb a monolith.

Around the corner, the sun is dazzling. The lichen on the warm south face provides a grip like Velcro. Swan has already hauled himself up out of sight, and I follow. The top is as flat as a table and about as small. It cranes over the treetops, literally the neck of the woods. Warm with sun, private since the Ice Age. We might be the first two humans on top. Ever. We sit gawking at the view. The panorama sweeps from the Atleo River in the east, all the way round the north end of Flores, past Hot Springs, Hesquiat and down the outer coast to Raphael Point. Not a cloud in the universe.

I can see moments from my life mapped out on the landscape below. At Sulphur Pass, Pierre the cop chases me as I run through the bush in my underpants. At Hot Springs Cove, I sit in a rock pool, warm as a pizza pocket on a freezing February night. Five miles out to sea, I shift from foot to foot at the wheel of my fishboat. And somewhere along that pristine beach below, I curl up against a genuine goddess of a girlfriend, knowing that I've never been so in love, and also that when we return to the human world, we will begin to drift apart.

Swan can see his whole history etched deeper in other places in the same landscape. Opnit, where his people were decimated. Raphael Point, where his great-grandfather harpooned the last sea otter. Hesquiat, where the first members of King George's tribe arrived in strange houses that floated on the water. Farther into the blue distance, the line between the sky and sea is blurred. Those are the whaling grounds, where one of the greatest of all human dramas once unfolded.

The place is epic. But what about the legends? Did they really die 200 years ago at Opnit?

I ask Swan. He hints that perhaps knowledge of the monolith still exists. "Why d'you think we found it so easy?" Later he says that for the Nuu-Chah-Nulth, some things must remain a mystery. It's part of their strength. Some stories are family secrets, passed only from the chief to his eldest son.

Right now, it doesn't really matter. Let part of every tale remain a mystery. All I know is that the monolith has been moved from fancy into fact. And somehow, on the way up the mountain, the line between the time of legend and the time of day seems to have vanished altogether.

||||||||||||||

ON THE TRAIL
OF GULO GULO

MARK ANDERSON

WINTER 2004

DREAMED OF *Gulo gulo,* the wolverine, last night. It was a terrifying nightmare, with the animals bounding across the lawn, clawing their way into the house as I attempted in vain to bar the door. I awoke relieved but exhausted.

Even now, several hours later, the dream remains vivid. I'm heading for the Ottawa airport, bound eventually for the small northwestern Ontario town of Red Lake, near the Manitoba border.

Perhaps I'm alone in this, but I enjoy flying and detest air travel. The difference? When you're sitting on a 524-seat Boeing 747, you're not flying, you're travelling, by air, in a mobile auditorium or theatre, depending on whether you can afford business class. When you book a ticket on one of Bearskin Airlines' 19-passenger Fairchild Metroliners, on the other hand, time compresses, and the miracle of flight reasserts itself in the smell of burning oil, the vibration of the turbo engines, the churn of the propeller.

The illusion of moving back through history, aviation and otherwise, compounds when your flight path takes you northwest, and the Ontario towns—Sudbury, Sault Ste. Marie, Sioux Lookout—get smaller and grittier, even as the country itself expands ad infinitum, until all that can be seen between refuelling stops is snow, trees, lakes, rivers, snow. The last stage of the journey, from Sioux Lookout to Red Lake, is undertaken in a plane smaller yet, a 14-passenger Beechcraft 99, with nine of the seats unoccupied.

WHEN THE residents of Red Lake—all 4,700 of them—first learned wolverines were being live-trapped and then released again on the outskirts of their town, their reactions ranged from "Neat" to "What's a wolverine?" to "Oh my God, my kids are playing outside!" The reactions, all three, are eminently understandable.

Even at the start of the 21st century, the wolverine, a.k.a. *Gulo gulo*, glutton, skunk bear, Indian devil, northern devil and *carcajou*, remains an enigma. Not many people even know what one looks like and very few have seen it in the wild. Some people might at least conjure up the image of the comic book hero of the same name, a Canadian beast-man whose superpowers include a set of retractable, razor-like talons and an ability to instantly heal even the most egregious wounds. The pop-culture reference is obliquely instructive, playing off the real wolverine's power and ferocity—reputedly the strongest animal, pound per pound, in the world, with a uniquely hinged jaw that gives it incredible chomping strength.

Here's the rest of the wolverine bio. It's the largest and least-known terrestrial member of the *Mustelidae* family, whose other members include the fisher, marten, otter, weasel and skunk; found mainly in remote mountains, tundra and boreal forests; females grow to 22 pounds, males average 35; massive paws are morphologically well-suited to travelling in the snow; powerful jaws and teeth can chew through bone and frozen carrion; has been known to take down animals many times its size, including caribou, moose and bighorn sheep; even known to challenge both bears and wolves when protecting a kill; low numbers, large ranges and great mobility make it extremely difficult to study in the wild.

The truth is, we don't know much more about wolverines now than we did a hundred years ago, when the late, great naturalist Ernest Thompson Seton had this to say: "The wolverine is a tremendous character… a personality of unmeasured force, courage and achievement so enveloped in a mist of legend, superstition, idolatry, fear and hatred, that one scarcely knows how to begin or what to accept as fact."

FACT. I encountered my first wolverine three years ago, in the remote Dene community of Trout Lake, in the Northwest Territories. I was casting flies in a river estuary at dawn, and there it was, no more than 50 feet away on the bank, dragging a buried fishnet from the sand. We sized each other up for a long moment. I wondered: How fast can a wolverine run? How fast can *I* run? How many steps would I manage before the animal landed on my back, dug its claws into my shoulder blades and ripped the tendons from my neck? It would be a nasty, gurgling, but at least quick way to go.

It would also be the first recorded case of a wolverine attack on a human, but I didn't know that at the time, and I'm hardly the first to succumb to morbid wolverine fantasies. The documentary film *Wolverine: Devil of the North?* features an interview with an Alaskan trapper who jumped into a beaver pond to escape a startled *carcajou*. "They'll take you," warns the grizzled furrier.

As it turns out, of course, they won't. They'll generally bolt in the opposite direction upon sighting humans, or, in the case of my Trout Lake specimen, return to worrying a fishnet from the sand.

Ever since that first encounter, I've become more and more intrigued by the mystery of the wolverine. So when I heard that scientists were live-trapping the animals in northern Ontario, I decided I had to make a visit. Which is how I ended up flying to Red Lake last March to visit Dr. Audrey Magoun. Magoun is one of the world's foremost experts on wolverines, having studied the animals in her native Alaska, as well as Sweden, Canada and the continental U.S. Two years ago she cobbled together a research team—comprising herself, Justina Ray of the Wildlife Conservation Society and Jeff Bowman and Neil Dawson of the Ontario Ministry of Natural Resources—to study wolverines in the lowland boreal forest of Ontario, the easternmost range of *Gulo gulo* in North America. (For some reason, yet to be explained, the wolverine population diminishes in the eastern part of the province, then peters out altogether in Quebec and Labrador, despite similar geographies, climates and ecosystems.)

The main goal of the project, which received $230,000 in funding from the Ontario Living Legacy Trust and the Ontario Species at Risk program, has been to examine the impact of logging on wolverine popu-lations, in advance of an MNR proposal to expand timber cutting north of the 51st parallel in Ontario. Magoun and her team are studying a 24,000-square-kilometre tract of land near Red Lake that is already being logged, and they've been attempting to get more detailed information on boreal wolverine habitat and behaviour by live-trapping, camera trapping, hair snaring and radio-tracking individual animals.

The first year of the study, undertaken during the winter of 2002/2003, was a disappointment, yielding but one photo from the camera traps. The live traps remained frustratingly empty, save for the occasional fisher, marten, lynx and opportunistic raven.

The 2003/2004 season, however, got off to a rollicking start with a December 14 capture of a 22-pound female, promptly named Joyce because it was trapped near Joyce Road. Joyce was followed, in short order, by Noel (trapped Christmas Day), Mary (caught near White Ass Lake, but even wolverines have feelings), Jack, Ranger and Maurice. Each animal was jabbed with a tranquilizing dart, fitted with a specially designed radio collar, and released back into the wild, where its move-ments could be tracked both by satellite and bush plane. After being blanked the first year, the live-trapping success in year two came as a wholly unexpected bonanza. It seemed a week didn't pass without a new capture, and the research team was fairly vibrating with excitement. The only prize yet to be taken, the Holy Grail of wolverine biologists every-where, was a denning female.

SHORTLY AFTER I arrive in Red Lake, I discover there are two main places to stay: the Norseman, named after the legendary, canvas-sided bush plane designed and built in this country from 1935 to 1959, and the Red Lake Inn. If you've spent any time in northern Canada, you'll immediately recognize the latter: a rambling, three-storey edifice with a moose head in the lobby, half a dozen buck heads in the ground-floor restaurant, and six drunks in the basement tavern, dubbed, appropriately enough, the Snake Pit. I love it at first sight, check in (no money down, no credit card required), briefly consider the Snake Pit, and opt instead for my room and bed.

In the night it snows, two inches of fluffy white powder, soft and silent and clean as a new duvet. While the people in Red Lake sleep, the wolverines nearby are moving through the snow, through the forest, across the logging roads, around the shores of Red Lake, hunting, scavenging, crunching bones, driven by hunger and the tightly wound spring that is their nature, which sets them in motion at birth and never, ever stops. The new snow will hold the record of their nocturnal activities in sharp relief, a snapshot lasting a day, a week, as long as it takes for the next squall to hit and for the next story to be written in loping tracks.

And maybe, just maybe, a line of prints will lead to one of the heavy wooden boxes set back from the logging roads, baited with frozen chunks of moose or beaver. There are approximately 20 such boxes strategically placed off two main trap lines, one to the northwest, one to the southeast of Red Lake. Not all the traps are set, but the ones that are have to be checked daily: not even 5x6-inch planks of solid hardwood will withstand the assault of a full-grown wolverine for more than a day.

Checking the trap lines is kind of like fishing or baseball: long periods of quiet anticipation, followed by occasional bursts of frenzied activity. The task usually falls to one of three field technicians, but today project manager Neil Dawson has arrived from his home base in Thunder Bay, and together we're going to be checking the south line trap sets, as well as camera sets and hair snares.

Dawson's tenure as a wolverine researcher in northern Ontario actually predates the current project. In 2001, as part of Ontario's Species at Risk program, he began setting up camera traps in the northwest quadrant of the province, hoping to define the lower end of the animals' present range. When Audrey Magoun heard he had successfully taken pictures of wolverines with those traps, she met with him and proposed expanding the scope of the research to include live-trapping and satellite/ aerial tracking. Justina Ray came on board within weeks, and during the last two years, the University of Toronto professor and Wildlife Conservation Society zoologist has travelled to six First Nation communities—both Ojibwa and Cree—gathering historical data on wolverine trapping activity, as well as legends and anecdotal evidence pertaining to the complex, age-old relationship between *Gulo gulo* and man.

It is, in some ways, an odd alliance to be studying the relationship between logging and wolverines. The MNR, Dawson's employer, has what some might consider a vested interest in seeing the timberline pushed north. As an agent for the Wildlife Conservation Society, Justina Ray has an equally vested interest in seeing habitat protected. And Audrey Magoun? Audrey's in it for the wolverines, pure and simple.

Dawson parks the truck at the side of Joyce Road and we immediately spot the tracks: wolverine, not more than a few hours old, leading into the forest in the direction of the trap. We follow the tracks for half a kilometre, hardly believing our luck. Within 50 feet of the box, however, the tracks abruptly veer off-line, as if the animal sensed danger. We can see at a glance that the trap itself has not been sprung, the heavy wooden lid propped open, the meat inside untouched. Next we check the hair snare, a length of barbed wire run around a tree trunk, above which the rib cage of a moose has been hung, looking for all the world like something out of *The Blair Witch Project*. The idea is that the wolverine will climb the tree to get at the bait, and in the process leave tufts of fur behind, trapped in the wire. Sure enough, a close examination of the barbs yields a few strands of brown and white hair—possibly, though not definitely, wolverine, says Dawson, dropping the hair into an envelope. If Magoun concurs that the sample is in fact wolverine, it will be sent to an MNR lab in Peterborough, Ontario, for DNA analysis, allowing the researchers to know if they're dealing with a new animal, or one they've already caught and released.

We spend the rest of the morning checking live traps on the south line, none of which have been sprung. In the afternoon, we strap snowshoes on our feet and head into the forest to examine camera sets. Snow's falling again, and there are fresh marten tracks everywhere, but no sign of their larger cousin. The camera traps consist of an infrared transmitter and receiver, placed about 20 feet apart. A pole is set diagonally between these points, with a piece of bait on top. The wolverine runs up the pole, stands on its hind legs to reach the bait, and consequently breaks the beam between transmitter and receiver, triggering the camera shutter and flash. The resulting photos are designed to capture the wolverine's distinctive chest markings, which can be used to identify individual animals. As with the live traps, however, the camera sets we check show no signs of activity: the bait is in place, the film unused.

"WHAT IS it about wolverines? Why not bears, or wolves, or field mice for that matter?"

We're sitting in the plush, second-storey living room of a rented house overlooking Red Lake, headquarters of Audrey Magoun and the wolverine research team. Outside, in the fading light of dusk, Pat Valkenburg, Magoun's bush pilot husband, races an Arctic Cat up and down the lake, compacting fresh powder into an X-pattern, which he then delineates with cut-pine saplings—runways for Valkenburg's single-engine, PA-18 SuperCub. Magoun herself is curled up on the couch, catlike, sipping a beer and considering my question. She was hooked, she says, from the time she wrote her Ph.D. thesis on wolverines at the University of Alaska, Fairbanks, back in 1985.

"At the time, there was hardly anything known about them, and they're still largely a mystery. They're rare, found only in wilderness areas, and they have this reputation for ferocity that makes them intriguing. But once I got working with them, I realized they're not at all the animal people think they are. They're really intelligent, hard working and tenacious, and probably no more ferocious than any other animal that's trying to make a living on the land."

Certainly, Magoun has overcome any fears she may have once had in dealing with wolverines in the wild. She recalls the time she was aerial surveying in Alaska and spied what appeared to be a dead wolverine half-buried in a snowdrift. They put the plane down, and she walked to within two feet of the animal, when it spun around, gave a terrific snarl and bolted off in the opposite direction. Experiences like this have led her to conclude humans have nothing to fear, at least physically, from the northern devil.

Still, the legends of the wolverine's strength and destructiveness are rooted in fact. The 93 elders and trappers interviewed by Justina Ray in her survey of northern native communities are united in their experience, almost always adversarial, with the wolverine. "You have some phenomenal damage stories," says Ray. "Someone will go and kill four moose for a wedding and can't carry them all out of the bush. They'll come back a day later and the carcasses are gone, dragged away and hidden, and whatever can be found has been pissed on and ruined."

It's the trappers, though, that really suffer. "They're always racing against time, because when a wolverine finds a trap, it just goes down the entire line, stealing the bait and eating anything that has been caught. And then there's no point continuing. You either have to shut everything down, or kill the wolverine, or move your traps to a different location. So there's this mixture of admiration, respect, disgust, fear and anger towards the animal."

As for the wolverine's reputation for ferocity and aggression, the jury's still out. Certainly, the stories of wolverines stealing human babies—a universal theme in native lore—are apocryphal, as, in all likelihood, are the stories of wolverines successfully standing down bears when protecting a kill or scavenging a carcass. More open to debate is the power struggle between wolverines and wolves. Someone once took some film footage that showed a pair of wolverines managing to fight off a couple of wolves, but an equal-numbers fight like this would be a rare occurrence in the wild, where wolverines tend to be solitary animals and wolves travel in packs. In such an encounter, the outcome would be all but certain. "Wolves are like an L.A. street gang," says Magoun. "They attack at once, from all quarters, and there are no survivors."

DAWN BREAKS snowy and cold, the land covered, yet again, in a fine white powder. Around noon the flakes stop falling and cracks of blue appear in the steel-grey sky. Pat Valkenburg and I pull on our flight suits and hike down to the lake where his plane's tethered and waiting.

There are small aircraft, and then there's the Piper SuperCub, a 150-horsepower Lycoming engine attached to a pair of wings and a coffin-like fuselage with just enough room for a pilot and a single passenger—me, in this case—wedged behind on a makeshift seat. What the plane lacks in creature comforts, however, it makes up for in performance: the ability to taxi and land on snow pack and extremely short runways, an impressive climb rate of 1,500 feet per minute, and unparalleled manoeuvrability. These features make it the perfect bush plane for wildlife surveys, and it's used extensively for this purpose in Alaska. It took Valkenburg five days to fly the craft from Fairbanks to Red Lake, the lengthening sun in his eyes the entire way. Since then, he and Magoun have been using it to track the radio-collared wolverines, compiling data on individual animals that will shed light on their movements, home ranges, relationships with one another and, it's hoped, relationships with the forested and deforested landscape.

Preliminary findings indicate that the largest home ranges have been staked by the two adolescent males, Ranger and Jack, at 3,800 and 5,700 square kilometres respectively. This was to be expected, as the youngsters seek out territory unoccupied by older males, who will not tolerate their presence. At approximately 2,000 square kilometres, the next largest range is held by the adult male, Maurice, whereas the two females, Joyce and Mary, each have a range of less than 1,000 square kilometres. (Noel, the Christmas Day female, met her end in an otter trap within a month of being captured, a personal tragedy for Magoun, but an all-too-common outcome when field research and commercial trapping intersect. Noel's collar was retrieved, and will be redeployed when another wolverine is live-trapped.)

As for the relationship between wolverines and logging, there appears to be a negative correlation. In a month and a half of aerial tracking, the collared animals have never once been located in anything but mature forest. "They're either not spending a lot of time in the logged-over areas, or they're using them at night when we're not flying," says Magoun. "It's too early to tell either way."

By the time we buckle ourselves into the SuperCub and taxi down Valkenburg's makeshift runway, the clouds are closing in again, the wind buffeting the wings. No sooner are we airborne, with the frozen expanse of Red Lake falling away like a giant unblinking eye, than the snow comes again. The effect through the windshield is mesmerizing and vaguely disorienting, but it doesn't bother the South African–born pilot: in 30 years of bush flying he's seen and done it all and is more or less on automatic behind the controls.

We head northwest of Red Lake in search of our first target animal, the young male known as Jack. As we approach the area of forest where he was last located by satellite, Valkenburg switches on the VHF receiver and we begin a series of low passes, about three kilometres apart. The transceivers embedded in the collars are supposed to have a range of about five kilometres, but wolverines are not delicate animals, and the antennas on several of the units have already been damaged, reducing their effective range by perhaps half. After 20 minutes of searching we've failed to pick up Jack's signal—not terribly surprising, given that he's one of the more mobile animals, and could be 50 kilometres or more outside our grid.

We give up on Jack and turn our attention to Mary. From the air, the endless expanse of forest, marsh, rock and lake all looks the same to me, but Valkenburg appears to know every hummock and hill by name, and guides us unerringly in the direction of Mary's last known whereabouts. After another 20 minutes or so, I hear a faint beeping in my headset. Valkenburg banks the plane sharply and performs a series of low passes until the signal becomes more pronounced and insistent. He then throws the plane into a tight loop, the left wing pointing almost directly to the ground, the tops of the pine trees no more than a hundred feet below. Somewhere amid the swirling vortex of green, Mary's hunkered down, possibly asleep, but in any event, not showing herself.

We circle a while longer, take down the coordinates, then pull out in search of the adult male, Maurice, who's been hanging around a thick grove of trees on an island in the middle of Red Lake and making periodic forays to a beaver house he's cracked. When local trappers told Audrey Magoun that wolverines in northern Ontario routinely claw their way into beaver houses in order to dine on the residents, she was initially skeptical: the behaviour is unheard of in her native Alaska and had never been scientifically documented—until now.

She and her husband made the discovery a couple of weeks earlier, following Maurice's tracks from the air as they curved along the shore of the lake. Sure enough, they led straight to a beaver house, outside of which the snow was stained blood red. They put the plane down, walked up to the scene of the crime, and discovered a neat hole bored into the side of the otherwise intact structure. Imagine the power and tenacity required to saw through two feet of mud and wood, frozen concrete-hard by the minus 40–degree nights. Imagine the terror and carnage when the inside wall was breached and Maurice's blunt head and massive fangs appeared, haloed in the cold light of day. As for us, we did a fly-by of the beaver house, but saw no fresh signs of the marauder.

IT'S THE morning of my last day in Red Lake, my final chance to see a wolverine up close. A storm blew up in the pre-dawn hours, and I'm driving in near-whiteout conditions with field biologist Richard Klafki, a young, tow-headed fireplug of a man with a penchant for coffee almost as great as my own. Our mission: to check seven traps on the north line and report any new captures back to HQ. With visibility reduced to about eight feet, it occurs to me that we shouldn't be out in this weather—that no one should be out in this weather. But set traps have to be checked daily, and so we drive the logging roads. And because we really, really don't want to surprise an 18-wheeler hauling a load of timber in the other direction, Klafki periodically radios our position to the loggers who are also working: "Half-ton, 12 kilometre, Nungesser Road."

After an hour or so we pull over to the side of the road to check a trap, and when we get back to the truck it's up to its axles in snow and won't budge. It doesn't help that we're towing a pair of Arctic Cats on a trailer, but then, by the look of things, we'll need the sleds sooner rather than later. We shovel out the undercarriage, cut pine boughs for traction, and eventually the truck lurches out of the drift and back onto the road. The wind's howling now, the snow coming down horizontally in big, wet flakes. One by one, we search the north line trap sets, driving, hiking and snowshoeing our way to each site; one by one, we're disappointed. By noon, with four of the seven traps checked and re-baited, I'm starting to get an appreciation for what the field techs go through each and every day of the research season: 400 kilometres of driving, interspersed with long hikes through waist-deep snow pack, the effort all for naught nine times out of 10.

By 3 PM we run out of road and unload the Cats. I haven't driven a snowmobile before, but Klafki explains that it's dead simple: a throttle, a brake and a set of handlebars for steering. With that he roars off at 80 kilometres per hour, hammering through snowdrifts and vanishing in a cloud of powder. I pursue as best I can, but quickly run into trouble when I fail to negotiate a fast corner and fly off the track into the woods, where the sled promptly bogs down in four feet of powder. Ten minutes later Klafki returns to rescue me and offers some further instruction. "You have to lean into the corners," he says, wrenching the sled out of the drift. "And not just a little, you really have to throw your weight in the direction you want to go."

A half hour later we park the sleds, pull off our helmets and hike into the forest to check one last trap, the last trap of my last day in Red Lake. Lo and behold, there are wolverine tracks everywhere. To find the trap sprung, to hear snarling and scrabbling from within, to smell the musky stench of the beast at this, the eleventh hour... it would be too much to ask, wouldn't it?

It would. The trap's empty. But a moose head that had been tacked to a nearby tree—an entire, four-foot moose head—has vanished, and not so mysteriously.

"Who stole from us?" asks an Ojibwa trapper in the 1930s-era documentary film *The Silent Enemy.* "The wolverine! Devil of the north."

I RETURN home. The wolverine researchers continue their work. A week later the luck that eluded me finds them in the form of a spectacular new capture: a lactating female taken on the south line, in the same trap that yielded Joyce back in December. The new animal, dubbed Jill, is collared and released, and the next day on an early morning fly-over, Magoun sees her running through the snow carrying one of her kits by the scruff of the neck.

"All this is brand new, and tremendously exciting," says Magoun. "When we started the research, we didn't even know if we had a resident wolverine population in Red Lake. Now we not only know we have resident animals, but we know they're denning, and we can describe the structure of the denning environment. None of this has ever been documented before in the boreal forest of eastern Canada."

Meanwhile, the question of whether wolverines can coexist with logging has not yet been definitively answered. Magoun is hoping that funding will come through to let her continue her study this winter with newly developed GPS collars, which would deliver more precise location data and help determine if wolverines make use of logged-over terrain, or whether they avoid it altogether. The good news, though, is that wolverine ranges in northern Ontario have actually been increasing over the past three decades.

As for myself, I don't know when—or if—I will encounter another wolverine in the wild. But if the moment comes, and I hope it does, I won't be afraid. I know it won't run me down, land on my back and rip the tendons from my neck. I know it won't "take me." Instead, I'll nod my acquaintance, maybe tip my hat: "Top of the food chain to you, *Gulo*." And the wolverine will regard me, perhaps recognizing a certain kinship—for are we not, both in our own way, relentless, vicious, insatiable? Then it will likely turn away, and shuffle off into the pine.

||||||||||||

SOME FUNNY THINGS
HAPPENED ON
THE WAY TO THE CARIBOU

JAKE MacDONALD

MARCH/APRIL 2001

IT'S A WARM summer day on the Barren Lands, and I'm sitting alone in the cockpit of a $1-million French A-Star helicopter. Through the polished lenses of my sleek Ray-Ban sunglasses, I can see the quiver and twitch of a dozen high-tech instruments, all of them monitoring the various functions of the thundering turbine overhead. The high-pitched pulsing of the rotors, the trembling of the airframe and the chattering scream of the exhausts all attest to the fact that the helicopter is primed for take-off. I reach down between the seats for my lap belt, but judging from the machine's dramatic reaction, I've grabbed the wrong thing. The helicopter starts to lift off the ground.

When something very bad is about to happen, the passing of time slows down to a series of ponderous and highly detailed images. This much I know—I'm sitting in the passenger seat, and I've inadvertently touched something that I wasn't supposed to touch. The rpms are rising dramatically and the pilot is outside the machine, tossing gear in the luggage compartment. My three travelling companions are back there too. As the helicopter begins to lift, I can see the whole accident that's about to unfold in terrible detail. The machine will rise, and the wind will get under the main rotor and tip the helicopter over to the right. The rotor will whack into the tundra, and the tail rotor will sweep into my friends. Gyrating wildly, the helicopter will begin beating itself to death while pink mist and body parts fly in all directions. With a feeling of regret, I decide that this is the worst thing I've ever done. With the same odd feeling of detachment I review the slow-motion accident footage and realize that I'm going to survive, which makes it even worse.

This trip has definitely had its surprising moments.

LAST AUGUST, my friend Tom Thomson and I decided that it was high time we travelled up to the Barren Lands to see the wildlife. Tom is a photographer and I'm a writer, and we were a little embarrassed, after all these years, that we'd never seen a wild caribou. I was also intrigued by the land; I'd always thought of the Barren Lands—that vast area in northern Canada between Hudson Bay and Great Bear Lake—as a sort of modern-day version of colonial Africa—remote, primitive and overrun with wildlife. When a mutual friend of ours recently came home from a visit to the Kazan River area in Nunavut's Keewatin District, he raved about the scenery and the wildlife, especially the vast herds of caribou. He also raved about his outfitter—a wild former Brit named Keith Sharp. "You've got to meet this guy," he said. "He's the real thing."

Beyond the obvious issue of cost—it's not cheap getting to that part of the country—Tom and I couldn't think of a single excuse for not heading up there. So we called Keith Sharp and arranged for him to take us to one of his outpost cabins in the heart of the Barrens.

There's nothing particularly risky about travelling in the modern-day wilderness. But once you get away from civilization, away from traffic lights and cell phones and the generalized monotonous regularity of modern life, you open yourself up to the possibility that *something* might happen. The only thing is, something might not happen, too. You might find yourself sitting in an airport for three days, weathered in by fog. The people who live there full-time seem to have an attitude of calmness, caution and good humour. "You learn to be humble," a bush pilot once told me. "The only one you can call for help is Mother Nature, and she's not picking up the phone."

OUR OWN particular lesson in humility starts with a flight from Winnipeg to Rankin Inlet, Nunavut, on the appropriately named Calm Air. The Saab 340 turboprop is full of government workers, teachers and nurses, and they all relax noticeably as the patchwork agricultural lands of southern Manitoba gradually turn to unbroken forest below us. Pretty soon Tom and I feel like we've gotten caught up in a grade-seven field trip. Passengers are wandering around the plane, table-hopping and yakking. Beer is being consumed in serious volume, and the pretty, uniformed flight attendant has kicked off her heels and is walking up and down the aisle in her stockings. I'm reminded that the North is somewhat of a distinct society, and one of its cultural understandings is that nobody stands on formality.

We stop in Churchill ("Polar Bear Capital!") for a couple of hours, then forge on to the town of Rankin Inlet, which sits on the northwestern shore of Hudson Bay. By the time we land in Rankin, the weather has turned grey and blustery. Our outfitter had promised to meet us at the airport, but he's nowhere to be seen. So we hail a taxi and ride through town—a maze of prefab metal buildings, gravel streets and rusty vehicles. Near the middle of town, not far from what looks like the world's largest Inukshuk, we check into the Sinniktarvik, the town's largest hotel. After we get settled, we call our outfitter's house, but get no answer. Only later will we realize that this is normal, in the sense that everything being all screwed up, all the time, is pretty much normal in the North.

TOM AND I shrug off the missing outfitter and head out to explore the town. Rankin Inlet—population 2,200—is built on bare rock, and the houses are scattered around like children's blocks. Each house has a sort of yard-sale look, cluttered with komatiks, gutted sofas, wooden pallets, discarded septic tanks, car bodies, dismantled snowmobiles, dried hides, and the bleached vertebral columns and shoulder blades of assorted dead mammals. Among the wreckage the children play. The preschool kids are ridiculously cute, with dark, almond-shaped eyes and open, trusting, friendly faces. Everywhere we walk, we're greeted with their curious waves and beaming smiles.

Down at the harbour, we meet three weather-beaten young Inuit guys who are just returning from a hunting trip. Their gear is an interesting mix of old and new. They're wearing Patagonia raingear and carrying rifles with composite stocks, rangefinder scopes and stainless steel barrels. One of them has a rusty old Captain Ahab harpoon, and all they have for food is a big hunk of *muktuq*—raw whale blubber. They tell us they've been trying to kill a beluga. "A whale will keep the three of us in meat all winter," one of them says. Belugas weigh 900 pounds, 400 of which is meat. But first you have to get one. The challenge is to move close enough to drive in a harpoon, then finish it off with the rifles. The guys have hunted for three days in their 22-foot skiff, but the whales have been spooky and hard to approach. When darkness fell each night, they'd anchored in the lee of a pure white quartz island, crawled under the bow and slept while the boat rocked in the swell. "It's a lot of work to kill a whale," one of them says. "We'll try it again in a few days."

It's late when we get back to the hotel, and we call Keith Sharp again. He still isn't picking up his phone, and we're getting a bit nervous. The next morning, we're eating breakfast in the hotel, wondering what to do, when a very large and somewhat frightening-looking guy comes in the door of the restaurant and hulks towards us. He has long, unkempt hair, dirty sweatpants, and is eyeing us with the gap-toothed smile of a road agent in a spaghetti western. He thrusts out his hand. "Nice to meet you, boys. I'm Keith Sharp."

Keith sits down, orders a coffee and apologizes in his thick English accent for not meeting us at the airport. He explains that yesterday, he'd been flying in a plane that had a "complete engine failure." This seems like an excellent reason for missing an appointment, but Keith doesn't try to get much mileage out of it. He says that he and his pilot were on their way back to Rankin in the Cessna 206, when there was a sudden crack of heavy metal breaking and a big puff of dust. "I know machines, and I knew that this was a major engine failure." They were cruising at 1,000 feet, and the young pilot kind of lost his cool. His hands started shaking and he didn't know what to do. They'd just crossed a long stretch of granite ridge, but luckily enough, there was a little lake just below them. "I pointed down and said, 'You'll be fine, just glide in there.' He dead-sticked it in, pulled off a half decent landing. We weren't hurt, so we radioed the helicopter and they came and got us."

Now the Cessna is stranded on a lake 80 kilometres west of here with a seized engine, and it won't be going anywhere until mechanics arrive, fly into the lake with a new engine and install it on the spot. "That was the plane we were going to use today," Keith says, making me realize I was one day away from experiencing complete engine failure. "Typical screw-up. It'll probably cost $80,000 to put that plane back in the air again."

Farther south, floatplanes are nearly as ubiquitous as taxi cabs. But Rankin Inlet is pretty much the ragged edge of civilization, and there isn't another float-equipped airplane in town. This means we won't be hobnobbing with any wildlife for the next few days, so we make a conscious effort to relax and enjoy Rankin. "Living in the North teaches you the virtues of patience," says Keith, as we pay our bill and head out to accompany him on some of his morning errands. "What you do in the North for most of the time is wait. You wait for the airplane. You wait on the weather. You wait and wait and wait, and while you wait, you hemorrhage money." Paying for our bacon-and-egg specials ($16 each), I begin to appreciate his point.

WE CLIMB into Keith's pickup truck, and as he drives around town he explains how he wound up working as a tour outfitter in the Canadian North. Keith grew up in Staffordshire, England, as a sergeant-major's son and spent a lot of his childhood reading escape novels like *Robinson Crusoe*. He always wanted to see the wilderness, and he got his first chance in 1967, when he came to Canada at the age of 28. He fell in love with the country and worked all over western Canada in construction, doing dams and bridges. "Anything you see with curved concrete in it, that's me."

When Keith arrived in Rankin in 1971 there were only 600 people in town, but there was lots of construction work and he met an Inuit girl named Alma, so he stayed. He says that it was a little rough at first getting accepted by the locals. "I was sleeping with an Eskimo girl, and that was a no-no in those days," he says. There was one building inspector who particularly disliked him. "He called me on the phone one night and started berating me. He said, 'You're a slimy Limey,' and so forth. I didn't really take offence because he was drunk. Then he said, 'You know what? You don't work for Baert Construction. You work for Fart Construction.' That did it. I went down to the pub and walked in, took off his glasses and knocked out six of his teeth. They called the police and charged me with assault. I happened to be friends with the local RCMP officer. We played poker together. So he went easy on me. But I couldn't get any construction work after that, so I just lived in a shack with Alma and trapped and fished for a couple of years. I loved being out on the land. The size of the country and its silence gets inside you. I could never live in a city again."

Later on, we arrive at Keith's place, a big windowless house. He introduces us to his Inuit wife, Alma, and to a couple of his daughters, and tells us the names of several of the fat little grandchildren toddling around on the floor. Then he fires up the stove and prepares us a lunch of Caribou à la Sharp—an inventive recipe consisting of one fresh-thawed bleeding hunk of caribou haunch tossed into a red-hot frying pan. Sawed into portions and dumped on our plates, it is nevertheless delicious—sweet as spring lamb and tender enough to be cut with a fork. Keith's kids qualify as Inuit, and as a family, they keep the freezer full by harvesting about 15 caribou a year.

The Sharps' kitchen is like one of those legendary restaurants in New York or San Francisco—sooner or later, everyone who visits this part of the North passes through it. "Pierre Trudeau sat right in that chair," Keith remarks, gesturing at me with a blood-smeared butcher knife. "Very quiet and courteous man. He came here with his boys to see the land." Keith says that General Norman Schwarzkopf ("a real redneck") and General Colin Powell ("a real gentleman") also ate lunch here en route to one of his outpost camps. During his 20-odd years in the business, he's had guests from all over. He says that people from Chicago are cranky, Germans are obedient and folks from Minneapolis "wouldn't say boo to a goose."

Keith—who was the mayor of Rankin in 1995 when the town lost the vote to become the capital of Nunavut to Iqaluit—has done almost everything you can do in the North to make a living. "I've built houses, hauled freight. I've made a million dollars several times over," he says with a sigh of regret. "But the money comes and goes. One day you're in the chips, next day you're broke. Everything is so bloody expensive up here, and as a territory, we have no idea where we're going. We've got this new political entity, Nunavut, and everyone is all excited about it. But be realistic, how are we going to support ourselves? Tourism? There's no bloody tourists. It's too bloody tough for the average tourist."

OVER THE next couple of days Tom and I get to know Rankin Inlet. Theoretically, we're waiting for the Cessna to be repaired. But that plot, too, is beginning to unfold like a rerun of an old Bing Crosby and Bob Hope movie—*On the Road to Nunavut*. Two mechanics from Thompson, Manitoba, have helicoptered out to the stranded airplane and settled into quarters that Keith has left for them—a soggy tent containing a rifle, a rubber mattress and a mouldy haunch of caribou meat. In the North, every chore assumes massive complexity. And once the mechanics start replacing the engine, they confront problems that might have stumped Archimedes. How, for example, are they supposed to lift the new engine into place, given that it weighs 600 pounds, they don't have a hoist and the nearest sapling of black spruce is 800 kilometres to the south?

The mechanics use their brains and somehow get the new Continental engine into place, start the plane and taxi it back and forth enough times to assure themselves that it actually works. Then they say a little prayer and take off, flying it back to Rankin Inlet. The Cessna is now parked on a lake at the edge of town. But they don't feel it's airworthy yet, and we aren't about to argue with them. They've ordered an oil gauge from the factory in Wichita. Every night in the coffee shop, they give us the update on the gauge's epic journey from Kansas to Nunavut. "Up here," one of them says, "it's a game of hurry up and wait."

While Tom and I wait, we get invited places. We go to a tent camp on a river north of town, and we eat whale blubber with an Inuit family that is catching and drying char for the winter. One of the old-timers in the group is recovering from serious injuries he sustained in an attack by a polar bear. It's the third time in his life he's been assaulted by a bear, but he seems philosophical about it. "There are good bears and bad bears," he tells us, through an interpreter. "The first bear that attacked me was a good bear. I was wearing white and it mistook me for another bear. The second bear that attacked me was a good bear also. She was a mother bear, protecting her cubs. The third bear that attacked me was a bad, angry bear. He was angry at the world. He was raised by a mother bear that had three cubs. A third cub is hungry all the time and he's angry at the world. He's the bear you have to watch out for. That was the type of *nanuq* that attacked me."

The next day, Keith invites us to an Inuit wedding. The ceremony is taking place inside a group of linked-up double-wide trailers called the Church of the Holy Comforter. As the crowd begins to gather, pretty bridesmaids roar up on ATVs, wearing high heels and the traditional hooded parkas called *motiqs*. Keith—who speaks Inuktitut—explains that the groom is moving a little gingerly because he has 12 brand-new stitches in his arm. "He went whale-hunting yesterday," says Keith, "and when he threw a harpoon at a beluga, the whale threw it back." The harpoon slashed the groom's arm but, as Keith reminds us, "the show must go on." So while the ceremony transpires, there's tittering speculation among some of the young women as to whether the groom will be up to his matrimonial chores this evening. Out in the parking lot, little kids pass the time by running around in the cold sun, blowing soap bubbles.

THE OIL gauge for the Cessna finally arrives from Wichita, and there's considerable incredulity and disgust from the mechanics when they open the carton and realize it's the wrong gauge. Keith takes it in stride. He says that he's been living in the North for so long that he's immune to the state of being pissed off. "Getting pissed off got me four heart attacks," he says. "Now I try to see it all as a comedy." He says that a local drilling company owes him a block of time on its helicopter, and he's prepared to call his note in. He has to make the trip anyway, in order to pick up a group of American fishermen that has been stranded at one of his outpost cabins ever since the plane blew up. Light helicopters lease out for about $1,000 an hour up north, and the chopper is based at a drilling camp about 150 kilometres west of Rankin Inlet. Since we're on a tight budget, it makes more sense to move us to the helicopter rather than move the helicopter to us. So Tom, Keith and I hitch a ride on a wheel-equipped Cessna that is heading to the drilling camp. There, we change into the French A-Star helicopter and continue.

As we thud along, the green, rolling tundra beneath us—interspersed with small lakes and rising flocks of sandhill cranes—looks unreal. The artificial appearance of the landscape is heightened by the artificial sensation of helicopter travel itself. The headphones dampen all noise except for the sound of the rotors overhead. And the Plexiglas walls of the machine afford such a wide-open view, it's hard not to think we're actually soaring over some computer-generated landscape at Universal Studios.

Finally we cross the broad, dark-blue Kazan River and flare in for a landing next to Keith's outpost camp, which is just a plywood shack perched on a sandy ledge above the river. The pilot leaves the engine running, and we hurriedly trade places with the American doctors who've been stranded here for the last few days. They look a bit like actors from the movie *Deliverance*, with sooty faces, whiskered chins and slightly crazed eyes. "Saw hundreds of caribou every day!" one of them screams over the roar of the helicopter. "Ran out of food but we ate fish! Bobby strangled a ptarmigan with his bare hands!"

The helicopter whisks the Americans away and we haul our bags into the cabin. There's a broken-down, 12-passenger Bombardier next to the cabin and Keith points to the smashed windshield. "A grizzly broke into it in the spring," he says. "Barren Lands grizzlies are not as aggressive as polar bears, but like all bears they're a bit unpredictable."

He leads us into the cabin, drops his bags on the floor and points to a rusty old 12-gauge pump leaning against the wall. "So that's for emergencies, if anyone needs it. Man, it's good to be here. Anyone want coffee?"

WE HAVE barely unpacked our bags when the first caribou appear. I have been glancing regularly out the window, hoping to see a miniature spot of life moving among the far-off hills, when a group of caribou walks right past the front door. For a few minutes they graze like Shetland ponies in the front yard, then wander down towards the river. Keith watches, chuckling, while Tom and I frantically dig out camera gear and slip out the door to get a shot. The caribou are feeding among some riverbank willows, and we keep the wind in our favour as we creep towards them. When we are about 25 steps away, the cow of the group raises her head and looks at us, as if to ask, "May I help you?"

The Kazan River is one of three major waterways that drain eastward across the Barrens, and Keith's outpost cabin is situated right between the calving grounds of the Kaminuriak and Beverly caribou herds. The animals are occasionally preyed upon by wolves, grizzlies and human beings, but the cows and calves display little fear of interlopers. The bulls tend to be more wary. Over the next few days we spot the occasional grand bull bedded alone on a hillside, in an exposed location with a good field of view in front of him and wind protection from behind. We try stalking close to these bedded bulls, but they always sense our presence and move off when we're still hundreds of yards away. Although large, the sheer size of bull caribou probably makes them more vulnerable to wolves, and that might explain their edginess.

Keith hasn't bothered bringing any food. After Tom and I get over the initial shock, we realize that there is food all around us. The so-called Barren Lands is actually one enormous larder, with so many berries growing underfoot that you can't kneel down without staining your pants, and hillsides that are alive with caribou, hares and ptarmigan. At mealtime, Keith smacks his hands together, glances at me, and announces, "Go fetch us lunch, will you?" Obediently, I grab my fly rod and head down to the river. Within a few minutes, I'm fighting a powerful 15-pound Kazan lake trout.

After a couple of days of us exploring, Tom still hasn't gotten his money shot of a bull caribou—image found on the 25-cent piece—so Keith takes us by boat down the river. The Kazan is a canoeist's dream, a broad smooth river that flows with muscular authority past endless gravel beaches and gentle green hills. On an August day, you could drowse at your station with the paddle across your knees, the warm sun on your shoulders, and the refrigerator breeze feathering your face. Even half asleep, you could average 10 klicks an hour on this river. But you wouldn't want to sleep too soundly. A few miles downstream from the camp, we hear the white-noise thunder of rapids.

Keith pulls the boat over to the bank well before the rapids and then insists on walking down the shore by himself to check for *akthuk*, the grizzly, which favours these rapids as a fishing hole. "They clean a fish so nicely you'd think it was done by a man with a knife," he says. "They strip off the fillets and leave nothing but a head, tail and backbone."

Once Keith is satisfied we have the rapids to ourselves, we walk the smooth rocks, worn into fabulous shapes by the age-old traffic of water and ice. The sun is warm and the breeze keeps the black flies away. We rest on couches of worn granite, feeling satisfied to laze a while in the late afternoon heat. "Last year," says Keith, "there were 10,000 caribou bivouacked here. They stayed for about four days. You could smell them from miles away, like a barnyard."

Keith is reclining on his side, curled up like a grizzly with his beard wafting in the breeze. "If you'd been here then, you would have got your bull caribou from 20 steps away. They were swimming the river and climbing out right in front of us, water pouring off them. Big antlers flashing in the sunlight. Magnificent sight."

"Do you think they'll be back this year?" Tom asks.

"Maybe," says Keith, with a shrug. "This is the North. You never know."

ON THE day of our departure, the Cessna fails to show up. Has there been another accident? We don't know, and we can't raise Rankin Inlet on the radio. It seems that sunspot activity has thrown the VHF radio out of commission.

"It sure would be nice to know when they'll get here," Keith reflects, trying the radio for the umpteenth time.

"Or *if* they'll get here," quips Tom.

We can't go off exploring in case the plane arrives, so there's nothing much to do except listen to the rain rattle on the roof. Outside, our bags are stacked in the lee of the cabin. We keep straining our ears for the sound of an engine. Is that just the wind? The plane might come in the next few minutes, or it might come next week, or maybe not at all. This is a great exercise in Zen and the art of equanimity maintenance.

Finally, late in the day, we hear an engine. From far across the river it comes, only it's not the plane, it's the helicopter. It lands in a roar of flattened vegetation. We run towards the chopper, hauling bags and gear, bending over as we run to avoid the ever-annoying problem of decapitation. The pilot climbs out, leaving the engine powered up and running, and begins throwing our bags into the cargo hold. Shouting over the roar of the engine, I ask the pilot if we should get in. He nods.

I climb into the front seat, get settled and that's when it happens. I reach down for my lap belt and accidentally pull the wrong lever. For perhaps one entire second the entire world goes cold, as the helicopter begins to chatter and shake and rise from the ground. Then the pilot dives through the open door beside me and jumps on the controls. For perhaps three more seconds the chopper shakes and trembles, like a stallion contemplating revolt, then it settles down quietly. The others climb in, and we strap on our belts and take off.

For the first 10 minutes of the flight the pilot is pale and stone-faced, saying nothing. And I don't say anything either. What are you supposed to say? How do you offer an excuse for the inexcusable? Finally he glances my way. "So how was your trip?"

"Fine," I say. "Very interesting."

He nods. Beneath us, a herd of muskox grazes on a hillside. It's raining, and the clouds ahead look like they're spoiling for trouble. We should be back in Rankin Inlet before nightfall, but I'm not betting on it.

||||||||||||

A KNIGHT'S TRAIL

MARK REYNOLDS

JUNE/JULY 2003

F

ROM THE VANTAGE of a sea kayak, the most mysterious chunk
of real estate in North America doesn't look like much. The island
stretches for maybe a kilometre, a low dark curve on the water, rag-
gedly packed with the oaks for which it is named. I could easily mistake
it for any of the 364 other islets scattered liberally about Mahone Bay,
except for one thing: the 650-foot stone-and-earth causeway that weds
Oak Island to Nova Scotia's mainland. That, and the fact I could get shot
if I tried to cross it. Hence, the kayak.

As I paddle the short distance to the shore, I feel a flutter of nerves.
All the stories I read about this place as a small boy come rushing back:
Pirate gold. Booby traps. A buccaneer's curse. Even 200 years after the
discovery of the notorious "money pit"—a mysterious shaft alleged to
hold privateers' plunder—Oak Island remains a forbidden zone. A secretive corporation of millionaires (known only as the Triton Alliance) owns
the money pit and remains embroiled in a bitter dispute over access with
two other property owners. Triton's on-island representative has been
known to chase off curious trespassers with a shotgun.

They can keep their pirate gold, though. I've come to Oak Island on
a quest more spiritual than mercenary—the only quest worthy of the

name. In my mind, my kayak has transformed into a mighty stallion, my life vest into a suit of armour, and my companion into a faithful page guiding me through unknown lands. I am Sir Galahad in neoprene, riding towards my long-sought, hard-fought-for and now nearly achieved goal: the Holy Grail.

Now let me be perfectly clear: I'm not here on the trail of a metaphorical Grail, the Holy Grail *of* something—the Holy Grail of Particle Physics, say, or the Holy Grail of Adventure. No, I am on a quest for the missing piece of Last Supperware made famous by mediaeval minstrels and Monty Python, the actual friggin' Holy Grail. And I'm not the only one who thinks it's hidden here in Nova Scotia.

EVERY SCHOOLKID in the Maritimes is taught the story of the first European exploration and settlement of Canada's East Coast: Champlain founding what would become Acadia before the English chased the lot away and filled the place with displaced Scotsmen. They also learn, a bit more eagerly, the legends of pirate gold hidden on Oak Island. What they're not told is that both stories are bald-faced lies.

I first heard inklings of Nova Scotia's "secret history" in my teens. One afternoon, my father came home with a tall tale that a golf buddy had spun about a Scottish lord, a secret society and the bones of Jesus. Dad often said some weird things after the 19th hole, so I didn't pay much attention. Years later, though, I stumbled across a book titled *Prince Henry Sinclair: His Expedition to the New World in 1398* and did the math: 1492 minus 1398 equals 94 years of missing history. I bought the only copy.

The book's author, Frederick Pohl, was an English teacher from New York who described himself as a "geographic detective." Today he would be labelled by academic historians as a "diffusionist": someone convinced that contact between the Old and New Worlds was far more common prior to Columbus than is generally accepted. Certain theories make sense: it's well established that the Basques were fishing off Newfoundland before Cabot sighted the island. Most strain credibility: Vikings in Minnesota, Chinese mariners in Chile, and King Arthur II founding an American Camelot a millennium before JFK.

Pohl was convinced that a Scottish nobleman named Prince Henry Sinclair had crossed the Atlantic in 1398 with a crew of more than 200. After landing on the coast of Nova Scotia, Sinclair supposedly explored the province and met its native population. He over-wintered along the Bay of Fundy, then navigated down the Gulf of Maine the next spring and headed home. The end.

This incredible journey would be grist for museum displays and Canadian Heritage Moments if Sinclair had returned to his castle, pulled out a sheet of vellum and inked down memories of his great adventure for posterity. But, alas, he didn't. With no authoritative account, Frederick Pohl instead relied on an Italian document called *The Zeno Narrative* as evidence of Sinclair's voyage. The 7,000-word travelogue, which lay hidden until 1558, describes how Antonio and Nicolo Zeno, two Venetian sailors of some renown, shipwrecked on the island domain of a "Prince Zichmni." According to the *Narrative*, Prince Zichmni convinced the two Venetians to accompany him on an expedition to a land of incredible natural wealth beyond the sea.

With a bit of linguistic legerdemain, Pohl interpreted "Zichmni" as Sinclair. Other diffusionists, building on Pohl's theory, wonder if Sinclair had more on his mind than just a visit to the New World. He had rumoured connections to the mysterious and powerful Knights Templar, the mediaeval forerunners of the equally secretive Freemasons, and might have made his voyage to our shores with a treasure of incalculable value to hide. Either way, his expedition supposedly set off across the Atlantic in 1398 and arrived sometime in early summer. The strange new continent, described as "Estotiland" in *The Zeno Narrative*, matches only one place on Earth: Nova Scotia.

I FIRST pick up the trail of Sinclair near Guysborough, a small fishing village tucked behind Cape Canso in Nova Scotia's northeastern corner. I'm rumbling along in a pickup truck with Jamie Grant, the vice-president of the Prince Henry Sinclair Society, on our way to Tower Hill, the alleged landing spot of the mysterious Scottish mariner. A retired history teacher with a gentle voice tinged by a Nova Scotian burr, Grant was just a young lad in 1951 when Frederick Pohl arrived in Guysborough to research his book. Grant still remembers the stir that the spare, grey-bearded American caused in the village. For a seven-year-old boy, having his hometown—an obscure coastal settlement of only a few hundred—named as the landfall of a genuine knight of the Middle Ages was heady stuff.

Like me, Grant grew up to become one of the biggest kinds of nerds this country has to offer: the Canadian history buff. We're not the sort of living-history devotees, however, who like to dress in pantaloons, chow down on bannock and recreate the Battle of Lundy's Lane. No, our historiophilia is both more romantic and more closeted. We prefer to read between the lines of soporific textbooks and spy a more thrilling, noble, even magical narrative. And then—amateur archaeologists, archival obsessives, historical revisionists—we troop across the countryside looking for proof of our alternate histories etched into rock and buried under root.

"I'm interested in it because this is basically a tale of adventure and courage," says Grant. He has other motives, too. "There's a certain amount of chamber of commerce boosterism," he concedes. "If this story were true, then wouldn't this be an ideal spot for a museum and tourist attraction? Call it a 'what if' centre."

Despite the efforts of the 200-plus members of the Prince Henry Society, government funding for such a what-if centre hasn't been forthcoming. And it won't be until the story gains currency with professional historians—which probably means never.

"There's a tremendous amount of inertia amongst historians," complains Grant. "There is no group more intransigent and accepting of authority. Truth doesn't come from denial for the sake of denial."

Still, the Henryites persevere. The society has published books, lobbied bureaucrats and raised money to erect three monuments outside Guysborough—all with the goal of restoring Bonnie Prince Henry's name to the annals of exploration. They've had the Zeno maps examined by the U.S. Air Force, received an endorsement for their quest from the Mayor of Venice and organized a symposium on Sinclair in Scotland. ("Three out of five historians on our panel said there was something to this, that the voyage probably happened," said founder and president

D'Elayne Coleman, a New York real-estate agent who summers in the area.) While they lack the money and land clearances, the Prince Henry Society would like to purchase 128 acres of property near Guysborough to dedicate to Sinclair and other pre-Columbian explorers. That park would serve as an anchor for the Sinclair Trail that the society hopes will trace the knight's route through peninsular Nova Scotia and become a tourist draw like Cape Breton's popular Cabot Trail.

Grant and I reach the top of the rise—Mile Zero of the Sinclair Trail-to-be—and get out of his truck. Barren, rocky and dominated by a fire lookout, it's the highest point of land for some distance, and while the clouds have been threatening rain all day, the visibility is still impressive. Below us lies Guysborough Harbour, and to the north, the low profile of Cape Breton. If Sinclair sailed across the Atlantic and landed near here, Tower Hill would be a logical spot from which to check out the local real estate. According to Frederick Pohl's interpretation of *The Zeno Narrative*, after Sinclair climbed Tower Hill, he saw smoke pouring from another hill in the distance. He sent 100 men to investigate; eight days later, they returned and described marching through "forest primeval" to a strange "smoking hole" on a creek that flowed from a "spring of pitch."

"They've been able to see fires as far away as Halifax County up here," says Grant of the vantage from Tower Hill. He points roughly to the west, where the gathering dark obscures a range of hills. "That's Mount Adams over there that Sinclair would have seen. The smoke would have come from Stellarton just beyond it."

The next morning, hot on Sinclair's trail, I drive to Stellarton, a coal-mining town about 100 kilometres west of Guysborough. While I hope to find evidence of the smoking hole, I'm pretty sure that someone has managed to put it out after 600 years. Coal Brook, near the edge of town, sounds like a logical place to look for a burning creek. It's not quite the "forest primeval" Sinclair's men encountered—I have to duck through someone's backyard and fight thorny undergrowth to reach the creek. It's hardly worth the trouble. The brook, in late June, is barely a dribble.

It's also black. The rocks, soil and exposed tree roots are covered with what looks to be tar. The "spring of pitch," which Pohl placed about a kilometre from where I stand, has leached enough bituminous material into the water over the years to paint the streambed a poisonous-looking hue. Unfortunately for my investigations, the source of this residue has since been grassed over with a baseball diamond. Still, if an exposed coal seam along the brook had been struck by lightning, it could have burned for decades. (One such fire near Pictou smouldered for nearly 30 years.) The black smoke would have been easily visible from Tower Hill.

Proof? No. But the geography fits so far.

AFTER HIS men returned, Sinclair—or rather, "Prince Zichmni"— allegedly sailed from Guysborough to the more sheltered harbour of Pictou, not far from Stellarton, and set up camp. Winter was approaching, so he kept a few small boats and then ordered most of his men home under the command of Antonio Zeno. With its author back in Europe, *The Zeno Narrative* contains no more about Sinclair's fate. But that didn't stop Frederick Pohl's historical sleuthing. He reconstructed the rest of the knight's tale using a variety of evidence: archaeological fragments, speculative reasoning, even the Mi'kmaq legends about Glooscap, the shape-shifting man-god who lived in the area. (Pohl interprets Glooscap's dramatic exit—he leaves Nova Scotia on the back of a giant whale—as a metaphor for Sinclair's own ocean-going vessel.)

This line of reasoning—the most tenuous in Pohl's argument—brings me to Cap d'Or, a natural redoubt that faces off against Blomidon, a similarly steep point on the opposite shore of the Minas Channel. If Sinclair had only kept small boats, Pohl hypothesized, he would have had to head inland from Pictou, crossing the isthmus that connects Nova Scotia to New Brunswick, until he arrived at the Minas Basin and the head of the Bay of Fundy. Then he'd need to follow the north shore before landing at Cap d'Or. Pohl figured that Sinclair built a fort here and constructed new vessels for his journey home.

In the town of Lower Economy, I meet Neil St. Clair, secretary of the Prince Henry Society. The 84-year-old from Orlean, New York, summered in the region with his wife before retiring here about 20 years ago. He treats me to lunch and agrees to give me a tour of Cap d'Or. The cape's cliff formation squats like a red-stone tower over the Bay of Fundy, topped by sparse scrub and marsh. "This place is awesome," says St. Clair.

The phrase could have popped off the lips of his grandchildren, but I have to agree.

In his book, Pohl claimed to have found stone foundations on Cap d'Or and argued they must have been from an old fortress, as no one else would have lived on such a forbidding promontory—the only building now is an unmanned lighthouse. St. Clair says he saw these foundation stones years ago, but—and here he hints darkly at a government cover-up—they've since been torn up to create a road through the park. He says he succeeded in convincing the provincial government to name one of the park trails in Sinclair's honour, but when we look for it, there's no sign to mark the route. "That means I've got to do some sleuthing and complaining," sighs St. Clair.

St. Clair doesn't have the hometown motivations of Nova Scotia–bred Henry fans like Jamie Grant, but there is still a family link: *St. Clair* is a variation of *Sinclair,* so Prince Henry may well be a direct ancestor. It's a link he discovered only after moving to Canada. When I press him about why he chooses to spend his golden years in a seemingly hopeless joust against the forces of historical correctness, he just shrugs and says, "No one else would do it."

We leave the park so that St. Clair can show me further fruits of his campaign in the nearby village of Advocate Harbour. On the waterfront overlooking the sea stands a commemorative plaque to Sinclair. It's actually an all-purpose nod to early settlers, lost fishermen and the nearby communities "claimed to be visited in 1398 by Prince Henry Sinclair." As far as official recognition goes, it's a bit of a hedge, but St. Clair takes what he can get.

I try to imagine what Advocate Harbour might have looked like in Prince Henry's day. A tide-break has cut off what must have been a salt marsh from the sea. Gentle hills, ideal for pulling a wooden boat away from the tide, rise from the water, while the looming cliffs of Cap d'Or shelter the harbour to the south. If Sinclair did build his ships here, he left no evidence. No slipways, no tools. The modern memorial is the only reminder of his expedition.

After a quick look around, I drive St. Clair home. As we wind through the hills overlooking the Bay of Fundy, he breaks from his habit of resolute non-speculation. "You know that they took Jesus off the cross before he died?" he asks. "He lived in France and had a family with Mary Magdalene."

I just nod. I've been blindsided by this odd line of speculation before. It's where the Sinclair saga morphs from an unappreciated maritime expedition into an international religious conspiracy and—pushed along by a lot of supposition—intersects with the mysterious chivalric order known as the Knights Templar.

The Templars were the adventure guides of the Middle Ages; their official mission was to protect pilgrims visiting the recaptured Holy Lands, but they were also rumoured to have plundered the Temple of Solomon and stolen the Holy Grail, variously interpreted as the chalice used at the Last Supper, the cup that caught Jesus's blood as he hung from the cross, a mysterious "stone of knowledge," or the remains of Christ—who had lived happily ever after with Mary Magdalene before finally expiring of old age. After the Muslim armies evicted the Crusaders from the Holy Lands, the political clout of the Templars declined. In 1307, King Philip of France, envious of their wealth, raided all their strongholds in his domain and tortured 200 of the knights for heresy. But the Templar fleet escaped with their treasure, and they were never seen again.

If the Templars had sailed north, as some people speculate, they might have sought refuge in distant Scotland. If they had the Holy Grail (Christ's remains, according to this interpretation), they would have wanted to hide it more securely: the Grail was—quite literally—the skeleton in the Vatican's closet that was worth killing for. After all, Jesus can hardly have ascended into heaven, body and soul, if his bones were still lying in some knight's suitcase. With the forces of Rome in hot pursuit, the remaining Templars knew they weren't safe in Europe. So they enlisted a sympathetic Scottish earl for a dangerous trans-Atlantic mission.

THIS GRAIL theory—a particularly rickety ladder of *ifs* and *maybes* that bridges vast gaps in the historical record—brings me to Oak Island. First I contact one of the main partners in the Triton Alliance and ask if I might visit the money pit. He is polite but firm: no one is allowed on the property, especially media. "Things are changing," he tells me cryptically. Several months later, I learn that, after 35 years of treasure-hunting, Triton plans to sell its share of the island. They're asking $7 million, a not unreasonable price for a 128-acre plot with such an enigmatic history.

With Triton a dead end, I convince Gord Tate, owner of Mahone Bay Kayaks, to guide me on a Grail-scouting trip around the island. When he hears the purpose of my trip, he says he can do better than just a floating peek-a-boo: he has a connection who can get me *on* the island. Like me, Tate was weaned on tales of Oak Island, and the notion of pirate loot off the coast of Nova Scotia still fascinates him. But he's concerned about recent local efforts to make the island a tourist destination and open it up to guided tours. His kayaking company would likely benefit from such a buccaneer boom, but Tate figures that Oak Island's true beauty lies in its mystery. Exploiting the island for quick bucks—a greater risk now that Triton plans to sell—would tarnish this allure.

"I'm worried about the Disneyfication of the island," he explains as we paddle across. "I envision pirate-themed gift shops and mini-golfs lining the roads."

Or how about a Templar Pub, where you can get a happy-hour Grail of Ale?

We reach the shore, and Tate's friend emerges from the woods to help us pull the boats up. Dressed in head-to-toe denim, aviator glasses settled on a wind-burned face, he looks like a treasure hunter straight out of central casting. In reality, Robert Young is an industrial designer from Toronto who took to Indiana Jonesing after he burned out on big-city life. He visited the area in the early 1990s, fell in love with the island and managed to convince another gold digger to part with one of the 32 lots. Young shows me and Tate around his four-acre property, marked on either side by "spite lines"—paths cleared in the forest by Triton flunkies to keep Young from setting foot on their property. He seems remarkably low-key about his work on the island, which he describes as more a spiritual stewardship than a treasure hunt.

"This place is special and it's only original once," he insists. "I'm one of the few people who's actually added something to the island. Some of these guys came in with backhoes and just ripped the place up. If the Smithsonian or some museum would step in, I'd be happy—this was my chance to contribute."

There is little evidence to connect Prince Henry to Oak Island, except various psychics' declarations that the buried treasure is of a holy nature and an e-mail I received from a Triton rep saying they had unearthed artifacts carbon-dated to Sinclair's time. Still, a belief persists that Sinclair's band of pilgrims used the island as a safety-deposit box.

"Yeah, I know the story," says Young. "It would be great if it were true, because that would mean there was something here far more valuable than gold. But I don't believe it."

Instead, Young thinks that after the sack of Havana in 1762, the British had too much treasure to store safely in the conventional ways, so they buried portions throughout Oak Island to keep prying fingers from the whole load. It's a convenient theory, because it means that Young's otherwise unremarkable lot might hold some loot. Most of his searching, though, has been limited to dowsing and combing the ground with a metal detector and ground-penetrating radar; so far, he has just turned up buttons and small metal items. He has made two small excavations; one revealed evidence of a well, Young says, and the other a fire-pit— interesting because his lot was never officially settled. The rest of his time has been dedicated to clearing his land of scrub and dead vegetation.

"Living trees are sacred," he says, patting one like an old friend, "and the oaks are king."

And so the search goes on. Superstition holds that a curse protects Oak Island's treasure, which will remain hidden until all its namesake trees have died (unlikely without dousing the island in Agent Orange) or until a seventh person dies in search of it (better odds, as six unlucky treasure hunters have kicked it already). On my visit, the island was plagued by mosquitoes and in little need of supernatural protection. But the golf buddy who first told my father the Sinclair story has another theory: no one will find anything until the Triton Alliance finally leaves. Far from trying to unearth the island's secrets, the corporation is a front for the Catholic Church and would rather keep them buried.

MY HEAD is swirling with conspiracies. It's time, I realize, to seek out some real historians—the intransigent, slavish-to-authority, academic rubes who have given Prince Henry's modern followers such a cool reception. I head to Cape Breton. My goal: the National Historic Site of Fortress Louisbourg. First I detour through Highlands National Park, mostly for the scenery—the low mountains and ocean views are the stuff of a thousand postcards—but also to see another possible Sinclair landmark: Smokey Mountain, perennially shrouded in mist, *also* could have been the "smoking hill" spotted by Sinclair's men. Considering how hard it would be for a trans-Atlantic expedition to *not* land on Cape Breton, rather than around the island in Guysborough, I wonder if this isn't a more likely location. The island's craggy hills might have struck the Scottish knight and his retinue—just as it would thousands of their compatriots four centuries later—as a home away from home.

It was the French, however, who first established a permanent European presence on the northeast corner of Cape Breton, and they used Louisbourg to control the Gulf of St. Lawrence, until the British captured the fort in 1758. Like the towns of Advocate Harbour and Guysborough, the fishing village outside the fort now has a waterfront plaque commemorating Sinclair's voyage. The evidence that Sinclair might have visited these fog-enshrouded environs lies behind Louisbourg's walls: a humble artillery piece called a *petrerra*. This primitive cannon came into use around the time Sinclair was supposed to have made his voyage, but the gun was quickly supplanted by more advanced technologies. One such *petrerra* was pulled from Louisbourg harbour in the 19th century—proof, according to Pohl and other Henryites, of a pre-French European presence on the island.

I wander among the reconstructed warehouses and mansions of Fortress Louisbourg, dodging the attentions of the costumed animators, before I meet with site historians Sandy Balcom and Bill O'Shea. They seem a little cautious; they've been dealing with Sinclair fans for years, and relations are strained. When I first called the fort and mentioned my interest in Prince Henry and his supporters, one expert spat: "I *hate* those guys!" Balcom and O'Shea are a bit more diplomatic.

"I think that maybe he did come here, but there's nothing here to prove it," says Balcom. "I don't discount the possibility, but I don't believe it either."

So what about the gun?

The *petrerra*, explains Balcom, would have been easy for even a reasonably talented blacksmith to make. "You didn't need a foundry to build these things," he says. "It's possible that a local blacksmith in the fort might have made them and sold them to privateers on the side."

O'Shea suggests another reason why the cannon doesn't prove Sinclair visited the island. Versatile weapons like *petrerras* didn't fall out of use just because newer and better guns came along, he says. "It's like you're on the beach and you find a 1960 nickel buried in the sand. It's still good currency. You don't know that it was dropped in 1960 —all you know is that it probably wasn't dropped five minutes ago."

Even O'Shea occasionally feels the strain between the local romance of the Sinclair myth and his own professional training. "I'd love this to be the landfall of Prince Henry Sinclair—I think it would be great for this area—but the proof's not there."

The two skeptics take me to the fort's archaeology building, home to the real relics and ruins of Fortress Louisbourg. The *petrerra* sits next to glass cases of 18th-century china, and the fluorescent light reveals its every rust pit and dent. I bend down to take a closer look. I don't know what I'm hoping to find. "Product of Scotland" emblazoned on the barrel? A MCCCLXXXXVIII stamp missed by everyone else? I see only black metal.

That's it then. The *petrerra* isn't a smoking gun, while the smoking mountain could have been from coal or even fog—neither of which is in short supply on either side of the Atlantic. The spring of pitch has been turned into a field of dreams, Oak Island refuses to give up its ghosts, and Prince Henry Sinclair remains as much of a mystery as when I started. I feel the Grail slipping from my grasp.

TWO MONTHS later, I'm standing behind the town library in Westford, Massachusetts, awaiting the Keeper of the Knight. I imagined a willowy Liv Tyler look-alike in a hooded cloak, but the Keeper turns out to be a petite 50-something library volunteer named Elizabeth Lane. She's originally from the Isle of Man, not far from Prince Henry's domains, and has agreed to show me what many think is the most solid piece of evidence linking Sinclair to the New World. To colonial ears, her English accent adds an air of authority to her courtly tale—although her version of the journey is more American Dream than mediaeval romance.

"The Templars were looking for a secure place to worship," she explains. "They were completely persecuted in Europe. It takes a long time to plan a mission like this, and they knew where they were going."

The part of New England in which Westford lies is replete with what Lane calls "sacred places." These include the equinoctial standing stones in Salem, New Hampshire (marketed as "America's Stonehenge"), and the Newport Tower in Rhode Island, which supposedly predates English settlement and measures up to Masonic concepts of "sacred geometry." According to Lane, Sinclair and his men would have known from their Templar connections how to find these places. After leaving Nova Scotia, they travelled down the Atlantic seaboard, sailed up the Merrimack River, headed up Stoney Brook and then landed at the foot of the hill on which Westford now sits.

Today, the main attraction in Westford, a sleepy town of 18,000, is the "knight" for whom Elizabeth acts as official guardian. We make our way down Depot Street to a spot where a length of chain prevents people from getting too close to a shelf of exposed gneiss next to the sidewalk. About 50 years ago, an etching was uncovered on the rock here, and rubbings suggest that it's an effigy of Sir James Gunn, one of Sinclair's retainers. Pohl thought the Sinclair expedition had climbed Prospect Hill to get their bearings and that on the march up, Gunn died, probably of a heart attack. (The hill is steep, and the poor schmuck would have been wearing a chain-mail shirt.) According to Pohl, his comrades hastily punched a memorial to him into the stone: Gunn is pictured in full armour, holding a broken sword (signifying his death) and his family crest. Recently, someone painted Gunn's shield as a visualization aid.

I stare at the rock.

"I think it's in the eye of the beholder, I really do," the Keeper apologizes.

Not this beholder.

The Knight's Keeper leaves me, still unconvinced, and I wander down to Stoney Brook. In the Grail romances, Sir Galahad only became worthy of his quest after meditating in the woods. He lived there as a hermit for years, but I only have a day before my flight leaves. I'll take what I can get. I follow a footpath along the banks of the brook—high even in late summer—as it meanders south towards the Merrimack. I try to envision a boatload of Scottish soldiers pushing their way up the waterway, tired, hungry, sweltering in their armour. I can't. I've exhausted my suspension of disbelief. Before I left Louisbourg, the two government historians showed me an article that convincingly argued the whole Sinclair story is a giant hoax, that Antonio Zeno likely never left Venice during the period when he was supposedly cavorting throughout Nova Scotia with a wandering Scotsman and his holy contraband.

On my way back up the hill, I decide to give Gunn one last try. I stare into the gneiss—it's a little like those eye-straining posters whose 3D images lie buried within a kaleidoscope of pixellation. And then something appears. It's a face—eyes and mouth askew, but definitely a face. I'm thrilled. I've finally seen my connection to Sinclair, however faint, through 600 years of history that has denied his achievement. I grab my notebook to make a quick sketch.

When I look back, he's gone.

THE MAN
WITH TUNNEL VISION

MIKE RANDOLPH

MAY/JUNE 2001

YOU'RE WALKING THROUGH the forest when you find it. A small pond that you know is not just a small pond. It's too round, too perfect, too near the other ones. This is a pond with a hole in it, like a washbasin full of water with a drain at the bottom—a sinkhole, where a subterranean water-filled tunnel came too near the surface and the roof collapsed. You had already found others nearby. You knew there had to be more.

You scan the portal to this other world of yours. It's dark in there, really dark, dark in a way that other people don't understand, black and unearthly. You dive in, kick to the bottom, find the opening, squeeze through. And then your helmet-mounted flashlight illuminates the walls of this cave for the first time. The first time ever.

Clinging to the rocky floor, you struggle against the current, hauling yourself along the tortuous passages, listening only to the gurgle of rushing water and the Darth Vader hiss of the regulator as you suck gas from your tanks. As alone as it's possible to be. The tunnel is too small to carry the tanks on your back like a normal diver, so you wear them on your hips; four tanks, each with its own regulator. When it gets really tight you detach the tanks and push them through the constriction first, squeezing through later, always paying out a thin line of nylon to show the way back. One wrong turn here means you won't ever see the sun again. Such a thin line.

The current is strong, and the water is cold and dark as Coca-Cola. You've been swimming for nearly a kilometre, through tunnels that braid like veins under the earth's hide. And you think: nobody has ever been here before. Nobody. And you love that feeling. You need it.

Will you discover yet another sinkhole? Or will you have to go back? When a third of your air is gone, the decision will be made for you. Go back. That's the rule: a third to go in, a third for the way back, a third for safety. You don't have to think about checking your air—you just do it because you've programmed it in. It's instinct now. You're in control. Focussed, singularly attuned to what you are doing, the way you always are, the way you are when you sit at home in front of the computer working on some paper, or entering some data, or replying to some e-mail and your wife, Dana, comes into the room and talks to you but you don't hear anything. You've always been like this.

Soon, light. The cave has been going up, the passage getting silty—you knew what was coming and then, yes, you're on the bottom of a river, and not just any river, but the mighty Ottawa. It *does* connect, you think. Fighting the current, you crawl across the bottom towards the shore, pop your head up out of the water. You take off your mask and spit out your regulator, draw a deep breath and look around to see just where the heck you are.

And just like that you're back in the world again.

TORONTO, MID-FEBRUARY on a grey, cold, sleety day. Dr. David Sawatzky, Canada's foremost cave diver, greets me with a crushing handshake and leads me through the antiseptic hallways of the Defence and Civil Institute of Environmental Medicine (DCIEM), a laboratory operated by the Department of National Defence where he has worked as a teacher and leading researcher on diving medicine for the past 10 years. Forty-seven years old, Sawatzky is trim and broad-shouldered with Popeye forearms, large weathered hands and piercing blue eyes. He wears his hair buzzed short, military style, though Major Sawatzky retired from the forces a few years back.

Sawatzky consults for the military now, keeping a small office here, with a computer, of course, and bookshelves lined with medical papers and binders detailing things like just how many nitrogen bubbles in the bloodstream it takes before a person is fatally bent. Along one wall lies a doctor's gurney, with the standard crinkly paper covering and a stethoscope hanging off a blood-pressure meter. These are for the guinea pigs— DCIEM is the only military lab in Canada where researchers use humans in experiments. "Good pay if you're a student, I guess," he smiles. Or sometimes just good fun—Sawatzky has volunteered himself when even money-hungry students have declined the tough assignments, such as sitting in a steel tub of ice-cold water until your core temperature drops, then letting someone cut out a plug of leg muscle so they can study it under a microscope.

By the door to the office hangs a map of Sawatzky's most recent project, the Ottawa River caves. Standing in front of it, he traces the passages with his thick fingers, recalling his explorations into the earth's plumbing system. "Here the current is way too strong to swim against. It *rips* through here.

"Here we laid some line in 1996 and when we came back the next year it was buried under a rock. I measured it. It was 18 inches high, 20 feet wide and a hundred feet long. The next year there was another collapse—five times that much rock. That kind of thing only happens every few thousand years.

"This passage was tight and filled with silt. After a few kicks with my fins, visibility would be reduced to zero. Zero. I'd be swimming along and suddenly bump into a three-foot sturgeon, scaring the heck out of both of us. They're pretty strong. They can boot you in the face, bam!" he says, punching me in the shoulder. "Hard, like that."

While most cave divers don't take the time to produce maps, Sawatzky feels that swimming through caves is meaningless if he doesn't carefully survey each passage. So for every five metres of forward progress, he had to stop, swim to the other side of the tunnel, measure the distance, the depth, take a compass reading, and record it all on his slate. Occasionally, he would discover whole new passages and suddenly there was more work to do, more cave to chart, but that never bothered Sawatzky. It would have suited him just fine if it went on forever.

But discovering the entrance to a cave and being able to dive it were sometimes two different things. Since some of the entrances to the cave passages were actually on the bottom of the river; the current filled them with massive piles of debris—rocks and gravel and waterlogged timber who-knows-how-old. On some trips, Sawatzky and his team spent more time cave digging than cave diving. But that never bothered him either. One of the divers who worked with Sawatzky on the project, Ralph Hoskins, later told me, "It was incredibly difficult, working in the water, pulling out these massive logs. But David loved it. No matter how big a log was, David got it out of there one way or another." Nothing could stop him. On one digging expedition, Sawatzky slipped and fell with his full weight on his arm, breaking a bone in his elbow. But he wasn't about to let that get in the way of doing what he set out to do. Pain was just an inconvenience. So he kept hauling out those logs any way he could, leaving the visit to the hospital until later, when he was finished.

After 14 years of diving and exploring the system, Sawatzky's unrelenting drive finally subdued it. So here is the map, in colour, detailed in meticulous precision. And it is *complete*. Sawatzky made sure of that, returning to the system even after they had finished, again and again, finding nothing each time except for the reassurance that every single cave entrance and every diveable passage had been checked out. Today, at more than 10 kilometres long, it's the largest known cave system in Ontario.

HOW MANY times have people said, "What are you, crazy?" You don't know. A lot, anyway. You try to make them understand, but they never do. It's just the way you are. How can you explain that? Even as a kid, you could never sit still. You never even slept in. You were always off in the woods, climbing trees; you loved climbing trees. That feeling of adventure, excitement, challenge. There weren't too many trees around Bowden, Alberta, you hadn't climbed. And canoeing? You'd covered 6,000 kilometres of Albertan waterways before you were 20.

The couple who adopted you, they never really understood, either. Your dad, he just shook his head. He was a conservative man, devoutly Christian. He'd come home from his job at the facility for wayward youths and half the time you weren't there. Off in the woods. *Again.* But he never said anything. He thought it was curious, this fire in you, but he let it burn. When you went for road trips with the family, Dad would pull over when you saw a tree or a cliff you wanted to climb. Your mom and sister would wait in the car while Dad kept an eye on you, shaking his head.

And then you discovered caving. In the newspaper, your dad had seen something about some dry caves near Jasper, told you about it, and soon every moment that could be stolen from something else was spent caving. You had that rope from the outdoor store, no real idea how to use it, and you just went, dragging your friends along. No helmets, just toques to dull the hits. Oh, it was low-tech all right, but so what? You still pushed a lot of new passage like that. That feeling, that experience of seeing some place that nobody had ever seen before, it consumed you. Soon you found new caves and you had to explore them, too. The fire never dimmed, not even in winter. Why would you stop caving just because the snow cover was three-feet deep? You had skis, and it was easier to ski in anyway.

Then, a few years later, you discovered Vancouver Island. More caves than anywhere else in Canada. Shangri-La. There was that day in 1978 when you and your friends discovered the Benson River Gorge Caves. That's where the fire got even hotter. Walking, running down that narrow passage when suddenly you fell into water up to your neck. Water so clear you never even saw it. It was the end of the cave for you, but it wasn't the end of the cave—it kept going, disappearing down a water-filled sump. It was so frustrating, being stopped like that. And that's when you *knew.* Someday, you'd be a cave diver. Someday, you'd come back to the island, right here, find out what was next, and then what was next after that. The fire burned hot. Not even water could put it out.

IN CANADA fewer than a dozen people dive caves on a regular basis, but there are places in the world where cave diving has become relatively popular, namely Florida, a state honeycombed with huge passages filled with warm water as clear as Evian. Unlike the sumps in Florida, however, wet caves in Canada are brutally cold, much more technically demanding (tighter passages), and visibility is often no more than 10 feet, as opposed to a hundred feet or more in places like Florida. Also, while in Florida you can literally drive to a sinkhole (some of them even have wooden stairs leading into the water), the approaches to Canadian caves are almost always arduous. The entrance to Vancouver Island's Mystery Cave, for example, lies up a rough trail that gains almost 700 feet of elevation. It's a minor mountaineering expedition just to get to the start—each diver has to haul more than 200 pounds of equipment, which means ferrying two truly backbreaking loads up steep trails. Once at the entrance, there's 600 feet of dry cave, then a 250-foot-long dive, then another 3,000 feet of dry passage to get to the next sump, which is where the real adventure begins. Castleguard Cave, in Banff National Park, is not much better. Just to get to the cave entails skiing 20 kilometres up the Saskatchewan Glacier on the Columbia Icefield, crossing a meadow, then dropping down 300 feet. The branch that Sawatzky explored then forced him to crawl on hands and knees through tight passage for a kilometre—wearing all his gear, at 7,000 feet of altitude, all to dive in water only one degree above freezing.

Aside from being merely exhausting, Sawatzky's dives are also extremely hazardous. Oftentimes, he has to swim in water so turbid he can't see the beam of his flashlight—can't even tell whether it's on or not. This, in places where getting lost is easy, and usually fatal. Then there's depth. For every 50 feet down, the narcotic effect of nitrogen equals a stiff martini on an empty stomach. In the controlled environment of the military's diving chamber at DCIEM, Sawatzky was once pressurized to 300 feet on air, almost three times the limit imposed on sport divers. "If that's anything like what street drugs do, then I understand why people take them. The air at that depth was so thick I could actually hear the blood going through my ears. I could have happily stayed right there listening to it forever, until I died."

But narcosis is not that comforting on a real dive. In 1997, Sawatzky pushed a passage in Vancouver Island's Devil's Spring, a satellite of the Devil's Bath system, to a depth of 202 feet. In an article he wrote describing the dive, Sawatzky said the narcosis was "frightening." He's not one to share his emotions very often; if Sawatzky says it was frightening, it was *frightening.*

After that experience, he resorted to using trimix, a breathing mixture that replaces some of the nitrogen with helium, thereby reducing the narcotic effect. It's a very advanced technique (Sawatzky's a certified instructor) and it worked quite well. But he feels the future lies in rebreather technology.

The navy has used rebreathers for decades, but now recreational and technical divers are joining their ranks. With regular scuba equipment, a diver draws air from the tanks and exhales it through a regulator into the water. With a rebreather, the diver's exhalations get fed into a compartment that removes the carbon dioxide and sends the rest back to the diver in a closed circuit—no bubbles. Since human lungs absorb only a tiny amount of the oxygen in a single breath, the diver need only carry a small amount. The advantages are that rebreathers increase range and decrease decompression time dramatically.

As a result, though the cheapest closed-circuit rebreathers on the market cost $10,000, they're becoming more and more popular. But rebreathers are highly sophisticated devices and require total understanding, as well as regular, comprehensive maintenance. "Quite a few people have already died using them," says Sawatzky. "And more will die in the future. There are more ways to kill yourself on a rebreather than you can imagine."

So why does he use them if they're so dangerous? Like everything related to cave diving, Sawatzky has thought this one over carefully. "Risk is different from danger. Risk is a reflection of how many things can go wrong and how serious the consequences will be. Danger is a function of the person doing the activity. Whether it's diving rebreathers or cave diving itself, for someone who is highly trained it's not terribly dangerous. For someone who doesn't know what they're doing it's suicidal." In an article he wrote for *Diver* magazine, Sawatzky states that people who dive with rebreathers "have to be just a bit obsessive and compulsive." Sawatzky certainly fits the bill. On his new rebreather, he will have already logged enough hours to become an instructor by July.

"He's a perfectionist," says Sawatzky's wife, Dana. As a Ph.D. in clinical psychology, she doesn't use the term loosely. But it doesn't take academic training to see that he sets extremely high standards for himself—and for others. Though he's patient, talking with him can also be intimidating. He chooses his words carefully, with confidence and directness. "You asked me that last time," he'd say to me when I repeated a question. There is no condescension in his tone, merely a flat statement of fact. "He scares some people," says Dana. "But he's a lot more social than he used to be. That said, he's still too honest and he's not big on tact. He just says whatever he thinks, and if you don't like it, too bad."

Dana learned this about David the first time they met. She was working as a commercial diver at the time (she's now a Toronto Police patrol officer in the infamous Jane-Finch corridor) and while diving a wreck in Lake Ontario, she got bent. The hospital didn't know quite what to do with her, so they sent her home. Knowing she was bent, Dana called DCIEM and ended up talking to David. Furious, David called the hospital and gave them a choice: either treat Dana in the dive chamber or he would do it himself, then report the hospital for incompetence.

"He doesn't suffer fools gladly," says his diving partner Ralph Hoskins. "God help you if you do something stupid. He'll let you know it."

Like most perfectionists, Sawatzky thrives on setting lofty goals, achieving them, then immediately setting new ones, achieving those, and so on and so on. Halfway isn't good enough. Three-quarters isn't good enough. It's a constant struggle for achievement. "When he sets out to learn something," says Dana, "he learns it. He studies it, gets to know it, practises it. His memory is unbelievable. I'll ask him a question about something and he'll take a few seconds, then come up with the answer. Then I'll find out that the last time he thought about it was in first-year med school."

Gripped by a military drive, Sawatzky never lets a moment pass without a fight. In addition to working at DCIEM, he studies caving research, maps his explorations, details every dive he ever does in a journal. For relaxation, he reads medical journals. Or he writes for them. Aside from papers related to hyperbaric medicine, he's also written hundreds of technical diving articles for publications such as the *Journal of Subterranean*

Metaphysics, Underwater Speleology and *Canadian Caver,* and he also submits a regular column for *Diver* magazine. He teaches diving to law-enforcement agencies, and for the military, he writes the manuals. He's on the board of advisors for seven diving-related associations and belongs to no fewer than eight societies of diving professionals. And then there's the one weekend a month he assists with emergency surgery at Humber River Regional Hospital. He's also a qualified flight surgeon, an accredited witness for the Coroner of Ontario in diving-accident investigations, and an instructor of advanced cave-rescue techniques. And then there's the cave diving itself. He spends at least two months a year on expeditions.

"He does everything," says Dana. "It's always something. Collecting rocks or coins or stamps. Or work around the house—he can plumb, do carpentry, dry wall, electrical. He's wound all the time. He's always got this edge to him. Sometimes I look at him and say 'relax.' But he doesn't know how. His idea of relaxing is going into the backyard and chopping wood that he's hauled from some snarled-up sump." Part of her understands, but the other part seems genuinely mystified. "And he works out in the gym every day, but it's like nothing is enough for him. His idea of having fun is most people's idea of torture."

YOU'RE IN Tobermory, Ontario. You, Ric Browning, your long-time caving partner, and the wives. The girls had a little dive vacation planned and Dana said, Come along if you want. But no caving. Open-water stuff only.

Okay, you said. No caving. But then you're up there and staring at the entrance to Little Stream Cave. Well, you thought, let's see whether it'll go. Just a little look-see for another time.

So you and Ric check it out. The sump is at the end of a dry passage. You dive down to the bottom, pry away the rocks and brush out the silt until it's big enough to get through.

Soon you're past this first restriction, in a small water-filled room. Visibility is bad thanks to your excavations, but you find a crack where the cave continues. It's tight. You put your feet in, but the passage turns off at a sharp angle. You contort yourself in an attempt to fit through, but the hole's just too small.

You go back up, tell Ric it doesn't go. He says he wants to check it out. Fine. Take my tank, you say. It's only down 300 psi; there's still enough left for a quick look. So Ric disappears down the sump. You hear the tank clanging against the rock walls, you can see the bubbles from his exhalations. But soon the noises end. The bubbles are gone, too. *What's going on? Ric's bigger than me—there's no way he could have made it through if I couldn't.* So you wait. Still, no more bubbles. Ten minutes pass, then 20, then 30. *What the hell's he doing? He doesn't have enough air to be screwing around like this.* Something's not right.

Time to get down there yourself. But Ric has the only tank, so you have to leave, get another one. It takes an agonizingly long time. Finally you scramble back into the cave, warding off bad thoughts.

You burrow into the water-filled room feet first, but Ric's not there. The thought of squirming through that crack frightens you, but you try anyway. It's a mess down here, like swimming in a chocolate milkshake. You struggle, more desperate now. How did he do it? Time is ticking away. But your main light is weak, your second is dead, and the third one is working only intermittently. *Shit, shit, shit.* Your small tank doesn't have much air left, either. You can't go on like this. You go back.

Ric had 45 minutes of air, tops. He's been down now for two hours. The cave was going deeper—just about no chance Ric would find an air pocket. He didn't have an exploration line—he must have gotten lost. *Damn it, Ric. You weren't supposed to go in. You shouldn't have gone in.*

Outside the cave, Ric's wife, Sandra, is sitting on the boat with Dana, soaking in the sun like nothing's wrong. Then they see you walk out of the cave, alone. And they know enough about cave diving to know something's gone horribly wrong.

You swim out to the boat. You want to tell them it's okay but it's not okay. "What happened?" asks Dana. You suck it up and tell her. "Ric went in and I couldn't follow him. He didn't have much air." Then she asks you what the cave was doing and you say it was going down. "So that's it?" she asks. "Yeah," you say. "That's it."

Fear washes over Sandra like a wave. She starts shaking. *Oh my God.* She starts crying. You see the terror in her eyes and then there's an ache in your stomach that you've never felt before. You grab the marine radio and try to call for help, but it's not working. *Why is this happening? It was working before, just this morning.* You motor to shore, jump out before the boat slides against the sand, tear up the beach towards some people. Somebody drives you to the police station. But what are they going to do? They're not cave divers. In an emergency they've been instructed to call *you*.

Soon, the Coast Guard joins the Ontario Provincial Police on the scene. But the rescue is still in your hands, so you focus. It's what you do best. You organize the operation, asking the help of two cave divers who happen to be there with all the right equipment.

Six hours after Ric first went down, you're once again at the sump entrance. One of the other cave divers tries to go down first. The rest of you wait, listening to him bang around. But soon he's back. He couldn't even make it into the water-filled room.

It could end right here, but you don't want to give up. Can't. So you go down again. This time, you try to get past the second restriction facing a different way, so you can bend your body around the corner. Slowly, you scrape your way in, thinking, God, this is tight. You're wondering whether you'll be able to make it back out. You could stop right now, go back, say you just couldn't make it. They wouldn't question you. You tried, they'll say. Even if Ric had found an air pocket, he'd be dead by now, drysuit or no drysuit—the water is seven degrees. Ric made a mistake. It's not your fault.

But that's your friend down there. If you go back now you'll have to live the rest of your life not knowing. And you can't do that.

Soon, your feet kick in open water. You enter a big void, shine the lights around, preparing to bump into Ric's corpse in the two-inch visibility. But there's only darkness.

Then, as you swim farther on, you see the roof of the cave rises upward. There's an air bell. An air bell. Unbelievable. You swim towards it, surface. The chamber is 10 feet long. You scan around with your light, but there's nothing.

Then, from behind you: "It's about fucking time you got here!" You spin around to see Ric completely out of the water, wedged into a nook. He's alive. You take your mask off, smile a funny smile. Alive. It's like it's not real.

When you exit the cave for the last time, you tell people Ric's right behind you. There's a pause, like it doesn't compute, like *huh?* It takes a while. Everybody thought they were on a body recovery, and then no, Ric's alive. No cheer went up, no fist pumping. It was all too draining for that. It's over, that's all anybody can think. It's over. One day, on a day much different from this one, the Governor General will hand you the Star of Courage, one of Canada's highest medals of bravery.

Later that night, Sandra hugs you, everybody hugs you, patting you on the back, thanking you, crying. But you don't say much. You've got nothing left. You're just waiting for the day to end. Two days later, though, it sinks in. As you sit at your desk, you start shaking. You remember the helplessness, the fear, the lack of control. And it scares you, deeply.

"SOMEHOW IT'S supposed to fit in here," says David Sawatzky. It's a Monday night in March and I'm at the Sawatzky home in North York. He's packing for a trip to Florida, where he'll be able to get some more time on his rebreather, but he can't seem to fit it in the crate that came with it. With the rebreather's turtle-like shell on the bottom, we try to tuck in the hoses and breathing tubes, but it just won't go.

"I'll figure it out later," he says, and with that we walk into his equipment room, which is a giant walk-in closet in the basement, filled with a neatly ordered arsenal of diving equipment. Thick pile union suits, wetsuits, drysuits, tanks of every size, piles of rope crocheted into perfect coils, masks, regulators, exploration lines, strange-looking tools. As he ferries pieces of equipment into the rec room, I ask him, cautiously, how long it took Ric to get back into cave diving.

"One week later," he says dryly. "It was our annual trip to Vancouver Island," he adds, as if that explained everything. But Ric accompanied David on only a few dives. The truth is it took many months for both of them to work out the psychological trauma, and another couple of years before things got back to normal. But Dana elaborated further. "I still don't think Ric's completely over it." Nonetheless Ric still dives on a regular basis.

Though the incident in Tobermory frightened Sawatzky, it never slowed him down. His latest project is the Devil's Bath system near Port

McNeill—the same cave system that includes the Benson River Gorge Caves, where his fire for cave diving was first ignited over 20 years ago.

On Vancouver Island, conditions for cave formation are nearly perfect: limestone bedrock—easily eroded into cave passages—and lots of rain to do the work. But diving here is ultra-demanding, even more so than the Ottawa River caves. While the water in caves on the Island is much clearer, the passages are far, far deeper. In 1999, while diving the Devil's Spring, Sawatzky set a record for the deepest-ever cave dive in Canada. Sawatzky and two other divers had been laying exploration lines for the previous five days. Then, on the final dive, Sawatzky reached a fearsome 262 feet.

Of course, for him, that's still not quite good enough. The passage was going down, and he thinks it may bottom out at over 300 feet before it comes back to the surface who knows where.

"I'm going back to finish it this August with the rebreather," he says. That'll be after he dives in Florida, England, Malta and the Caymans, where he's planning a dive on his rebreather to over 400 feet.

"And once we finish up in the Devil's Bath," he says, "there are lots of other systems on Vancouver Island that are too far back in the bush to dive with tanks. But with the rebreather, it's a different story."

A different story, and yet the same story. David Sawatzky just doesn't know how to take a break. "It's addictive," he says. "Going where nobody has gone before—that's what it's all about. Once you've experienced what that's like, you just can't give it up."

OUT OF THE HOLE

BRUCE RAMSAY

JANUARY/FEBRUARY 2002

0:58:87

They don't even see the finish line. As the sled carves around the final corner, the driver turtles beneath the fibreglass cowling, squeezes the steering rings and counts off in his head the last stretch to the timing beam: one-one-thousand, two-one-thousand, three-one-thousand... On cue, the brakeman rocks back and drives the rake-like blade into the ice. The sled lurches hard to the right as it slows. Ice chips fly in their faces, and the chill air rips tears from their eyes as the four bobsledders crane their heads to catch sight of the electronic scoreboard. Time freezes on the board.

FOURTH PLACE. After four runs in two days, an accumulated time of 3:54:12 leaves the Canadian team a mere eleven-hundredths of a second out of the medals and twenty-two-hundredths away from the gold. Squeezed into the sled, a disappointed Ken LeBlanc watches as the clock resets and their time is forgotten.

A day before the final race, LeBlanc was sitting at a table in the Olympic cafeteria with Prince Albert of Monaco, captain of his small nation's bobsled team and unofficial ambassador of the sport. The two bobsledders—one a lean, patrician blue blood, the other a stocky, tattooed Metis— swapped stories from their high-speed escapades, on and off the track.

LeBlanc's next engagement with royalty arrives just 12 days after the closing ceremonies in Albertville, France: an invitation from the Court of Queen's Bench to stay in a 10′ × 10′ cell at the Ottawa Regional Detention Centre. Back home from the 1992 Winter Games, LeBlanc falls into the middle of a murder investigation when crown prosecutors charge him with threatening a witness. For 14 months, he will sit alone in a jail cell, refusing to cooperate, and wonder how his dreams of Olympic glory could fall to pieces in just a blink of an eye.

THE FIRST time I heard of Ken LeBlanc was when I started bobsledding in the winter of 1993. Too many afternoons watching *Wide World of Sports* had filled my imagination with the names of exotic alpine towns like St. Moritz, Cortina and Winterberg—the icy homes to the most exciting 60 seconds in winter sport. And although I was well past any sort of athletic prime, I was delighted to discover a recreational bobsled league in Calgary where hacks like me could live out their fantasies.

The Canadian bobsled community is small, so I ended up "competing" beside some of the best sledders in the world. That first year, all I heard about the Ken LeBlanc story were fragments: "Some guy... this fucking hood... had killed... threatened to kill... had been killed... and was in jail... doing life... on the lam." Still, I reserved judgement for four years. Only then did I decide that I didn't like LeBlanc.

In 1997, the national program was coming off three successful World Cup seasons. An upbeat atmosphere reigned at the practice track and hopes were high for the upcoming Winter Games. Dave MacEachern, a good friend of mine, was favoured to be the brakeman at Nagano. But Ken LeBlanc suddenly emerged after more than four years of rumour-plagued retirement, and his return meant that Dave might not get the Olympic ride he deserved. I wasn't the only one to wonder what right LeBlanc had to disrupt the national program at the precise moment it seemed poised to reach the top. He was a common street fighter, with little respect for the law, and had no business representing our country—or taking Dave's hard-won position in the Canada One sled.

When I first encountered him, LeBlanc lived up to his reputation. He was large, aggressive, cold, hard, distant—an iceberg of a man drifting through the fragile national team. Later that year, when he walked away from the Nagano Games amid yet another storm of controversy, I felt vindicated in my judgement of him.

I'M WAITING, in the living room of his Calgary home, to hear Ken Le-Blanc tell his version of the dark myth that has shadowed his career. He finishes up a phone call and wanders back into the room. Built like a line-backer—6′1″, 235 pounds—he walks with a gait that's perpetually on the balls of his feet, predator-like, cocked for the final pounce. His complexion, narrow-set eyes and long hair bear witness to his native blood. Tattoos cover his body—dragons, damsels, warriors, a miserable face etched across his back to prevent blindside attacks. I don't expect to see his photo on a Wheaties box anytime soon.

LeBlanc describes to me how his days revolve around the steady, often tedious process of reaching peak conditioning and preparing for the upcoming Winter Games in Salt Lake City. Mornings, he heads to push practice; then he's off to the gym with his strength coach. Afternoons are taken up with physical therapy or massage and perhaps more sprints. If time allows, he'll hop on his rebuilt custom Harley and disappear into the nearby mountains. He spends most evenings at home with his dogs, an American Staffordshire bull terrier and a Rottweiler, watching *The Simpsons* or a movie on TV.

"I'm pretty happy cuddled up with my dogs," LeBlanc tells me. "You can't beat the unconditional love of a pet."

I bite my lip at his confession. *This* is the bad boy of Canadian bob-sledding?

LeBlanc grew up in the Carling/Merivale area of Ottawa, a tough neighbourhood he describes as "the projects"—and a far cry from the national capital's tulip-lined tourist image. "Someone could come along and punch your lights out just because they didn't like the way you looked," he recalls. When LeBlanc was eight years old, he was jumped by a group of older kids, who fractured his ribs and left him to crawl four blocks home. He learned how to take a beating and how to dish one out—to protect himself, his friends or his family.

LeBlanc's mother had moved to Ottawa after her family's farm in Carlsbad Springs, Ontario, burned down. Ann Brown met the local paperboy, Lee LeBlanc, a Metis with ties to the Six Nations Confederacy, and a few months later they married. Ken was born February 13, 1968. He was followed two years later by Bryan—now serving a life sentence in Stony Mountain Penitentiary—and then, in 1977, by Mark, who has since joined his oldest brother on the Canadian bobsled team. Despite economic hardships, Lee and Ann LeBlanc did their best to keep the family together. Ken's father worked two full-time jobs and took courses part-time. "We didn't see him a whole lot," says LeBlanc. "He did what he had to do—his work lifted us out of the projects."

At school, while the other kids daydreamed about playing for the Montreal Canadiens or the Ottawa Rough Riders, LeBlanc drew inspiration watching the 1976 Games in Montreal—especially Cuban runner Alberto Juantorena, the gold medallist in the 400 and 800 metres. "When I watched Juantorena on TV, I remember telling my family that I'd be in the Olympics one day," he recalls. The young LeBlanc would race anyone he could and starred in every sport he played—track and field, football, wrestling, basketball, water polo. He was even an Ontario finalist in badminton. I struggle to imagine the hulking, tattooed athlete flailing away at a birdie.

"Hey," LeBlanc protests, "I was a sneaky badminton player!"

In 1987, Chris Lori, a former decathlete who'd switched to bobsledding, was developing talent for the upcoming Winter Games in Calgary. He'd heard stories about a young running phenom from Ottawa with long hair who'd warm up for his meets in cut-off jeans. When Lori saw LeBlanc race, he was struck by the strength-to-weight ratio of the 170-pound runner—his ability to generate power comparable to that of athletes with 20 to 30 pounds more muscle mass. Perfect bobsledding material.

The national bobsled program took him right out of his seat at Laurentian High School. "I was sitting in class, drooling on my desk, and I got a call to see if I wanted to push a sled," recalls LeBlanc with a laugh. "They were supposed to wait until I finished high school, but the call came. I picked up my books, got my plane ticket and flew out to Calgary." He was whisked away to practise running and jumping in sleds at a hockey rink. Five days after touching down in Cowtown, he was racing in a World Cup race.

The speed and balls-out nature of bobsledding hooked LeBlanc immediately, and the next year he competed in the Calgary Olympics in one of Canada's two four-man sleds. While Canada failed to medal at its home track, LeBlanc caught the attention of both coaches and athletes. His explosive starts, combined with Chris Lori's improving skills as a driver, helped Canadian bobsledders rise in the world rankings over the next few years until they were competing with the very best European sledders. "Ken arrives and we start consistently moving up to top-five finishes," Lori explains. "Without these results, we don't receive any profile—no profile, no recruiting." A 14-year bobsledding veteran, Lori believes LeBlanc is the finest athlete who has raced for Canada.

In 1990, LeBlanc and Lori needed a win in the final World Cup race at Cervina, Italy, to steal the four-man title from German über-slider Wolfgang Hoppe. The last time Lori had competed at the Cervina track, however, he'd failed to duck into the sled when it lost control and struck the track wall. The wreck put him out of competition for the season and left a six-inch scar down his left cheek. The memory of the accident only compounded the pressure of a potential title win and had been brought into further relief for the Canadian sliders when they'd crashed during their two-man run five days earlier and LeBlanc had fractured his collarbone. A lesser team might have splintered under the tensions of injury and uncertainty. "Everybody's sphincter is puckered when you race at Cervina," admits LeBlanc. "I knew that if we could push past the fear everyone else was feeling then we could win."

And that's just what the four-man crew did. The Canadians outpushed the German superstar by just under a tenth of a second. A lunchbox crew of good ol' Maple Leaf–wearing boys met the Old World veterans on their home ice and scrapped their way to the top. Most of Europe viewed the victory as a huge upset in a sport long dominated by Swiss, German and Austrian athletes. But back home in Canada, news of the win was met with a resounding, "Honey, what time is the Leafs game on?" To capture the attention of a nation still in a post–Ben Johnson malaise, the team would have to strike Olympic gold. Given their new status as world champions, that ambition seemed realistic. They'd get their chance in just two years at the Albertville Games.

0:27:53

The growl of the descent is deafening as the bobsled rockets on its four steel runners through a straightaway and towards a curve banked at 90 degrees. As the sled rides up the side, five Gs of force squeeze the crew—internal organs slam against the inside of the body, blood drains from the brain and the lungs compress until grunts are forced from each athlete. The sled flashes through the exit of the corner, and each racer jams his helmet firmly into the back of the person in front so it doesn't jackhammer too hard against his teammate's spine. The rushing air forces the acrid smell of muscle-warming balms through the sled. Wintergreen stings the eyes. They ignore the discomfort and try not to move or even breathe. The vehicle's balance is so precarious that the most minuscule shifting might send it careening out of control.

BOBSLEDDING CONFOUNDS people. To many observers, the sport seems like little more than a glorified toboggan race, its most enduring image that of the plucky Jamaican team from the movie *Cool Runnings*. The sight of four grown men spooning each other while separated by only a thin veneer of lycra has prompted more than a few snide comments. Despite our national success—two Olympic gold medals, numerous World Cup victories—Canadians know little about bobsledding and less about its athletes.

For centuries, Europeans used sleds, in one form or another, for recreation and transportation. But bobsled racing didn't officially begin until 1877 when sledders in Davos, Switzerland, attached a steering mechanism to a wooden toboggan. In 1897, in St. Moritz, the Swiss founded the first club for bobsledding—which took its new name from the unusual bobbing motion crews once used to accelerate—and the sport spread to winter resorts across Europe. By the turn of the century, more durable and sleek steel sleds had replaced their splinter-inducing forerunners. Swiss ski instructor Emile Cochand built Canada's first run at Montebello, Quebec, in 1911.

In 1924, in Chamonix, France, six teams competed in the four-man bobsled race—one of 14 events at the inaugural Winter Olympics. (The Swiss took gold.) The two-man event was introduced at the 1932 Games in Lake Placid, New York. Crashes were more common back then, and the atmosphere around the track had the feel of a stock-car race. In these salad days, the sport remained the pastime of those wealthy enough to gather at the alpine resorts where the tracks were built. These athletic dilettantes rarely trained for races: they simply rented or bought a sled, went for a few runs as a passenger and then took over the controls.

By the fifties, crews had clued into the profound effect mass has on velocity. At the 1952 Olympics, a German team of four, shall we say, Rubenesque sliders (averaging 250 pounds each) applied this simple law of physics to flatten the competition—not to mention terrorize finish-line workers. In response to the tubby Teutons, the Federation Internationale de Bobsleigh et de Tobogganning introduced a maximum-weight rule to move the emphasis from bulk back onto athleticism and stop the sport's slide into the ridiculous. Meanwhile, teams discovered the importance of the explosive push-start and began recruiting high-calibre—rather than just high-calorie—athletes.

While the bobsled's mechanics remained largely unchanged, the aerodynamics of the sled bodies continued to evolve. At the 1980 Olympics in Lake Placid, sleds were wide and flattened, with a profile like a whale shark, and could reach relatively safe speeds of around 130 kilometres per hour. By 1990, European designers had developed sleds with a missile-like appearance that could push upward of 170 kilometres per hour. Sleds are now bound by design standards of length and width to keep them within safe speeds. Inspectors ensure that the sleds have not been altered to add suspension or improve handling. They also check the shape of the bobsled's steel runners and determine that they haven't been heated prior to a run to make the sled travel faster.

With sled design standardized, the deciding variable of bobsled racing has become the ability of the athletes who push and drive the sled. Modern bobsledders are likely former track stars, football players, even professional wrestlers. Coaches try to develop a team that possesses both the explosive strength to accelerate the bobsled over the first 50 metres and the agility to leap into the speeding vehicle without knocking it off course.

While track designers have all but eliminated the chances of a sled launching out of the icy chute, bobsledding isn't without risk. Most injuries happen when the driver fails to bring the sled down at the exit of a turn and it tips over in a *Dukes of Hazzard* barrel roll. All a crew can do then is brace themselves inside the upside-down, out-of-control sled— still travelling faster than most cars on the Trans-Canada—and endure most of the flip on their backs, heads and necks until the sled skitters to a stop. Bobsledders rarely wear protection other than helmets, so the friction will burn any body parts that drag across the ice surface. And bailing out of a sled just isn't an option.

FOLLOWING THEIR breakthrough season, LeBlanc and his Canada One teammates were sliding well, with top-10 World Cup campaigns in 1991 and 1992, and had high hopes for a medal. In the four years since Calgary, the Canadians had developed into serious contenders, and even the European powerhouses were looking over their shoulders. But then the Canadian team suffered what has become a quadrennial tradition: the pre-Olympic meltdown.

Bobsledding decides winners by laughably small margins, so most teams avoid naming their Olympic teams until the last possible moment, to be sure not to exclude a crew member peaking just before the Games. In the month before Albertville, LeBlanc had been suffering nagging back spasms that required treatment, but he had raced in pain before. At a race prior to the Olympics, John Graham, one of his sledmates, approached members of the Canadian delegation and questioned whether the ailing LeBlanc should slide with Canada One. When he learned of this meeting, LeBlanc was incensed and—after confronting Graham—told the coaching staff that he refused to slide with anyone who doubted his readiness.

The crew stayed together until Albertville. But it was clear from their slowing push times that the quarrel was having a negative effect. Finally, coaches swapped the crews to split up the feuding members; Dave

MacEachern and Cal Langford joined Lori and LeBlanc in Canada One. It was the first time the foursome had raced together, yet they still managed to finish fourth, a whisper off the podium. LeBlanc still wonders what might have been if the Canadian team hadn't succumbed to infighting.

He didn't get too long to ponder that missed medal. "We got home from the Games and I spent a couple of days out on a frozen Ontario lake ice fishing," says LeBlanc. "Then I went to visit my brother in Ottawa and within 48 hours I was sitting in a cell."

He takes a deep breath and descends into the tale. "My brother is like me: we both do things 100 per cent—he just applied it to a different path. He worked for various Italian families who needed protection. He was—" LeBlanc pauses to consider his words. "—a bodyguard of sorts." Someone was killed. Bryan got charged. Ken came to his brother's defence.

The crown prosecutor claimed that Ken had threatened the star witness, and he was charged with obstruction of justice. LeBlanc says that by locking him up and scuttling his athletic career, the prosecutor hoped to pressure his brother into admitting to the crime, as investigators had only turned up circumstantial evidence. But the LeBlanc family loyalty didn't cause Bryan to roll over. Instead, it worked in reverse.

"I told them that I would sit," says Ken. That's what he did, alone in a cell, for the next 14 months.

LeBlanc had been in jail twice before, for less than six months each time, on assault convictions. "I knew what to expect, and there were others from the neighbourhood on the inside," he says. "But I had gone from sitting at a table having dinner with Prince Albert to a prison cell in less than 14 days. That's a pretty serious roller-coaster ride."

At his bail hearing, Ken's aggressiveness on the track and his ability to block out pain were thrown back at him as evidence he was capable of intimidating a witness. If so, he wasn't the only one. Ben Morin, then the executive director of Bobsleigh Canada, spoke as a character witness (along with Cal Langford) on LeBlanc's behalf. "Several members of the police made phone calls to my home and let me know that they weren't pleased that I was testifying," he recalls.

Bryan LeBlanc was convicted by a judge of first-degree murder and given a life sentence, which he's currently serving at Manitoba's Stony

Mountain Penitentiary. Less than 24 hours after his brother's conviction, all charges against Ken were dropped.

The biggest shock was yet to come. LeBlanc walked out of the Ottawa Regional Detention Centre and discovered that the Canadian Olympic establishment had washed their hands of him. In the 14 months he'd been detained, the Canadian team had moved on. Sheridan Baptiste, another Ottawa native, had joined Chris Lori's two-man sled, and Dave MacEachern, LeBlanc's surprise teammate in the almost-medal run at Albertville, had taken over the role of Canada's top brakeman. While LeBlanc was never officially cut from the program, his funding was withdrawn the moment he was charged. Still wobbling from the Ben Johnson controversy and the Dubin inquiry, Sport Canada administrators didn't want to be attached to another athlete-gone-bad story. "There was no innocent until proven guilty," says LeBlanc.

Not everyone shares LeBlanc's belief that Canadian sports authorities abandoned him. "We were unequivocally behind Ken," explains Ben Morin, now a director of the Canadian Olympic Association in Ottawa. "At the time [of his arrest], we were working to help Ken unlock his incredible potential as a leader to match his athletic strengths. We knew who Ken was, where he had come from, his neighbourhood and his family. The truth is that the average Canadian cannot relate to him."

Nevertheless, LeBlanc retired from bobsledding to a 120-acre plot of land, with his wife and her two children, in Beaverton, Ontario. He worked in construction and as a gardener, and helped start a gym in town.

"I certainly didn't feel free or released," says LeBlanc of walking away from the sport. "I had built up a lot of bitterness and dark feelings about the system, the country and people around me. I was pretty much finished with everything."

0:00:42

The racers explode out of the blocks, and the sled jumps as if it were violently rear-ended. Their bodies are airborne, eyes fixed on some spot downtrack as their feet catch the ice and power them up into a running position. Spikes claw the frozen track and ice chips rooster-tail as they power out of the starting gate, through a cacophony of coaches, wives, teammates, bullhorns, bells. The racers feel the handles begin to accelerate from their grasp and they give one last powerful exertion before swinging their legs into the sled, shuffling neatly into place like a deck of cards, and rumbling towards the first curve.

ON A warm September morning, I walk through the doors of the Ice House, a three-storey glass-faced warehouse beside the Trans-Canada Highway on Calgary's western edge. Inside this building—a $4.1-million facility opened in February 2001—are three artificially frozen tracks; two are designed for luge, the other for bobsledding. As I enter the practice area, I'm confronted by a 50-metre-long frozen downhill straightaway—an exact replica of the slope and surface of the Calgary bobsled track's start area—a small transition zone and then a steep uphill braking stretch. It's a good bet that Ken LeBlanc can be found here most mornings, honing his start technique. The theory: every tenth of a second gained at the start will translate into three-tenths of a second advantage at the finish line. In a sport where hundredths of a second can separate the heroes from the zeros, it's impossible to overstate the importance of the work being done here.

LeBlanc's teammates in the Canada One sled include driver Pierre Lueders, Lethbridge-born twins Ben and Matt Hindle, and Ken's youngest brother, Mark. As I watch the team practise, I can't help but consider the intimate dynamic in front of me. The politics of bobsledding can be a vicious game of musical chairs, as a handful of athletes jockey for one of the two or four positions in the leading sleds. Drivers will swap or dump crew members on slim notice if they think they can gain even a hundredth of a second—or for less competitive reasons. Rumours swirl through the starthouse and weight rooms about athletes who are hurt or out of shape, who are taking drugs, who have cut deals with coaches or are favoured by officials.

Most days at the track, it's impossible not to be dragged into this black hole. Yet as I watch Canada One train, they're like a family around the dinner table—there are insults, tensions and accusations but all are out in the open. That this team has remained largely unchanged for the past three seasons is testament to their loyalty. It must also be a record for a

Canadian program that erupts into more chair-throwing hissy-fits than *Jerry Springer.*

Lueders is still recovering from an off-season injury—a hernia from lifting weights—so he operates the clock and records the times. The Hindle brothers take turns running the icy 50 metres with the sled. As Ken LeBlanc stretches and warms up with some sprint drills, the Hindles begin a game of chronological limbo, casually slicing away hundredths of a second from the other's best time: 5:90. 5:84. 5:78. 5:71.

LeBlanc finally takes the start block. He wears a simple grey sweatshirt, "Canada" printed across the back. Black tights wrap large thighs that taper to impossibly thin ankles. On his feet are bobsled start shoes, hundreds of tiny spikes packed between the arch and the toes in three rows. Lueders pushes a button and the clock spins to read 0:00. Ben Hindle stands behind LeBlanc and offers only one short sentence of encouragement: "Drive out of the hole, Ken."

That's what bobsledders call the first five metres of the start: the hole. In a moment of sustained explosion, LeBlanc breaks inertia and fires the sled down this frozen barrel.

It's his first run since a hamstring injury suffered during sprint training in August. He runs over the crest, disappears from view and breaks a timing beam at the bottom. Lueders records the time—5:67—shakes his head and smiles. "He doesn't quit," he says of his teammate. "When you're winning, he'll race harder. If you're losing, he'll race harder. With Ken you are never out of it. He works through the pain and then works through the consequences later."

AFTER BURSTING onto the scene in 1993, Pierre Lueders established himself as Canada's top bobsled pilot. He won the overall two-man title in his first year as a driver as well as the combined title that year. Since then, he has collected 34 World Cup medals, 16 of them gold. In short, he likes to win—and he recognizes the talent and tenacity required to do it. That's why he wanted LeBlanc, even with a rap sheet, in his sled.

In 1994, Lueders wrote a letter to LeBlanc asking if he'd like to race together once he was released. He never heard back. "Then in 1997, I returned home from a workout and my mom said that I had a message from Ken LeBlanc." LeBlanc was tired of watching bobsledders whom he knew he could beat racing for Canada, so he met Lueders in Calgary that summer. "Ken looked at me," says Lueders, "and said that he was ready to get off the couch."

LeBlanc's wife joined him on his drive back to Calgary that September. She understood that Ken couldn't be kept down on the farm once he'd been offered a shot at returning to the Olympics. Both figured he'd go to Nagano, win a medal and return to Ontario, ready to move on with his life.

"What can I say," he shrugs, four years later. "She's out east and I'm still here in Calgary."

Lueders understands why some people felt uneasy about LeBlanc's return. "All they see is the long hair, the tattoos, the big guy—they see trouble." But he believed that LeBlanc had made his mistakes, done his time and was ready to move forward—and he thought LeBlanc was still the best brakeman in Canada.

Others connected with the sport disagreed and describe LeBlanc as a short-tempered bully who openly intimidates other athletes. Last season, at a World Cup race in Austria, he got into a fight in the starthouse after another athlete moved his equipment bag—a breach in the steroid-age etiquette of amateur competition—and then had to cool off in the local jail. "He is, plain and simple, a hoodlum," says one Canadian official, "and he had better watch his back." Considering LeBlanc's penchant for punch-ups, it's little surprise his critics prefer to remain anonymous.

Malcolm Lloyd, former head coach of the Canadian team, has a more balanced perspective on LeBlanc's sometimes fiery character. "Ken is the most loyal and talented athlete I have worked with. But he is misguided at times," Lloyd explains. "Any trouble he has ever gotten in has been for what? Friends, family, teammates—all those things that he sees as good reasons."

On his return to bobsledding, LeBlanc quickly silenced his critics. In his first World Cup race with Lueders—his first race since being placed in a cell—he struck gold. After that initial victory in Calgary, though, Le-Blanc suffered through a series of hamstring injuries that kept him off ice until late January, 1998. Lueders went on to two more World Cup victories with two other brakemen.

Dave MacEachern, one of the athletes who shared the podium with Lueders, had started with the national program in 1991 and, while LeBlanc was away from the sport, the Charlottetown native had established himself as one of the top brakemen in the world. The amiable MacEachern is the light-spirited Superman to LeBlanc's dark-souled Batman. As the Nagano Games approached, the two former sledmates found themselves in a battle for the brakeman's position on Canada's leading two-man sled. In public, MacEachern and LeBlanc played down the controversy. At the track, things were different.

"Ken wanted to go head-to-head with Dave to prove who was the best," explains Lueders. When that showdown finally happened, MacEachern narrowly beat the injured LeBlanc and earned the right to push Canada One at the Nagano Spiral. LeBlanc felt disappointed but realized that his time on the injury list had hurt his chances.

Things got worse. Six weeks before the Olympics, LeBlanc's father died suddenly at the age of 50 from Creutzfeldt-Jakob disease. Still on the World Cup tour, Ken couldn't return to Ottawa for the funeral. "[My father's death] was definitely not expected and, to be honest with you, it's something I haven't dealt with," admits LeBlanc. "He used to shake his head at things I did. But even as a kid, when I thought that track was my thing, he'd drag me out to meets and let me run. His last words to me were, 'You've always had to be number one ever since you were a kid.' In the end, he was pretty proud that despite all the shit I'd been through I had persevered."

At Nagano, Lueders and MacEachern won Canada's first Olympic gold in bobsledding since 1964. But the post-medal glow was short-lived, as the national team descended into yet another soap opera over who would compete in the four-man event. Chris Lori, the driver of Canada Two, was incensed by Bobsleigh Canada's decision to let Lueders have first crack at filling his sled for the four-man race. In practice, the driver chooses his crew, but coaches will alter line-ups if they see problems developing. Lori felt he had contributed more to the program over the years and, as the more skilled four-man driver, he shouldn't have to deal with the seconds. He drew a line in the snow and demanded to be allowed to switch his crew. When the coaches balked at his request, Lori parked his sled for the first two days of official training and refused to slide. Without a backup driver and unable to force Lori to take to the ice, the coaching staff decided to wait out the controversy—leaving LeBlanc and the other Canadian athletes caught in the middle.

After the sledders missed a second training session due to the stalemate, LeBlanc packed his bags and exchanged his plane ticket for a return flight home the same day. "I didn't put my family and myself through hell to make a comeback just to get a 'Participaction' badge," he says of his decision. "I was incensed by the complete lack of leadership and desire found on the team." He returned to Calgary and gave his Olympic jacket to a friend.

DESPITE HIS gold medal in the two-man event, Lueders admits he should have been more loyal to LeBlanc as a teammate, a lesson driven home by a disappointing ninth-place tie in the four-man race. "I asked him to consider staying in the sport, and we made a commitment to move on together," says Lueders. "Before 1998, I would juggle crews to gain a hundredth of a second. Since then, I'm not willing to do that. I want to work with people who are loyal to one another—Ken demands that a team operates this way."

Lueders and his teammates credit LeBlanc's determination with keeping Canada One together during their difficult post-Nagano years. LeBlanc, in turn, says Lueders's leadership and the ever-competitive Hindle twins have helped the team persevere. Over the last two seasons, the squad has been so wracked with injury—LeBlanc: hamstrings, back and knees; Lueders: hernia and concussion; Ben Hindle: achilles tear; Matt Hindle: rebuilt ankle—that they've been nicknamed Team Tape and Tensor. Last season it was the sled, four years old and ancient by World Cup standards, that slowed them due to steering box failures and a cracked frame.

"The last couple of years haven't been the easiest," admits Ben Hindle. "But Ken has been through much worse. Sometimes knowing that makes it easier to deal with the obstacles."

What the team doesn't seem to suffer from anymore is the internal strife that scuttled other promising Canadian squads. It remains to be seen whether this battered solidarity will be enough to win gold in Utah this February.

The bobsledding venue for the 2002 Winter Olympics is cut into the slopes of the Wasatch Range above the resort town of Park City. The track resembles Calgary's in its technical difficulty and long banking turns but differs from other tracks in that the designers have implemented two uphill sections, which cause the sleds to become momentarily weightless—a mistake here and chances for a medal evaporate. The steep start area rewards teams that generate velocity quickly and then settle smoothly into the sled—like Lueders and LeBlanc, who placed sixth at a World Cup race there last February. Still, to medal at the Games, the Canadians will have to knock off the heavily favoured Swiss and German teams and fast-rising American star Todd Hayes.

LeBlanc won't speculate on his chances of standing on the podium in Park City. Chris Lori, Pierre Lueders, Ben Hindle, former coaches and officials—all told me how much they hope LeBlanc will finally win a medal at these Games. And Lueders has stated flat out that LeBlanc will be racing in Salt Lake City, regardless of his health. But in one of the fastest events at the Winter Games, time is running out. These Olympics—his fourth—will be LeBlanc's last.

ON THE face of things, life has been simple for Ken LeBlanc. His job description has contained one simple entry: push a bobsled faster than anyone else in the world. It's a skill he's excelled at for 15 years. To hone this talent, our government pays him $1,100 a month; add to this salary maybe another $500 to $700 a month in prize money. This set-up can make for a Spartan existence, but LeBlanc has never complained. Many other athletes and pundits bemoaned the financial plight of Canadian competitors after the medal drought of the Sydney Olympics, and they will likely do so again if expectations aren't met in the mountains of Utah. LeBlanc agrees that amateur sport in Canada lacks something. But he's learned the hard way that it isn't money.

"The bottom line is there is no sense of patriotism," says LeBlanc. "What follows patriotism is loyalty and camaraderie, and it needs to be at all levels—administration, coaches, sponsors, athletes. We Canadians aren't real good at the patriot thing."

I glance around LeBlanc's modest rental house. The walls are bare save for greying paint and framed prints of a cheetah and two wolves—one creature known for its explosive velocity, the other for its loyalty to the pack. Out of the front closet spill the meagre spoils of the elite amateur athlete: a pile of athletic shoes of every description, some with the tags still attached, to be saved and bartered. There's no trophy case, no displays of his many achievements. Aside from the shoes, there's little evidence that a three-time Olympian and gold-medal hopeful lives here.

"I'm not comfortable asking people for money and using the sport to get rich off of sponsorship," LeBlanc tells me. "I know that the only thing I have to answer for is my ability, my genetics. Sure, it would be nice to not have to worry about budgets, but that isn't what motivates me. I'm in it for the fight, and nothing beats race day."

0:00:00

In the hole, the racers slowly coil their bodies behind the sled. Their hands twitch on the push handles as they find purchase, balance. They exhale and fix their eyes down the track, shoulders just above the top of the sled, feet on the blocks. The clock resets. For a moment time holds still, compresses to a single point, turns in on itself. Then a green light signals that the track is clear. The driver flips down his visor. "That's back!" the brakeman yells. His left calf trembles like a sewing machine, anxious for release. And then it all begins.

POSTSCRIPT: Just prior to the start of the 2002 Winter Games, the decision was made to remove Ken LeBlanc from Pierre Lueders's two-man sled and replace him with rookie brakeman Guilio Zardo. LeBlanc's last Olympic race was as a member of Canada's four-man crew, along with Lueders, Zardo and Pascal Caron. The sled finished ninth.

||||||||||||||

ONE GIANT
LEAP... MAYBE

BRUCE GRIERSON

JULY/AUGUST 2002

IN **THE WARNER** Brothers cartoon *Ready, Woolen and Able,* Wile E. Coyote's alter ego, Ralph Wolf, discouraged with the recent results of his Acme leg-muscle vitamins, hits upon another way to gain an advantage over his prey.

He orders a couple of Acme bedsprings, which arrive in a crate with a warning on the side: "For mattress use only: not to increase one's jumping ability." Undeterred, he fastens one to each foot, assumes a hurdler's position, and almost immediately the steamhammer boinging sends his haunches well overhead. A lusty anticipation spreads across his face; he is about to break the back of a long history of humiliations.

It's impossible not to think of those bedsprings when your Exerlopers arrive in the mail. Exerlopers might best be described as spring-loaded boots, although the boot is really a sleeve your own shoe slips into. The spring is a couple of elliptical plastic shells with a "tension band" sandwiched between them. The shells compress to take your weight, then recoil. Just standing in them adds six inches to your height. Giving them a little stationary test-flex, you can compress them an inch or two. Walking in them, you naturally fall into a variant of what Tom Wolfe called the "pimp roll"—a sort of exaggerated ghetto swagger as you rock over your centre of gravity.

But these boots were not made for walking.

IN THE late-1970s, Gregory Lekhtman, a neurophysiologist from Moscow who'd immigrated to Montreal a couple of years earlier, had an Archimedes-like insight: *Human beings are not designed to run.* Across the Western world, the first wave of injuries had beset jogging's early adopters: shin splints, knee-cartilage tears, hip pointers. In his work designing medical electronics—chiefly heart-rate monitors and biofeedback devices—Lekhtman had calculated that the signals that travel from the environment to the central nervous system and back to the muscles are quite slow. So slow, in fact, that when we run, the muscles can't contract quickly enough to absorb the force of impact. A lot of that force is transferred to the bones and joints, and gradually it wears them down. "So if we're going to run," Lekhtman said, "we're going to destroy our skeleton."

What we ought to be doing instead of *running*, he determined, is *loping*: covering ground with long, jarless strides. While this may *seem* evolutionarily backward, like something we as a species grew out of, in theory it's just the opposite. Consider: In the beginning we swam. Then we crawled. We ambled on all fours, we walked upright, we ran. And now, with spring boots, we can leave the earth entirely, if briefly. The boots add another coil to the spring that is the human body.

But for Lekhtman there was a more immediate point of interest. Running was on its way to becoming one of the century's more powerful addictions—so compulsive that its practitioners keep doing it even as it takes them apart like a clock. What if there was a product that could extend their habit, allowing them to get their fix for another 10 or 20 years? For such a gadget, wouldn't a runner pretty much be prepared to write the inventor a blank cheque?

In 1981, Lekhtman and his brother, David, filed for a patent for a device of their co-design. So unusual was their "sporting and exercising spring shoe," it sent the patent examiner digging nearly a century back into the files to find potential ancestors. Lekhtman would have to defend his Exerlopers against, among other things, an early roller-skating boot, a flexible ice skate and a turn-of-the-century spring used to dampen the shock in the Model T.

Which he did—and he was soon knocking on the door of running-shoe manufacturers. Lekhtman hit the engineers with the language they understand: numbers. "Every stride you take delivers to the body a force equal to three times body weight," he explained. Only a quarter of that force is absorbed by the muscles. The shoes pick up a little, but not enough. The rest falls on the frame.

He tried to get Reebok interested. This wasn't a competing product, he explained, but a complementary one: it fit over the shoe. The company president was not convinced. "But soon they were talking about air cushioning," Lekhtman remembers. "I said to myself, 'Hey, guy, good luck.' Yes, you'll absorb impact, but only maybe 20 per cent. You won't take away impact completely, because you need space. That's why you need the springs."

Lekhtman took his prototype boots on the road, and by the late 1980s they had become the talk of inventors' conventions in the U.S. and Europe. He won gold medals at events in Belgium, Switzerland, Germany, California and Pennsylvania. In so doing, he attracted the attention of Dr. Yoshiro Nakamats, the world's most prolific inventor and a titan in Japanese popular culture, who invited him to Tokyo for the World Genius Convention in 1989. Lekhtman bagged a gold there, too. With Ginza Street closed to traffic and network-TV cameras competing for angles on the swarthy Russian from Quebec, a beaming Dr. Nakamats hung the medal around his neck. Watt had his steam turbine, Edison his tungsten filament, Dr. Nakamats his floppy disk. Now the world's most recently designated genius took his place in the inventors' pantheon's back row, standing a half a head above the rest in his six-inch heels.

But these first-generation Exerlopers were still not, in Lekhtman's estimation, up to scratch. He knew the secret lay in creating a spring that could "collapse to zero." The theoretical breakthrough was that the user should not so much *spring* as *roll,* fluidly converting muscular energy into forward movement. The solution existed in Lekhtman's head, but the technology did not.

"It took me about three years to develop the plastic," he says, one Friday evening in Montreal. "I started to work with DuPont on how to do a spring which will not break. It took us at least five more years until we perfected it."

Still tinkering with the formula for the resins, Lekhtman released his new improved Exerlopers on the market in August 1992, patent pending. In October, he founded a company called Unique Life and Fitness Products, based in Lachine, Quebec, built on the promise of U.S. patent #5,205,798.

Then things got really interesting. Through a mutual acquaintance, he met a woman. She was blonde and smart and spoke Russian. And she *loved* the boots, bouncing around in them near her home in Vancouver's Kitsilano neighbourhood whenever she could find free time—which there isn't a lot of when you're prime minister of Canada. Lekhtman and Kim Campbell dated all through 1993 while she was on the re-election trail. In her memoirs, Campbell recalls cavorting in the Exerlopers on the lawn at the PM's country residence at Harrington Lake, a few days before she called the election that would collapse the Conservative Party to two MPs.

So for the better part of a year, Lekhtman was in the enviable position of dining with heads of state; for a brief few minutes he had the ear of the first of the jogging presidents. Had he casually slipped mention of a device that prevents knee injuries, who knows what would have happened when Bill Clinton felt the first twinge of pain down there, and his mental Rolodex brought up the intense face of the boyfriend of that funny Canadian prime minister; and his strange boots—what were they called again? Lekhtman, however, refused to exploit his access to the levers of power. In fact, he hardly ever mentioned his invention. Acutely uncomfortable around the kind of people who pin you with their gaze as they size you up, he rarely emerged from the shadows.

As it turned out, Exerlopers didn't need help from the PM; they were cooking pretty well on their own. That year, *U.S. News and World Report*, the *New York Times*, the *Boston Globe*, *Forbes* and *Fortune* gave them a plug. ("Only a Russian emigré would dream up contraptions like these," gushed *Forbes*, "and one did!"). The word "Exerlopers" would appear in the third edition of the *American Heritage Dictionary of the English Language:* "impact-lessening running shoes mounted on elliptical springs."

The new, new thing, then. But Exerlopers also seemed to have value beyond their novelty: they appeared to be at least as aerobically challenging as running. Studies conducted at Montreal's Concordia University and at Idaho State showed heart rates and oxygen consumption climbed higher when you ran in the jump boots than when you ran in your regular sneakers. If you could have bought stock in what the *Scotsman* called "the latest fitness craze to sweep through the Western world," this would have been the time.

Today you might be glad you didn't. Nearly a decade later, Exerlopers are still available, but they've all but vanished from the tracking grid. And Gregory Lekhtman is a 55-year-old inventor and businessman, quietly living and writing poetry in a cluttered apartment, unknown to just about everybody but his friends and the mailman.

What happened?

THE PROCESS by which new products are embraced by the public is almost geologic in its complexity. An idea is born, someone turns it into an object and takes it to market, and then depending on a staggering number of factors—the economy, the cultural fit, who adopts it, who endorses it, naming, marketing, patent defence, luck—it catches on or it doesn't. Conditions converge and a sub-sea volcano erupts and the lava forms a cone that breaks the surface, becoming suddenly and for thousands of years a point on the map. Or one stage of the chain reaction fails and that point of land never appears, and the world never knows anything could have been otherwise.

Rollerblades were not "new" when a couple of Minnesota brothers named Scott and Brennan Olsen launched them by that name in 1979. The British inventor Robert John Tyers patented a crude version of them in 1823, before his design was abandoned in favour of ever more sophisticated roller skates. The Olsens took a step back in order to leap forward, and then they sold their fledgling company to someone with enough money to iron out the design flaws. So the right people (hockey players yearning for some off-season action) stumbled onto the right thing (a pair of Tyers's ancient skates) at the right time (when new technology existed, chiefly polyurethane for the wheels, to make them nimble) and did the right thing with it. Remove any element from the equation and the story of in-line skates is suddenly quite different.

More like, say, the story of Will Wilkinson's Power Walking Sticks. These collapsible poles were the American inventor's great hope for a sporting revolution. Like Rollerblades, they offered a no-impact aerobic blast. They gave a little against resistance, making walking a "full-body exercise." Wilkinson sold the distribution rights to his invention to mighty NordicTrack, and that's where the promise dissolved—as eventually did NordicTrack, which went bankrupt in 1999. (Wilkinson was vindicated when Reebok picked up one of his forgotten fallback inventions, plastic stackable "steps"—igniting the trend of "step aerobics.")

An industry rule of thumb is 10 misses for every hit. For every pair of Rollerblades there are 10 Power Walking Sticks. For every Razor scooter there are 10 unicycle–roller skates, pontoon skis or motorized pogo sticks. Not to mention mountain boards, disassemblable dumbbells or light-emitting basketballs for nighttime play—inventions on which posterity has yet to cast its vote.

But in some ways it's unfair to compare jump boots to in-line skates or Razor scooters, global breakouts that are really just modifications of long-established concepts. Because jump boots have, until recently, existed only in myth. The story is always the same. In magic boots, an average schlub becomes a Nietzschean superman—Zarathustra vaulting over the canyons—a symbol of humanity's transformation to a more advanced stage of consciousness.

But actually *building* spring-loaded boots, ones that have any practical value, has proven to be a bitch. Somewhere along the line, all the inventors who dreamed the dream Lekhtman dreamed before Lekhtman dreamed it ended up stalled in the breakdown lane, a cloud of magnificent expectations issuing from under the hood. The long list of failed attempts includes things called "leg-extension jumpers," "jog springs" and "amusement shoes." Now, of course, Nike is trying to get in on the act with what are colloquially known as its "boing sneakers," the Nike Shox, wherein pillars of foam absorb impact and, in theory, create spring. (The running-shoe watchdog Kicksology.com pretty much put to rest the idea that they actually help you gain altitude.)

"Everybody was thinking about putting a trampoline on your feet, to jump higher," Lekhtman says. "But nobody was thinking about how to make a shoe to eliminate the problem with human running." In the postmodern age of sampling and borrowing and tweaking, Lekhtman's leaf-spring jump boots are an astonishing rarity—a product *sui generis*. They're like nothing you've seen and, when you try them, like nothing you've felt.

Of course, having a unique product that actually works is no guarantee of success. Dr. Nakamats, who had awarded Lekhtman the Genius Gold Medal in Tokyo, spelled it out in a Web site conversation a few years ago. There are three components to every successful invention, he said: *suji, pika* and *iki. Suji* is the base of knowledge, *pika* the inspiration, and *iki*, basically, the sales job. The marketing. It's the *iki* that has proven to be the jump boots' biggest challenge.

AT A subterrannean café in Vancouver's Gastown, Douglas Hetherington boots up his laptop. Video footage blooms on the screen. An empty road in a rain-misted forest, a runner slowly rising into the frame, like the '56 Chevy in *Mississippi Burning*. And on his feet are jump boots. But they're not Exerlopers. They're Kangoo Jumps—for which Hetherington, as VP Sales and Marketing of Jump Canada Inc., works full-time promoting. If you happen to see a pair of spring-loaded boots flash past you on the street or in the rainforest these days, Kangoo Jumps is what they're almost certain to be.

The reasons for this are a bit tricky, but they unwind from developments back in Montreal, circa 1994. It's high summer. Gregory Lekhtman is on a roll. Churning circuits around Mount Royal's Beaver Lake in his Exerlopers, he's flush with hope for his beloved invention. But he is about to run into a spell of bad luck.

He strikes a deal with NordicTrack, giving them exclusive distribution rights to his boots. What he doesn't realize is that NordicTrack has no intention of distributing them. Believing them competition to their ski machine, the company sits on them, freezing them, delaying Lekhtman's progress for a year and a half. At the same time, Lekhtman's efforts to penetrate the physiotherapy industry—seemingly a dream clientele—are coming to nothing. He has advertised repeatedly in the trade magazines, without a bite. Puzzled, he collars an orthopaedic surgeon he met once. "Why don't you prescribe my product to your patients?" he says. "What about my business?" the doctor replies, not quite concealing a grin.

All the big-media press for the boots *does* draw a raft of eager potential distributors. One of them is Denis Naville, a soft-spoken Swiss businessman whom Lekhtman appoints as exclusive European distributor. According to Lekhtman, Naville signs a non-infringement, non-competition agreement but is soon in business with his own variant of Exerlopers. He files for a design patent for "Kangoo Jumps" from Geneva ("Swiss engineered!") and starts cranking them out in a factory in Taiwan.

Lekhtman considers suing. "And then I said to myself, 'Hey, what am I going to gain? People don't even know about Exerlopers.' At least what he's doing is promoting my invention."

Denis Naville has a somewhat different take on events. "We tried to work with [Lekhtman] but he obviously didn't want to improve the product," he says by phone from the south of Spain, where he spends his winters to avoid the chill of Geneva. Naville claims that Lekhtman never respected their planned business agreement and that his original patent hadn't been registered in Europe and may not even be valid in North America, opening the way for a new, improved jump boot. "We had already imported quite a few of his Exerlopers and all of them, every single piece, broke—and he didn't even want to replace them. We suffered a huge loss. And since he didn't want to hear anything about it, we decided to move on with the Kangoo Jumps." (Lekhtman, in turn, says he refused to send more Exerlopers only after hearing from suppliers that Naville was planning to market a variant of the original boot.)

Naville argues that another problem with the Exerlopers was their lack of spring. "So we took this item over and developed it so that it really has a very satisfactory rebound power," he says. "There's no other way to get the rebound than with the patent we registered."

In fact Exerlopers and Kangoos *do* feel a bit different. It is, you might say, the difference between a cough and a sneeze. Both get the job done, but the Kangoos definitely have more kick. Whereas Lekhtman eventually settled on a one-size-fits-all arrangement, with a sleeve you slide your own running shoe into, Naville went with a moulded Rollerblade-like boot in different lengths.

Believing Lekhtman hadn't done enough to either improve or promote his Exerlopers, Naville vowed not to make the same mistake with his Kangoo Jumps. He piled on the *iki*. Distributors were lined up. Press releases were prepared. An omnibus, it's-a-floor-wax-*and*-a-dessert-topping approach was struck ("Kids off the streets, adults off their seats!") emphasizing the boots' versatility. Launched in Europe in the mid-1990s, Kangoo Jumps immediately caught the zeitgeist, sparking a fitness mini-trend called "Kangoorobics" (exactly what it sounds like).

In 1998, Naville launched Kangoo Jumps in the United States—where Doug Hetherington spotted them at a sporting-goods store called Johnny's. Hetherington, a Vancouver-born telecommunications engineer who was working in Silicon Valley at the time, dismissed the boots as further proof of the prevailing stupidity of Californians. And then... couldn't get them out of his mind.

The next day he bought a pair for himself and one for his partner, psychologist Alice Pauline. Hetherington was an utterly sedentary man. He smoked. When he climbed a lot of stairs, he filmed up like a bathroom mirror. He took his boots out for an inaugural bounce in San Francisco and almost had a heart attack, doubled over and fish-gaping as a small group of inner-city youth looked on with concern.

But he was hooked. He wore them in the office. "Suddenly I had reasons to jump across the office and send a fax!" Within days he'd made a decision. The fibreoptics business was at its zenith, but Hetherington was done with it. It was one of those moments when you see your way clear. He was leaving an industry built on wild speculation and slippery bandwidth swaps in favour of the simplest, low-tech enterprise this side of farming—a business where nobody gets rich (at least not immediately) but everyone goes to sleep with a healthy glow and a clean conscience. Where a grown adult can make a living acting like the entertainment at a party for kids under six.

He called up Denis Naville in Geneva and successfully pointed out that Canada was a separate country from the U.S. and therefore ought to have its own distributor. Soon after, 1,200 pairs of Kangoo Jumps arrived on a container ship in Vancouver, and Hetherington was in business—with most of the couple's life savings in the balance. With no actual outlet stores, and few merchants brave enough to take the boots on consignment, Hetherington and Pauline began to demonstrate them in malls. This way —unlike Internet selling—they could take the pulse of the people. What did folks really think of a nearly 50-year-old man and a 60-year-old woman bopping around in spring-loaded boots? And more importantly, would people swallow their egos and give it a go?

Bouncing seven days a week, Hetherington quickly shed 20 pounds. One night a customer called him up and bellowed into the phone: "These boots you sold me—you charge $299 for these?" "You don't think that's fair?" Hetherington said. "Hell, no!" the man replied. "You should be charging $20,000. These boots changed my life!"

But the reaction wasn't all positive. A lot of mallwalkers laughed outright—a not unreasonable response, when you think about it. Smartass yuppies rubbed their hands as they passed and stage-whispered: *There's a personal-injury lawsuit waiting to happen.* "You wouldn't believe how many times I've heard, 'I'd break my neck. Oh, I'd break my tibia. I'd break my elbow. I'd break my nose,'" Hetherington says. "It dumbfounds me how many parts of the body they can come up with."

Kangoo Jumps were also facing some challenges on the international front. After the East German distributor moved to Texas with 400 pairs of boots and declared himself the American distributor, Naville had to nip a potential branding disaster in the bud, gently reprimanding the man, "You don't even speak English!" In the fall of 1997, high-profile British radio morning host Chris Tarrant donned the boots to play soccer with his kids—and broke his leg in two places. ("He was using the boots for something he shouldn't have," Naville said.) Comic Howie Mandel tried them on his own short-lived variety show. Unfortunately, they were sized wrong for him. "So he gets up there and there's no more bounce in them than the shoes I'm wearing," Hetherington says.

But lately, Kangoo Jumps have been riding an uptick. New York City's fitness mecca Crunch now offers Kangoorobics classes—though they call it "urban rebounding"—with music specially calibrated at the 115 to 120 beats per minute the boots naturally align to. Little Kangoo Kiosks are opening in California malls, and potential distributors are being urged, via the Internet, to *Act now!* so as not to miss out on this amazing marketing opportunity. Last summer, the boots made a cameo at the opening ceremonies of the World Track and Field Championships in Edmonton. Before a TV audience of millions, 200 teenage kids bounced in choreographed moon strides to the Parachute Club's "Rise Up."

The Kangoo camp has pretty much given up on the mall audience. ("We realized people were laughing *at* us, not *with* us," Hetherington says.) That leaves actual athletes—the folks Lekhtman insisted spring boots were meant for all along, those people who would quietly shudder when they heard the line *Human beings are not designed to run.* Recently, Doug Hetherington gave Kangoo Jumps to Paul and Lynn Williams— both former Canadian middle-distance Olympians—who now carry them in their running shop in the Vancouver suburb of White Rock. The marathon crowd, a continuously running river of cash, is the obvious, ultimate target. No-strain training is the idea, even if you don't actually run the race in them. Though some folks have. Jodie Luther, a 35-year-old professional trainer from Palm Beach Gardens, Florida, has completed eight marathons in jump boots. In each case, she says, she has felt chipper enough afterward to resume training *the next day.*

Luther is in the unique position of being on the spring-boot train through every whistle stop, promoting Exerlopers for Gregory Lekhtman and now Kangoo Jumps for Denis Naville. Shooting a promo video for Kangoos recently, she was "discovered" and cast on a reality TV show called *Matchmaker* (with the boots, of course, as a quirky-character prop). She once hawked Exerlopers on the Canadian Shopping Channel; more recently she took Kangoo Jumps onto CNN. "I don't like to do that until I'm sure the company can and will support whatever efforts I do out in the community," she says. "Because if you can't provide people with product, it's fruitless."

Is the infrastructure finally there?

"Absolutely," Luther says. "It's ready to rock."

Though only about 3,200 pairs have thus far found their way to Canada, Denis Naville estimates there are hundreds of thousands of

Kangoo Jumps extant. And the company's own market surveys indicate the fitness-club industry, where it's made its European inroads, represents less than one per cent of the potential market worldwide.

Lekhtman won't divulge how many Exerlopers he's sold. "I don't want to give my competitors—my *infringers*—any ammunition," he says. "I've given them enough." His voice betrays a certain weariness. "When I started the company, and Exerlopers started getting written about in magazines and newspapers, a lot of people said, 'Gregory we will help you, Gregory we will partner with you.' This is how all my problems started. If I would have continued independently, Exerlopers would today be an incredible item."

Like Rollerblades?

"*Much* bigger. How many people do you know who can properly skate? But I'm going to tell you: everybody can run."

If Lekhtman and Naville are working parallel grubstakes on the bend in a river, each sees the other as ultimately wasting his effort, and lawyers for each man are ready to snap into action, if need be. Two competing products that fizzle will likely never land their inventors in patent court; it's usually when one really takes off that litigation begins.

"A patent is a tool of offence, not defence," Lekhtman says. "In other words, I as the patent holder can go after anybody without being sued myself." So, hypothetically, if Kangoo Jumps break out next year? "Then what you do is send that file to a nice patent attorney, and he will take them to the cleaners."

I HAD canvassed the opinions of some folks whose opinions ought to matter, including the chief exercise physiologist for the American Council of Exercise and the former doctor to the Vancouver Grizzlies (both of whom showed a kind of guarded optimism about jump boots), and Dusan Benicky, who keeps a dozen Kangoo Jumps for "core training" at North Vancouver's Human Performance Centre and speculates that NHL star Pavel Bure (whom Benicky helped come back from a blown anterior cruciate ligament) could have avoided injury had he used the jump boots. Still, I decided due diligence was not quite complete. It was time to take both models for a test bounce.

The Kangoo report: Around the Stanley Park seawall in 60 minutes instead of the usual 45, 35 alien stares, general feeling of exhaustion (in a good way). One sore foot. Several new muscles awakened from slumber, down in the region where losses continue to lead gains by a wide margin. (The Kangoos drew less comment than I thought—which probably tells you more about Vancouver than about the boots.) Kangoo Jumps are about as springy as pogo sticks; you probably couldn't dunk a basketball with them, unless of course you could before.

The Exerlopers are pretty convenient: you don't even have to take off your shoes. Running at night in them, past the vacant volleyball courts of Spanish Banks, clop-clop-clopping like a Clydesdale, I was reminded of Lekhtman's pitch—"You're producing this workout effortlessly because you're not working against pain!"—and the Ron Popeilish enthusiasm with which he delivered it. The Exerlopers were more comfortable than Kangoos, but the plastic sleeve seemed less likely to hold up. The springs felt a bit soft.

And so the question arises: what if the chip off the block is better than the block—more durable, more fun?

"Let me tell you the story of Polaroid and Kodak," Lekhtman says. "Ten years ago, Kodak made their own Polaroid camera. It was a completely different camera. It was an improvement. It was much better than Polaroid's. It was 15 years in the making. It was much fancier, and people preferred to buy it over the original. Well, Polaroid sued Kodak, and they won. Kodak had to pull their product out of the market, and they paid Polaroid 900 million dollars. Kodak had to discontinue the product.

"This kind of litigation goes on every day," Lekhtman says. He slows the tempo for emphasis: "You're. Not. Allowed. To. Improve. Unless. You. Have. Permission."

One person convinced of Exerlopers' patent primacy is Daniel Taylor, CEO of Jump America and the world's most successful marketer of bouncy boots. For four years, Taylor was the American distributor of Denis Naville's Kangoo Jumps—he'd become a convert after losing 40 pounds using them. Then Lekhtman appeared on his doorstep with copies of his patent and the non-infringement contract that Naville had signed.

"Even after investing millions of dollars in Kangoo Jumps, it only took my attorneys and me two hours to decide that we didn't want to build a future nest egg on the loose sands of Denis Naville's product," says Taylor. "My attorneys told us we could get stung. We'd sold more Kangoo Jumps than anyone else—50,000 boots—but we dropped them like a hot poop." Jump America bounced back to square one. Taylor has since signed a licensing and royalty deal with Lekhtman and will begin marketing a new line of boots under the name "Jumpers, by Exerlopers." In March, he filed a $24-million lawsuit against Naville.

SO NOW, nearly a decade after they first made jaws drop in trade shows, the curious jump boots with the elliptical springs—the gizmos that were going to change the way we run, train, heal and relieve stress—haven't caught on. No quarter-million-dollar book deals have been proffered, no software magnates have stepped forward to predict that whole cities will be designed around boots with springs. The great unspoken possibility is that they will fall into the sump of forgotten fitness products, alongside the Stair Climber in a Briefcase, the Bollinger's Sports Exercise Putty, the Superstar Human Gyroscope, the Slam Man, the Versaclimbers, the Suprabar, the Dynabee, the Yankeebike—products that have all but vanished, not necessarily because they weren't good, but because they never reached critical ignition temperature.

Neither Lekhtman nor Naville seem particularly concerned. It takes time to hatch a revolution. Lekhtman's company, Biosig Instruments, which supplies heart monitors in 70 countries, would do fine even if he threw Exerlopers over the side and relieved his headache. But he doesn't seem inclined to do it.

"My vision of the product is many, many miles ahead of [my competitors], who are stuck with a product which I designed and put on the market 10 years ago," Lekhtman says. "When things start to happen for them, I will come forward with a very advanced product, which will spread all over the world."

For now, the Montrealer lies low. Like the proverbial restaurant that closed down because it was getting too busy, he has stopped promoting Exerlopers in order to weed out the customers who just don't get it—which is most of them. The interviews for this story are the first he has given since 1996. The market, he says, is still not ready.

When will it be?

"When there are lots of people with damaged knees. When people start to scream, they're going to start looking at Exerlopers. And when they start looking at Exerlopers, they're going to start to understand the product. There's only one person who understands completely the story of Exerlopers, and that's me. Maybe one day I will write a book explaining what it's all about. Maybe one day they'll make a movie out of this."

||||||||||||||

GRUELLING, ON
A SUMMER AFTERNOON

JERRY KOBALENKO

JULY/AUGUST 2002

IT'S WEDNESDAY MORNING, just past eight, and a small crowd is gathered at the marina in the town of Roberval, Quebec. A few locals are in the water, swimming their daily mile. On the docks, a middle-aged man limbers up with arm swings while puffing on a cigarette. He strips into his swimsuit, sucks in his gut and dives off the pier into iron-stained Lac St-Jean. His form's not bad for an amateur.

The serious swimmers—those who've come from around the world for the 2001 edition of the Traversée Internationale du Lac St-Jean—are easy to spot. They're the ones never without a jumbo squirt bottle in one hand; as if they don't spend enough time around water, marathon swimmers are constantly rehydrating themselves. After a light workout in the marina, they hang around the lakeside bleachers and chat. Professional marathon swimming is a small world, and everyone knows everyone. While it takes weeks to recover from running 26 miles, swimmers race almost that distance every weekend during the busy core of the marathon season. Last week, most were either at Lake Memphremagog, on the Quebec-Vermont border, or at the world championships in Japan. Now they are eagerly discussing a rumour that the 2004 Olympics in Athens will include a 10-kilometre swim, a move that could up the profile of this otherwise obscure sport.

They also talk about the water. It's been windy lately, and even in the protected marina, the water temperature is a breath-sucking 17°C. Most of the swimmers keep their concerns to themselves, but Fabio Fusi, a well-sculpted Italian, is noticeably spooked. These days, relative newcomers such as Fusi are weaned on warm-water events, like those in Argentina and Egypt. They no longer expect cold to be a factor. Among the major marathon-swim races, only Lac St-Jean has the potential to be truly dangerous. In three days, the 25 swimmers will slip into its chill waters and test the resolve of both body and will. Ten competitors will be defeated by the lake in their attempt to cross it. One of them will nearly die.

LAC ST-JEAN sits 200 kilometres north of Quebec City, on the edge of the boreal forest. Roberval, a pulp-and-paper town at its southern end, bursts into provincial prominence on the last weekend of every July, when it hosts the Traversée. Thanks to Lac St-Jean, marathon swimming is a big deal in Quebec, and some years the race winner even graces the front page of the Montreal papers.

The Traversée began in 1955, a year after Marilyn Bell electrified the nation with her swim across Lake Ontario. Until then, swimmers in Quebec had been scared to attempt Lac St-Jean. "She showed it was possible," says Jacques Amyot. A barrel-chested 78-year-old who still swims three times a week, Amyot was swimming a relay in front of the Canadian National Exhibition on the same day that Bell did her historic crossing. The following year, he and six other Quebec swimmers attempted the inaugural 26-kilometre Traversée. Waves and cold water thwarted the others, but Amyot prevailed in a time of eleven and a half hours.

Amyot's improbable feat made him a local celebrity and established Lac St-Jean as a world-class marathon swim. It also inspired a host of other prestigious Quebec races, including a 24-hour relay at La Tuque, a 40-kilometre crossing of Lake Memphremagog, and a swim in the frigid sea at Paspébiac, off the Gaspé Peninsula. Except for Memphremagog, all these events eventually folded. Marathon swimming, to put it kindly, is not a telegenic sport. Sponsors are largely local, and the organizations depend on the continued goodwill of volunteers. In the mid-1990s, even the Traversée came close to bankruptcy.

The race always ends at the marina in Roberval, but the course has changed several times over the years. In the late 1980s, for example, it was a gruelling 64-kilometre double crossing. Competitors began at 10 PM the previous evening, with light sticks in their swimsuits so that their boats could keep track of them in the darkness. "It was hard on the guides as well as the swimmers," says Denis Lebel, mayor of Roberval and a long-time Traversée aficionado. Currently the route is 32 kilometres long and begins four kilometres up the Péribonka River, on the north side of the lake.

Unlike the English Channel or Lake Ontario, Lac St-Jean does not have a history of dramatic solo swims—it's always been about the Traversée. Nevertheless, in 1996, Jeffrey Blufford, an American in his late thirties with no history of marathon swimming, came to Lac St-Jean and enlisted the help of one of the experienced Traversée guides. On the same day as the race, he set out to swim a slightly different route across the lake with the guide and the guide's son. It was a stormy day, according to one observer, "with waves like white sheep" that rocked the solitary little boat. Near the end of the crossing, an exhausted Blufford grabbed the gunwale of the boat and capsized it. The guide managed to swim to an island, but Blufford drowned, along with the guide's son.

THE PRE-RACE favourite for 2001 is Stéphane Lecat. Each year, marathon swimming crowns an overall champion, much like Formula One racing, based on the accumulated results of about 10 races. Lecat has reigned for the last two years; the aloof, goateed Frenchman is also the two-time defending champion at Lac St-Jean. His winnings, combined with sponsorship in his homeland, give him an annual income that fellow swimmers estimate at around $70,000 U.S. Most of the others at the race swim to break even or for the experience of travelling the world after their careers as pool racers.

Lecat's main competition is Petar Stoychev, a dour Bulgarian who broke Lake Memphremagog's record last week. (Lecat was racing in

Japan.) Among his peers, Stoychev is about as popular as cheerless Czech star Ivan Lendl was on the 1980s tennis circuit. Bulgaria's Alice-in-Wonderland economy makes marathon swimming's modest prize funds real money for him, although it's rumoured he has to turn 80 per cent of his winnings over to his coach, an even more dour figure with the bedside manner of a Soviet-era figure-skating czar. Stoychev says that he swims in order to own nice clothes, cool sunglasses and a Mercedes. When asked if he ever plans to swim the English Channel, he looks puzzled: "What for?"

His good finishing kick—he swam for Bulgaria in the 400 and 1,500 metres at the Sydney Olympics—means that if he can keep up with Lecat in the early going, he might be able to outsprint him at the end. Gabriel Chaillou of Argentina and Stéphane Gomez of France have beaten both frontrunners before and are considered potential spoilers.

Rookie Tim Cowan is the lone Canadian male at the Traversée. A 23-year-old 1,500-metre pool specialist from Calgary who comes just shy of national team standards, Cowan heard of these marathons through a friend. Every year, such Olympians *manqués* make up a small but consistent percentage of the field. With 10- and 25-kilometre races now part of the world championships and marathon swimming threatening to become an Olympic sport, the longer distances offer a last chance for these athletes to fulfill a lifelong dream of representing their countries. Lac St-Jean is a step along that path.

The women's field is dominated by Dutch super-swimmer Edith van Dijk. Her one rival in the speed department, the slender German law student Britta Kamrau, hasn't beaten her in two years. Van Dijk is so far ahead of her competition that she usually swims with the lead men's pack. Although she typically finishes around seventh overall, she's beaten most of the men at least once.

"In marathon swimming, it seems to be okay if a girl beats you," admits Tim Cowan. "That never happens in a pool." (Not everyone is so gracious: after van Dijk edged out Stoychev at a race in Argentina, he didn't speak to her for a week.)

The four Canadian women are all from Quebec. Here, swimmers have grown up with the mystique of Lac St-Jean and tend to regard it as an end in itself rather than as a backdoor chance to represent their country. Three of the women are veterans, while 19-year-old Melissa Doyle from Aylmer, near Ottawa, was offered a spot after a last-minute cancellation, thanks to her strong showing at Lake Memphremagog. When she passed the 32-kilometre mark at this longer but less-storied race, her first thought was, "Now I can do Lac St-Jean." She's thrilled and a little scared to be part of the grand event.

THE TRAVERSÉE is the pièce de résistance of Roberval's week-long summer festival. Blue and yellow bunting, the official Traversée colours, drape local stores and houses. Kids get their faces painted and slide down the backs of inflatable dinosaurs on the makeshift fairground by the lake. Live music draws thousands to the adjacent bandstand, and poutine stands do a brisk business. One evening, the main street closes for a street party at which the athletes are introduced.

During these hectic days before the race, the swimmers are billeted in private homes. They relax, swim a little, sign autographs. Quebec is not quite as marathon-mad as Argentina, which accords the swimmers the status of celebrities, but little Roberval pulses with excitement as Saturday approaches.

A year earlier, the Traversée took place during a hot spell, and Lac St-Jean had been like a swimming pool. Swimmers shattered records that had stood for 20 years. The fastest maintained a five-kilometre-an-hour pace. That's the equivalent of clocking one minute and 12 seconds per 100 metres—for six and a half hours. But this year the challenge will be to survive, not to smash records. The lake has warmed slightly since Wednesday, yet the water remains dark and uninviting. The slender, speedier swimmers become pensive while the more plodding but better-insulated swimmers pray for waves and wind and cold, their one chance at Traversée glory.

On Friday afternoon, the swimmers and their coaches pile into two yellow school buses and drive to a boarding school on the far side of the lake near the starting line, where they will spend the night. They continue to cling to their water bottles like security blankets. Many have already withdrawn into themselves. Fabio Fusi and Melissa Doyle look scared—the Italian because the cold water has psyched him out, Doyle because of the magnitude of the test ahead of her.

The mood in the cafeteria is quiet as they eat a last supper of dried-out lasagna. Most of these swimmers do 70 to 120 kilometres a week in training, which makes them capable of equally prodigious feats of eating. Josh Santacaterina, an incredibly thin Australian, tells me that for breakfast he typically has 10 pieces of toast, four bowls of cereal with fruit and three or four sandwiches. One of the Canadian women loves chocolate chip cookies and puts away about 40 of them a day. Another swimmer once ate a whole chicken and a large pizza the morning of a race.

Tonight, whether owing to pre-race butterflies or the withered lasagna, no one has more than two helpings. Most of the swimmers soon retire to their rooms to mix their drinks. They'll consume about a litre an hour during the swim, in quick gulps every 15 or 20 minutes. Mainly they use carbohydrate fluids like Endurox, a thick peach-coloured drink, or Boost, a nutritional shake. Some supplement this with a couple of bottles of flattened Coke, for the caffeine. Others dissolve three or four aspirins in half a litre of water as an anti-inflammatory.

A GREY dawn breaks at 5:30 AM as the swimmers come down for breakfast, clutching their favourite cereals under their arms. Everyone speaks softly. A few continue to look scared.

"It's raining," mutters the Italian as they board the bus for the short drive to Péribonka.

"So what?" shrugs Edith van Dijk. "We'll be wet anyway."

The swimmers take shelter inside a yacht club and strip to their suits, as race officials go around writing bib numbers on their arms in indelible black ink. Many of the swimmers already have numbers from previous swims reverse-sunburned onto their skin. Using surgical gloves, the swimmers apply lanolin or Vaseline to their bodies. The grease doesn't protect much against the cold but it gives psychological comfort and it will keep armpits and thighs from chafing during the seven- to 10-hour ordeal ahead. Despite the packed room, everyone carefully avoids bumping into one another. No one wants grease on their hands, because then they won't be able to adjust their goggles without fouling them.

Most are wearing ordinary swim trunks, but Lecat and van Dijk opt for the long-sleeved racing suits that made their debut at the Sydney Olympics. Grease applied, Lecat sits in a corner listening to music on a Walkman. Van Dijk looks intense and focussed. A well-proportioned 5′10″, she has neither the anorexic runner's bony frame nor the swimmer's muscularity. She looks like a normal slender person rather than a great athlete. Lecat and Stoychev also seem slender, but "they're not as 'dry' as they look," van Dijk remarks, using the swimmer's term for no body fat.

At precisely 8 AM, after brief introductions to about 150 umbrella'd spectators, the 25 swimmers jump off the dock into the dark Péribonka River. They clutch the starting rope with one hand and wait for the pistol. The most dangerous part of a marathon swim is the mass start. It is worse in a triathlon, with thousands of participants, but even with two dozen swimmers it is easy to get a hard kick in the face or to lose a pair of goggles during the wild opening melee.

The pistol goes off and the frontrunners sprint madly for 200 metres to get clear of the thrashing pack before settling into their race rhythm. Each of the competitors will be accompanied by a small red-and-white motorboat holding two people—a local guide and a coach who will feed the swimmer and (except for the Bulgarian coach) scrawl encouraging words on a slate. A flotilla of larger vessels, including a dive boat for real disasters, will keep close tabs on the field as it stretches out, in touch with each other by radio. Within a few minutes, all the boats fall in alongside their swimmers and the race is on.

I hop aboard one of the roving security boats. Now and then we run off to fix an engine that has conked out on one of the other boats; mainly we stay in the thick of the action. It's the ideal platform from which to watch a marathon swim: we can follow one swimmer or another, as the drama unfolds. Spectators at the finish line only get a faint taste of the cat-and-mouse games, the battle against cold and the herculean effort of the swim through periodic summaries over the loudspeaker.

A digital readout on our boat's console gives the surface temperature of the water. The Péribonka River is 19°C—cool but not cold. Even a thin athlete can tough out 19°, roughly the temperature of an Ontario cottage lake in early July. The water gives an opening shock when you jump in but is manageable afterward. Still, it's a far cry from the 29° of a heated swimming pool. Water drains body heat 25 times faster than air, and an experienced swimmer can tell when the water temperature drops even half a degree.

Lecat, Stoychev and Fusi seize the early lead. Lecat, known for his fast starts, maintains a blistering 82 strokes a minute, a few body lengths ahead. Stroke rate is the only way open-water swimmers know how they're doing. Everyone has a natural range. Some big, albatross-winged men average barely 70 strokes a minute, while shorter women may flutter at 90-plus. When your stroke rate drops, you're getting tired, or having a bad day, or in trouble. One of the jobs of the coaches in the boats is to keep the swimmers informed of their stroke rates.

After 45 minutes, Fusi has dropped back the length of two football fields but still leads the second pack, which includes Edith van Dijk. Gradually, Stoychev reels in Lecat. As Stoychev draws even, Lecat—in a little psychological move—stops for his first drink, proffered in a cup at the end of a long pole. Two seconds to drain the cup, then back to 82 strokes a minute. By the end of the race, hundreds of plastic cups are floating in Lac St-Jean.

UNTIL RECENTLY, marathon swimmers have been more heroes than athletes. In the public mind, swimming 30 to 50 kilometres ranks somewhere between going over Niagara Falls in a barrel and wheelchairing across the country. Canada's best-known swimmers—Cindy Nicholas, Vicki Keith and Marilyn Bell—accomplished feats of endurance that made the front pages, not the sports pages. Bell, in particular, became a national icon for completing the first swim across Lake Ontario in 1954. By comparison, few have ever heard of Greg Streppel, a world champion in the early 1990s and the best marathon swimmer that Canada has ever produced.

The Mount Everest of the swim-as-spectacle has always been the English Channel. Pioneer marathoner Matthew Webb breast-stroked from Dover, England, to Calais, France, as far back as 1875. But it wasn't until 1927 that long-distance swimming reached Canadian shores. That year,

Wrigley's Chewing Gum sponsored a 21-mile closed-circuit race in Lake Ontario, during the Canadian National Exhibition in Toronto. The big event, with $50,000 U.S. in prize money—still the largest purse ever for a marathon swim—drew fledgling pros from around the world. Ernest Vierkoetter, a German swimmer, won in just under 12 hours. Until 1964, with a couple of hiatuses, the swim remained a highlight of the CNE. But when an offshore wind stripped away the warm surface layer, Lake Ontario could be so cold that some years almost no one finished.

The cold waters of the early professional circuit, which included Lake Michigan and the bracing Pacific Ocean off California, required what might be called the Channel Swimmer physique. Even in late summer, the English Channel is consistently cold, around 15°C, so its conquerors have always been walruses, not whippets. Some of the most famous marathon swimmers of the 1960s had, in their prime, beer bellies rather than six-pack abs. No amount of outdoor training, mental toughness or applied grease can make up for the simple fact that in cold water, only body fat defeats hypothermia. Consequently, all the figures from the heroic age of marathon swimming were on the chunky side.

In recent years, marathon swimming has changed dramatically. Wet-suits are still forbidden (unlike in triathlons), but the swims themselves are much warmer: at the world championships in Japan last week, the water temperature was a balmy 30°C. The sport seems to be going legit. The professional circuit is even sanctioned by FINA, the same international swimming federation that governs pool events. Among its rules, an open-water race cannot begin if the water is below 16°C.

So a widening gulf has opened between the traditional marathon swimmer and the current crop of professionals. The beefy traditionalist attempts to solo Lake Ontario or heads for England, where the swims are all bone-chilling. Some ambitious soloists continue to sell marathon swimming as a spectacle. In 1987, 180-pound Lynne Cox of California swam four kilometres across the Bering Strait in five-degree water. In Canada, Vicki Keith made a name for herself by butterfly-stroking at a mile an hour across Lake Ontario. In England, currency trader Alison Streeter reigns as the Queen of the Channel, with 39 crossings. All are solid accomplishments, but to professional marathon swimmers, they're hardly deserving of worldwide acclaim. "The measure of an athlete," says Greg Streppel, "should not be a measure of the amount of body fat."

Edith van Dijk, the most dominant swimmer on the marathon circuit, agrees. "We're athletes," she explains, when I ask how today's pros differ from the heroic figures of the past. "We swim to win, not just to finish."

THE RAIN stops as the swimmers emerge from the Péribonka River into the lake. Roberval is 28 kilometres away, and the steeple of the Church of St-Jean-de-Brébeuf near the finish line wavers like a mirage, never to be reached. That's a prophetic vision for some, because the water temperature now begins to drop steadily: 18°, 17°, 16.4°, 16.2°, 16°. Sixteen degrees is no longer cool, it's seriously cold, like a cottage lake in early June; one does not swim in it except as a brief test of hardiness. It remains to be seen how the thinner competitors—the transplanted 800-metre and 1,500-metre pool specialists—will handle these English Channel conditions.

Around the two-hour mark, guide boats—no longer accompanied by their swimmers—begin to file past the security flotilla and across the lake towards home. Their swimmers have given up and are wrapped in blankets, shivering convulsively, on one of the larger vessels. We learn the "abandons" from their names stencilled on the passing guide boats. The Italian, Fabio Fusi, is one of the first retirees—no surprise. The willowy German, Britta Kamrau—van Dijk's chief rival—follows. Our boat is alongside when a Yugoslavian swimmer gives up. He seems in an almost catatonic state in the water. Divers in wetsuits jump in and haul the rigid-limbed swimmer to a waiting security craft. Even Stéphane Gomez, one of the top four contenders, fails to survive this belt of cold water. In a span of 15 minutes, five swimmers concede defeat.

Meanwhile, leaders Lecat and Stoychev continue to swim side by side, sandwiched between their two boats. Drafting—following on the heels of another swimmer—was once part of the tradition of marathon swimming, and one of the great Egyptian champions of the 1960s, the euphoniously named Abdel-Latif Abo-Heif, was known for his strategy of clinging to a rival until it suited him to forge ahead. But drafting is not allowed under FINA rules. The organizers of some races turn a blind eye because drafting lets slower swimmers keep pace and makes for a tighter contest, but the Traversée is strict.

After three hours, Josh Santacaterina, the skinny Australian eating machine, is pulled from the water; the race doctor determines that he's got a hypothermic core temperature of 30.6°. Then word comes over the radio: Edith van Dijk is struggling. Her stroke rate has dropped from 80 to 72 a minute, not a good sign this early in the race. Sensing blood in the water, half a dozen security boats circle her like sharks, watching. She stops for a drink and a quick chat with her coach. Five minutes later she stops for another drink. Before the race, she had told me that she didn't get negative voices any more—those tricky, left-shoulder demons exhorting you to quit for seemingly good reasons. "When I'm really cold, I know that everyone else is, too."

But now, during her increasingly frequent breaks, she keeps staring incredulously at her white hands, a sign that blood is abandoning her extremities to protect the vulnerable core. *You can do it,* her coach scrawls on the slate, swinging his arms encouragingly. *Netherland women are the toughest.*

She stops again. She's shaking in the water. She vomits. Marathon swimmers often vomit from seasickness, but van Dijk's stomach is in turmoil from stress. Perhaps she's remembering one of her early river races, when a hypothermic swimmer abruptly sank from sight. The race was stopped as swimmers and officials frantically dove for him. They found him after 10 minutes. He was in a coma for a week but miraculously recovered.

At the three-and-a-half-hour mark, van Dijk calls it quits. "I'm sorry, I'm sorry," she sobs, as she's lifted aboard the security boat and quickly wrapped in blankets.

News of her departure sends a shiver of excitement through the remaining women. With van Dijk and Kamrau out, it's now anyone's race. Australian Shelley Clark whoops with joy when her coach writes #1, her new ranking, on the slate. Traversée neophyte Melissa Doyle now finds herself unexpectedly in third position. She's in a groove, she will later admit, and the swimming feels easy. The upbeat melody of "I'm a Believer," the old Monkees song, begins playing in her head, in time with her stroke rate.

By now, nine swimmers have succumbed to the cold. All the slender ones are gone, except rangy Tim Cowan of Alberta, who seems somehow immune. Around mid-lake the swimmers hit warmer water. Soon the temperature is back to 18°. Roberval is still hours away, but the steeple of St-Jean-de-Brébeuf has begun to sharpen on the horizon.

The withdrawal of van Dijk and Kamrau has stratified the field into the surviving men followed by the surviving women. The speedy Argentinian veteran, Chaillou, briefly joins leaders Lecat and Stoychev, but soon falls back. Three times, Lecat puts on a half-hour sprint in an attempt to shake Stoychev, without success. Likewise, Stoychev twice tries to pull ahead but cannot tear loose from the dogged Lecat. They swim side by side, stroke for stroke, hour after hour, in a classic duel.

The sun appears, and the clearing sky gives the rust-coloured water a clean blue look. As the leaders finally approach Roberval, a mere handful of klicks away, the number of accompanying boats multiplies into dozens. Swimmers now have to deal with the taste of fuel in the water, as well as cold and fatigue. During this last hour, Lecat drinks every five minutes, hoping to gain an edge for the final sprint. Just before the racers enter the marina, my security boat drops me off on shore so I can watch the last leg from ringside.

The two pairs of windmilling arms clear the breakwater together and enter the calm waters of the marina. The guide motorboats, jobs done, hang back as their swimmers fight out the final 800 metres. After swimming 31 kilometres in seven hours, the Bulgarian and the Frenchman are still dead even. Now they have to swim 400 metres along a chain of roped buoys, turn around and swim madly for home.

A thousand Quebecois cheer on the two leaders from the stands. Stoychev edges half a body length ahead of Lecat and then grabs the inside track, next to the rope. At the turnaround to the final 400 metres, Lecat makes a desperate attempt to overtake the Bulgarian, but Stoychev forces him wide. The announcer screams the finale racetrack-style. Lecat tries to swim over his rival's legs to the inside, but Stoychev blocks him and begins to pull away. Thirty metres. Twenty. Ten. Kicking strongly, the Olympic swimmer slaps the finish board ahead of Lecat and pumps his fists in the air.

"In the old days they'd be too tired to raise their arms like that," says Mayor Lebel. "But now they're so strong."

Stoychev has touched the floating finish board in seven hours, three minutes, 45 seconds—seven seconds ahead of Lecat. It's the closest Traversée finish in almost 30 years.

GOGGLE MARKS aside, Stoychev looks none the worse for wear after his ordeal. Lecat is disappointed but graceful in defeat. Four minutes later, an exhausted Gabriel Chaillou touches the finish marker, then slowly crawls out of the water. "You want to know what pain is?" an Australian coach remarks. "Look at him—he can barely stand."

In the next 20 minutes, three more men finish. Around the eight-hour mark, the crowd begins to buzz with news from the lake: Shelley Clark, the lead woman, has just passed a struggling Tim Cowan. Meanwhile, Melissa Doyle has edged into second place. Clark reaches home in eight hours, 33 minutes, 52 seconds—an hour and a half after Stoychev. Doyle, still singing "I'm a Believer" to herself, touches six minutes later, followed by the veteran Quebecoise, Nathalie Sauvageau.

Doyle feels so fresh that she tells me she could jump right back in the water and swim back to Péribonka. She's even disappointed that she didn't finish first among the women: at one point she was only 25 metres behind Shelley Clark, but Doyle paced herself conservatively and had too much left at the end. Her only cold-water complaint is that the little finger on each hand is numb. "You could cut them off with a knife and I wouldn't feel anything," she says. After more than seven hours in the lake, many of the swimmers look like bloated corpses when they emerge from the water. "I never look at myself in the mirror right after a swim," admits Doyle.

Then a stunning development: a kilometre from the marina, after eight and a half hours in the water, Tim Cowan is in serious trouble. He is disoriented, his eyes rolling in his head. When his coach asks "How many fingers?" Cowan takes 20 seconds to give a slurred response. He keeps veering off at right angles to his boat. His coach waves a red flag, signalling trouble. The race doctor comes and takes one look at Cowan, whose fingers are now rigid like claws. The doctor orders Cowan plucked from the water. He takes his temperature and gets a reading of 25°C, the very edge of heart failure. Cowan is rushed to the hospital. He regains his senses by evening but stays in the hospital overnight for observation.

"I remember nothing of the last three kilometres," he later admits. Cowan does recall the race up to that point. After the first two hours he was shivering in the water—mostly in his legs. He began taking warm drinks, but when the shivering went away after another hour and a half, he told his coach he was warm again and didn't need any more warm feedings. In fact, the cessation of shivering can be a danger signal, indicating the next, more serious phase of hypothermia. "I remember being surprised every time one of the big names got out of the water," he says. "I didn't know my own limitations."

In the end, eight men and seven women complete the 32 kilometres across Lac St-Jean. Petar Stoychev will go on to wrest the overall 2001 championship—and its $12,000 bonus—from Stéphane Lecat. Undeterred by his near-death experience, Tim Cowan will race again in 2002; Lac St-Jean, however, won't be on his schedule. Melissa Doyle, spurred by her success, will double her training from 40 to 80 kilometres per week. "I wasn't even trained for that race," she says cockily.

Edith van Dijk handily wins seven of her eight races in 2001; only Lac St-Jean eludes her. After the Traversée, at the gala evening held at the marina grounds, we sit down and talk for a couple of hours.

"It's so hard to know whether you're being smart or just weak," says the Dutch titan of her difficult decision to quit.

Perhaps that fine line is the beauty of the Traversée. Every year, marathon swimmers race against each other with the tactical finesse of Olympic competitors. But like the epic soloists of their sport's historic past, they also face an interior struggle that modern warm-water marathons have all but eliminated. On the one hand, they don't want to give up prematurely because of the specious arguments of a shivering body. On the other hand, they don't want to cross into the twilight half-world of hypothermia, like the too-courageous Tim Cowan—or beyond. They swim to win, yes. But sometimes, locked in a long embrace with Lac St-Jean's northern waters, winning still means just finishing.

WHO HAS SEEN
THE (GODDAMN) FISH?

MARK SCHATZKER

MARCH 2005

NEW BRUNSWICK'S MIRAMICHI River is probably the world's best Atlantic salmon river, and to get there from Toronto, you travel east-northeast in as straight a line as possible for about 1,400 kilometres. The journey should take no more than two days, not nine years, which is how long it took me.

It started with a flight to Reno, Nevada, of all places, back in 1995. Reno isn't a great place to go if you want to catch a salmon. You might easily catch a disease there, or a debilitating case of ennui, but what little salmon there is in Reno all arrives by plane.

Nevertheless, this is where my quest for a transcendent fishing experience began. (Though, truth be told, it started with trout, which are distant relatives of salmon.) A friend of mine was attending a conference in Reno and suggested that I fly there, hop in his car and drive north to Wyoming and Montana to fly-fish some of the finest trout streams in the world. This would be different than those minor-league streams north of Toronto I was used to, stocked with dwarf brook trout and choked with agricultural runoff. This was the West.

I had a lot of romantic notions about the West back then. I pictured myself standing knee-high in some gin-clear stream winding its way through a sun-dappled field of blond grass, snow-capped peaks above me and a trout wriggling free from my gentle grasp. It turned out my romantic notions were uncharacteristically on the money. The streams were gin-clear, the peaks were snow-capped and the fields of grass were indeed sun-dappled. It was all very memorable and beautiful, a high-flying buddy adventure to be sure, except for one fundamental and overarching flaw, which had to do with the part about trout. There were plenty in the river, jumping, sipping flies or just hovering in the current. But I didn't catch a single goddamn fish. Not once did I get to feel a trout wriggle sweetly out of my hand. In fishing parlance, I got skunked.

My winless streak didn't end there. About six months later, I went fly-fishing with my 73-year-old uncle. It was deep winter by this point and the two of us were standing on opposite sides of an ice-fringed creek a ways south of Calgary, casting into a pool. There were about 10 good-sized rainbow trout in plain view lolling on the surface, their fins poking out of the water like Jaws (with trout, the effect isn't nearly as menacing). They were sipping tiny midges and generally making the most of a grey winter day.

My uncle, who had never fly-fished before, caught one on his third cast. A few minutes later, I caught one, too. But there was an important difference. Whereas my uncle hooked his trout by the mouth, which is where you are supposed to hook a trout, by some dint of happenstance I hooked mine in the anus. The physical damage was, mercifully, minor. After I unhooked it with surgical delicacy, the fish swam vigorously away and rejoined its friends, no doubt the object of their ridicule for months.

If, during that grey afternoon, that fish raised its eyes skyward and asked some higher power why he was cursed, he wasn't the only one. The obviousness was undeniable: I could catch a fish, but only by accident.

DRIVE PAST any stretch of Canadian farmland and you run a good chance of seeing a sign. "Fresh Eggs," "Sheep Manure," "Puppies for Sale": the blameless if somewhat fecund products of farm life. Drive past a stretch of New Brunswick farmland, though, and you'll see a different sign: "Salmon Flies."

The farmers aren't the only ones who erect unusual fish-related signage. So does the government. Every few kilometres of highway, there's a blue sign that depicts a fish jumping out of a river. There is no writing featured on the sign, nor are there numbers or symbols that convey any kind of specific information. Often, the signs stand surrounded by forested hills and there won't be so much as an arrow indicating where the river might be. And yet, for a government sign, its message is uncharacteristically enthusiastic: salmon!

New Brunswick is also the only province in which the government has its own salmon lodge. It is a luxurious wood-panelled cabin on the Restigouche River with a great stone fireplace and plenty of comfy chairs. Running it costs almost $1 million each year. To this lodge, the government invites powerful people from around the world—past guests have included George H.W. Bush, Brian Mulroney and Norman Schwartzkopf, not to mention an untold number of hand-rubbing provincial MLAS—so they can smoke cigars, catch fish and determine the course of history. The lodge is called Larry's Gulch, which strikes some people as an odd name for a government-owned institution, though I think they should carry the theme to other ministries, such as Larry's Healthcare, Larry's Revenue and Larry's Highways.

Canada, we all know, is a country rich in natural resources, but New Brunswick is the only province where the people are actually obsessed with one of those resources. Not every Albertan has a favourite beef or oil story, and not every British Columbian can spend three hours talking about pot (though in fairness, a lot can), but every New Brunswicker can and will gladly talk about salmon. A person can't so much as mention to a waitress in a downtown Fredericton café that you just went salmon fishing without the restaurant owner pulling up a chair five minutes later to have a sit-down. The province has even gone so far as to erect its own salmon museum.

There are two reasons for this. The first is that the Atlantic salmon is a fish of legendary quality: silver and athletic when fresh out of the ocean, powerful, prone to acrobatic leaping, rare in number, delicious when smoked and electrifying sport on a fly rod. The second, far less well-known reason is that they're hard to catch. The truth is, you catch an Atlantic salmon the same way you get audited or fall in love: by accident. (Which, it hardly needs saying, is why I decided to visit.)

The reason comes down to lifestyle. Atlantic salmon have chosen a different—some might even say deviant—lifestyle compared to most fish. Instead of spending their lives in fresh water or salt water, as most fish do, salmon choose both. They hatch from an egg on the river bottom and spend two years foraging for food. Then they hit puberty. Their bodies change, they experience new and sometimes frightening urges and at three inches in length, weighing no more than a few pieces of lettuce, the salmon head into the ocean, where they gorge on sardines, sand eels, shrimp and other such Atkins-friendly goodies. After six months at sea, a salmon can gain as much as six pounds. Sometimes, a salmon will return to its river of birth after only a year; these fish are called grilse. Salmon that spend more than one winter at sea are called—get ready for it—salmon. It's not that grilse aren't salmon. Technically they are. But they're not salmon in the awe-inducing, holy-crap-that's-a-huge-fish sense. A true salmon, you see, can weigh as much as 40 pounds.

It's when the salmon return to the rivers that fly fishers try and generally fail to catch them. There's a good reason they fail: the salmon aren't hungry. From the time they enter the river until well after they've laid their eggs, salmon do not eat anything. (This is nature's way of ensuring that the mature salmon do not gorge on the population of young salmon.)

So, whereas fishing generally involves the presentation of something that either is or resembles fish food, Atlantic salmon fishing requires you to throw this central premise out the window. A salmon fly, in fact, is a fly in name only. Unlike trout flies, a salmon fly doesn't even look like an insect or some small aquatic creature. A salmon fly doesn't look like anything, other than other salmon flies. No one really knows why it is that from time to time, when a particular mood strikes, a salmon will bite one. Make no mistake, the fisherman is trying to catch the salmon. But when the salmon strikes, it's seemingly without rational cause. It is what a philosopher would call an accident.

THE PROBLEM with accidents is that they don't always happen when you want them to, as I learned to my continuing fishing chagrin my first day on the Little Southwest Miramichi, a branch of the fabled salmon river. It was a nice day—I'll give it that—and my guide, Brett Silliker, who hails from the town of Silliker (Brett is a Canadian with some seriously deep roots) and who comes from a long and storied line of salmon guides, was explaining the various theories of why a salmon will take a fly. "There are three main theories," Brett said. "The first is that the fly reminds the salmon of something it used to eat when it was young. The second is that the salmon is annoyed and strikes at the fly as a way of saying 'Get out of my face.' And the third is that the fly just looks appetizing."

"Sort of like a canapé?"

"Exactly."

Already that morning I had learned much about salmon fishing. The first thing I learned is that you don't need to be a very good fly fisherman to be a good salmon fisherman—good news for me. It requires nothing in the way of technique besides the ability to lay down a middling cast. The second thing I learned is that I'm not a good salmon fisherman.

We started the day on a stretch of the river called 94 Pool, so named because that was the year a mid-winter ice jam carved out said pool. Pools are very important to salmon and, hence, to salmon fishermen, because salmon ascend the river in sustained bursts and rest in the pools. But if there were any salmon resting in 94 Pool that June morning, they weren't telling either me or the other two fishermen at the pool. The three of us just stood there, laying down cast after useless cast.

I developed a theory: there were no salmon in this river. There were no salmon because there were too many other fish. Every 10 seconds, a gaspereau—a somewhat coarse and reputedly inedible member of the herring family—would break the water. I would hear a small *plop,* turn my head to see rings, and Brett would say, "Gaspereau." There were also big silver fish cruising upstream, circling around boulders and scuttling through riffles. These were shad, a bony and rather ugly fish, which is revered in some parts of the U.S. but is generally frowned upon in the salmon-rich Miramichi. At the time, I didn't know they were shad, and when I saw two big silvery fish shoot past my legs, I dropped my rod and yelled, "Salmon!" One of the other fishermen there, an old Acadian who smoked constantly and had a hacking wet cough that echoed off the rock cut, grabbed his net and started running. He was about to plunge it in the water when he saw the fish were shad. Disgusted, he tossed the net on the bank and said in a barely comprehensible accent, "If that had been a salmon I'd a grabbed it by the tail and put it in me fuckin' bag. Cocksucker!"

With the weight of empirical evidence firmly on my side, I presented my theory. "Brett, how do we even know there are salmon in the river?"

Brett was sitting on a boulder on the riverbank, smoking a cigarillo. Without so much as turning his head towards me, he replied, "They're there."

"But how do we know?"

"We just do," he said, and returned his attention to his cigarillo. A minute later, the other fisherman, who had healthier-sounding lungs, began pointing at the water just downstream of the pool. Something was stirring there. There were ripples and waves out of keeping with the gentle turbulence of the river. The four of us all saw it at the same time. A salmon, its head, fin and spade-like tail sticking out of the water as the big fish—absurdly big, given the depth of the water—swam in slow, lazy circles.

I turned to Brett with an open-mouthed look of idiotic wonder. "It's rolling," he said. "Salmon do that."

Later that day, I got a fish on the line, although I don't like talking about it, because the fish was only on for 30 seconds. It struck the hook and moved like a torpedo upriver, shaking its head and peeling line off my reel. Brett kept saying, "She's a grilse, alright. Keep your rod tip high! She's a grilse for sure. I said keep it high!" And as quickly as that fish got on, it got off. My line, just like my spirits, hung limply. The general sense of deflation was downright palpable as Brett and the other two fishermen switched into the past tense. "It was a grilse, alright."

Nevertheless, this was big news back at Upper Oxbow Outdoor Adventures, the lodge where I was staying. Thanks to a lack of rain, the fishing had been bad for more than a week. Lew, a retired medical and dental sales rep from New Hampshire, who had fished for more than 50 years and would still be fishing his beloved Penobscot River in Maine if there were any salmon left in it, was enduring his fourth day of a five-day skunking. His wife, who'd been fishing for 30 years, had merely equalled my first morning's catch over the course of her four days. She also had a grilse on for 30 seconds.

Thus was I congratulated on my loss, which was examined in great, almost loving, detail. ("He did everything right, but that fish just kept shakin' its head." "There wasn't a thing he did wrong.") From there the conversation drifted, as I sensed it often does, to Salmon Stories of Note, vol. 167. Everyone with a salmon story told it, sometimes more than once, while everyone else listened attentively and nodded in agreement. There was the old-timer who, a couple of years back, was found dead on the riverbank with his rod in his hand, a fish (also dead) on the end of his line, and a smile on his face. There was the salmon that drowned an osprey. There was the guy floating down the Little Southwest Miramichi one sweltering afternoon in an inner tube, locked in a trance-like state of relaxation, when a salmon jumped out of the river and landed on him. "There were fish scales in his chest hair."

Talking, however, is different than doing, and over the next two days—my final two days on the Little Southwest Miramichi—I didn't do a whole lot of doing. On day two, Brett took me back to 94 Pool, and I got nothing. On the third day, we drove inland for about an hour to a special spot on the south branch of the Big Sevogle River, a little-known canyon of gnarled blue shale, grown over with conifers whose roots looked like arthritic talons biting into the rock face. The trees clung to the cliff face with such tenacity as if to say "So long as you have a view of the river, any perch is a good perch." The trees had a point.

We fished the Big Sevogle for a few hours under a heavy drizzle. The forest and grass were green, the air was moist but the salmon weren't in the mood. I fished two pools and then got bored, so Brett tied on a dry fly called an Orange Bomber, and I cast it into the current and watched as little brook trout took insanely suicidal runs at this strange and foreign morsel as big as they were. Then I fell in the river and soaked my left arm and chest. It didn't take long before I got cold and we decided to leave.

And that was it. Skunked again.

FOR MOST of the next few days, I drove. I drove with the windows open and the radio turned up loud and tried to forget about my continuing streak of failure. I drove up and down the Acadian coast, stopping for deep fried Atlantic haddock, stopping twice for a lobster dinner, and stopping in the town of Bouctouche to see what a town with a name like Bouctouche actually looks like. (It looks okay.) But there were glimpses of ocean, glimpses of other rivers, and when I saw water, despite the open window, despite the radio, I would ask myself a question I often seem to ask: what's wrong with me?

According to Brett, nothing. According to Dale and Debbie, who run Upper Oxbow Adventures, nothing. Merely having a grilse on counted as a fish in their books. And it was better than Lew did. Sensing my distress, Debbie cornered me at one point and said they thought I should be happy. But I wasn't, and not because I didn't catch a salmon, not because I wasn't going to be able to boast about catching a salmon. I was unhappy because I just wanted to see a salmon.

As it turns out, there is a place you can go to do just that: see salmon. You can see hundreds of them in fact, big and small, swimming around in circles. The place is the Miramichi Salmon Conservation Centre, in a town called South Esk, which is close to the mouth of the Miramichi. The people of the Miramichi Salmon Conservation Centre are doing good work. Every year, they raise 500,000 fingerlings (salmon, not potatoes) that help sustain the Miramichi's flagging population. (No one knows why, but despite the elimination of the commercial catch and a vigilant program of stream conservation, Atlantic salmon numbers are dwindling.) If you want to see big fat salmon hovering in an outsized wading pool, eating food pellets and waiting to spawn, then this is the place to go. But if you crave a glimpse of the salmon's silvery beauty, its sea-fresh effervescence, then the Miramichi Salmon Conservation Centre will leave you muttering, "This isn't what I had in mind."

So I made my way to a place called Boiestown to visit the Atlantic Salmon Museum, hoping that a salmon museum—specifically its aquarium full of live salmon—could satisfy my salmon thirst. The aquarium was a disappointment, and I probably should have expected as much. The salmon were listless and pallid and appeared well beyond the reach of Prozac, suggesting that a glass-walled enclosure, as popular as it may be in modern architecture, doesn't appeal to salmon.

I had higher hopes for the other half of the salmon museum, which contained no less than $140,000 worth of salmon art. This amounted to $140,000 worth of wood carvings, fish portraits, wilderness dioramas, mounted fish, old photos of strapping young woodsmen from wealthy American families holding dead salmon, and depictions of salmon leaping through waterfalls. There were a large number of paintings that you might fit into a category called Heavenly Fishing. They all depicted scenes of rapturously beautiful angling: gently flowing water, salmon jumping, grey-haired men who looked like they would probably drive cars with atrocious fuel economy, guides standing dutifully at their side, net in hand. Sometimes there would be a canoe in the painting, but not all the time.

It was harmless, unthreatening art, suggestive of a serenity in both nature and people that I don't think you find much in either. The best pieces were a series of underwater photographs taken by a man named Gilbert van Ryckevorsel, who went for a swim in a big pool in Quebec's Grand Cascapedia River. In his photos, the salmon didn't look stunned and moronic, the way they do when photographed out of the water. (It's hard to be photogenic when you're gasping.) And unlike the fish in so many paintings, his salmon didn't look angelic to the point of stupidity, the way Jesus Christ is often depicted in bad stained glass. Mr. van Ryckevorsel, I later learned, spent so long in that pool that a large male salmon, almost four feet long, got so used to him that he swam over and let Mr. van Ryckevorsel stroke him.

I think it would be nice to stroke a salmon.

PEOPLE HAVE their reasons for catching fish. Some anglers—not very many, thankfully—seem to view fishing as a way to prove their manhood (which always seems to be in need of being proved). These are the people you see wearing camouflage-print T-shirts on casual Fridays. Then there are the anglers—the majority of fishermen, in my opinion—who see fish as a noble adversary. They live for the "thrill of the fight," the opportunity to test themselves against nature and then either boast about their victory or speak reverentially of the one that got away.

And then there is a marginal group made up of people who simply like fish. I am one of these. I have long found fish to be cute, even lovable.

This is why I fish. It's strange, I realize, and hard to reconcile, but fishing is the only way I know of saying hello to a fish. It just isn't enough for me to look at a river and know there are fish in it. I have to catch one.

So it was with a certain amount of sadness that I realized, as I drove through New Brunswick doing my best not to think about it, that as much as I like fish, fish don't like me. Just like the trout in Montana and Wyoming, the Atlantic salmon of New Brunswick were doing their best to avoid me.

As with women, it turns out that winning the affection of a salmon may simply be a matter of demonstrating your love. And in my case, although it hasn't always worked with women, and certainly not trout, it did work with salmon. You see, I changed my plans. I went back to the Little Southwest Miramichi, and that, it would appear, was the devotion the salmon were looking for.

It happened my first day back on the river, late in the afternoon, so late that shadows were creeping almost to the opposite bank and all the other fishermen had gone home for dinner. I hooked a 10-pound salmon. There was no reason to hook this salmon. I'd fished the same pool for over two hours, and there was nothing I did differently that would suggest a reason for the salmon striking when it did. It happened by accident. And when it did, that fish pulled hard. It ripped line off the reel, swimming deeper and deeper into the current, the whole drama narrated by Brett Silliker. "That, my friend, is a *salmon*. Not a trout, not a bass. But a *salmon*." The salmon jumped twice clear out of the water and pulled more line off until it was too tired to fight anymore and we coaxed it into Brett's awaiting hands. He revived it by holding its head into the current and when the fish finally swam away, I felt like I was saying goodbye to a friend.

The message from the salmon to me was unequivocal: we like you too. The next day, the message was downright absurd, a mass flowering of love not seen since the famous "I'd like to buy the world a Coke" commercial of 1971.

It started with another salmon, this one eight pounds, hooked almost directly in front of the lodge. Minutes later, it was followed by a grilse, which I lost, and then by another grilse, which I landed. But that was all very minor compared to what would happen later.

That afternoon, we headed upstream from the lodge to a large, calm pool in a slow stretch of river. On what was, I think, my tenth or eleventh cast, there was a swirl in the water followed by a violent bending of my rod. Line started peeling off so fast that the reel, as fishermen say, "screamed," although the truth is that it sounded more like the reel was squealing. There was something big and very powerful on the end of my line, and it was now swimming as fast as it could downstream. About 200 feet downriver, the salmon jumped. And even from that considerable distance, its size was evident. Then the fish continued swimming downstream. It bolted so far, in fact, that I had to bolt after it, sprinting in knee-deep water while holding my rod tip high in the air. The fight carried on this way for about 40 minutes, replete with trembling hands and liberal use of the lord's name in vain. It was the kind of fight that some fishermen live for—protracted, hard-fought and intense. I would be lying if I said I wasn't massively thrilled, but it's what came at the end of the fight that giddied me the most.

When the fish began to tire, I could see only its immense tail thrashing in the water. Then its flank came into view, and I realized A) I'd hooked it in the mouth, thank god and B) this was a really big fish, a fish of the size that up until now I'd only seen at a fish market, a fish of a size that only the ocean can produce, and yet here it was, far inland, on a gorgeous stretch of river. And then I saw its head, scarred down one side, perhaps from a long-ago fight with an osprey or an illegal net. The fish looked at me. For one eternal-seeming moment, its eye met mine.

There was a look on that salmon's face, a look that some people would take as one of defeat, but in which I saw something else. The salmon looked tired, it looked pissed off and, more than anything, it looked like it wanted to stay in the river, swim upstream and spawn. Which is precisely what it ended up doing. As it cruised past my feet, the salmon, which we estimated at nearly 25 pounds, shook its head back and forth one last time. The line made an abrupt snap, the fly shot out of the water and with a sweep of its large tail, that big salmon disappeared into the green.

CATCHING A salmon that size is a rare enough event that it is followed by a congratulatory round of beers back at the lodge. Everyone sat down on the porch, cracked into a cold one and listened as the story of the day's fish was told and retold, then counterpointed with cautionary tales of guests getting skunked. The spirit of Lew hung in the air. At one point, Brett said, "Four fish in one day. And you haven't even paid your dues, buddy." Brett, as you can see, knew nothing of my angling history.

Nevertheless, Brett was inspired. Brett, who hardly ever fishes himself, despite spending about a hundred days a year on the river, disappeared for half an hour and then returned wearing his fishing gear. As we sat on the porch of the lodge, sipping beer and telling stories, we looked down towards the river every now and again to see Brett standing in the green water, casting his line into the current, waiting for an accident to happen.

CONFESSIONS
OF A HERPETOLOGIST

LESLIE ANTHONY

APRIL/MAY 2003

T WAS OCTOBER 1997, and a few of us were having dinner at a walk-up chophouse in the centre of old Hanoi. Five Royal Fish featured a rather catholic menu by Vietnamese standards (meaning it didn't specialize in dog, monkey or snake, like neighbouring establishments), and was thus frequented by the growing tide of foreigners who washed up on the shores of the new Vietnam. Unlike other more mercenary patrons, however, my companions and I weren't peddling generator-driven televisions to bored jungle-dwellers or convincing Hanoi's millions of bike commuters to mortgage their souls for a two-stroke scooter. No, we were herpetologists, a peculiar subset of biologists dedicated to the mysteries and marvels of reptiles and amphibians.

We had come here to demonstrate that the rapidly vanishing primary forests of this tiny country were home to an astounding six per cent of the world's entire biodiversity. And that with a little care—well, maybe a lot of care, a new government, a tad more literacy, an end to logging and somehow convincing a poor, protein-hungry population of 74 million not to eat everything that moved—Vietnam could become a paragon of conservation in Southeast Asia. It was a crucial mission, though such noblesse oblige wasn't the stuff of our dinner conversation. Instead, after six weeks in the jungle, the gang was sharing war stories.

I'd largely been ignoring the epic tales of drunken frog capture, but when talk turned to the irresistible macabre of snakebite, I perked up. Nikolai Orlov, a burly curatorial technician at the Zoological Institute of the Russian Academy of Sciences, was explaining through mouthfuls of carp how he'd once been bitten by a viper of the genus *Callosellasma* in Vietnam's Central Highlands, a million miles from anywhere.

"Ees like beink hit by truck," he said gravely, describing two days spent sweating, vomiting and hallucinating in a jungle hammock, unsure if he'd live to tell about it. "You cannot believe pain." He shook his head and stared at the notched end of his middle finger.

Across the table, Ilya Darevsky, doyen of Russian herpetology and Nikolai's boss, held up the permanently hooked digit where he'd once found a deadly Lebentine viper dangling by one fang as it pumped venom into the tissue. He professed not to recall the details of how this had come to pass, but Darevsky's encyclopedic scientific knowledge was exceeded only by his absent-mindedness. He could be missing half a hand and not remember how he'd lost it.

Bob Murphy, a lanky, bearded Texan and the curator of herpetology at Toronto's Royal Ontario Museum, nodded smirking assent while clutching chopsticks with his own misshapen index finger, courtesy of some carelessness with a black-tailed rattlesnake as a grad student. That bite had led to a frantic drive-for-life through the desert to the nearest hospital, an arm that turned black and swelled to the size of a watermelon, the almost total destruction of his immune system and lifelong allergies to virtually everything except beer. Then Murphy recited the long list of people he knew who'd lost life and limb to snakebite.

Maybe it was the critical mass of these tales that hastened my epiphany. Or maybe I just wised up. But it was here, at Five Royal Fish, that it finally hit me: if I continued playing Wheel of Misfortune with these maniacs, I could be next.

IT HAD all started innocently enough. As a kid, I loved snakes. They were fast, sneaky and well camouflaged, required stealth and thinking to hunt, always fought, frequently bit and expended the rest of their energy trying to escape—at which they often succeeded. But my personal version of Snakes and Ladders wasn't just catch-as-catch-can. Early on, as I cut my herpetological teeth in the ravines and railway rights-of-way of Toronto, I paid attention not just to where I found the animals, but how. Like fly fishermen studying the food of their quarry, I noted what snakes were doing and eating, and more subtle signposts such as soil type, vegetation and even time of day. From studying snakes, I learned not only how they fit into the puzzle of a local ecosystem, but that there even was a puzzle to begin with. It's no leap to say that I owe a lifelong fascination with the natural world and a built-in affinity for outdoor adventure to snakes. (I'd say thanks, but snakes don't have ears.)

To this day, though, my mother has never quite understood this fascination with all things slimy. She still remembers the toads and lizards and turtles I collected that somehow escaped to terrorize her housekeeper, gardeners and neighbours. And the phone calls from camp counsellors, teachers and babysitters to update her on my latest bites and subsequent tetanus shots. And especially the time the family was late for Sunday mass because my prize garter snake made its way from a cake-box in the trunk to the dashboard vent, where its head protruded like a prairie dog. The priest told her it was the devil at work.

THE STUDY of reptiles and amphibians has long been a noble pursuit among history's great biologists. Cope and Agassiz were de facto herpetologists, Linneaus a heavy dabbler, and even Lamarck and Darwin took a few whacks. Herpetology once counted among its ranks the world's pre-eminent paleontologists—before someone decided dinosaurs were birds and handed the portfolio to ornithologists. (Honestly, what's some pantywaist who studies warblers gonna do with *Albertosaurus?*)

Most biologists—with their studies of salmon fecundity or duckling behavior—are earnest, bespectacled types, destined for safe jobs in some campus lab or government ministry. But as I soon discovered after embarking on my own academic career, herpetologists are a little different. More accurately, they're a weird collection of nerds, freaks and misfits. In fact, an inordinate number of bikers, strippers and devil-worshippers count herpetology among their hobbies. Go to a meeting of the good ol' boy Herpetologists League or even the more mainstream Society for the Study of Amphibians and Reptiles, and you'll see snake-skin belts, poison-arrow-frog T-shirts and necklaces of crocodile teeth. By way of contrast, ornithologists' conventions do not feature feather headdresses and eagle-talon jewellery, and no self-respecting mammalo-gist would be caught dead in a coonskin cap. Neither discipline can boast an equivalent to the popular herp bumper sticker, "My python is bigger than yours."

But despite all this, herpetology offers a potent cerebral draw. The rabid individuality leads to much lateral thinking, resulting in a lot of original ideas that later flow into the scientific mainstream. Herpetolo-gists remain at the cutting edge of theoretical work in taxonomy, system-atics and biogeography—the sciences of naming organisms, establishing their relationships and describing their distribution. When herpetolo-gists present their findings, they frequently combine theory, laboratory wizardry and adventure—often in the world's wildest landscapes—into a powerfully addictive blend. It was at such a talk that I first met Robert W. Murphy.

For his dissertation at UCLA, Murphy had spent months roaming Baja California, collecting hundreds of lizards and snakes, and compar-ing amino-acid sequences to determine origins and relatedness of the various species. From these data, he had marshalled a grand theory of dual-continental and oceanic origin for the herpetofauna of the enig-matic Mexican peninsula and its offshore islands, some of which showed Galapagos-like patterns of colonization and diversification. Big news in the snake world.

In the summer of 1986, shopping for a Ph.D. supervisor at a meet-ing in Victoria, B.C., I watched Dr. Bob (as I came to know him) deliver his groundbreaking theory with a trademark mixture of barely dis-guised vitriol and laconic wisecracking. Grumbles of skepticism rippled through the mostly suit-clad audience and erupted into open contempt during question period. Slouching in a black Motörhead T-shirt and rat-tler belt buckle, and buoyed by his recent appointment to the ROM in Toronto, the new Punk King of Herpetology deftly rebuffed challenges with a blizzard of data-analysis mumbo-jumbo. Arguments over methodology broke out. When one obstreperous doubter pressed him on his interpretations, Murphy responded with a shrug. "You can believe what you want," he levelled. "But you're a complete fool if you do."

Where did I sign up?

Later, at a sushi bar, Murphy and I shared histories of childhood snake-chasing and our disdain for both religion and mainstream academia. As we drank long into the night and ate intertidal creatures that neither of us knew existed—things the chefs kept for themselves and the waitresses winced over—I became Murphy's new grad student.

WHEN I was a kid, my first encounter with a blue-spotted salamander was singularly uninspiring. Plucked from under a woodpile at the cottage, it hung there in my fingers, blinking stupidly in the cold light of day, dirt clinging to its moist skin, and made no attempt to escape. A dull animal to be sure—certainly not one to sponsor fascination in an eight-year-old. (At least red-backed salamanders parted company with their wriggling tails when you grabbed them. How cool was that!) So, unlike many creatures that found their way into my hands at that age, I let the blue-spot go, returning it to the muck of its existence.

How ironic, then, that I would later spend a decade studying more than 10,000 of the things, crouching in the nighttime woods in the rain and snow every spring, watching their migrations. For much of this time, I was working on a study of blue-spot breeding that formed the nucleus of my dissertation. More specifically, I was working towards a molecular elucidation of why this particular group displayed tendencies towards unisexuality (too many females), hybridity (too much sex, wrong partners) and polyploidy (too many chromosomes). You can't even imagine the title.

Dry as it sounds, the study was not without its hazards. Among others, these included getting lost in the vastness of the Ontario bush, being charged by a moose and spilling −196°C liquid nitrogen on your skin. But perhaps the biggest danger was falling through the ice, and one spring I had the pleasure of watching Murphy—poster boy for the law that bears his name—go straight down into a beaver pond, dip net and all.

Though a reptile specialist and confirmed desert rat, Dr. Bob was willing to help me with my study in the bug-infested, rain-soaked, cold-enough-to-you-know-what boreal ecosystem of our great country. While staying in a remote cabin, we spent the daylight hours catching up to 500 salamanders a day and the nights creating the world's first scientific rock opera—which we would later produce with talent from Toronto's herp community. Incorporating a real set of data and biological in-jokes, our musical morality tale told the story of a bumbling graduate student caught between two conflicting theories—one promulgated by his (good) professor and another by an (evil) rival. We wrote original lyrics for the almost 20 songs, based on the music from The Who's landmark album *Tommy*. In a nod to Dr. Bob's association with the Royal Ontario Museum, we called it *Rommy*.

The international herp community has always viewed Canadian herpetologists as rather pedestrian cousins. It's true that the herpetological landscape in Canada is predictable (almost every proper species name sports the prefix "Northern," as in Northern green frog, etc.). It's also true that we spend a lot of our time studying things such as cold tolerance and hibernation physiology. Still, given the prohibitions of climate, we nonetheless have surprising numbers of reptiles and amphibians here. And despite the paucity of venomous snakes (the now rare massasauga rattler in southern Ontario, and the Prairie and Pacific rattlers, whose ranges edge just north of the border in those respective areas), it's still possible to get into trouble.

Such as when you rub your eye with the hand that just picked up a poisonous red-bellied newt on Vancouver Island, so the eye goes numb and won't work for hours. Or when you climb down into one of Manitoba's famous snake pits to marvel at several thousand garter snakes merrily mating in a hole the size of a hot tub, only to find you can't climb out because your shoes are slick with their foul-smelling shit. Or when a 60-pound snapping turtle latches onto your leg like a bear trap and starts backing slowly into deeper water.

But despite hundreds of non-venomous snakebites on my ledger, I hadn't really come close with the lethal ones. Not when a rattlesnake curled up under my tent on Manitoulin Island in Lake Huron. And not even when Murphy had broken the necks of a half-dozen rattlers to immobilize them in the shower stall of our hotel room in Baja, where I discovered them—not quite as immobile as they should have been—on a late-night stroll to the bathroom.

"This is nothing," drawled Dr. Bob after yet another close call. "Wait until you get to the jungle."

MY FIRST jungle work came in 1994, when I joined Dr. Bob's expedition to the lost forests of Vietnam. We were an international team, including Nikolai Orlov and Ilya Darevsky, and the first group of scientists allowed into the former North Vietnam since the French were punted from Indochina in 1954. Luckily for me, Orlov and Darevsky were more than happy to handle the big snakes, while I rounded up frogs and took pictures. We found undescribed species of lizards and snakes everywhere, including at least a dozen creatures that turned out to be new to science. My only scary moment came when our van hit a pothole, and a bag of cobras landed on my lap.

By the time I consented to a return mission in 1997, Murphy had been to Vietnam six times. But when it came to obviating the perils of jungle collecting, most of Bob's experience amounted to a hill of rice, and we had to contend with the usual litany of uncontrollable elements—bloodsucking critters, incompetent humans, and the wildly varying and unpredictable behaviour of snakes. To wit: we still got covered in leeches, our "guides" still got us lost, and various and sundry malevolent serpents found their way underfoot, overhead and out of supposedly secure bags into bunkhouses, hotel rooms and moving vehicles.

Not long after our dinner at Five Royal Fish, we headed out on our last night of jungle work. To cover more ground, the group split up. I joined Murphy's current Ph.D. student, Amy Lathrop, and we followed our guide down one ridge while the rest followed theirs down an adjacent one. We planned to meet at the streambed in between. Naturally, we got lost. By the time we realized there was no trace of the trail we'd been following, it was too late.

Clawing on hands and knees through a bamboo thicket, we looked up and met the primeval gaze of a large specimen of *Protobothrops mucosqua-*

matus—an alarmingly agile tree viper. As we struggled to manoeuvre our snake-catching sticks in the dense brush, the delicate brown-and-gold-banded serpent wound menacingly through the branches towards us before it dropped to the jungle floor in front of Amy and charged with its head held aloft. In the end, sweat stinging her eyes, Amy won the face-off and pinned the metre-long beast to the ground. I held the bag open with shaking hands and weakening bladder while she deposited the writhing creature—fangs gleaming under my headlamp's beam—with a pair of tongs no longer than a hairbrush.

Our deadly booty in tow, we finally located the appointed stream but were still several hundred feet above it with no trail down. So, as in a scene from some action-adventure film, we found ourselves hurtling down a slick, vine-covered slope into the valley. Sliding feet-first, often out of control, we dodged thick, looping lianas that could pop a knee or ankle like a chicken bone. The slope was studded with upward-angled, razor-sharp bamboo *pongos,* and Amy rattled off curses as we shot past them. All I could think about was whether we'd tied off our snake bag tight enough.

And suddenly we splashed into the gorge, where Dr. Bob and the others were well into a show-and-tell session, displaying their latest catches as though they were hockey cards. Our recently endured hardships evaporated as we joined them, trumping their motley collection of run-of-the-mill kraits and cobras with our flashy new *Protobothrops.*

As we stood there, I realized what I love so much about herpetology and why I'm willing to keep such dangerous company. It's the childlike thrill of playing hide-and-go-seek with the products of 300 million years of evolution—the limitless adventure of trashing through the unknown, looking for the unfindable, and trying to understand the unfathomable.

At least that's what I tell my mother.

IN SEARCH
OF THE GIANT EEL

MIKE RANDOLPH

MAY/JUNE 2002

THE WAIKATO RIVER, east coast of the North Island, New Zealand. Our first official recon mission has taken us a ways upstream from the mouth of the river, into sheep country, not surprisingly. The water is clean but milky blue with sediment carried from the high volcanoes on the western horizon, where the Waikato rises from melting glaciers. With our boat nudged onto one of the many sandbars braided through the river, my friend Steve and I dig out our lunches and collapse onto the sand. We hear a droning over the whitewater, then, from upriver, the first person we've seen all day—GQ Man, as we would later call him—roars into view in a small beaten-up jet boat, bounces over the rapids, carves a stylish turn through the big eddy in front of us and pounds his boat up the gravel a few feet away.

"The name's Glen," he says with a big smile, clambering out and reaching into his pocket to roll a cigarette. "Good to meet you." He has messy blond hair, second-day stubble, and is sporting a smart-looking pair of knee-high boots and tan moleskin pants—Abercrombie & Fitch meets the Marlboro Man. He takes one look at our admittedly pathetic sandwiches (peanut butter) and offers us something else instead. "You blokes want some sheep's tails?"

I figure they're sausages or something. "What are they?"

"Sheep's tails," he says.

"I know, but what are they?"

"*Sheep's... tails*," he repeats slowly, his face wrinkling into a light-bulb smile. "You're not from around here, are you?" With that he walks back to his boat, rummages in a muddy, tattered garbage bag and returns with two handfuls of sheep's tails, as in, the actual tails of sheep. I can honestly say that until this very moment, I had no idea sheep even had tails, much less that people ate them. "Throw them on the fire to burn the hair off, brush away the ashes and nibble at the meat between the knuckles. A little bit of salt and pepper helps. I always take a bunch in case the fishing's no good."

Steve and I exchange glances. This, clearly, is our man: a fisherman, a local and someone of wide-ranging culinary tastes.

"Say, maybe you can help us," I start. "Would you know where we can catch some eels? We're looking to cook up a few of them."

The man who has just deposited two handfuls of bloody, mud-flecked sheep's tails by my feet blinks and cocks his head. He scans my face as if deciding whether I am kidding, crazy or just plain stupid.

Steve breaks the silence. "We heard the best way to find the big ones is to swim the river, so we brought wetsuits and everything. Any suggestions?"

"Yeah," he chortles. "Forget it. I'd rather swim with white sharks than eels. Had a big one attack my Labrador retriever, hunting ducks last year. Tore all the hair off its hind leg. Bloody thing wouldn't let go, so I shot it with my 12-gauge. Believe me, you don't want to swim with those things. Ever seen one, mate? Huge mouth full of teeth. Slimiest, ugliest, meanest bastards on the face of the earth."

We talk for a spell, exchanging pleasantries about the countryside, until at last GQ Man flicks his butt on the sand, shoves the bow of his boat back in the river and jumps aboard. Just before he guns it, he looks back one last time, shaking his head.

"You guys have some balls," he says with a bemused smile. "But if you want to keep them, I suggest steel-mesh underwear."

WHEN I first heard that the clear, mountain trout streams of New Zealand are home to giant eels, I didn't believe it. Come on, I thought. But after a little fact-checking I discovered it was true—eels, big ones, black, slimy, six feet long and as thick as a football.

My friend Steve and I were already in Australia, and we were looking for a good reason to visit New Zealand. Giant eels seemed like an *excellent* reason. I quickly developed a plan. We would swim with the eels. Masks, snorkels, the whole bit, floating down some gorgeous clear river. I've done it before in B.C. with salmon, which was great, but eels would be even better.

It would also be something of a tribute to one of the most fascinating scientific expeditions I've ever read about. A few years ago, Clyde Roper, a zoologist at the Smithsonian National Museum of Natural History, mounted an expedition off the Great Barrier Reef in search of giant squid, 60 feet long with eyes the size of dinner plates. Nobody had ever observed one in its natural habitat, only washed up on beaches, dead. (Giant squid are like giant eels in that they really do exist, which never fails to surprise people.) Roper, whose specialty is cephalopods (squid, octopus, cuttle fish), failed to observe one. But giant squid live in the dark ocean depths; eels are a lot more accessible. And how many people have swum with giant eels?

I also had another reason to admire Roper. A true Renaissance man, he doesn't limit his research to the laboratory. He takes it one brilliant conceptual leap further: to the kitchen. As Richard Conniff says of Roper in his book *Spineless Wonders,* "Having delivered an enthusiastic description of the differences among various cephalopods, he is liable to conclude, 'Which one tastes best depends on how much garlic you use.'" Roper, apparently, likes them best with hot Thai peppers. He's eaten just about every kind of squid and octopus that swims and once even made an important discovery by this commendable method; he had eaten a section of giant squid a colleague found washed up in Newfoundland and found it bitter and ammoniacal, which suggested the muscles were rich in ammonium ions. That turned out to be true, leading him to deduce giant squid can maintain buoyancy without expending energy.

So, yes, we would eat some wild giant eel. I'd always wanted to try fresh eel, and here was an opportunity for culinary discovery. I'd had it smoked, but fresh it's considered one of the best things you could hope for on a plate in front of you. Except, of course, in squeamish North America, one of the only places in the world where eels exist but haven't caught on as tablefare. The monks at Our Lady of Spring Bank Cistercian Abbey (who operate a Web site called MonksOnline, which offers, among other things, a few unusual recipes) hint at the possible reasons: "If the serpentine sliminess of the body is not enough for you, take a look at the head. Its wolfish grin is enough to make anyone swear to vegetarianism for life." Bad looks aside, there are still other issues. The venerable *Larousse Gastronomique* says that eel flesh spoils quickly (and, interestingly, that raw eel blood is poisonous if it gets into a cut on your hand), so for grilling or frying, eels should be bought live and killed at the last minute: "To kill an eel, seize it with a cloth and bang its head violently against a hard surface." I think it's safe to say that's a procedure you won't be seeing on *Emeril Live!* any time soon ("Let's kick it up a notch! BAM!"). Preparation also seemed to demand a stout constitution. From *Culinaria France*: "Suspend by the head so that the blood can flow from the tail, and then remove the entrails. Pour the blood in a container [for the sauce], mix with some red wine to prevent coagulation."

Clearly, there would be challenges to overcome. But such is the nature of all great expeditions. To be sure, we would be ready, by which I mean to say we would be hungry. Appetite, as some wise person once said, is the greatest sauce of all.

AND SO, after striking out on the Waikato, we follow GQ Man's advice and head for Tongariro National Park. We arrive on a rainy, deathly black night. It's early November—springtime in the Antipodes—and we check into a place called the Grand Chateau, an elegant hotel built in 1929 in the style of CP hotels in western Canada. With the ski season over and the hiking season still around the corner, we have the place nearly to ourselves. We drop our bags in our rooms and retire by the hearth in the dimly lit Ruapehu Lounge downstairs, sipping beer and talking to the porters about eels as the wind whistles outside and streaks the windows with fat raindrops.

"Well, now," says Tekarehana, an aristocratic-looking Maori man with a meticulously trimmed beard fringed with silver. "You've certainly come at the right time. The eels come out at night, you know, and most often when it rains." He places another log on the fire and jabs the coals back to life with a poker, sending sparks drifting upward. "There's probably a few of them slithering around right now, if you're game enough."

The concierge, a charmingly foppish man, overhears our conversation and comes over to join us. His name is Mike Hutchinson. "They're lovely to eat. Fatty, they are—put some weight on you." He tells us that eels are 25 per cent fat by weight; salmon, which are fatty enough, are less than three per cent. Hutchinson also confirms something else we'd heard before. "They've got teeth, you realize, and they're not shy about using them."

"We've heard that," I say.

There is a pause as he digests our plan with restrained, but unmistakable amusement. "Swimming with eels," he says wistfully. "I'd like to see that."

He then recounts an episode from the Grand Chateau's distant past, when the hotel's chef dispatched local kids to procure some eels for an important dinner with visiting royalty from England. "Oh yes, it was to be a smashing occasion," he says, looking off in the distance, smiling fondly. "But the chef, a French chap, left them in a pot in the sink, still alive naturally, and by the next morning they were all gone. Oh, it was terrible," he says, shaking his head. "The eels roamed the hotel for ages." Once, a large one appeared beneath a table in the dining room, to the horrified shrieks of well-heeled patrons. The smaller ones got into the drains and lived there for months, until finally the manager called in a plumber to flush the pipes. They never did find them all.

WE WAKE the next day to low clouds, more rain and only a vague idea of where to begin. But eels turn out to be a great conversation opener and we soon meet lots of people eager to share their wisdom regarding the apparently lost art of eeling. Unfortunately, however, I am beginning to discover that when it comes to eels people have a hard time reaching any kind of consensus. "You should have gone to the South Island," someone says. "You should have gone farther north," someone else says. "Wrong time of year," laments another. Luckily, though, Steve bumps into a Maori woman whose husband, it turns out, is an avid eeler who works as a porter at the Grand Chateau. "You should talk to him," she tells him. "He goes eeling all the time."

We track him down. When Alan Wilkinson learns of our quest to catch and eat an eel, his face breaks into a huge smile. He is a big man, exuberant and friendly, and he warms to our mission immediately, taking us under his wing with great enthusiasm. Speaking slowly and deliberately so we won't miss anything, he says, "We have been brought up by Tuna. That's the Maori word for eels. I come from a big family—eighteen. Nineteen, actually. That's why we went eeling as kids. To feed everybody. You see? We'd come back with a big basket full of them and we'd boil them with onions and all that. And salt. Or we'd put them on a wire and lay them on the embers. And that's it. You want to go eeling? Tomorrow we will go. But first, it is our custom to take you to where I am from. Because that is our custom. Then we will go out and play."

According to Maori legend, Tuna is the eel god. He had a daughter named Hine, who married Maui, a nasty sort who ended up killing Tuna by smiting his head off with an axe. Tuna's severed head fled to a river and gave birth to all freshwater eels; his tail swam out to sea and gave birth to the congers.

Imaginative explanations for the rise of eels span many cultures. Aristotle devoted a large part of his *Natural History* to eels and their mysteries, suggesting that eels sprang magically from the mud of ponds. Later, Pliny contradicted him, writing that baby eels came from the scrapings left over from mature eels that rubbed themselves against rocks. An old Irish myth explains that eels rise from horse hairs that fall into the water. Wherever they occur, eels have inspired fanciful myths for thousands of years.

The truth about eels, however, is only slightly less improbable. Until less than a hundred years ago, all that was known about European eels was that they lived in rivers for most of their lives, descended to the ocean, and some time later, baby eels, called elvers, returned to the river. And that's about it. The whereabouts of their spawning grounds remained a mystery until, finally, a persistent Danish biologist named Johannes Schmidt (with funding from the Carlsberg beer company) triumphed in his quixotic bid in 1922. Schmidt had combed the Atlantic and discovered that small eel larvae could be found only in one spot, the Sargasso Sea, located, appropriately, in the Bermuda Triangle, an astounding 6,500 kilometres from the coastline of continental Europe.

How the eels find their spawning grounds in the Sargasso is a mystery, though the most popular hypothesis is that ocean salts act as a guide— eels can detect minute differences in salinity, thanks to a faculty so acute it surpasses all man-made instruments. How the elvers manage to navigate through myriad ocean currents back to the land of their ancestors— a journey that takes two years for European eels—is not known. How eels transform themselves from deep-travelling ocean fish to shallow, freshwater fish—and then back again—is also not known.

The long-finned eels of New Zealand are similarly mysterious. They live in the rivers on both the North and South islands for up to 60 years, much longer than their European and American cousins. They spawn only once, at the end of their lives, when they descend their home rivers and, biologists believe, swim 2,000 kilometres to a spot somewhere off the coast of Tonga. After the elvers drift back on ocean currents to New Zealand, they swim upstream, and their ability to get around obstructions is legendary; long-finned eels, apparently, are not easily discouraged. The small ones have been known to scale the concrete walls of dams, and the larger ones simply crawl out of the water and go it on land, squirming their way around the obstruction and back into the water. Eels, having gills, are most definitely fish and not reptiles as was once thought, though one species of eel has lungs and can't breathe without coming to the surface. But even the freshwater eel can get by on land for long periods of time. Eels can breathe through their skin when it remains moist and for this purpose they produce huge amounts of slime. As long as they're not caught out in a hot sun, eels can survive out of water quite comfortably. There has been one substantiated case of a farmer discovering eels in his field, eating peas. Usually, however, they are carnivorous, eating trout, ducklings, small hapless mammals. The truth is, eels eat just about anything they can fit into their mouths, which, I am honoured to add to the limited body of eel knowledge, sometimes includes the hind legs of Labrador retrievers.

"I USE mutton," says Alan Wilkinson the next day, when I ask him what eels take as bait. "Or any kind of seafood. Peppies. They are a flat, clam-like thing."

After touring the strangely beautiful volcanic landscape near Alan's village, we drive to his home and meet the family in his small, basic kitchen. They want to hear our stories, so we tell them about who we are and where we're from. Alan shows us a video of the New Zealand All Blacks, the national rugby team, performing the traditional Maori challenge, or Haka. "*Ka mate, ka mate! Ka ora, ka ora!*" shout the players fiercely, beating their chests and stomping their feet in unison.

"It means, 'It is death, it is death. It is life, it is life,'" says Alan.

Long after dark, we head to the garage and set to work making a gaff. Alan selects a large fish hook and secures it in a notch in the end of a stick. "It has to be strong," he says. Afterward, we drive along dirt roads to the river, bundled in layers against the chill, rain-whipped night. Gripping flashlights, we descend a steep muddy bank to the river's edge, slipping and sliding. Aiming the beam of his flashlight into the water, Alan searches in the nooks under rocks and beneath sunken logs. Nothing. "They hide in burrows, but once they smell the bait, they will come out."

Steve fishes out the bait from the bottom of a supermarket plastic bag. Fresh lamb chops. We rig up some handlines with heavy sinkers and lob the works into the water with a loud plonk. And we wait. And wait. Alan is wearing a fleece jacket, which unfortunately is doing a good job of sopping up the rain. We huddle behind a bush to get out of the wind. And we wait some more, blowing on our fingers to maintain at least a little feeling. Steve and I have agreed to give this spot a good try before we move on somewhere else tomorrow, so we stick it out. Every now and then we shine a flashlight into the dark swirling water, only to see nothing. We pull up our lines to check whether the lamb is still on the hooks; it is, but it has turned whitish and shrivelled in the cold water. It looks the way I feel.

After a couple more hours of this, Alan seems to be losing hope. Steve and I had lost faith a long time ago, but felt compelled to pretend things would turn around any minute. We seize the opportunity and convince Alan to give up. We climb back in the car, soaked, defeated and hungry. Driving back, we wish we'd just stayed at Alan's house in the first place and eaten the lamb chops ourselves.

THE CHOPPER slows and shudders as the pilot flares on approach to the landing strip, which is not really a strip at all but a patch of cleared brush barely big enough to accommodate the skids, on a high knife-edge saddle in the mountains.

With the wind blasting over the tight pass, the pilot wants to get the hell out of here as soon as possible. "You'll find the cabin down that trail," he yells over the thump-thump-thump of the rotors. "Good luck!"

We snap some pictures of the helicopter as it lifts off and U-turns back along the snaking river valley, and we listen until the whir fades into silence.

"Well," says Steve, rubbing his hands together and smiling, "this is it. We're finally here."

Yesterday, in a last ditch effort to find a river full of eels, we visited the department of conservation in Turangi. A friendly Swiss expat by the name of Michel Dedual seemed eager to help. The Rangitiki had the biggest eels, he said, but the place was also a training ground for the military and it was doubtful we'd get permission to go there on short notice. "But the Mohaka is also good. Lots of eels in there. It's in the wilderness, though; you can't walk in. You'll have to fly in." Michel had swum the Mohaka before to survey trout populations. "Take a stick with you," he warned. "The eels will attack your legs and it helps to whack them away."

The Mohaka valley is like nothing else we've seen so far of the North Island—wild, steep mountainsides covered in thick jungle and not a sheep to be seen. We schlep our gear down the switchbacked trail until we enter a clearing, where we first set eyes upon the "cabin." A crude sign made of a hunk of worthless lumber announces it as Mohaka Manor.

The cabin is disappointing, to put it politely. It has a hard plastic sheet for a roof, filthy green tarps for walls, no door and a dirt floor. The kitchen table is a plank of greasy black wood that is clearly also the favourite toilet of a team of small but well-fed mammals. The wood-framed bunks are just as bad, strung with wire and covered by dank cotton sleeping pads. Calling this squalid rundown hovel a "cabin" is a cruel joke. It's more like a port-a-john with bunks. For this, we are paying $50 a night.

Steve turns to me. "Before we leave this place, I say we burn it down," he says, only half joking.

Disgusting though it is, there is no option but to stay. This will be our home for the next four days. That the cabin is a pit of despair is one thing the kind people at the charter service did not mention. But we soon discover another problem—it isn't even near the river. It sits on a shelf in the mountainside, a good hour's trek from the water via a trail that leads down a cliff so steep we sometimes have to face the mountain and descend using the roots of trees like the rungs of a ladder. Then, we have to fight through a tangled wall of lush jungle undergrowth on the valley floor—all vines, giant ferns, rotten, punky logs that crumple when stepped on, twisted trees covered in lush beards of wet green moss—before crossing a swamp with man-eating mudholes of stinking ooze. The final descent follows a narrow path cut into the side of another mountain like the spirals of a screw, which is decorated by moist, bright-purple mushrooms right out of the imaginations of the Brothers Grimm.

The river, though, is just the way we thought it would be. Clear, green and fast, flowing over clean stone. The first day we leave the diving gear behind, figuring we'll need a day to scout the best section to swim. When we finally make it to the water's edge, Steve, who has gotten there first, says, "Look, man: floating rocks."

At first I think he's kidding, that they're hunks of smooth wood that look like rocks. Then, no: rocks the size of softballs and bigger, swirling on eddies by the bank—floating. Using a stick I fish one over and pick it up. It's rough and weighs nothing. Volcanic pumice, filled with air pockets. Figures that a river that has giant eels would also have floating rocks.

We thrash our way downriver for a kilometre or so, finally coming to a deep pool where the river piles into an undercut cliff, changing directions. The current is strong and dangerous. We can't risk swimming close to that wall, where we could get pushed under and trapped, so we move on, spending the rest of the day scouting downriver, occasionally spotting giant brown trout finning in the shallows, but no eels. It doesn't seem like a good sign. To top things off, the rain has returned, and you can just tell it isn't going away any time soon.

The next day we stuff our packs with wetsuits, masks, snorkels, fins and lunch, then head for the river. Sure enough, the rain continues. We suit up for the long hike and when we reach the river, we explore upstream. There are no trails at all; we simply bash our way through the jungle. After a couple of exhausting hours, however, we spot a sandy beach through the trees. Parting the branches and stepping onto the sand, we enter a small canyon with sheer walls of green on the opposite side. Mist hangs in ghostly patches along the tops of the tallest trees. Walking along the beach we turn a corner and find a pool of deep water connected to a fast-flowing but smooth run. It's perfect, the one place we have seen that doesn't look suicidal to swim.

With the reality of swimming in eel-infested waters upon us, however, the river suddenly doesn't look so inviting. Nevertheless, we struggle into our wetsuits, spit in our masks and high step into the shallows with our fins on. I plunge in and enter an alien world of sound, muffled, muted, with a far-off swishing of watery commotion. The cold water stings my head, hands and feet. Worse, the current is stronger than it looks, even in the flat sections. Visibility is not good, either, maybe 20 feet. From above, the river looked clear as distilled water but underneath the surface, bubbles and bits of flotsam obscure the light and make things look soupy. Somewhere in here, I think, are giant eels, lurking. With my field of vision cut off by the mask, I snap my head side to side, sure that I'll catch sight of a monster eel bearing down in the cloudy water, jaws open. I swim down the middle at first. Nothing. Then I get braver and approach the banks, scanning the inky blue holes under tree roots and rocks looking for any sign of life. In one dark mess of jumbled wood, I see something move, and for an instant my heart jumps into my throat. But it's only the roots of a tree swaying in the current.

The river soon carries me dangerously close to a set of rapids I have no intention of descending, so I fight my way to shore and pick my way back over the rocks to the head of the pool, where Steve has just gotten in. We swim this section of river again and again. No luck.

After a while we reconvene by our gear on the bank. It's raining harder now, with real gusto, and we sit in the mud wearing our soaked wetsuits, waiting for it to stop long enough to put our clothes back on. My face, feet and hands have turned blue. Mosquitoes and sand flies swarm around our heads. We hunker there for some time, shivering and miserable, without saying a word. It's getting late. Finally we decide to hike back wearing our wetsuits, something we've been avoiding, but now it's obvious there's no choice. Everything we own is wet, anyway. My cameras have been fogged for hours. With every step we feel the clammy suits against our skin and at this moment it's hard to imagine ever feeling comfortable again.

THE NEXT day is pretty much the same. Plodding through the jungle, scouting spots to swim; swimming, not finding any eels; then plodding back to camp, wet, tired and fly-bitten. By the last day, I can't take it anymore. Screw the eels. I have my fly rod with me and damned if I'm not going to catch a big beautiful brown. The barrel-fermented Hawke's Bay Chardonnay I have been saving for our eel meal will be opened in short order if I manage to fool one of these big trout on a fly.

Wading barefoot into the piercing cold water, I stand on a submerged dune of fine light-coloured sand, trying to cast a Yellow Humpy into the riffle in front of me. But the river's edge is so overgrown I can't get off a decent cast. When it doesn't snag on a branch behind me it lands in a pile of tangles on the water. Nevertheless I soldier on, switching flies and trying every trick I know.

Disgusted, I finally wade ashore. Steve has been dappling his fly over a boulder in the river, and after no luck, he decides to give my spot a try. I lie back on a moss-covered log swatting flies as he beats the water to a froth, probably scaring every trout for miles, if I haven't already. Then he gives up, too.

That's when I see it in the water, only a few feet from Steve, black and utterly creepy, undulating its snake-like body above the sandy bottom. It's huge.

"Steve!" I scream. "There's an eel right beside you!"

He doesn't believe me.

"Where?" he asks in a dubious voice, splashing towards the bank just in case.

"Look, look," I point. The eel has swum a little upriver towards a tangle of logs and rocks. "There! Right there!"

"Oh my God," he says, spotting the long black body.

There's no time to waste. A few days ago a man at a fishing store sold us what he considered an appropriate size gaff for eels, a hook so big it looked like the anchor on a small boat. But we hadn't yet bothered to fix it to a stick, so Steve retrieves a branch from the forest and sets to work carving a notch the way Alan taught us to. I dig out the handline and bait, a package of second-rate lamb cuts that was outdated when we bought it. After sitting unrefrigerated for three days in a zip-lock bag, it assaults me with a cloud of stink so putrid I can taste it.

As Steve puts the final wraps of twine around the gaff, I scramble upstream to the log-jam to keep an eye on the creature. I can't see it. Then, right by my feet, I spot its massive, wolfish head poking out from under a log, and it makes me shudder.

Steve gets into position. The handline I'm using is made of cotton, 40-pound test, wrapped around a thick wooden dowel. I spear a chunk of rotting lamb onto the hook and fling it in the water. Suddenly, out of nowhere, there's a whole bunch of eels swimming towards it, circling into a writhing ball of black slithery flesh until one of them opens its jaws and swallows the bait whole. I lean back into the line to set the hook and when the beast feels the tug it rears its ghastly head out of the water and starts twisting around the line, twisting, turning, gaping its mouth as I look on in horror, forgetting all the wonderful things I've heard about eels, staring only at this sinister, evil, evil devil fish crawling up the line towards me and suddenly—it just comes out of me, I don't know—I shriek at the top of my lungs. I pull back hard, the eel pulls back hard and then the line snaps.

"Gaff it!" I scream. "Gaff it!"

Standing precariously on the bank above it, Steve—normally a humane, animal-loving man—starts strafing the gaff through the water in a maniacal frenzy, again and again with no luck, then finally the big hook sinks into flesh and a primitive battle ensues, Steve struggling to hold on, the eel wrapped partly around a log, every bit a match for Steve, and then, just as suddenly as I had, Steve lets out a terrible shriek.

"Aaaarrrruuuuggg!!!"

At last, grimacing in revulsion, Steve wrenches the beast loose from the log, and with the giant eel wound tightly around the gaff like a boa suffocating a pig, we scramble up the muddy bank, slipping on fallen leaves until we get to a clearing of flat ground. The eel is nearly five feet long, probably 25 pounds and the most revolting creature I have ever set eyes upon.

"Well," Steve asks, "what now?"

"Kill it," I say.

"How?"

"Pick up that rock over there and bash it on the head."

The preferred method for killing eels is a matter of some controversy. Alan had said an axe to the neck is the best way. The man who sold us the gaff hook suggested we put it in a burlap sack, suspend it from a tree and have at it with a cricket bat. Without these resources, however, we decide the rock is the way to go.

Steve lifts up the rock, which must weigh 20 pounds, and drops it on the eel's head. It bounces right off. The eel tries to make a break for the water, but Steve picks up the rock again and bashes it once more. Again, it simply bounces right off. The eel's head is wide and fatty and, apparently, unbelievably strong. I've never seen anything like it. I'm used to trout, which are so delicate you can practically kill them with a mean look. If they don't expire on their own in a minute or two, a little rap on the head is all it takes. But the eel seems indestructible. We both feel sorry for the wretched thing, but by now it's definitely injured so we have no choice. Again and again Steve pounds it. I can feel the impacts through the ground. The thing just will not die. It is turning into a hideous ordeal, a mediaeval beat-down, like the penultimate scene in *Casino* when Joe Pesci and the other guy get brutally clubbed to death. All we want is for it to be over, so I look around for a bigger rock. It's dark now and I can't see very much, but finally I find one. I can barely lift it. Waddling over to the eel, I struggle to heft the massive stone over my head. Then, with a one-two-three, I hurl the great rock down. We know it's all over when we hear a loud, sickening crunch.

WITH THE butter sizzling in the pan, I cut the mushrooms and pour two glasses of wine.

"To the eel," I offer.

"To the eel."

Steve leads us in a moment of prayer to the eel gods. It seems appropriate given the nature of the encounter. Then we sit there, wordless, shell-shocked. Though it's been two hours since the death scene, we haven't really discussed it, concentrating only on trudging back in the darkness. It was, by any measure, a deeply unsettling encounter.

"Well," I say after a while, by way of an ice breaker, "you sure did a good job of gaffing the hell out of that thing."

"You're the one who unleashed that boulder on its head," he responds, instantly indignant.

Another long moment of reflective silence passes.

"It wasn't exactly what I had in mind," Steve confesses, and I have to agree. Then more silence.

"You hungry?" I ask Steve.

"No, not really. How 'bout you?"

"Not really."

This, I can tell you, is incontestably true, though we haven't eaten since morning. But the only thing we can do now to redeem ourselves is to eat the damn thing, which is why I start sautéing the mushrooms, big fat portobellos I've been keeping for the occasion. I cut up some potatoes for a Spanish omelette and in another pan, slice some red peppers, onions and garlic. Prior to flying in here, we had to decide on a cooking method. Everyone we had spoken to about eating eels offered their own recipe, but in the end we had decided to go traditional, the way Alan had recommended, which also had the attraction of being easy.

Now it's time to grill some eel.

We walk over to where it's lying on the ground. It's been dead for at least three hours, but when I take a knife and slice into it, the eel lifts its tail off the ground, slowly but deliberately, then uncurls it back down just as slowly.

"Oh, man," says Steve. "That's all we need right now." Seeing even a façade of life in something you know was dead some time ago—and in something you're just about to eat—does not please.

Steve immobilizes the tail by stepping on it with his boot, and I hack off a huge steak, slicing it in a few places to tuck in pieces of lemon, then throw it on the grill.

Unfortunately, I've grossly miscalculated the time it takes to grill eel. Eel flesh, I discover, resists heat quite well. It takes almost 40 minutes to cook through, during which time fat drips and sizzles, drips and sizzles, non-stop. It's like trying to grill a five-inch-thick slab of beef fat.

Finally, the moment arrives. I re-warm the mushrooms, peppers and onions, serve them up on two plates and carve into the eel steak. The flesh is white, firmish, and the flake is very fine. We dig in. It's chewy, bursting with oil. I look over at Steve, who's trying to subdue a large mouthful, leaning forward over his plate and wiping his mouth as the juices squirt out. After a few moments of effort, he finally gets it down and I ask him what he thinks.

He considers it for a few moments. Then, in a measured way that hints he's still undecided, offers, "Interesting."

This seems like an accurate assessment.

For my part I have decided, at least, that portobello mushrooms are not the ideal accompaniment to eel. Their texture—soft, chewy and slippery—is too similar to the eel flesh (which alone is pretty much all the fatty texture you can stand on one plate). But the onions and peppers seem to cut the flavour a bit, which helps. The eel flesh itself is okay, but when you get a mouthful of fat, which is hard not to do, the taste is strong and, I'm afraid, a little off-putting. Maybe it's the circumstances. Nonetheless, we finish the eel, chewing just to get it down, as though it's punishment for our crime.

With bellies full of eel, we hunker around the fire in our musty, filthy clothes. For the first time in over a week, it looks like the rain has finally stopped. But then it comes back, drizzling just enough to dampen whatever spirits we have left. We stare at the fire, mesmerized by the embers, flaring and glowing white, a lick of flame coming to life here and there, then dying, then coming to life again, then dying again. *Ka mate, ka ora.*

BY THE afternoon of the next day, we're back in civilized country, in Hawke's Bay once again, our last night in New Zealand. It feels really good to be back, clean and showered and dry for the first time in five days. Really good. We're at a fish-and-chips place that thankfully has no eel on the menu. For less than five bucks each, we have a mountain of crispy French fries made from properly aged potatoes—not too sugary—with two huge slabs each of perfectly cooked, delicately battered, absolutely scrumptious Pacific kingfish. We're sitting outside on the patio near the wharf, and at long last, the sun is shining for real, and we sit here in our shirt sleeves, luxuriating in the warmth.

"You know," I say to Steve, digging into the fish, "I don't think we should rule out eel just yet. Who knows, maybe breaded and deep-fried is the answer."

Steve looks up at me, glaring. It's clear he doesn't want to talk about it, doesn't want to take the bait. Like a soldier back from the front with a thousand-yard stare, he can manage only a few words, a single sentence actually, but one that says it all.

"Pass the tartar sauce."

THE WET COAST TRIAL

J.B. MacKINNON

MARCH 2003

IT'S RAINING. IT'S raining like a thousand hands thumping the Old Testament. Well, what did you expect? Sunshine? Chorus girls? This is the ragged fringe of the Pacific coast. The freaking *rainforest*. In the middle of the freaking *monsoon*.

I splash past signs that read "Trail Closed" and "Bridge Out." Up ahead, a thick five-o'clock-shadow of cedar and salal plays peek-a-boo games behind a curtain of mist. There was a fella who said it right back in 1906, when his lifeboat made the shore and he staggered into the forest with a handful of other shipwrecked survivors. It was January, and I can imagine them shivering in their wet woollens, wondering whether they've stepped from the frying pan into the fire. And then this fella, probably a glass-half-full type, he says, "By God, I think there's a trail in here."

Back then it was known as the Mariner's Trail, there to save the lives of stranded sailors. Nowadays we call it the West Coast Trail, there to save the souls of urban warriors who crisscross the planet in search of hard trekking. They come in droves all spring and summer, peaking at a flow of 60 per day, and then, on October 1, they vanish. The trail is officially shut down, and for the next six months, the landscape belongs to the storms and the gulls. And the rain.

So I get moving, heading up the first slope above Pachena Bay. I check my watch. There's only half a day of winter light, and 12 kilometres to the first camp. Right away I'm pushing it, even jogging awhile. It feels good to be under the pack, and it's actually a relief when the first deep puddles overflow my boots—no more sad games of hopscotch to keep my feet dry.

The trail steers into the forest, but I can still hear a sea-lion rookery—old curmudgeons griping about the weather again. Then comes Pachena Lighthouse, where I can finally absorb the open ocean's violence: huge waves rolling in from Japan that strike with the sound of a temple bell. I press on—a man with a mission—and make the Michigan Creek campsite with daylight to spare. Keep going? Why not? I'm already on the bridge when I realize it ends halfway in shattered wood and splinters. I climb down the broken planks to the water, and wade.

Beyond the creek, a tidal shelf stretches into the middle distance; I follow runnels of sand through a seaweed field. It's still raining, of course. Raining as though nature wants to dissolve herself. Soaked to the skin, I have to remind myself to drink—a miserable chore, like eating ice cream in a snow cave. But finally, as the sky shades from dark to darker grey, I reach kilometre 17 and Tsocowis Creek camp.

I haven't seen a soul all day.

The camp is full.

It's a trail maintenance crew, from the looks of the cork boots and tools. No one is home, but I can see some figures down the beach, and an upwind breeze carries the smell of marijuana. I back off—plenty of room for everyone—and pass back beneath the rusting stern of the freighter *Uzbekistan*, grounded here since 1943. Working against the falling light, I clear a patch of swamp beside Orange Juice Creek. There isn't time or comfort enough to cook, so I eat some fruit, some crackers, and I crawl into bed.

Shortly thereafter, I get the big-time heebie-jeebies. Is that someone playing harmonica? And drums down the beach? A woman calls my name. Was that a car horn? Was that the Number Nine bus passing by on Broadway?

And then I'm suddenly awake. A new sound. Something moving outside. (Isn't there always the sound of something moving outside?) No, this time it's real. I can hear footsteps on damp earth, and air through a wet nose. A bear? (But it's the middle of winter.) A wolf? A cougar? Osama bin Laden? I need a plan. Somewhat irrationally, I put on my headlamp, snap open my buck-knife and wait for the creature to pass the front hatch.

With the knife in my right hand, I whip open the zipper, snapping on the light with my left. With every atom in my body I attempt to express terrifying authority and willingness to fight. My eyes snap into focus on the enemy.

Two coal-black eyes.

Hot breath in cold air.

The cutest little fuzzy-face you ever did see.

THE GOOD people at Parks Canada do not want you to hike the West Coast Trail in the winter. Take, for example, the woman who answers telephone calls of inquiry.

"Is it illegal to hike the West Coast Trail in winter?"

"The trail is closed."

"I understand that the trail is closed. But is it actually illegal to hike the trail in the winter?"

"It is definitely not recommended."

"But is it illegal?"

"We've gone in there in the spring and found bodies."

That is only the first of the hurdles. In the summer, the trail is a logistician's dream. You reserve a departure date for $95, and when the time comes, you drive to Port Alberni on Vancouver Island. From there, it's two hours of dirt road to Bamfield, an isolated outport. A few kilometres from town, you park at the trailhead and register with the park wardens. Then you spend a week or so drifting through a series of epiphanies induced by crashing surf, primeval forest, and the blue pills you take on a sunset beach with three naked hippies from Denmark. Seventy-five kilometres later, you get ferried across the San Juan River to the village of Port Renfrew, where a shuttle bus whisks you over logging roads and back to your car. That's when you get to the hard part: the reluctant return to reality.

The off-season is different. In the winter, the 90-kilometre road from Port Alberni to Bamfield can be extremely rough on, for example, a 1991 Dodge Colt, so a better bet is the MV *Lady Rose,* a 1937 packet freighter that takes five hours to chug up Alberni Inlet. Assuming all goes well on the hike—and remember, where there is no cellphone signal, no one can hear you scream—you then end up in Port Renfrew. There's no shuttle to your car; in fact, there's no public transport, period. To get back to your parking spot at the *Lady Rose* dock, you'll have to hitchhike to Victoria and hop busses to Port Alberni. Total connect-the-dots: more than 200 kilometres.

But let's backtrack. You're not going to make it to Port Renfrew. Not unless you can walk on water.

The midpoint of the West Coast Trail is Nitinat Narrows, a tidal rapids. In the summer, a Ditidaht family shuttles hikers back and forth in a motorboat, but Parks Canada forbids the family from arranging passage in the winter. You're on your own across a few hundred metres of water that, depending on the tide, might be churning at 14 knots—fast enough to strip off your swim trunks as you cling to your overturned driftwood raft. The water, incidentally, is cold enough to freeze the brass balls off a dead prime minister.

There's more. Suppose you make it across the narrows. At the end of the trail, where the lights of Port Renfrew twinkle across the bay, you still have the San Juan River to cross. You might try to arrange a pickup with Brian Gisborne, skipper of the Juan de Fuca Express Water Taxi, but the Parks Canada people have gotten to him, too. And he will say this about finding your own way across Port San Juan: "In a southwestern blow, you can end up pretty deep in the rhubarb."

And it's always a southwestern blow.

At this point you might remind yourself that a kind of elitism has crept into the West Coast Trail experience. Yes, in the 1970s, it was a world-class trek, an epic that introduced the world to the Canadian rainforest and inspired a generation of environmental activists. "You should prepare for the worst," reads the 1972 Sierra Club guide, "and the worst on the west coast of Vancouver Island is beyond what most people have experienced." Back then there were no boardwalks; you crossed the wider rivers on hand-built rafts, and the recommendation for one steep descent was "just squat down and sort of slide."

Today, the critics say, the trail has become a tick-list adventure, a bureaucratized "experience" of "wilderness." Book your space, line up to register, follow the crowd down the dotted line. In fact, one former hiking guide sneered, there are three ways to follow the West Coast Trail. You can take the path up the middle, or you can follow the cairns through the woods to either side. What do the cairns look like? Each one is a little mound with a white flash of toilet paper sticking out of the top.

So why, on a grey mid-winter morning, did the chorus of complaint sound so much like a failure of imagination? I was sitting on the *Lady Rose*, which can—and in summer often does—carry up to 100 passengers. In winter the boat runs just three times a week, and I was one of only eight passengers, not including a cat and a dog. These few locals gave me a pitying look as I fiddled with my tide charts and topo map. I had a plan for Nitinat Narrows, but not one that could be honestly described as "fail-safe." I was even less sure about the San Juan River. And both my would-be partners had bailed out with soft excuses ("got a job" and "moving to France," respectively).

I got off the boat and within 10 minutes had arranged for a lift to the trailhead in exchange for a single Sir John A. Macdonald. And there I was. Damned if it didn't feel like an adventure.

SO FUZZY-FACE was a dog. She was the kind of dog that would look great in a woman's largish handbag. Maybe something in a monochrome—a Toronto red or a Los Angeles yellow—because the dog itself was a pure white pom-pom. Seeing this Yorkville dog, this Robson Street or West-mount dog, standing in the black rain on the sleepless Pacific, was too unreal to absorb. I scratched her on the head, zipped the tent and went to sleep.

She was still there in the morning, looking, as only dogs can, delighted to see me alive. More delighted, in fact, than I was myself. Sunrise had come with only the slightest brightening of the sky; the few forest birds had held off, hoping for better, then burst into song for the feeble dawn. It was raining, of course. Raining tears for all the dead that ever did die.

I pulled on my wet clothes, packed, and stamped down the beach trying to beat blood into my feet. I figured the work crew would be anxious about their little mutt, and the happy reunion began just outside the camp—a young malamute came bounding down the beach, sending pom-pom into twirling circles of joy.

Tsocowis camp has a cabin, where a large, off-duty logger-type was leaning on the rail. He had the wise, weary look of a person who has concluded that the world is completely insane, but what the hell, they're still paying union wages. We locked eyes, and at precisely the same time, we said:

(Me) "Guess you're missing your dog."

(Him) "So you're the mysterious dog owner."

We stared at one another. And then:

(Together) "These aren't your dogs?"

It took some effort to sort out the story. The malamute had shown up the previous afternoon. The white dog must have followed, trailing behind. Somehow, both animals had arrived, separately, at a camp almost 20 kilometres from the trailhead. Where they came from, nobody knew. It was a mystery, and one that I was happy to leave to the trail crew. I was here to hike the West Coast Trail, fast, light and solo. House pets didn't fit with the plan.

The dogs, however, had other ideas. The moment I headed down the trail, they followed. I tried running, yelling, throwing small clods of dirt; they simply stared back at me with chase-a-stick eyes. Finally, I walked them back to the camp and asked two sturdy lumberjacks to hold back the hounds.

I ran. I scrambled up a rough staircase and thundered over a suspension bridge. I ran with the backpack sending shockwaves down my spine, until I was out of breath and spattered with mud. When my chest was heaving and my knees were wobbly, I slumped against a tree and listened for the pitter-patter of paws.

They came loping around the bend.

Delighted to see me.

God how I hated those dogs.

It was time to apply a more logical approach. Studying the map, I noted that the broad Klanawa River was just a few kilometres away. I would lose the dogs there. They would stand on the north bank, yelping, while I flew over the water in the cable-car. Then they would remember the smell of bacon at the work camp, and they would fade into the forest. The conquering hero—that's me—would forge onward alone.

In the meantime, there was the climb to Valencia Bluffs. We wound our way up, the malamute ahead, the puffball behind. At the top, we all looked down to where the sea and the shore seemed to fight in slow motion. Here, on the night of January 22, 1906, the steamer *Valencia* ran aground and was beaten apart by the waves over two appalling days. Of 173 passengers and crew, only 37 survived, including the lucky fella who made it ashore and found the Mariner's Trail. All the others—136 souls— were lost. Some of the last to go tied themselves to the rigging to keep from being washed off the decks by the surf. It was probably a day like today, with rain falling from a funereal sky. The trees moaned and the sea lions keened and the wind said the rosary through the leaves. And then the boat broke up, and the last survivors were dragged, crucified, into the Graveyard of the Pacific.

The two pooches looked up at me with sparkling eyes and did their merry jigs. Pretty great dogs, really.

But my heart leapt as we descended to the river, which was wide and fast-flowing. Without pausing, I climbed the ladder to the cable-car, the dogs whining below my feet. I loaded my bag, climbed in and cast off. Rolling out into open air. Feeling the freedom. Looking back to see two dogs swimming through the rapids.

Oh sweet Jesus. Little pom-pom was going to die.

On the south bank, I jumped onto the platform and scrambled down the ladder, noting with relief that the malamute already had his footing in the shallows. Out in the middle of the flow, though, foam was cresting over a bright white head. I ran to the water's edge and started to shout, slap my thighs, make good-doggie noises. The little snout was beginning to point downstream, and I started to wade in, and then she caught the shore eddy and came swirling to my feet. She stepped out daintily, shook, and turned some happy circles. She and the malamute headed down the trail.

It is strange how the focussed mind works towards a goal. I had prepared myself for storms, washouts, bitter cold, rogue waves and the creepy sound of ancient trees in the wind. I had never considered the possible challenges of spontaneous dog care and handling. This new reality simply didn't fit. All I could think was that, somehow, I would push these animals another 50 klicks. Or I would break them, and they would wander the long haul back to Tsocowis camp. Either way, I would go on. I had the trekker's equivalent of summit fever.

But on the banks of the Klanawa, something had shifted. Now I shared my food with the dogs; we drank from the same creeks. Watching the pom-pom eat junk fish on the beach, I settled on nicknames. The puffball would be Flotsam; the malamute, Jetsam. When they lagged behind, I glanced back half-hoping they had turned around. But only half-hoping.

Meanwhile, the trail was working its magic. The rain softened to silken sheets, and the tide pulled back to give us miles of beach. Bonaparte's gulls, wearing the twin teardrop markings of their winter plumage, skipped along the tops of the breakers, where the wind lifted salt mist into the trees. Eagles wheeled overhead—keep close, Flotsam, keep close—and seals stared from slack water behind the sea stacks. I was deeply, idyllically alone, and at the same time in good company. For the amusement of my friends, I belted out a sea shanty in full voice.

A cluster of red buoys marked the point where the trail steered back into the forest. The next stop, I knew, was the Nitinat Narrows. The true test. Would the tides be pumping? Would a whirlpool be turning below the bottleneck where I hoped to cross? I caught a sidelong glimpse of green water through the trees, but refused to look again until the trail made its way to the rocks along the shore.

And it was perfect. From my charts I had predicted a slow inflow towards Nitinat Lake, and here were two mergansers slowly drifting inland, the still water reflecting their colours exactly. In my pack I carried a small, inflatable raft, barely big enough even for a single person. It was my secret weapon. And it would work. I could make it.

The water, though, was deep and cold. The dogs stared at me, and then out across the lonely distance to the faraway bank. Flotsam's brow wrinkled into a chevron of anxiety. She was a beauty queen once, and now just look at her. Muddy and matted. For the first time I noticed that she was favouring one leg, and when I checked I found a worn patch of pink flesh on her paw. If she somehow swam the narrows, we still had half the trail to go, including a half-dozen rivers and a series of ladders.

I looked back at the water. Everything so right.

Is the end of a trail worth a dog's life?

Without an ounce of regret, the whole team turned around.

IT WAS five kilometres back to the nearest camp. We marched hard along the shore, but the rising tide chased us back into the woods. Finally, at the top of the long stairway down to Tsusiat Falls, the sky opened up in an unfamiliar blue and a sunset beamed on the trail's most perfect scene: a bridal veil waterfall tumbling from sky to sea. In the warmer months, Tsusiat is an all-too-human place, where primal meditation has given way to hackeysack and singalongs. It can be, as Ian Gill wrote in *Hiking on the Edge*, "a dreary reminder of the press of civilization." Not today. I had the beach to myself, and for the moment it was bathed in crystal winter light. I had reclaimed Tsusiat in the name of spaced-out thoughts.

To wit: *rain is some powerful stuff, dude*. All over the world, people pay their year's savings to wander deserts and jungles, or to stand at the poles. We have a hunger to test ourselves against the earth's extremes, but rain, somehow, remains a final frontier. The village of Bamfield gets nearly 10 feet of precipitation a year (picture yourself standing at the bottom of the deep-end of your local swimming pool), and 85 per cent of it falls after the tourists go home. In the winter, the coast is lashed by 10 to 15 storms each month. It is a place to test yourself, as surely as Antarctica or the Empty Quarter. It is a place of humbling natural primacy and gothic magnificence. It can also be, as one coastal logger put it, "the asshole of the world." How you feel about the winter rainforest depends on whether a steady cascade of cold water down your spine marks the line of adventure, or of suffering.

We had crossed that line. With numb hands, I fumbled with the stove, cooking black beans and rice for three. I combed out the dogs with a bristly twig, and chatted in spite of the language barrier. The twilight stretched sublimely, but I had trouble on my mind. Flotsam had started shivering, and then shivering hard. *The dog is going to die,* I thought. *Prepare to suck bad karma.* I tried to dry her, then to lure her into the tent. She refused, curling up instead with Jetsam beneath the driftwood.

I woke up heavy with dread.

I heard the sound of a moppet shaking out her fur.

I felt a deep sense of gratitude.

Still, there was something about the morning that didn't feel right. The sky was mainly clear, but rain would come suddenly in ballbearing gusts, fierce snarls of weather spun from the purple horizon. I had decided to walk the dogs to Bamfield, preferably in two days. It was 35 kilometres from Tsusiat Falls.

Around midday we reached the Tsocowis crew camp, where the scene was exactly as I'd left it. The gentle giant was there, leaning against the rail. He listened to my turnaround tale and nodded his approval. Then he fiddled with some gear and said, offhand, "So what's your plan for today?"

"I thought I'd camp up the beach, and get these dogs out to Bamfield tomorrow."

"You *could* do that," he said. His choice of words suggested the likelihood of a preferable option. He shifted weight, as though physically uncomfortable telling someone else what they should do. "There's a storm coming," he said. "Better tarp 'er down tight."

He paused to let that settle, then looked at me with one fixed eye. "They're sending in a chopper to take us out."

The message was unmistakable, and I got the team moving. The tides were tipped in our favour, giving us endless sand flats, but as the day wore on the signs of the impending storm grew clear. The squalls had a cinematic violence, and the surf sawed at the shore in tall, tight sets. The horizon, and eventually much of the western sky, was the same colour you see in that last instant before you go unconscious.

The day had just become too long when we saw the mist rising from Pachena Bay. On the last leg to the trailhead, the dogs began to lead out. I knew then that they were close to home.

We dragged our feet along the dirt road into town. Already, we had covered more than 30 kilometres without a break. Even Jetsam, the unstoppable malamute, was lolling his tongue. Finally, a van came rumbling up the steady slope that was slowly sapping my will to continue. It stopped, and a door slid open to reveal fresh-faced young women in Helly Hansen overalls.

"Wanna ride into town?"

I resisted the urge to collapse into their laps. "I'd have to bring these dogs," I said. Exhausted and fumbling, I gave them a nutshell version of my last three days.

The women gave the mutts a closer inspection. "We know these dogs," one shrugged. "They're locals." The van erupted into an energetic discussion of tell-tale markings and recent encounters. The dogs might have an owner, they said, but more than likely they don't. When they look skinny, someone feeds them; if they look matted they get brushed; if they look cold or wounded, someone takes the time to care. I had done good by the dogs, bringing them home. But there was nothing, really, I could do from here. We were just outside of Bamfield. The dogs could smell it from here. And anyway the dumb mutts wouldn't get into the van.

We pulled away and I stared out the rear window as my two friends chased after the wheels. Then we crested the hill and Flotsam and Jetsam winked out of sight.

I STEPPED into the Bamfield Motel and the woman at the desk said, "You're the fella who went out on the West Coast Trail."

I had never seen this woman before in my life. I did not want to talk to her. I did not want to explain myself or share my story. I wanted a shower, a bed and a thermostat over which I had totalitarian control.

"We made bets on how long you'd last out there."

"Is that so?" I said sharply.

She handed me the key.

When I stepped out of the shower, the world had changed. The windows were rattling with wind, and outside, the treetops were wagging like accusing fingers. It was raining; it was raining like you just plain wouldn't believe. I said a quiet prayer as I dressed in warm, dry clothes. Then I opened my door, fought the gale to close it, and made my way back to the motel's front office. The woman was there, fiddling with something under the desk.

"Who won?" I said.

"Pardon?"

"Who won the bet?"

She bent her head to cover up a small smile. "Well," she said, "I guess I was the lucky one." She looked up with bright eyes. I nodded towards the window, where a streetlight was catching raindrops blowing sideways in its beam.

"I figure I had some good luck, too."

"Yes," she said, "I suppose you did."

THE BOYS AND
THE BACKCOUNTRY

IAN BROWN

WINTER 2002

ON THE QUESTION of whether to include a single woman in a group of seven married men who are ski-mountaineering out of a tiny hut on a remote icefield in the Rocky Mountains of British Columbia, let me offer, dear reader, one small piece of advice: do not tell your wife, by way of pacifying her about the imminent presence of said woman on your ski trip, that the woman is a lesbian. Especially do not do this if the woman is *not* a lesbian. No one will believe you anyway, and when they find out you lied, they will mock you mercilessly, referring to your untruth at every opportunity, ski-related or otherwise. Your foolishness will be the talk of the village. Months later, should you happen to say, "I met an interesting woman at the peace conference in The Hague last week," people will say, "Oh, yes, was she a lesbian?" and derisive laughter will ensue. Or you might say, over breakfast many years later, "The woman at the dry cleaners gave me a hard time when I complained about my missing shirt." There will be only one reply: "Well, she must be a lesbian."

Anyone who goes ski-mountaineering with the same middle-aged men every winter for nearly 20 years knows that the reasons for doing so are amorphous. The reasons change, too. The longer you do it, the harder it becomes, the more theories you have as to why you still want to do it. But you cherish your days in the empty white rooms on the top floor of the earth more with each visit. Needless to say, with one's head in the clouds, having a single woman along is not something one thinks about even for a moment. In a way, that's the point: one is freed from such obligations as lust and attending to the desires of women. But to the faithful mates and partners you have left at home to tend the fires of income production and the tears of your babes, any woman who shows up on a previously all-male ski trip is a tart and a jezebel. So lesbian or non-lesbian, you cannot win. And this is only the first thing you will discover on top of the world in the company of friends.

ANOTHER DISCOVERY available to the glacier traveller is that the theme of every adventure story is the same: *It seemed like a good idea at the time.* I can't say this one was any different. The idea was to fly in a ski plane onto the Clemenceau Glacier, one of the longer, wider, remoter and less-yielding fairways of ice in the Canadian Rockies, out of Golden, B.C. Golden is a lumber town that is thriving despite the American tax on softwood lumber because Golden is also home to Kicking Horse, one of the newest and most exciting downhill resorts in North America. We could have skied there, in other words. But no, we had to haul 500 pounds of food and 150 pounds of fuel and all our personal gear on our backs up into a region that is famous for its bad weather even by the high bad-weather standards of interior British Columbia.

Three of us had tried it 15 years earlier, so we really ought to have known better. Back then, the plan was to ski from the vast Clemenceau Icefield to the vaster Columbia Icefield, a trip that, according to published records at the time, had been accomplished only twice before. (Now it seems to happen about once every other year.) On that trip, weather had forced us to abandon the attempt. But the experience of ascending the crux of a giant wave of ice known as the Apex Glacier with a 75-pound pack on my back had lodged itself in my memory like a hot, sharp, permanently disfiguring splinter.

Hence the improvements this time around. Now we were all in our late forties, older but (for the most part) richer (if you don't adjust for inflation). Instead of carrying a tent and sleeping on the snow, we'd make camp in the Alpine Club of Canada's cozy Lawrence Grassi hut. Instead of carrying heavy packs, we'd fly in, on a fixed-wing aircraft no less, and have food and fuel dropped. Instead of making mind-numbing decisions about snow safety and cooking food in a snow bank, we'd high-grade the whole operation. We hired John Buffery, an internationally acclaimed guide (he often advises movie productions on climbing scenes and makes sure no one dies). Then we hired a second guide/cook to make gourmet meals in the comfort of the hut while we sat around drinking gin and tonics and discussing the technical niceties of that day's summit.

Anyone who knows anything about adventuring will recognize instantly how radical an approach this was. Did I say radical? It was a total repudiation, a slap in the balaclava of centuries of explorational wisdom. *Pain,* we were saying to the gods of the mountains, *is not necessary to find pleasure in remotest nature. Man*—even middle-aged man—can triumph over adversity *by avoiding it altogether.*

As I say, it seemed like a good idea at the time. The guide/cook's name was Hilary. She was blonde, an indefatigable skier, a trained wilderness nurse and 28 years old.

THE FIRST hitch in our beautiful plan was that the plane, a laughably small Cessna, could only carry three passengers at once, given all our gear. With the guide and the cook, this meant three trips. I was on the first flight. Hilary waved goodbye to me from the runway. "Hope we see you up there," she said. "If not, you had a good life." I respectfully suggest this is not the sort of ironic breeziness you want to hear from the mouth of a blonde whose trail-riding-toned thighs could crack hazelnuts between them, *not that I know anything about that.*

The second hitch was that even the Cessna couldn't get any closer than seven kilometres from the hut, which meant that at the age of 48, I once again found myself carrying a 60-pound pack on my back and hauling a hundred pounds of diesel fuel and white gas on a Norco plastic toboggan that seemed to be attached to my inguinal canal. Perhaps you know the feeling associated with watching a small plane disappear in the sky, while you come to the unavoidable realization that it was your last available exit from the middle of goddamned frozen nowhere for the foreseeable future. John Buffery, our guide, who despite his renown resembles Gene Wilder in *Young Frankenstein*, was at the front of the first party, laying track through 18 inches of fresh powder. I was at the back of the first party, keeping my eye on Colin MacKenzie, a Toronto newspaper editor and friend who, while fit and keen, hadn't ever—and this was an oversight—actually descended a field of fresh mountain powder on skis. Mind you, in his capacious and always interesting mind, he *had*, both conceptually and theoretically: he was just a little light on actual feet-on-snow experience. Two hours down the first glacier from the Cessna's landing strip (a row of wands tipped with fluorescent orange plastic tape), MacKenzie informed me that he was about to turn 50. "Yes, yes," he said. "That's why I wanted to do this, before the gruesome date itself." Pause. "By the way, is there any way the heels of these boots lift up when we're going uphill?" He had spent the morning traversing a glacier with his heels locked down.

Two hours later, we'd descended the Tusk Glacier and were starting up Reconnaissance Ridge, an endless dorsal fin of rock and snow that offers some of the best (albeit unheralded) turning terrain in the Rockies. The hut was now 2,000 feet above us, and about two kilometres to the northwest. If the Apex had been agony at the age of 32, this was agony times three, given that Reconnaissance Ridge is even steeper. I'd been training rigorously in Toronto, at least by my 15-pounds-overweight standards. But out here in the whiteness, the day getting on, I couldn't take more than 20 steps without resting. Even Buffery was having a hard time carrying a pack and pulling a sled up the steep incline, which I admit made me feel better. We briefly considered climbing packless and setting up a pulley system to haul the packs over the crux, but we decided in the end to shuttle our respective loads one by one up the ridge.

A couple of hours later, we made the hut. Buffery and I headed down again to start shuttling the remaining piggish packs while the rest of our party made their way over the ice from the airstrip. MacKenzie stayed behind, happily volunteering to shovel the hut—a two-storey Quonset—out of the snowdrift in which it was almost invisibly buried. There were three windows and a door, all similar. His first job was to find the door. He got it on the fourth try.

This is the second lesson—no, wait, the third—of the wilderness ski experience: it doesn't matter how much money and how much help you have. In the mountains in the winter, you work for everything. I am told that eventually this seems like its own reward.

DID I mention the weather? It snowed. It snowed for five days straight. "I've never seen this much fresh snow at once in my whole life," MacKenzie said one morning, staggering in with yet another bucket of the fresh white fluffy stuff to melt for coffee.

This shouldn't have been a surprise either. Mount Clemenceau, the boss mountain of the region, was first sighted by a white man in 1892. The white man was A.P. Coleman, a peripatetic explorer in the Canadian Rockies. The mountain wasn't seen again for four years, so even the second sighting rated a mention in the *Canadian Alpine Journal*, where the 12,000-foot Clemenceau, the fourth-highest peak in the Rockies, was considered (in the *Boy Scout Manual* prose that still characterizes a lot of Canadian exploration writing) "the greatest prize awaiting conquest in all the Canadian Rockies." (The mountain was named for Georges Clemenceau, the brilliant French journalist, Germany-despiser and two-time premier who inspired France to victory during the Great War.) "Awaiting conquest" was the right phrase: the Clemenceau Glacier—and its icy siblings the Tusk, the Apex and the Shackleton, all of which curl around each other like cold, hungry wolves in a lair—is so remote, so difficult to get to (three weeks of bear-infested bushwhacking by foot), and its weather so uncompromising, that the peak wasn't climbed until 1923. And a first winter ascent had to wait until 1977. When the shovelling-challenged MacKenzie finally burrowed his way into the hut for our party, no soul had set foot in it for two years. That's a rare degree of isolation, even in the Rockies.

The isolation and the weather were only the beginning of our travails. By evening of the first day, Hilary was in a single-minded fury of kitchen organizing. Meanwhile, Norman Bishop, one of the strongest skiers in our party, was out cold in bed thanks to dehydration after "blowing chunks across the Rockies." Two other members of the party had come down with the racking cough that Hilary had brought along, while Mac-Kenzie, who for reasons unknown to science disdains sun block, resembled a well-broiled tomato.

The next morning, with Bishop in bed, Hilary still maniacally reorganizing the hut's spice rack, and the cough threatening to spread still further, two of our party decided to take action to save our corporeal and mental health. They began building what was to be the techno-civilizational triumph of our expedition—the portable sauna.

The rest of us skied up Reconnaissance Ridge. It was a long ridge. As we trudged upward, visibility was 20 feet. Then we skied down the other side, onto the Cummins Glacier. Visibility was now 10 feet. Setting off downhill entailed handing your fate to the gods the way you might hand your car keys to a parking valet. Sometimes the snow disappeared beneath your feet and you sailed through space, at least until you found yourself upside down and de-skied in a bottomless bank of soft white confounding hell—a delirious flight usually accompanied by a small, surprised "oh." Shortly after lunch, Buffery decided to check a slope for its avalanche potential and told MacKenzie to wait behind him. Mac-Kenzie moved a few feet back, and I heard the "oh" again. MacKenzie had fallen 10 feet off a cornice and broken his binding. (It was fixed that evening in a bout of ingenuity by Buffery and Will Randall, the Argentinian farmer in our party. Randall fashioned a new binding plate out of an empty white-gas can while the rest of us watched intently from perches around the hut, like medical students observing their first heart transplant from the gallery of an operating theatre. It occurred to me that the Ski Repair Channel has a future on cable.)

MacKenzie's ski technique, however, was not solvable by mere repair. He was terminally afflicted the entire trip. He sailed off down the slopes admirably enough, never wanting to keep us waiting, but then leaned back, fell, lost his ski in the snow, got up, sailed off, got scared and leaned back, fell, etc., etc., all the while muttering "fuck fuck fuck fuck," like a mad speckled hen suffering from both Saint Vitus's Dance and Tourette's.

I know the frustration MacKenzie felt, because I wasn't exactly dominating the slopes myself. My problem, Buffery insisted, was that my telemark turns were missing a proper pole plant. "The pole plant is the key to all skiing," he said gently, albeit oracularly. "And the steeper the terrain, the more critical the early pole plant is." The plant comes first, then the weight shift, then the commitment to the legs, that delightful telemark sensation of hurling yourself downhill face first—not the other way around as I had been performing it. "You start with the pole, the upper body follows," Buffery said.

Wonderful. I'd been telemarking for 15 years, and I still hadn't mastered the basic pole plant.

BACK AT camp, fuelled by sheer gumption and something they found in one of the packs, the stick-in-the-huts were going about setting up the sauna.

The sauna was another concession to advancing middle age and our love of comfort—or, to put it another way, we refused even to be dirty in the remotest mountains. John Mitchell, one of the original Edmonton-based members of our annual ski-mountaineering party, had made it his mission on the trip to perfect a portable *steamhaus*. There was no reason to believe he couldn't. Mitchell, after all, was the genius who had designed our glacier pigs, the modified Norco toboggans that we used to haul heavy packs over the glacier. The original portable sauna prototype, tested in the Tonquin Valley in Jasper National Park several years earlier, was modelled roughly—very, very roughly—on the ancient concept of the native sweat lodge, except that where the natives used fire-heated rocks, Mitchell—with a nod to fossil-based fuels and his background as an oilman—employed a double-burner Coleman stove boiling two full kettles of water inside a two-man North Face High Sierra tent covered with two sleeping bags. This contraption was hot enough to make three men want to run outside into the sub-zero evening and roll naked in the snow. Drawbacks included a persistent threat of scalding and a two-by-four headache due to methane gas collecting off the stove inside the tent.

A second model developed a few seasons later incorporated the same tent/stove design, but located the Coleman safely outside the tent.

The kettle nozzles were then clamped into clear, reinforced PVC tubing, which was fed into the tent—not a steam*haus* so much as a steam*hose*. This model was safer, or at least reduced the scalding threat, and was less noxious; alas, it produced the same rise in body temperature as two aspirins in Coke.

With Model III, the one to be field-tested on the remote unlit plains of the Clemenceau Glacier, Mitchell figured he had all the kinks ironed out. True, the Baboonmaker—as it came to be known—required its own sled and most of the afternoon of Day Two to assemble, but these were minor sacrifices to the progress of comfort. The newly rethought design brought the stove and kettles and boiling water back into the tent, thus retaining the high sauna temperature and the scalding threat. It also retained the PVC tubing technology—except this time as breathing tubes venting to the fresh outside air, as two or even three grown humans sat inside the tent around a flaming Coleman stove and two steaming kettles, sucking in fresh air from the outside. The laws of gasiform physics made it important to remember to breathe *in* through the tube and *out* into the tent to avoid hyperventilating and near-certain death, but the godliness of ski-trip cleanliness would have felt less valuable if it had been easy.

Results and discussion: Two days later, everyone had Hilary's cold; the tubes, which we all shared, were the Indianapolis Speedway of germ-sharing. As for the brume in the sauna and the frightening dark water that condensed on the floor of the tent after a couple of skiers had steamed away a day's sweat and willnots—well, let me say that I made the mistake of slipping in it that first experimental evening in the steamer. Two days later, I had the worst case of baboon ass I have experienced in 30 years of outdoor life. Baboon ass, of course, because of the brilliant red calluses the steam juice fetched up on my hiney. And painful? Imagine your own anus as the rusted-out gear of a giant pepper grinder. That begins to describe it.

"I don't know," Mitchell said one night over dinner, "it might be more trouble than it's worth."

"Well," said Bishop, who by now had stopped puking, "at least no one has died yet."

DESPITE ALL this, maybe even because of it, we enjoyed ourselves. "Best trip yet," we all said, every day, which is what we say every year, and every year we mean it more, if anything.

For instance, there was the first run of Day Three. It was still snowing slightly, after 36 hours, and visibility was too poor for serious glacier travel. But Buffery moved us out quickly onto the snow anyway. We shot straight up Reconnaissance Ridge and then down a thousand feet of the deepest lightest powder I have ever skied. It was one run, and I suppose not much by the standards of helicopter skiers. But it was the one run I had never had before. There were others, too, in rapid succession, almost as good, but the snow was setting up, becoming fractionally heavier with every descent as the temperature rose, permitting the distinction between truly excellent and timelessly sublime skiing—a distinction very few people are lucky enough to get to make.

Or there was the day two days later, the only one describable as sunny, with the new snow load approaching 14 inches, or 35 centimetres. Buffery operated on a rough "30 by 30 by 30 rule": 30 centimetres of new snow loaded by a 30-mile-an-hour wind on a 30-degree slope equals an avalanche. Buffery and Hilary had, as a result, spent a morning digging a snow pit and analyzing the structure and stability of the slopes we were skiing. Satisfied, he led us right to the top of the ridge, and then down the steepest runs I have ever skied, much less telemarked: 42 degrees, by Buffery's estimate. I have to say it was one of the more intense moments a life can provide: that breath-sucking lurch your stomach does as you come to the yawp of the steep, where the slope falls away and away and away; the way the snow released by your turns cascades down the pitch around you. All the famous attendant phenomena occurred: time stopped, and I felt no more or less than what I was, a tiny being making his way safely, sneakily down the vast shoulder of God, because for a moment God wasn't looking, or wasn't angry. "It's quite strange," observed Allan Kling, my attorney and the person who first took me skiing in the mountains nearly 20 years ago, as we made our way up through the prelude to another whiteout. "You can't tell one plane from another." He meant that with the fog and the snow, it was hard to tell where the

slope beneath our feet ended and the sky began. He's right. You're trudging up a hill or soaring down a slope, but the thing that makes the winter
mountains what they are and nowhere else is that you are always moving
through the sky.

One afternoon we climbed down to the frozen waterfall at the foot of
the Shackleton Glacier. The icicles were five storeys high, an enormous
knife drawer in the sky. Above us light was leaking across the glacier
like spilled cream, and snow had blown into every crack and fissure and
cranny of Mount Tsar, a Jackson Pollock painting on the most massive
scale imaginable. I always want to assign consciousness to the mountains at times like that, as if they know what they are displaying for us,
and why—as if the ancient emptiness, the austere uncaring silence of the
high winter wilderness is a message, a warning not to become too ambitious or too prideful. This rock and ice has been here a long time, after
all. Of course I know this is illogical: nature is a system, even an intelligence, but not a Being with human intent. But something in me wants the
mountains to be alive. Probably it's just the effect of that churchy white
grandeur on a suggestible consciousness; that there's no one else around,
and that this really is the last place left on a shrinking earth that can truly
be called wilderness; or that you have to earn every step and take care
of the necessities, which in turn puts life in the needlessly complicated
city in clarifying perspective. As I said before, one's ideas on the subject
change constantly up there. But it is a place that gives you ideas; it makes
you think. And maybe that's the mountains' most lasting appeal.

I COULDN'T wait to go out skiing every morning, but I liked returning as much or more—the unmatchable camaraderie as we climbed the
ridge back to the hut for the last time of the day, this time without our
heavy packs, openly admitting to the thrill of being up high, amid this
random empty pure beauty, banded together—I wax sentimental here—
by conversation, friendship, years of habit and tradition and relying on
one another, inspired by the thrill of once again doing something you've
always done, and will always want to do, but have never done the same
way twice. You could call it love, if you had to; that familiar but never-
familiar rhythm, when the sun comes out and it seems that progress, or

at least a little clarity, might be possible. Or you could just say that we were once again brothers against the terrible dark fall; because that day comes too, eventually, when we aren't together anymore. So we flirt with danger and are happy when it spurns us.

While I'm on this embarrassing subject, I should also admit that one of the best parts of every day, no matter how good the skiing has been, is the time in the hut at the end, after the steamy unbootings, after the dinner is underway, after the gin has been poured. I realize this isn't the sort of thing one is supposed to make a big deal about by the strict standards of expedition writing, where the preference is always for bravado and technique and a slim witticism at most, as if real everyday emotion had no place in the rarefied life of the high-altitude adventurer.

But this is the truth of it: I love the tin of smoked oysters that gets broken out each year as an appetizer, the luxury amid necessities, the glacier-hut equivalent of dressing for dinner. We've been breaking out this tin of oysters for years. More than the oysters, I love the idea of the oysters, that someone thought of it. We even had MP3'd music this time around, which I can't decide if I like or not: I may prefer the more old-fashioned, non-digital necessity of silence. But it made the hut seem more like home. Is that what we want—for the womanless wilderness to feel more like home?

Mostly we talk. People claim men don't much, but my experience skiing in the mountains is otherwise. I am talking about a cave of blabber-mouths. On Friday night, for instance, according to a list in my notebook, we talk about Argentina's troubles, as the aforementioned Señor Randall runs an *estancia* there; about corruption and what a terrible thing it is but how sometimes it's the only way to do what has to be done. (Our conversations are rarely moralistic.) We talk about getting old, and about our fathers, but not about dying. Norman Bishop and John Barber (a more recent addition to the trips, but an excellent skier) hive off into a side conversation about the blues (Bishop plays in a band when he isn't lawyering in Edmonton), while for the rest of us there is a stout debate about whether it is better to own a cottage or rent one. We talk about the death of idealism in big cities, about God, about whether, given enough good-will and serious effort, maybe there is no such thing as failure. We talk about our children—one of the Bishop teenagers is already snowboarding with the Alberta provincial team—and about the modesty that gradually surrounds one's efforts the older one gets, and what a relief that modesty can be. We talk about whether men over 45 are ever again even passingly attractive to women under 40 and about whether having power in the workplace makes a man (I'm not mentioning any names) more attractive to aspiring female colleagues. (Split decision.) Three stories about excretion receive their annual retelling. (We've heard some stories 20 or 30 times before, but we always laugh anyway; it's the chance to laugh that we re-enact.) We also talk about fidelity and infidelity, how they seem like cousins, estranged and bitter, each wanting what the other has. We're solicitous (as always) of one another, opening doors, getting up to refresh each other's drinks, each gesture a small complement to camaraderie. You watch out for each other on the slopes, and then you do it again in the hut at night, if only to demonstrate that it can indeed happen under both circumstances.

By 11 we're in bed, though more of us suffer from insomnia now. Mitchell listens on an earpiece to the CBC and relays the news into the blackness. This night's dispatch, slightly louder than necessary due to the earpiece, concerns the Americans. "They're putting intense pressure on the Israelis," Mitch announces, "and telling them to get the fuck out of Dodge."

I can't sleep, so I listen to the snoring. You can say what you like: there is nothing on Earth or anywhere else that sounds like nine people snoring at night in a hut. On my right I can hear Bishop's patented double-purr, and MacKenzie's gasping, anxious intake, followed by a huge sucking drain noise, which would be Randall. Upstairs Barber is dropping long, low, slowly deafening depth charges.

Sometimes the ebb builds instantly and ferociously and everyone's snore goes off at once, and then it sounds like the homemade soundtrack of a World War II film. A lot of snores sound like cries for help.

WHICH BRINGS me, at long last, to the woman. I know what you're thinking. You're thinking: so along comes a woman into this male simulacrum of domesticity, and she destroys the illusion of their competence and togetherness.

But that is not the story I have to tell. All right, admittedly, she was a stronger skier than any one of us, and that could perhaps, theoretically, I suppose, have been a little embarrassing. She was also 20 years younger than us, which meant that whenever someone mentioned a record—John Mayall's *The Turning Point*, for instance (a perfectly fine record!) a look of confusion and…yes, say it…pity crept into her eyes. That hurt.

What happened was something else. All I can do is tell you that one evening—this would be Night Two, over spaghetti and meatballs that Hilary had whipped up from scratch—the conversation turned to our wives. We are all married; in fact, we are all still married to our first wives, a fact that does not go unrecognized or even uncelebrated. We've often wanted to bring our wives onto the ice, but only two or three could manage the skiing, and the idea of bringing some wives but not others has never caught on. I'm not sure if this is because it might offend some of the wives, or because it might upset some of the husbands; and if it did upset some of the husbands, whether it would upset the husbands whose wives were there, or those whose wives were not, or both; or if even the presence of some wives would tear the delicate fabric of our all-male camaraderie by realigning our icefield loyalties back to their everyday suburban configurations. It's a complicated subject. I realize, too, that our wives have their own ideas about "the penis trip," as it is called: that they savour the week to themselves, for instance, and that we all return more pleasant husbands.

In any event, Kling said, "I'd love to get Tecca up here, but I don't think she'd come. And Johanna, Brown's wife, wouldn't come either. They don't like the cold, for one thing, and the skiing would intimidate them."

Then everyone started weighing in.

"It's about roughing it, and maybe they've gone beyond that."

"Been there, done that, you mean. After labour, nothing seems hard."

The room went silent. It was a subject Hilary knew something about. She'd dated some of the more prominent wilderness adventurers in the Rockies and put her singleness down to the fact that very few men who share her interest in the outdoors tend to settle down, at least with women like Hilary. Maybe she thought we were complaining. In any event, she put a plate of nachos on the varnished plywood table, and said:

"But you guys are all outdoorsmen. Keeners. Why then did you marry them, if they didn't share your interest?"

A longer pause. "Well," Kling finally said, "I don't think it would have been a deal-breaker even if I had known ahead of time that she wouldn't like ski-mountaineering."

"I'm not sure I'd even want my wife to be here," someone else added. "I like her, but I relish my time alone as well."

"And anyway," Barber said, "children change everything."

"I'd like to think I'll be able to be a good mother and include my children in my outdoor life," Hilary said—testily, I thought, though it could well have been the gin.

"You don't know what you're talking about," Barber muttered, and Hilary must have heard him, because she didn't say much to anyone that night. Every man in the hut figured she was mad at him, personally. By the morning she'd forgiven us. But it snowed all night just the same. I lay there in the darkness, thinking. I thought about whether Hilary would be able to organize her adventuring life the way she imagined, life resisting organization as it does. After all, even something as manageable as trying to take the easy way into the Clemenceau had backfired. I thought *women presume life will work out, whereas men are surprised when it does*, followed closely by *that's the kind of line that gets you crucified at dinner parties*. I thought—and here I think I was onto something—*maybe we go away from our wives so we can return to them*. It's one of the best parts of a trip, according to Ulysses.

I started to fall asleep. Frank Sinatra's *Duets* was playing on the portable CD player. Mitchell was in bed, listening to the radio in the dark as he fell asleep. "Palestine," he said with finality, "is being eradicated." One more homeland gone.

THE PLANE never made it in to pick us up. Instead, as a five-day storm set in—we had a day's food left, and no diesel fuel—we dropped down into the valley of Cummins Creek, the backdoor of Clemenceau, and got picked up by helicopter. The next day we skied the lifts at Lake Louise, especially on the back side at Temple Lodge. It was at Temple, 15 years earlier, that I had learned, as Mitchell puts it, to "telemark in both directions. Which meant you could then descend any run." That day I had skied to the bottom, into a crowd of young girls in ski boots and bikinis. I wanted to go back.

But I overdid it, and tried to keep up with some young downhillers on my telemark skis, and forgot to drink water, and overheated, and arrived at that by-now-not-unfamiliar psychological unpaved shoulder of the soul where I thought I was about to have a heart attack. "Impending sense of doom," Hilary said, when she finally found me, sitting on the deck of Temple Lodge. "Do you have an impending sense of doom? That's a sign of heart attack."

"Hilary," I said, "I always have an impending sense of doom."

Hilary set off skiing again, insultingly less than worried. As she did, a pack of old-guy skiers in their late sixties clumped onto the verandah of the lodge and sat down, turning as they did to look up the hill they had just skied—much the way dogs immediately examine whatever they leave behind, I thought. The oldsters were taking their annual ski trip.

"Let's do that again," said one.

"Oh, I don't want to do that again, I want to ski the other side of the mountain," said another.

"Well, we can, but that's later in the day," said a third.

"I have an idea," said the fourth. "We can ski here one run, then go over, then come back."

"Too complicated."

"You're sure," said the fifth, "that these are all green runs?"

"Yes," the others replied in unison. "They're all green runs."

It was the wimpy guy who made me see it, because he sounded so much like me. They were us, 20 years from now. All of us were there, just in older bodies: the leader, the wandering contrarian, the wimp, the conciliator, the detail man. It was as if I was being shown the future: things never change, you are who you are, no amount of glacier travel can change it. Or maybe it can, just not the way you hope. At least these old geezers were still coming out.

"Have you been skiing together a long time?" I said.

"Forty years," they replied.

"That's good to see," I said.

"Hey," the old wimp said, "that's AC/DC on the PA system. Christ, that song came out when my kids were young. Who'd have thought I'd be listening to AC/DC all my adult life?" Then he sang a few words. "Not bad. That was good music."

"Not like now, though," the silent one said. He was clearly the honest crank of the group, their Barber. "These young kids, you can't tell them anything. Whole different crowd. They think they're never gonna die." He looked pissed about the possibility.

They *are* gonna die, of course: they just don't know it yet. Whereas later, you know it, which makes you fearful. Not weak, just fearful. There's a difference.

INTO THE
HEART OF WINTER

JILL FRAYNE

WINTER 2003

SURPRISE LAKE IS a skinny grin 25 kilometres long and less than two wide in a huge jumble of mountains at the top of British Columbia. It's a Gold Rush lake, the creeks feeding into it burgled for gold and clogged now with mining waste, big gravel mounds that look out of place in the wild disorder of the mountains. A few people still have claims on some of the creeks, and there may be a cabin or two tucked here and there. But from the west end where the road comes in, the lake stretches away between the mountains, vanishing at the edge of sight without any sign of habitation.

The day of our trek up the lake, winter is feeling its oats. Minus 20 with a knifing wind. I follow behind Jack on aluminum snowshoes, carrying a pack with the lighter gear and pulling the heavier stuff on a fibreglass sleigh. Jack drags "the Noodle," a nine-foot plastic toboggan that's worn out its welcome. It has no directional stability at all. If we weren't moving in a straight line over flat ground, the toboggan would slide off the trail, twist and flip over, right away. I've suggested we drop it off a cliff, but because it was my birthday present to him, Jack is dogged about keeping it, a position that can't last.

Today the Noodle is docile, having exactly the conditions it prefers. It makes a tidy train ahead of me bearing its load of eight-by-ten cotton tent, 20-inch woodstove, equipment duffle, fibrene tarp. By luck, a snowmobile has been through recently, and we follow its packed trail. A north wind streaks into us. I feel it through my hide mitts. If I fall any distance behind Jack, his trail starts blowing in. I have my parka hood pulled forward as far as it will go, but I can't keep my left cheek from freezing. I trudge with my mitt against my face, like someone with a toothache. After a while, plodding into the wind is simply work. The world is very small. I see the disappearing end of Jack's toboggan, the trail it makes within the faint larger trail of the snowmobile. I keep my head low. If I look up, snow needles into my face. There's nothing to see but the white swarm of wind. I don't think about anything. The task of hauling is too consuming for thought, a mental state I have come to crave when I'm back home.

At least we've already picked a site. We found it a few days ago, scouting for a likely spot. Likely, for us, means enough trees. We need standing dead timber for poles and stove wood. What we found on our reconnoitre down the lake was mostly dense, verdant spruce, but Jack spied a spot on the south side behind a little point where the ground was flat and open and there were a large number of dying pine. Some insect has been attacking pine in the region, and most of the trees in this solemn grove were afflicted. It would suit us fine.

THE SMALL town of Atlin in northern B.C. sits 90 kilometres off the Alaska Highway, about three hours from Whitehorse. The community began when two prospecting partners, fooling around in 1898, found gold in Atlin Lake and started the uproar that birthed the town. Back then, Atlin's population quickly grew to about 5,000. These days, the number of citizens is down to 500.

I've been coming to the Atlin area for years. The first time was in 1990 when I drove down from Whitehorse in a rented car and stayed in a campground on Pine Creek, a bracing little stream that is still undefeated after all the Gold Rush mayhem. It runs out of Surprise Lake, squirming its way west through the mountains and shoving through willow scrub into Atlin Lake. At the time, the campground was marked by a sign that read, "$3 per day. Pay any Atlin business." Campsites were lined up along the bank for a view of Atlin Mountain, a three-crowned colossus across the lake. Atlin Lake itself is beautiful past anything, a 130-kilometre glacial trench ringed in mountains.

When Jack and I got together a few years ago, I brought him out to Atlin with me, and he promptly blew out the boundary of everything I had ventured so far by skiing eight kilometres across the lake to Atlin Mountain and scrambling up the rock glacier at its throat. We've come north this time in March, when the ice is still good and light is returning. We've left plenty of good firewood and snow in Ontario for the joy of living in our tent and the chance to ski in the mountains. Jack lives to telemark. For him it comes as close to being a bird as humans can get, an elegant, weightless swoop down a slant of snow. I am not the skier Jack is, but I have a tap root in Atlin and will face a drive across the country to get here any time. Even in winter. Especially in winter, when the land is open and available as at no other season. At this time of year you can see distances, contours in the land that are invisible in summer. On skis, you can glide into a swamp that is impassable, unknowable except in winter. There are no bears, no bugs, no crowds. No people at all. Cold is the only bane.

In supreme cold, Jack finally veers off the snowmobile trail and heads towards shore. He has recognized the spot we found the other day. We drag our sleds off the lake, Jack's toboggan promptly toppling over at the unwonted change in terrain, and work our way into the trees. If we'd brought our nylon summer tent, we'd now be close to the end of our labours. We'd dig out a patch in the snow, hook the tent to its aluminum poles, drive in a few stakes and fire up the stove for tea. Twenty minutes' work. As it is, we're just switching ordeals. The first time we set up our cotton tent—designed for seven or, in a pinch, three poles—it took us two and a half hours. I reported our endeavour to Craig McDonald, the ex-forest-ranger who sold us the tent, and he remarked dryly, "You'll improve on that," but we never have. We're already at the limit of what we can drag in by hand, so we have to harvest and limb trees at every camp. It takes forever.

This spot has plenty of long, straight pine, and I choose a site among them, cover being the main thing. In a stay of several days, we'll have wind from any direction. Protection is more important than view or sunlight or even close access to water because of the risk of fire. Wind can whisk sparks from the stovepipe onto the tent and, even with its fire-resistant tarp, that's a worry. When we're living in our tent, we keep a knife handy. If the tent caught fire, we'd slash the likeliest wall and escape, hopefully, but we'd like to avoid that.

I start levelling the ground, tamping down a big square of snow with my snowshoes. Jack takes the axe and goes hunting for poles. Our tent is a typical wall design, no floor, a flap entrance with a hole in the front wall for the stovepipe. The cotton is an extremely fine weave, creamy white, all the seams tightly stitched and bound. We can stand in it, the peak just reachable with stretched fingers, a real luxury if you've ever spent a week crawling in and out of a hoop tent, getting dressed seated on your Therm-a-Rest mashed against your partner.

Today's pitch again takes two and a half hours, pushing against night-fall. When the tent is as squared and secure as we can manage, we start fashioning the inside. We dig out half the floor for stove space, heap snow in the other half for a sleep bench and cover it and the floor with boughs. While Jack assembles the stove, I start sawing up a couple of dead pine that Jack has knocked down, panting at the work of it, grateful for the heat it pushes into my body. Most outdoor jobs have this heaven and hell mix.

Jack's last vital chore is water. In heavy dusk I hear him out on the lake with his ice spud, pounding a hole in the ice. He brings back a nylon bucket of beautiful water and we drink. He goes into the tent and lights the candle lanterns. From the black trees where I'm standing, I see the glow. I put aside my saw and go in. He lays his lighter to the kindling in the stove, the wood snaps and catches. In a minute the air in the tent begins to warm. We look at each other and grin. We are never too far gone to love this moment. Now the night can come on. We're safe and sound.

CAMPING IN a nylon tent in the cold never offers this feeling of harbour, though we do that, too. This kind of camping has its place. We don't always want to haul a nine-foot load on a perfidious toboggan or take three hours to set up. It was camping in the cold, though, that convinced me to look for an alternative. Jack and I used to take our summer tent in winter, counting on body heat while we zoomed around all day, coping as best we could at night with a campfire, which is smoky, uncontainable heat, or doing without a fire. By the third day, I'd be nauseated with fatigue. I was looking for a way to stay out longer, last in the cold and be able to renew energy instead of wearing out keeping warm. I wanted to be able to dry out sweaty clothes at the end of the day and get into boots in the morning that weren't frozen stiff. The search for a winter tent and stove led me to Craig McDonald, a winter-camping vet and one of the only suppliers of Egyptian cotton in North America, living right under our noses in Algonquin Park. Craig's basement had everything we needed. My gift of the toboggan, wretched as it turned out to be, prompted Jack to go in with me on a tent and stove.

Our first day in camp on Surprise, snow continues to stream and we stay close to home, recovering from the long day that getting in always is and organizing the fine points. Eight by ten is a small living space. Not much can be stowed inside. We each have a foot of turf at the end of the sleep mats for personal gear, an ever-shifting heap of books, maps, reading glasses, headlamps, hand cream (my pile), toilet kits, spare mitts. Sometimes a stack of pots and pans accumulates on a ledge across from the stove; otherwise, everything stays outside. Jack builds up a wood supply by the door, shielded by my overturned sleigh. His duffle holds the food bags, roughly organized into breakfasts, beverages, lunches, dinners, snacks. On long trips we cook from scratch: flour, an assortment of grains, spices and seasonings, packaged soups and plenty of fat—nuts, olive oil, butter, cheese, salami, Swiss chocolate. In the cold, the food rules reverse. Eat rich and heavy. Even at that we'll lose weight. Nothing beats hauling a load into a headwind at −28°C for slimming.

For lunch on the second day, we have rice crackers and the peerless Mennonite salami we brought from home that slices frozen, tastes rich and dense, and quells hunger like nothing on Earth. In the afternoon, we bundle up and ski a few kilometres farther up the lake, the views shrouded and the north wind keeping the temperature down. We can barely glimpse Surprise today, but it is a beautiful lake, 3,000 feet above sea level, rimmed with mountains in the 6,000-foot range, the rock at certain points piling sheer out of the lake. Across from us, Ruby Mountain looms and vanishes in the gusts. Ruby is one of the domed variety, buried under ice 10,000 years ago and rubbed smooth. It has a huge base. I can ski up the lake for miles and not get past Ruby.

We get a better look next day. The storm has passed and the air around Ruby is crystalline, glinty points flashing in the extreme cold. The whole sky shines. At this time of year, the mountains have their full raiment of snow. A wavering scarf of spruce spreads across the base of Ruby, strands of trees trailing up where they can take hold in the rock furrows, giving out at last, giving way to the broad white dome that arcs over the lake. Mountains change every moment, mountains on water being the most mercurial. Viewed across the ice, Ruby seems to float. Over the time we're here, I come down to the lake many times to look, trying to take Ruby in, memorize it, but like all mountains, its character is evanescent, unknowable. Last thing before I get into my feathers at night I go to the edge of the lake, the moon muffled, Ruby figured and luminous in the dark, its features distinct and private, a language in code.

The third day, Jack and I have separate outings. Jack wants to ski farther up to see if he can find a way through the trees to the open snow-caps. I am thinking about footwear, the inadequacy of my mukluks in this cold and the walloping blister I got on the trek in. My Sorels, back in a friend's cabin in Atlin, would be a better choice. It's a regrettable use of time, skiing out to get them, but temperature organizes existence. I dab wax on my skis, shove all the usual survival gear in my daypack and retrace the route we took two days ago, now completely blown in. The weather is calm and brilliant, but before I go I take a compass bearing, just in case. In this great cold, even a four-kilometre ski down the lake and back seems a significant outing. I tremble a little, setting off without Jack. I have the feeling again and again of being on the margin of what we can manage. In this extreme place, there is no sure rescue from mishap, no quarter if we are caught out when night falls or the weather changes.

In Atlin, people are cheerfully digging out after the storm. After trading in my mukluks, I pick up a few groceries, fresh food already a luxury after two days, and stop in the Pine Tree Restaurant for an all-day breakfast that I am too nervous to eat. I drive back to Surprise and make the return ski in an amber hoop of late sun, the day cooling and turning violet by the time I reach camp. Even at a distance I can tell Jack isn't here. His skis are gone. I take off my backpack, tuck an avocado I just bought into my undershirt so it won't freeze and set out again, following Jack's trail. The wind has come up, the warmth of the day draining fast. I ski in his track until I have a view of several miles. I know I'll ski till I catch sight of him. This gulping anxiety is the flip side to the luxury of our tent, a razor's edge from the warm glow of it, us inside, propped in our feathers, reading by candlelight. Everything stops, the world holds still while I find Jack. Finally I do see him, a tiny moving speck against a cliff, the only moving thing in a panorama of falling night. Time resumes its slide. I turn and ski back. It's safe now to put in a fire and rummage for supper.

There's no avoiding the extremity of these swings. The physicality of the life, the heat in our bodies, working or striding along on skis, or buried in our puffy bags, is one extreme, an extreme of happiness and exhilaration, and the other, just as reliable, is dread. Knowing we could die if we're not careful.

In the night, the wind shifts and drops. I notice the change in my sleep. I don't have to burrow so deep. We get up mid-morning, the cold disinclining us to leave our bed till the last possible moment, bladder-wise, and we make a long breakfast of bannock, butter and jam. This morning is a treat: baths. We load wood into the stove, bring all the pots to a simmer, pour the water into the yellow basin. We take turns kneeling on our Crazy Creek chairs, the bowl of hot water on the ground. First the shampoo, then a sponge bath in the soapy water. I use a cotton dishrag to dry off. Jack brought his towel. When I push back the flap and step outside, my wet hair turns to ice hanks in two minutes.

This afternoon we make a short climb on snowshoes up our back hill, the trees changing as we gain height. I see these spruce put more oomph into girth than height; they are thick, strong-bodied, with close, dense branches. A steep drop beside us is broken by tracks—caribou or moose—the choice of ascent so curious and awkward I think the animal must have been chased. We come to a plateau, heavy-going to traverse, tangled willows under the snow giving way under our feet. I skid to my hips more than once. We reach a level with good views of the surrounding mountains, sombre today under a low sky, a white and black day, the only sunlight a brief gleam on the mountaintops to the east.

Our camp looks homey and familiar when we come down. This is our best pitch ever, our fourth I think, and we got it right. I like these soldiery, stiff-armed little pine, dying and all, with their scabby black-and-silver bark and orange skin underneath. They're giving us good firewood, easy to saw and split. Jack likes the chore. When I was gone yesterday, he dug in a lintel over the entrance to the tent and laid a split log footrest along the stove as a brace against melt. He's in his element in camp. If we stayed long enough in any camp, he'd probably square everything.

In my way, I'm in my element too. I am settling into what feels like the most natural and untroubled rhythm for a human in winter. Big mammals slow down in winter. Some go out of circulation altogether. I feel the pull. After a day of exertion, my body fed and warm, a long night of sleep comes easily. Marathons of sleep. As much as 11 hours. At first, we lie awake in our sleeping bags, waiting for them to warm. The moon is waxing and, through the pale walls, the tent glows. That's its beauty. There are no windows, no view outside, but the cloth is so fine and permeable, it seems translucent. We cannot see outside but we are not cut off. We always have what light does. In my bag, I fidget awhile, arranging my hot water bottle and various down items around my body before drifting off. Through the night, in deep cold, I register every turn, tucking carefully, but mainly I'm asleep all those hours. My dreams teem with absent friends. Awake, I have one companion, one only, in a black-and-white landscape. My dreams, hectic and full of colour, give the balance.

We stay six days in this camp. The time is a mix of housekeeping and adventure, a balance that's comfortable even when the temperature falls to −28°C, which it does our first two nights. We have good feather bags and do not keep a fire in the stove through the night, warmth in the tent ebbing quickly until the temperature indoors equals the temperature outdoors and a rim of ice forms around the breathing holes of our sleeping bags.

Mornings tend to be domestic: many rounds of tea, a slow grill of bannock or pancakes on top of the stove, or a porridge of millet, couscous, figs and honey. We tidy up, restock the woodpile, get out the maps to pick the day's outing. On one of our days, we ski up the lake for a better look at Four Crown, a scrabble of mountains on the south side that merge in a long bowl tipping into the lake. Jack is yearning for a way up onto these mountains, their broad, rolling domes perfect for telemark skiing. I'm happy to stick to the lake, filling my eyes. The effect of so much space is thrilling. On the lake we're in the centre of a huge, shining ball, ice and sky meeting, any way we turn, on a horizon of soaring rock. It's a feast for the eyes, for all the senses. The ears absorb the silence. Every bird cry registers, every breath of wind. The skin wakes up, heat and cold commanding and acute. When we're living outdoors in an intense environment, mind and body reverse prominence. Mental activity is anchored in the present and in the body. We attend to physical sensation all day, and this strums existence. We feel more alive because, literally, we're using more of ourselves—more than the sparky brain is at work. Fibre, muscle all over the body tweaks and thrums. I push along on my skis, heating up, gawking at the mountains, and that's all there is.

My relation to myself changes when I live outdoors—more body, less brain—and my relation to my companion is altered too. Jack and I are in a different key outdoors in winter, involved in a different way. In the evenings, confined in our tent, we gab in our usual way; during the days, we hardly speak. Today, for example, I'm breaking trail, Jack close enough behind me to talk to, but we exchange only short sentences. Our days are full of short sentences. I don't know why this is. I believe being outside brings the couple thermostat down, takes the emphasis off. It may come with the territory. Winter camping is the territory. It rules. The currents of a relationship flatten in the space and vibrancy of the outdoors. We're deep in our bodies and our senses. The beauty of the natural world tops everything, quiets the mind, raises perception. We move into a mode of apprehending and responding that is more compelling than anything. Conversation is a distraction.

I don't mean we are silent. Jack and I keep each other posted. This is important. But our commentary is very specific. It has to do with how we're faring in the moment. This is for safety. We are alone in territory without help and we need to know each other's condition. We communicate when we're hot or cold or hungry. We stay present to each other, wired together in an intense endeavour that's physical, not verbal. I find this brand of contact, so skinned down in words, intimate. Because of our reliance on each other.

If one of us is injured or sick or lost, there is only the other to help. That was the rumble in the belly the other night when Jack was so long getting back. If he needs me, will I be able to help him?

In a grand-scale place, any separation from Jack makes me anxious, but, of course, separations are inevitable. We have different yens. Jack always wants to go farther and stay out longer than I do. The day we ski past Four Crown, we're following the south shore, a long lap of dense bush on our right, watching the far shore where sheer orange cliffs shoot to a ridge above the lake. By mid-afternoon I'm footsore. I tell Jack I've had it, I'm ready to turn around. How is he doing?

"Just about. I want to ski on a bit for a look at those cliffs. Just that bend up there. I'll be right behind you."

And so we part, me glancing over my shoulder, watching him shrink to a dot on the lake. I ski into a gold sky, gliding in my own track. Every run is different, even ones that retrace. The day will have advanced, melting or freezing the trail. Wind will have shifted, the sun have a new slant. On the trip back I ignore my cramped, hot feet and get my earflaps out of the way. I remember to stop and drink water. I can see a long way. I am the only one in this huge, silent afternoon.

Except a snowmobile. I hear it behind me and am not astonished. We know there is a prospector overwintering on the lake. Someone made the trail we marched in on. A bundled man on a Skidoo Tundra comes to a stop behind me, two mutts loping behind him. Dave has a cabin on Quartz Creek, where he stays year round, hiking in and out on an old mining road during the season between water and safe ice, when he cannot paddle or use his snowmobile. He tells me about the summer winds colliding on the lake, waves ramming into each other.

"That's when you want to be on shore."

His face is sun-dark and his eyes have the extreme brilliance of people who don't watch television. A front tooth has gone black. He's cutting firewood farther down and soon shoves off, summoning one of his dogs.

"Let's go, Boner."

Jack doesn't find a way up Four Crown this trip but he gets his ski a few weeks later, after we've moved back to Atlin. Ruby Creek, the other side of the lake, has a five-kilometre trail into a beautiful bowl where Jack skis solo many times, returning exhausted and ecstatic. On a day in April, I go back to the lake and ski to our old campsite. Spring has come in the meantime, the sky low and mild, the lake ice still a foot thick but collapsing into mushy puddles on the surface. I ski to a point beyond our site. Our trail is still there, two frail spines of ice. I look at Ruby, snow tracings vanished, plain brown rock in a new season, waiting for rain, waiting for open water and for the long, long days ahead.

THE MYSTERIOUS
CASE OF THE
TAHLTAN BEAR DOG

ALISA SMITH
JUNE 2005

OMETIMES ADVENTURES BEGIN humbly, like this: it was a rainy day and I was alone in my dreary bedroom in Vancouver. Well, not all alone. I was following the venerable American nature writer Edward Hoagland on a journey to Telegraph Creek, British Columbia, in 1966. Telegraph Creek came into existence 100 years earlier, as part of a grand scheme to link New York and London by an overland telegraph line. Hoagland went north to see this most remote outpost of hubris. What he found was the continent's fading frontier, its vanishing wilderness.

His book, *Notes from the Century Before*, was not a happy read—especially the part about the dogs. "What are there, only two or three left?" Hoagland wrote. "Before the last of the grizzlies are exterminated, the last Tahltan Bear Dog will be dead. One wants to record them for the future—that they were black and pint-sized, skinny and gutsy, that they moved on springs, lived by their wits, darted about, apprehensive as well as courageous, and that they seemed to know, in those final few years, that they were doomed as a race."

Hoagland mourned and moved on. But this creature I'd never heard of before stuck in my mind. When the Tahltan bear dogs died out, Hoagland seemed to be saying, the wild North itself would be dead. Still, not all of Hoagland's gloomy predictions had come to pass. The grizzlies, for one, had survived to see a new millennium. So why not these remarkable little dogs? Suddenly, I had to know.

I phoned the Canadian Kennel Club, the authority on all things canine. "Ah yes, the mythological Tahltan bear dog," the club's Andrew Patton answered from Toronto. "There haven't been any registered since 1953." In fact, after they became an official breed in 1942, only 13 were ever registered.

A few days later, Patton sent me an old file that contained, among other gems, the official breed standard. It described every part of the dog from neck to hindquarters, including temperament (bold and cunning). An enclosed sketch showed a black-and-white canine, only 12 to 16 inches at the shoulder, with a fox-like face and pricked-up ears, a dense mid-length coat with a longer ruff around the neck and, most distinctively, an upright tail shaped like a shaving brush. This codification was, for the most part, supplied by RCMP Sergeant J. Blackiston-Grey, who had been posted in Telegraph Creek in the 1930s and had become obsessed with the unique breed. Besides the Inuit dogs, the Tahltan bear dog was the only one of seven North American canine types from the times before Columbus to survive into the modern era. I refused to believe it could be snatched from existence before I had a chance to know it.

Reading on in the file, I learned that the dogs' habitat once ranged from northwestern B.C. to the southern Yukon, the territories of the Tahltan, Sekani, Kaska, Tagish and Inland Tlingit tribes. But, as their name suggests, they were most closely associated with the Tahltan people, sub-arctic Athapaskans who, before 90 per cent of them were wiped out by disease in the late 19th century, numbered about 3,000. Today, there are roughly 5,000 Tahltan, with about 1,000 still in their traditional territory, which includes the villages of Telegraph Creek, Dease Lake and Iskut, B.C. Living a mountain range away from the Alaska Panhandle and the Pacific Ocean, they've straddled two cultures. Traditionally, they wore the coastal button blanket for ceremonial dress and depended on the salmon that came to them from salt water, but, like inlanders, they favoured beaded buckskin and moccasins, trapped for pelts, and hunted moose and bear. This was where the feisty little dog excelled. A hunter carried his dog in a pack so it didn't get tired, then released it to run lightly over the snow crust while the bear sank and floundered. When two or three leaping, yapping dogs cornered the prey, the hunters moved in and released their arrows. The dogs' bravery is celebrated in the region's myth-history. In "The Girl Who Married the Bear," a dog rescues a young woman who had been kidnapped by a bear in human form. When the woman comes home, she teaches her people the sacred ways of dealing with a bear after it is killed.

Fearless in the bush, the dogs seemed to have just one weakness: even before white men came, the Tahltan said, they died if taken from their home territory to the coast. Certainly, later removals proved fatal. In the early 1900s, wealthy Americans who came to Telegraph Creek to hunt big game couldn't resist the little dogs and frequently took them home. But whether it was the change in climate or diet (they were used to dried salmon and fresh game), or simply a broken heart, the dogs always died when they left the North. The *Guinness Book of Records* tracked them as the world's rarest dog until 1982, when the listing of the last three in Atlin, British Columbia, quietly disappeared. The Tahltan bear dog was extinct.

At least, that was the official word. Canada Post even issued a wistful 1988 stamp bearing the dog's portrait. But something still didn't sit right with me. It seemed strange that only 13 were ever registered. I wondered if First Nations people would have wanted to deal with the Canadian Kennel Club, a white man's institution based thousands of miles away or, for that matter, the *Guinness Book of Records*. What if the dogs somehow lived on among the native people, unofficial and unrecognized?

I called a friend in Whitehorse. "Everybody up here seems to know someone who's got one," he said. "You see them advertised for sale in the newspaper sometimes." It was just what I wanted to hear, but I could scarcely believe that reality in the North differed so radically from the official version. My friend gave me a name, which led to another name, and pretty soon I was talking to Shirley Quash, a Tahltan woman in Telegraph Creek. "I've got four of them," she said. The breed had survived, she explained, because the Tahltan had long ago hidden some of their dogs from the white people, who thought they had to take them away to save them. This exactly fit the vision I'd had. Now I imagined a land of lost dogs nestled somewhere in the vast North, and I vowed to go there and maybe discover a mythical beast that was right under our noses, riding shotgun in a pickup truck, sniffing the breeze.

A PLUME of dust rises behind my red hatchback as I drive through the Yukon's boreal forest south of Whitehorse. I'm on my way to the First Nation community of Tagish to see a man named Art Johns. In all the band offices and villages I phoned across the North, Johns is the most widely reputed to own Tahltan bear dogs. When I'd phoned him a few days earlier he'd said fine, come visit anytime, but I haven't been able to reach him since. Luckily, he and his partner, Elaine Ash, are well-known local figures, and I soon find her at the Southern Lakes Justice Committee, where she's the coordinator for a native community sentencing circle. "I'm his *ex*-partner. I live in the cabin behind his," says Ash, a stocky Caucasian woman with a ready grin. "Come by later if you want to see the dogs."

Just before a long bridge over the river, I turn onto a side road leading to Tagish, which turns out to be not so much a town as a cluster of houses nestled among the trees. I drive under a wooden archway with "Art Johns" etched into it, pass a relatively new, varnished log cabin and park by a weathered grey one. Ash's domain. Dogs bark, feisty little dogs that leap and caper. Tahltan bear dogs? Could they be? I feel as if I'm looking at relics, museum specimens come to life. They stare up at me with a cold curiosity, and delicately sniff my hand.

Sitting in her kitchen surrounded by worn furniture and the oldest operating refrigerator I've ever seen, Ash tells me her dogs are descended from a purebred named Schwatka. Now dead, it belonged to Johns's aunt in the 1980s and was named for the American explorer who charted the Yukon River and, most famously, found the long-lost Franklin expedition. During the last two decades, Ash has searched for breeding stock and found a handful of what she considers good bear dogs amidst more dubious claims. "I don't know about the Ross River line," she says huffily. "They're funny." In turn, she's had to weather challenges to her own dogs, such as a vet proclaiming they were some kind of Chihuahua. "Chihuahua?" she cries, pushing back her exuberant frizz of grey hair. "What do they know about Tahltan bear dogs?"

Feature for feature, Ash insists, her dogs match the Canadian Kennel Club standard. There's just one flaw, she admits with a sigh: only one of her dogs ever had the erect ears. "But their size is good. Their short coat too. And the black-and-white colouring is just right." As a case in point, she picks one up. "They aren't like other dogs. Their intelligence is almost human. They can jump as high as a truck window. And look at that shaving brush tail." I nod, transfixed by the possibility that these are mythical animals I can reach out and touch.

But as I back my car down the dirt driveway and the dogs' yipping fades, so does Elaine Ash's spell. It begins with the shaving brush tail. Yes, it was white with a black tip, but it would never raise a lather. And the dogs' eyes were buggy—like, well, a Chihuahua's. I pull over and peer at the photos of Blackiston-Grey's dogs, as reproduced in a 1949 article that I'd recently found in the Yukon archives. These are obviously the animals on which the Kennel Club based its codification. Alas, the overall impression is quite different from Ash's dogs. Clearly, hers are not the purebreds I'm in search of, but that doesn't faze me; I have many more towns to visit, many more names on my list.

In fact, my next stop has great potential: Atlin, British Columbia, the last recorded home of the bear dog. Dusk is falling as I head southwest and, after an hour and a half, pull into a cute clapboard town by a huge lake with a mountain rising from the far shore. Atlin styles itself the Switzerland of the North, and German tourists are mad about its frontier charm. But this means nothing to me compared to the word that Sandra Jack, a Tlingit woman here, owns Tahltan bear dogs.

The next morning I drive to the far side of the lake. The native part of town begins just beyond the burnt shell of the Aurora House brothel, which marks where respectability ended in the white man's geography of a hundred years ago. Jack's house on a hill is a nondescript grey, small and plain like the others around it. I knock and a pretty woman with an open face and a cascade of curls opens the kitchen door. "You're lucky to catch me," she says. "I just got back from the moose camp." She smiles as her two dogs race towards me. Two wildly opposed dogs. One is robust, perhaps 40 pounds, with a thick black-and-white coat, bushy tail, erect ears. The other is tiny, maybe 10 pounds, with a short beige coat and buggy eyes.

We walk across a linoleum floor old enough that a hole has worn through and sit in her cozy, tidy kitchen. On the far wall a poster reminds her to listen to the elders. Jack, who develops native language curricula for local schools, says she is still working on her Tlingit, which she lost in residential school, but regained from her grandmother. The large dog walks over and she scratches his ears fondly. "It's from a part Tahltan bear dog and a Karelian bear dog," she says. "When I took it to Telegraph Creek—I have relatives there—the elders told me they thought it looked the most like a Tahltan bear dog of any they'd seen for years." Karelian bear dogs come from Finland and, though much larger than the Tahltan breed, have similar colouring and are also used for hunting. Be that as it may, this cross-breed of Jack's is a long way from the one-hundred-percenter I was seeking. And, as for his little bug-eyed friend: "It's one of Elaine's dogs, bless her heart," Jack says. "She means well, but those things are mostly Chihuahua."

PARKED ON the other side of the lake, I open my file folder once more on the cheerful foxy face and teasing eyes of Blackiston-Grey's dog Etzerza. Perhaps I have been too rigid in insisting on an exact match. Are there other ways of identifying the essence of a Tahltan bear dog besides the Kennel Club standard?

First, I consider what I've learned of First Nations lore. Most people have said that the dogs had been around as long as anyone could remember, but various twists had them coming from Russia, perhaps as recently as the 1700s, while one Tahltan man thought they had interbred with local foxes. Not much help, and neither—despite tantalizing but ambiguous hints—was science. I'd gone to see Susan Crockford, an archaeozoologist at the University of Victoria, who'd done some work on dogs indigenous to North America. She decided to include the Tahltan bear dog after she found skin and bone samples in the Royal British Columbia Museum. This was the mid-1990s, when she was the first in her field to use the new technology of DNA analysis. She discovered that the

Tahltan bear dog, along with the other New World dogs, is different from all modern breeds. She found enough North American wolf genes to suggest that they were domesticated on this continent. While this is still being debated, scientists agree that the thousands of years the dogs spent isolated here made them genetically unique. "I tell you, it's the most complicated thing I've ever done," Crockford said. Unfortunately, there is not yet a DNA map, because it was difficult to get full DNA sequences from the old materials available, and, more crucially, there are no archaeological remains from before European contact.

Fortunately, DNA is not a gift given in entirety or not at all; though the physical evidence can vary greatly, it flows through all descendants. If there are dogs with only 10 per cent of the original genes, wouldn't it still be worth it to collect them and preserve what is left of the boldness and cunning, the fox-like yip, *anything* for the future? Even the finicky Kennel Club hasn't closed the door on this idea. "Maybe you could breed back the traits, if they came out true for seven generations," Andrew Patton said. "But could you call it a Tahltan bear dog? That's a thorny question." No more thorny than the one posed by Curtis Rattray, a local history expert in the Tahltan office at Dease Lake. "What's a purebred anyway? Whether dogs or people?" he asked. "I don't think there's any such thing."

Despite all that, I still can't help dreaming of a eureka moment when I find a match for that damned Kennel Club standard. Sometimes, the most extravagant hopes are the most stubborn.

BY THE time I approach Carmacks, 175 kilometres north of Whitehorse on the Klondike Highway, I'm also approaching bear dog burnout. Over the last two weeks, I've seen mutts that look like miniature huskies, small labs, large Chihuahuas, lightweight bulldogs and stripped-down terriers—but nothing that could pass for a pure Tahltan bear dog. The grapevine pointed me to Carmacks, where Hannah Kruise was supposed to have one, though when I phoned she said she got it from the pound in Atlin. As unlikely as that sounded, I decided to check it out anyway.

I bypass the town's highway presence—a couple of gas stations and a motel featuring the decidedly unglamorous Gold Dust Saloon—and turn left towards the wide, brown Yukon River, which is lined with a pleasant boardwalk and a row of houses. When I pull into a dirt drive-way, Kruise and her younger sisters are loading horse gear into a pickup in front of their barn-red plywood house. My eyes widen as a small black dog runs towards me. Fox-like face. Ears at the perfect angle. Brushy tail. Ruff around the neck. Amazingly, this stray is the closest thing to Blackiston-Grey's dog I've seen.

Kruise had never heard of Tahltan bear dogs until she took her new pet to the local roadside café she owns. Native elders sipping coffee told her it looked like one and brought pictures to show her. Now, she's come to fully appreciate Shasta, as she calls him; he's a real northern dog. But on closer inspection, I find a few flaws. He's at least 10 pounds too large; though Kruise gamely holds him in her sturdy arms, he's clearly no por-table pooch. As well, his fur might be too long, too silky. But he's enough to restore my enthusiasm. Why shouldn't the closest thing yet come from a pound in Atlin? After all, it's a historic hotspot for the breed. The genes are no doubt lurking in many of the town's mongrels, which, like most northern dogs, habitually run loose. Shasta is clearly an important throwback.

I remind myself to mention Shasta to the Eastmures. Besides Art Johns and Elaine Ash, Lori and Dick Eastmure are the people most often named as a source of Tahltan bear dogs. They've been trying to breed the dogs since 1990 and have sold at least eight litters.

After an hour's visit with them in their spacious log home southeast of Whitehorse, I discover that they too began with Schwatka, the founder of Ash's dynasty. They crossed Schwatka with a terrier because they thought the feisty qualities were compatible, and like Ash, they sought out any canine with a claim to being a Tahltan bear dog. But they've reached the end of the line. They can't find any credible bear dog that isn't related to theirs.

Lori Eastmure, who works as a faculty advisor in Yukon College's Native Teacher Education Program, still checks out any bear dog she hears about, answering newspaper ads and visiting the pound, but the claims are usually delusion or fakery. "You wouldn't believe what people would say is one," she says. They charge as much as $500 for their fakes, far more than the ones she and her husband sold on the understanding that they only had "the bloodline." She pauses, and then speaks hesitantly. "I think we're the main reason you hear about so many Tahltan bear dogs in Whitehorse now. Our dogs are out there and people get carried away and just say they're Tahltan bear dogs." When the owners sell or give away the puppies, people don't know their true history anymore.

She pats Suki, their little black dog with white chest and paws. "You know, I think I know why they went extinct. These dogs are cursed. So many of ours have died, killed by coyotes or packs of larger dogs, mostly. And a lot of them have turned out to be infertile. We only have one left now."

THE ROAD into Telegraph Creek is like no other. From the Alaska Highway junction with Highway 37, it's 250 kilometres south on patchy pavement, punctuated by single-lane bridges, to Dease Lake. From there, the last 115 kilometres west take two-and-a-half hours on gravel and wrenching mountainous switchbacks. At one point, you can stop on a thin high wedge of land: down one cliff face is the plunging canyon of the Tahltan River, down the other is the Grand Canyon of the Stikine. This beauty takes on a melancholy cast when I think that I've come here no longer hoping to find a last lonely stash, but to unravel the bear dogs' demise.

I reach Telegraph Creek in dense rain and park in the mud in front of Shirley Quash's large, well-kept house. A cacophony of five barking dogs greets me. Four of them have characteristics of Tahltan bear dogs. The fifth, Quash jokes, is "barely a dog." He's a strange fellow, all right, like a cross between a terrier and an old monk, with long grey hair on his chin and brow. As I step into the house, I survey the other dogs with a jaded eye. Quash obtained the matriarch, Kitty, after spotting a hand-lettered sign—"Tahltan bear dog for sale"—in a town window. "But then we found out the lady, Delores Smith, had already moved to Whitehorse, so we drove there," Quash says. "And then we found out she'd gone to Vancouver. But we really wanted that dog, so then we drove there, and at last we got her." (Smith's dog came originally from Ross River, Yukon.) Quash then asked her father to look for a dog in Telegraph that seemed to have promising characteristics for breeding. Since then, Quash has distributed a few litters of these bear-dog descendants, as she calls them, to family and friends throughout Tahltan territory.

"Some people in town don't believe it; they don't want to hear that there are still Tahltan bear dogs. But that's their problem, not mine. I think it's possible to bring back the breed." Quash's dogs are jumping up and down now, sitting on her ample lap or fidgeting on the flowered couch. "We're going to breed Kitty with Snoopy, her son. My dad says that's the only way we'll get the characteristics back."

That evening I stop by the house of Pat Carlick, Quash's father. He was the man to talk to, many Tahltan recommended, if I wanted to know about bear dogs. Serene and portly in his early sixties, he's ensconced in an easy chair. Tahltan is his first language and his accent renders "bear dog" as "beer dog." "I was born in the bush and raised there," he says. "My grandparents had bear dogs. I think the last one in Telegraph Creek died in the 1970s. It's sad to think they're gone now. I don't see any that look like them anymore."

I show him a copy of a 1963 photograph that a Tahltan man in White-horse emailed to me. "Hey, that's my grandfather's dog, Ah Chin Dat Oak," he says, fingering the paper with delight. "What smart dogs they were. They would do anything you asked them in Tahltan. They had different barks for different kinds of game. Then you would know what they'd treed when they were outside on their own. No, you would never starve if you had a Tahltan bear dog." If you wanted to train a pup to hunt a certain animal, you would prick its nose and rub the blood of it there. "Ah Chin Dat Oak was a good dog. He followed my uncle everywhere, even to church. I bet he followed him to heaven, too."

"What happened to the bear dogs?" I ask. "How did they disappear?"

"I don't know. We always thought there were lots, they were always around. Then one day people realized there were none left." He shrugs helplessly. "That was it."

I HAVE one more stop to make, Dease Lake, to visit Liz Edzerza, an 84-year-old Tahltan woman who, Sandra Jack's sister told me, knows exactly what happened to the last of the bear dogs.

Edzerza sits in an easy chair in a cramped living room, her knitting—kelly green socks—on a table by her hand. The TV mumbles in the background as we talk. "The Tahltan bear dog is all gone, all dead," she says. "It makes me angry when people say they still exist." I ask her why they keep saying that. "They want it to be true, I guess. It's a feeling of something missing from Tahltan culture. But they don't know. They never even saw the dogs. I did. I know." She looks at the photos of some of the dogs I've seen. None meet her approval. "Look at that one. Too big. Or that one's ears. Too far apart." The Carlick dog, Ah Chin Dat Oak? Not a purebred, she says. "Look at its muzzle. It's too long." Even the ones in the Blackiston-Grey photos don't fully stand up. "That one there, also too big. It must have been a cross already. There were so few left—what could you breed it with? But that fox face on the black one, that's right. That's how they were."

In 1942, she says, there was a flu and measles epidemic in Telegraph Creek, and many elders died. They were the main ones who still owned bear dogs, whose place in the hunt had long been usurped by rifles. "When they were gone there was no one to look after the dogs, and they were just running around. So they were shot. Charlie Callbreath shot them. Charlie and I were just talking about it last summer. He's a very old man now, 94 I think. You should go visit him in Prince Rupert. He remembers everything."

A couple of weeks later I do go to Prince Rupert. As always, it's misty and raining. I walk past the downtown mall to Charlie Callbreath's concrete apartment block near the sea. He stands in his doorway, a short, stooped, washed-out man. His clothes, an indeterminate blue-grey, are washed out too. "I'm half blind and half deaf," he announces as we sit at his kitchen table. "I'm the oldest Tahltan still living."

He remembers many things about Telegraph Creek. The paddle-wheeler that brought the mail on the 5th and 20th of every month. The time the pioneering New York–to–Nome (Alaska) flight stopped at his father's ranch. That Mrs. Agnes Simpson used to own bear dogs, Ben Cameron and Jack Russell too.

"So," I ask, "there was a flu epidemic during the war and a lot of elders died then?"

"I don't remember anything about that," he says.

"And the dogs had to be shot?" He seems not to hear, and I repeat the question.

"I don't remember anything about that," he says again. "I left Telegraph 51 years ago."

ON THE morning train heading east from Prince Rupert, I stare into the mists above the Skeena River and wonder again if Charlie Callbreath shot those dogs. It plagued me all last night, but perhaps it doesn't matter. One way or another, the Telegraph Creek dogs seem to have disappeared around that time. W.G. Crisp, a white Hudson's Bay fur trader, reported that they were common when he lived there in 1931, but only mongrels were left by the time he returned in the 1950s.

The train whistles. It's a sound that summons regret. If only I'd gone on to Teslin, if only to Ross River, maybe I'd have found a purebred Tahltan bear dog. But no. Impeccable sources in those places—a leading elder and an aged bush priest—told me they had not seen bear dogs for many decades. I've searched diligently in northern places obscure enough to satisfy any explorer—and I've come up empty. If I adopt the mindset of a scientist or a bureaucrat, I have to admit that the Tahltan bear dog is extinct. The exact configuration of DNA that once trotted alongside Tahltan hunters has vanished. There is no pure breeding stock, no little black-and-white dog uncontaminated by European influence.

"The Tahltan bear dog is pretty watered down now," a Tahltan man with startling blue eyes told me, "just like the Tahltan people." Indeed, my journey has brought home to me that whatever purity might be, it's not the prerequisite of authenticity. In their traditional territory, regardless of whatever intermixing has gone on—and the tribes of North America were intermixing long before Europeans arrived—the Tahltan and other northern First Nations have maintained their unique cultures. They now have satellite television, sure, but they go to the moose camps, the men hunting and the women preparing the meat and skins, and they dry salmon on hand-hewn racks in riverside smokehouses as they have for thousands of years. Throughout the North, I met native people working to preserve their languages and traditions by "listening to the elders."

What does it matter if a key cultural message comes, as in Sandra Jack's kitchen, from a framed poster instead of a button blanket?

In a very real way, I did find the Tahltan bear dog. It was lurking in the legendary Schwatka and his lineage, in a rescued stray from Atlin that was the image of the Kennel Club standard, and most of all in the unshakeable belief that a motley band of animals scattered across the North are descendants of this unique breed. Not everything has been lost. The dog remains in traces, but even more so as an idea that is a pillar of northern identity. And the dogs themselves? They don't care what name we call them. They will still yip and scamper across the spring snow, fighting against the odds.

REQUIEM
FOR A RARE BIRD

WAYNE GRADY

JULY/AUGUST 2002

AT THE END of February 2002, I came south after spending the better part of four months in the Yukon, which explains why I was thinking about acclimatization, the propensity of a species to tolerate sudden drastic changes in climate. I made a brief stop in Vancouver, the evergreen city, in which thoughts of acclimatization often lead to a yen for adaptation: I could get used to this, I thought.

Acclimatization intrigued Darwin as an engine of evolution. He had observed that some individuals within a species tolerate sudden changes in climate much better than others: take a handful of, say, rhododendrons from high in the Himalaya, plant them along the roadsides of England (as botanist Joseph Hooker had done in 1850), and some grow as though nothing had changed while others are suddenly rendered "unfit" (to use the phrase invented by Herbert Spencer, not Darwin, although Darwin approved of it and used it himself in later editions of the *Origin*) and die off. Why? To Darwin, it was "an obscure question."

There is, or perhaps by now I should say there was, an instructive example of acclimatization in Vancouver—the city's unique population of Crested mynahs—and I lingered there a few days to observe it. And also to observe acclimatization's opposite: extinction.

THE CRESTED mynah (scientific name: *Acridotheres cristatellus,* which means crested locust-hunter) is not a native North American bird. It was introduced to Vancouver from Southeast Asia in the late 1890s. There are several murky legends about how this came about, most of them involving Chinese immigrants and birds in fragile bamboo cages. One tells of an exasperated sea captain who, tired of the mynahs' constant chattering, smashed the cages and released the birds as soon as he caught sight of land. Because of their mimicking skills, mynahs—not just the Crested variety but also the more aggressive Indian Hill mynah—were popular in Vancouver from the end of the 19th century until well into the postwar period. An advertisement placed by the Vista-Variety Store in the *Vancouver Sun* in April 1958 notified customers of a shipment of Indian Hill mynahs: "Young, tame birds 3–4 months old, finest talking strain. $45 each f.o.b. Victoria. Limited quantity. Free advice on how to feed and train these wonderful talking birds."

(The word "mynah," by the way, comes from *maina,* the Hindi name for the bird, having been anglicized at the same time that India was, around 1770. I opt, by the way, for the spelling "mynah," with the terminal "h," rather than swinging to the more modern version, "myna," or reverting to the original "mina," as given by the OED. I do so on no solider grounds than that there is nothing wrong with the letter "h." We leave it on other Hindi-derived words, such as verandah and pooah, a fibrous plant of North India, on "Hurrah!"—the battle cry of the Prussian army during the War of Liberation in 1812–13—and on the names Sarah, Jonah and Winnie-the-Pooh, so why not leave it on mynah as well?)

However the Crested mynah's introduction came about, there were feral birds zooming over the city streets by 1897, and it was formally identified as a local breeder—citizenship status for birds—in 1904. Despite the drastic climate change, the population soared. By 1920, there were 20,000 Crested mynahs in the city. By 1935, its success so alarmed the United States Department of Agriculture (USDA) that that august body issued a special report urging that "every precaution should be taken to check the spread of this species and prevent its spread into the United States." Crested mynahs were the suspected terrorists of the 1930s.

The USDA needn't have worried, for the mynahs never ventured very far from Vancouver. They couldn't make it over the mountains. But even had the birds spread like Japanese knotweed the USDA would by now have relaxed its vigilance, for the Crested mynah has declined steadily since 1950. From its 1920 high, the population plummeted to 906 by 1971; in 1980 the figure was 630. The Christmas count in 1985 turned up only 98 mynahs. Recent numbers are even more alarming. Last fall, a brief article in the *Globe and Mail* declared that the total number of Crested mynahs in Vancouver had dwindled to "seven, or maybe five." I realized that if I wanted to see a Crested mynah without having to fly to Taiwan, I had better hurry.

THE LARGEST single roost of mynahs in Vancouver, comprising more than 1,000 birds, had been located at the corner of Cordova and Carrall streets, and that's where I went first, on the chance of seeing a remnant of that enormous flock. It was noon, still cold in the shadows, a faint warmth when the sun came from behind a cloud. There wasn't much bird life at the corner. The massive buildings had seen better days. Some scaffolding blocked part of the sidewalk. I stood and looked up at the Lonsdale Building, an imposing, three-storey edifice built in 1889. The upper windows were blank, the ground floor occupied by an Army & Navy outlet. A solitary crow landed on one of the upper windowsills and eyed me as though waiting for me to drop a sandwich or a slice of pizza. One of the shops on the corner was a take-out chicken joint, and Crested mynahs were often found scavenging around such establishments—not, as was supposed, because they liked junk food, but because they ate maggots, thus doing the city a valuable service. I poked hopefully around a dumpster behind the chicken place, but there were no birds of any kind on the ground. High above, a few gulls wheeled up from the harbour, and a squadron of pigeons flew over in formation, as though rehearsing for an air show. But that was it.

I walked up a block to Hastings, where a group of street people wrapped in grey blankets sat cross-legged on the pavement, their backs against a formerly grand bank building that had evolved into the Treasure Island Bargain Centre, its treasure of odds and ends spilling out onto the sidewalk like costume jewellery from a trunk. More pigeons strutted about outside, pecking at a handful of seed someone had tossed them. No mynahs. At one point a small black bird flew down from a leafless tree and joined the pigeons, but it was a starling. I glared at it for a minute, then drifted back to Cordova and continued down to Water Street, the next corner. Here the storefronts tended to cafés and curio shops, although it was early in the season for tourists. A few sidewalk tables had been set out, so I sat in one across from the statue of Gassy Jack Deighton, Vancouver's first hotelier, ordered a decaf Americano, took out my binoculars and watched the starlings.

The decline of Vancouver's Crested mynah population began with the arrival of starlings in 1950. The European starling (*Sturnus vulgaris*), closely related to the mynah, is also an introduced species. Fifty of them were let loose in New York's Central Park in the 1880s by a drug manufacturer named Eugene Schieffelin, who'd been struck by the dubious notion that North America should have every bird mentioned by Shakespeare. There are now an estimated 50 million starlings in North America, devouring grain and ousting native songbirds from the best nesting places. It was the startling starling experience that had turned the USDA against the Crested mynah in 1935.

Ironically, starlings helped solve the mynah problem. They ate the same foods and promptly took over all the ideal nesting sites—in Vancouver, that meant the unheated eaves of wooden houses. The weather conspired with the starlings to doom the city's mynahs. To a bird from Southeast Asia, anything but a year-round 25°C is cold. Female Crested mynahs usually lay clutches of five eggs, but because they come from relatively tropical climes, they don't feel obliged to sit on them for 24 hours a day, as more northerly birds—such as starlings—do. Mynahs, male and female, spend only about 50 per cent of their time incubating their eggs. The rest of the day they hang around the local McDonald's and KFC, checking out the dumpsters for maggots. This means that only two of the five eggs in the clutch actually hatch. It also means that the nest site is undefended half the time, and after 1950 a lot of mynahs must have flown home from the chip wagon to find a pair of starlings settled in where their own nest used to be.

Gastown turned out to be a good place to think about acclimatization. Up on Hastings, homeless people wrapped in blankets crouched on the sidewalk, or on car seats propped in numberless doorways, or cruised the darkened alleys wearing Sorel boots and zipperless winter coats with the hoods up. Here on Water Street, two blocks away, cyclists in yellow Gore-Tex jackets and spandex shorts basked in the sunlight, sipping lattes. Both groups seemed comfortably in synch with their worlds. Who were the long-term survivors?

After an hour I'd had my fill of Gassy Jack and cold coffee, and took a taxi to an address on the other side of False Creek. Local birders had started a Crested mynah hotline in the early 1990s, and word soon got out that the species' last stronghold, their local Alamo, was a small, red-brick building at the corner of First and Wylie, the offices of the Best Janitorial & Building Maintenance Company. As I stepped out of the taxi beside the south entrance I heard some shrill peeping from a row of cedars flanking the building, and just in case, I spent a few minutes poking among the branches before finding a cluster of house sparrows celebrating the spring-like sunshine against the brick wall.

When I emerged I found a man near the entrance, leaning against the wall smoking a pipe and reading a book. He looked up as I came out of the trees.

"Looking for our mynahs?" he said.

"How could you tell?" I asked, brushing cedar fronds off my shoulders.

He grinned. "They never go in the trees," he said. "And they aren't here right now. They usually don't show up until later in the afternoon. They were here yesterday."

His name was Cliff and his office was on the third floor, second from the right. His window was at the same height as two exterior light fixtures, one sticking out of the brick just to the left of his window and the other two windows over, above the cedar hedge. Between Cliff's window and the far light fixture was a hole in the brick wall where a third, central light fixture had once been. Cliff pointed these features out carefully. The mynahs perched on the light fixtures, he said—I could see a fan of white guano on the wall under each metal pole—and they nested in the cavity where the third fixture used to be. Cliff could watch all three sites from his window and was thus probably the most experienced observer of Crested mynah behaviour in North America.

"It gets very hot in the building during the summer," he said. "Even in early spring, this south wall gets a lot of sunlight. That's probably why they like this building."

I asked him how many mynahs he'd seen this year. "We're down to three," he said sadly. "Last year we had five: two males, a female and two hatchlings. The females don't sing as much, and their crests are smaller. I take it the two hatchlings were females, and something bad happened to the males over the winter, because now there are only three, and all three are female."

When Cliff returned to work, I crossed Wylie Street and fixed my binoculars on the nest cavity. It seemed to go in and up, probably connecting with a larger hole deeper in, where warmth from the building would nurture the eggs. This would give these birds a slight advantage over other mynahs, whose nest cavities were in trees or the eaves of buildings that did not exude so much heat.

Here's how Darwin thought acclimatization should work in the case of Vancouver's Crested mynahs: when the birds started reproducing in 1904, most of them spent 50 per cent of their time incubating the eggs, but a few would spend 53 or maybe 55 per cent. Those that spent more time on their eggs would have a slightly better chance of producing young. Perhaps the 50-percenters would successfully raise one chick, while the 55-percenters would raise two or three. Gradually, the 50-percenters would disappear, and the population would be made up entirely of 55-percenters. Among this population, a few 60-percenters might emerge, and gradually they would ease out the 55-percenters. Over time, the Vancouver Crested mynah would have acclimatized into a new subspecies that sat on its nests much longer than the original Asian population.

I hung around, but no mynahs appeared. When the sun dropped behind the Maynard's Auctioneer building behind me, it began to get really cold. At four o'clock the police officers in the Canine Division compound across First changed shifts. A few minutes later a thin man in a light jacket pushed a shopping cart up to the Best Janitorial dumpster and started rummaging for plastic bottles and aluminum cans. He whistled as he worked. He said a friend of his was going to give him a brand-new, 28-inch TV set, and that all he had to do was go and pick it up, which he planned to do the next day. "You don't have a car, do you?" he asked me. I said that regretfully I did not. Like the mynahs, I said, I was just passing through. When he left, I looked up at the nest cavity and the light fixtures one last time. Is this what extinction looks like, I wondered? All day watching an empty hole in a brick wall?

THE NEXT day I arrived shortly after noon and stayed for an hour, then left for lunch. When I returned at three o'clock, I settled in for another vigil. This time, however, I was rewarded. At 4:20 two black birds flew towards the building from the direction of the Cambie Bridge and landed on the light fixtures. At first I thought they were starlings—their white wing flashes were not very visible when their wings were folded—but when I looked through my binoculars I could see the tuft of feathers at the point where the tops of their beaks met their foreheads. They had large beaks, and their eyes were bright red. They looked about them with nervous inquisitiveness. Two female Crested mynahs. I could barely contain my excitement. I waved at Cliff's window, between the two light fixtures that held two-thirds of the entire North American population of Crested mynahs.

Darwin thought that acclimatization would gradually lead to adaptation, that as Vancouver's Crested mynahs, say, became more habituated to a colder climate they would adapt to it physiologically as well, and over vast stretches of time, they would evolve into a new species. "Let this process go on for millions of years," he wrote, "on millions of individuals…." But recent researchers think it could happen much more quickly. Jonathan Weiner, for example, in *The Beak of the Finch,* suggests that adaptation "need not be as gradual as Darwin imagined." Citing Darwin's finches on the Galapagos Islands, whose beaks adapt to differences in seed availability from one year to the next, evolutionary changes could take place within a few generations.

It's possible that, left alone for a few more years, Crested mynahs could have become better acclimatized to Vancouver's climate and might even have figured out a way to spread beyond the mountains and thus fulfill the USDA's worst fears. Sitting on a nest for an extra hour or two a day is hardly a huge adaptation. A few years ago, two UBC evolutionists, Craig Benkman and Anna Lindholm, conducted an experiment on crossbills, a type of seed-eating finch whose bills curve sharply at the tip and do not meet, like a pair of badly made nail scissors. The birds have adapted to opening a particular kind of hemlock cone; when Benkman and Lindholm clipped their beaks, the birds could forage open cones, but were unable to open tightly closed cones. As the beaks grew and became more crossed, the birds were gradually able to open closed cones again. It thus became clear that beak alterations had occurred gradually in nature and that the birds would have had to change in many subtle ways to take advantage of the changes. Citing the UBC experiments, Weiner posits that crossbills with slightly altered beaks would have needed to refine their instincts for cone hunting, learn to recognize new types of food, develop new muscles to operate their new beaks, and so on. These physical changes would eventually lead to social and reproductive changes (as females chose mates with well-adapted beaks), and before long the world would have a whole new species of crossbills. Something similar might have happened with Vancouver's Crested mynahs.

But it didn't. Starlings happened instead. As I watched, the two Crested mynahs left their perches on the light fixtures and flew to a nearby telephone cross-tree, obviously hoping to roost for the night. Within five minutes they were assailed by three starlings. One of the mynahs scooted along the beam, chasing two of the starlings off, but the starlings merely flew up onto a wire and then returned to the cross-tree. Before long two more starlings arrived, and both mynahs moved grudgingly back to their light fixtures, perhaps to protect their nest, but it seemed more as though they had just given up, realized that there was nowhere else for them to go, that wherever they tried to roost they would be ousted by starlings. Not violently, not aggressively, just edged out by force of numbers, made uncomfortable, unwanted, forced into retreat.

That, I realized, is what extinction looks like.

THE BIG MELT

ANDREW NIKIFORUK

SEPTEMBER/OCTOBER 2004

PETER LEMIEUX, A glacier and mountain guide on the Columbia Icefield, has been watching his workplace shrink for the last 20 years. Every day during the summer, the thin and jaunty 52-year-old takes tourists on guided walks of the Athabasca Glacier, next to the Icefields Parkway, where he shows them mysterious mill wells and yawning crevasses and streaming rivers of water. And every day he swears his walk gets a little bit shorter. In fact, the glacier is melting so fast that tramping on the Athabasca is a bit like entering one of those Internet sites in a state of constant redesign. "The changes are really getting dramatic," says Lemieux. "It's shocking."

Lemieux likes to begin his tour by taking his visitors up to a moraine with a post that reads 1982. He then asks the crowd what they were doing that year. After the assembled walkers offer the usual lifetime landmarks (graduations, marriages, divorces), Lemieux explains that in 1982, the toe of the Athabasca, now a five-minute walk away, reached this very spot. Then he mentions that 150 years ago, the glacier stood about 300 feet tall where they are now. There are *oohs* and *ahhhs*, and sometimes disbelievers.

During the course of the ice walk, Lemieux rhymes off more astounding figures. In the last century, the Athabasca Glacier has beaten a

Napoleonic retreat of more than 1.5 kilometres. Every year it gets thinner by about 70 feet or more. The glacier now loses 565 million cubic feet of ice more than it regains in new snowfall. And so on.

At the end of his tour, Lemieux takes out a Mars bar to demonstrate what he calls Glaciology 101. First he bends the bar to show how glaciers hang off an icefield. Then, after talking about the layers and movement of glaciers, he asks if anyone has heard of global warming. Everyone offers a polite yes. "Well, that's when entire glaciers disappear," explains Lemieux. He then plops the chocolate bar into this mouth.

AS A Calgarian and frequent mountain-goer, I wish that Lemieux's Mars bar lesson was an example of mere dramatic licence. But the terrible truth is this: the glaciers in the Rocky Mountains are leaving us, one by one. Like spilled ice cubes on a hot sidewalk, they are melting and vanishing at a pace that is decidedly unglacier-like. Even the mighty Athabasca could wither and be gone within 100 years.

The ramifications of this sudden retreat are staggering. When our great-grandchildren visit the Rockies, much of what is currently called alpine habitat—with its lush green meadows and technicolour wildflowers—will have been replaced by something quite different. And if our descendants live on the prairies, well, God bless them, because they will have less water to drink. Less water to fish. And less water for irrigation. The alpine oases of Canada's prairies are drying up and there will be hell to pay all the way from Banff to Lake Winnipeg and from Rogers Pass to Vancouver.

FOR A million years, glaciers covered most of Canada like a Hudson's Bay blanket. When these ice sheets last retreated some 25,000 years ago, they left behind a few calling cards. Some of the most remarkable of these now rest in my backyard: the glaciers of the Rocky Mountains. The last time they advanced was at the end of the Little Ice Age around 1850. Ever since, our glaciers have been shrinking and disappearing. Nobody really knows how many glaciers Canada has now (government data is remarkably poor) but the best estimates say we still have more ice than any other country except Greenland. But no scientist I talked to thinks we'll keep that record for long.

Mike Demuth, in particular, has some grave concerns about the future of our glaciers. The 43-year-old Calgary-born scientist caught the glacier bug while climbing Mount Logan in 1981 and has been measuring and thinking about ice ever since. Today he is Canada's number one glaciologist at the Geological Survey of Canada, where glacier researchers are almost as endangered as glaciers. There are fewer than half a dozen scientists studying Canadian glaciers, and as Demuth puts it, "We could use some extra help."

Last year Demuth wrote a disturbing but little-read paper on climate change and glaciers on the eastern slopes of the Rockies. He concluded that glacier cover in western Canada is reaching its lowest point in the last 10,000 years. "Everything is thinning," notes Demuth. "The mass balance is negative, which means the glaciers are losing more water than they are gaining." Demuth says that the area of glacier cover has become so much smaller in the last 50 years that even their ability to regenerate is in doubt. And the primary culprit, of course, is climate change.

Although scientists agree that the Rocky Mountain glaciers started to thin out naturally 150 years ago, recent wasting has clearly been driven by man-made events. In fact, most of the serious melting has taken place since the 1980s. "It's on par with what we would expect from the greenhouse effect," says Demuth.

Experts say that the mean annual temperature in the Rockies today is 1.4°C higher than it was in the 1880s. This change (and scientists expect the increase to double or triple within the next 20 years) has triggered a number of important changes. First, the winters rarely get cold enough now to give the glaciers a true rest from melting. Second, during the summer, the warmth of day now lingers far into the night. (Last year, for the first time ever, summer climbers reported that the Wapta Icefield dripped all night long.)

Dan McCarthy is an alpine ecologist at Ontario's Brock University who fell in love with glaciers as a young ski bum in Jasper. For the last 25 years, he's spent his summers in the Rockies poking around glaciers and monitoring lichen growth (an excellent indicator of glacial retreat). McCarthy has calculated that in B.C.'s Glacier National Park, more than 50 per cent of the glacial ice has melted away in the last century. The smallest and lowest-elevation glaciers (those about one square kilometre in size) have suffered the greatest wasting. All in all, McCarthy calculates that the glaciers in the park have probably lost enough ice to fill a water tower at least five kilometres tall by five kilometres wide. "In these days of global warming," says McCarthy, "the wasting of glaciers is the most obvious environmental change you can see."

IN JULY, I decided to check out some glacial wastage myself and went looking for Peyto Glacier. Next to Glacier National Park's Illecillewaet Glacier, Peyto is probably the most studied glacier in the Rockies, which isn't saying much. Canada only has three so-called sentinel glaciers in the eastern Rockies, and the scientific literature makes pointed references to "the poverty of modern measurements" in Canada. But Peyto is an exception. It has been so well studied that researchers have even built an outhouse with a million-dollar view above its leaking snout.

To get to Peyto, I hopped in my truck and drove up the Icefields Parkway to Peyto Lake, about 30 minutes north of Lake Louise. I grabbed a stick and some lunch and walked in the glacier's debris-ridden wake for four hours. I knew that Peyto had retreated two kilometres since the explorer Walter Wilcox first photographed it in 1886. And I also knew that Peyto's tongue once extended Mick Jagger-like into the valley and almost far enough to lick the very shores of the emerald Peyto Lake. What I didn't realize is how effectively a wasting glacier can hide itself from view.

I tramped down the slopes of an old spruce forest but saw nothing. I marched across a boulder-strewn plain hoping to catch a glimpse, but still no luck. I goated up a roaring gorge where Peyto's waters rushed by, the colour of milky tea. But still no glacier. I traipsed across a log bridge and then lost the trail in a rock slide. I scrambled up a vertical piece of bedrock and nearly earned myself a Darwin Award, the honour given posthumously every year to those people who have died in the stupidest ways. At the top I found a narrow path best suited for sheep on the right side of a towering moraine. But still, no sign of ice. After another kilometre climb,

I entered a broad alpine bowl. And there in the middle, crouching behind another moraine, lay Peyto, making the sound of mountain water.

Looking for Peyto, however, was more fun than finding it. There simply isn't much left. As Mike Demuth notes, the ice is positively gnarly and unhealthy. "It's not really a classic glacier anymore." Demuth calculates that Peyto has now lost about 75 per cent of its volume. That means it has bled out 3,000 years of water savings in just a couple of decades—no mean achievement.

IN 1887, 27-year-old Mary Vaux and her brothers, George, 24, and William, 15, all members of an illustrious Philadelphia family, visited the newly constructed Glacier House near the summit of Rogers Pass. That's when their fascination with glaciers, and specifically the Illecillewaet Glacier, began. George, Mary and William started to measure and photograph the Illecillewaet with a 19th-century thoroughness that few have equalled since. They noted that the sharp surface of the glacier was unkempt, dirty and pockmarked by "little round holes about an inch across and two inches deep." They found, as I did on Peyto, that each hole contained soft sticky mud, soot or rocks. They also observed that "little streams trickle" down a glacier's face like the tears of a giant. They saw what I saw, but with one difference. On Peyto and other glaciers I visited, these opalescent streams now roar with enough force to wash away a full-grown man.

The Vauxes were the first people to wake up to the fact that Canada's glaciers were retreating. Seven years after their first trip to the Illecillewaet, they noticed that the great glacier had receded at a ferocious pace. "But sorrowful to say the distance is constantly becoming greater owing to the very rapid melting away of ice," wrote Mary Vaux in the *Minneapolis Journal* in 1898. In the last decade of the 19th century, a period of extensive drought on the prairies, the Vauxes reported that the Illecillewaet retreated 452 feet. Since then it has barely stopped to catch its breath and has now receded two kilometres.

Two years ago, Henry Vaux Jr., the grandson of George and a well-known California irrigation economist, returned to the very spot where his ancestors had lovingly photographed the Illecillewaet Glacier over the years. Armed with a copy of one of their black-and-white photographs, the 64-year-old could hardly believe his eyes. What had once been an easy stroll for his ancestors to the toe of the glacier had turned into a four-hour scramble. Where his relatives had once seen layers of majestic ice, Henry stared at bare rock.

These days, Parks Canada hands out a brochure informing tourists that "Your vacation photos may be the documentary material of the future!" As Henry Vaux discovered, it's no joke.

NO ONE really knows if the Illecillewaet and Peyto glaciers are reliable harbingers of a calamitous retreat or just precocious wasters. Mike Demuth is still working on modelling that might indicate just how quickly our glaciers will disappear in the next 50 years. But if you want to get a better idea of the future of Canada's alpine glaciers, you can take a trip to Montana's Glacier National Park, about three hours south of Calgary. Glacier, which borders Canada's Waterton National Park, is located at the southern tip of the Canadian Rockies, and looks and smells a lot like parks such as Banff and Jasper.

Daniel Fagre, an ecologist with the U.S. Geological Service, explains that the situation in Glacier is "a precursor of what's going to happen" to Canada's glaciers. In 1850, the area now occupied by the park boasted 150 glaciers, which explains how the park got its name. Today the park has fewer than 26 glaciers left. The ice that once occupied 99 square kilometres of real estate is fighting hard to hang on to 27 square kilometres, and losing. The park's famous Grinnell Glacier, for example, lost 23 per cent of its coverage in just eight years. "That raised a lot of eyebrows," notes Fagre. When the park's final glacier wastes away—expected to be sometime around 2030—the park might have to change its name. "It's going to happen in my lifetime," says Fagre.

The Minnesota-born ecologist, who has been studying this glacial retreat for 11 years, says that glaciers are probably the best and saddest signals of climate change in the world. He notes that animals and plants can essentially pick up and move when faced with rapid climate change. In fact, there is now a mass migration of animals towards the polar regions in search of cooler climes. But glaciers, fixed as they are to mountains of rock, don't have that freedom.

He likens glaciers to old men at the dinner table who are slow to catch on to new drifts in the conversation. So the melting we see today is merely a response to climate changes that occurred 10 to 25 years ago. When visitors ask him what can be done to save the glaciers, he reluctantly tells them that the time for effective greenhouse gas reductions was 30 years ago. "There is nothing we can do directly now," he replies. But he hopes that the great glacial melt-out might stand as an ominous warning. "Maybe we might get smart about our footprint on the planet and how to manage it."

IT WON'T be long until we in Canada start to notice the fallout from the unexpected departures of our glaciers. One of the most obvious changes will be the loss of the sheer beauty of our ice-draped scenery. The Rockies will look pretty drab without their ice. Imagine Lake Louise without Mount Victoria's crowning snowfield at the other end. Or Mount Edith Cavell without its Angel Glacier.

Daniel Fagre expects fir trees will march into our alpine meadows where they will displace the wild flowers. High-country wildlife such as the pika and maybe grizzly bears will disappear because, as Fagre dryly puts it, "Not too many animals eat trees." One Canadian study predicts that a further increase of 3°C could polish off anywhere from nine to 62 per cent of all mammals in montane habitats.

The wasting of our glaciers is already affecting those who come to play in the mountains. Bob Sandford, a vice-president of the Alpine Club of Canada, and the Canadian chair of the United Nations International Year of Freshwater in 2003, says mountaineering routes are changing by the hour. "The Alpine Club can't keep up with everything," notes Sandford. "Routes that were formerly ice or mixed climbs are now rock." Once-passable crevasses have become gaping chasms. Even the Lake Louise approach to Abbot Pass, which used to be a straightforward haul, has turned into a hazardous trip. Meanwhile, backcountry skiing in many areas has also become more dangerous.

Tourist operators have little idea what's about to hit them. For example, in a few years, the big lumbering SnoCoaches that take 600,000 visitors onto the Athabasca Glacier each year will likely find the glacier unnavigable. Yet few operators that cater to those tourists seem prepared for how climate change will rearrange their businesses, all within their lifetimes. Lee O'Donnell, the manager at Num-Ti-Jah Lodge, is typical. "If it doesn't affect the bottom line for next year, we're really not thinking about it." O'Donnell says he gets long reports from Parks Canada about new rules and regulations, but he's never read one about "glacial recession."

Then there are the downstream effects. To appreciate these, it helps to first understand that glaciers are probably Mother Nature's most elegant and economic system for storing freshwater. They build up water over time in the form of snow and ice, and then, come the dog days of summer, release it slowly just when it's needed most. According to Mike Demuth, we've already lost much of the reliability of the glacial water supply from the Rockies—these glaciers can no longer be depended upon to top up our dwindling rivers by 50 per cent in late summer. The flows of the rivers rushing out of the Rockies are in steep decline and will just get lower. That means less water for Calgary and Edmonton alike, and Demuth predicts that communities up to 3,000 kilometres away from the Rockies will be affected. "A continuation of this trend will exacerbate water shortages that are already apparent across many areas of Alberta and Saskatchewan owing to drought."

In the end, this means dry land will just get drier and many of our valley forests will burn like matches. On the prairies, water-starved hydro stations will produce fewer kilowatts (Calgary currently gets 17 per cent of its hydro from the Bow River) and irrigators that once grew water-slurping crops such as alfalfa for cattle feed will need to switch to drought-proof carrots or simply find another job. And as mountain-fed streams lose their glacial chill, their cold-loving trout will vainly search for cooler waters.

For those of us living on the prairies, our glaciers couldn't be leaving us at a worse time. Scientists studying lake fossils and tree rings have learned that droughts are pretty much a staple of the West. They've also learned that Europeans settled the prairies during the wettest century in the last 2,000 years. No white man, in other words, has ever stared aridity in the face. We also now know that the drought of the Great Depression was a minor dust-up and that there's a 40 per cent chance we'll be hammered by a whammy drought by 2030, which could last as long as 45 years. At the same time, more and more people are spilling over the plains to settle in Edmonton and Calgary. Unlike the Blackfoot and the Cree, who understood the importance of travelling light, we newcomers are gambling and trading up our vulnerabilities. Meanwhile, the temperature is rising and we are losing our glacial insurance.

Of course, what's happening in the Rockies is just part of a global trend. During last summer's heat wave alone, Europe lost a whopping 10 per cent of its glaciers. The melting ice on Mont Blanc, the highest mountain in the Alps, made that peak virtually unclimbable. Many experts expect all of Switzerland's glaciers will be gone by 2050. Glaciers in Peru retreated 32 times faster between 1998 and 2000 than during the 20 years from 1963 to 1983. Water and power shortages are already dogging Andean villages. The glaciers of the Tien Shan mountains between Russia and China have shrunk by 22 per cent in the last 40 years.

In Africa, it appears that Ernest Hemingway wrote about the snows of Kilimanjaro at just the right time: its glaciers are now 82 per cent gone. Even the glaciers in the Himalaya, the world's highest range, are disappearing. In Nepal, they've had to drain as many as 40 swollen glacial lakes so they won't flood the villages below. And the Khumbu Glacier—which flows down the valley below Everest base camp—has retreated five kilometres since Sir Edmund Hillary and Tenzing Norgay first climbed the mountain 51 years ago.

ALL IN all, glaciers provide 50 per cent of the earth's citizens with freshwater. Or did. So if you think it sounds like there's a crisis ahead, you're right. But you wouldn't know it from the world's politicians. Here in Canada, despite the fact that our glaciers contain more freshwater than the Great Lakes, our federal government doesn't seem to understand the significance of what losing our glaciers will mean to 10 million folks in B.C., Alberta and Saskatchewan. And Alberta, the province most dependent on glacial melt in the country, has no provincial glaciologist and only the vaguest notion of how the disappearance of 1,300 or so glaciers will affect water availability and supplies on its side of the Rockies.

Although most scientists agree that it's probably too late to save our glaciers, no one suggests we should stand still. Sustained reductions in greenhouse gases could still save a lot of ice in the Arctic and Greenland. As Demuth notes, "Any action that reduces greenhouse gases is a good thing." In his recent bestseller, *Boiling Point*, Pulitzer Prize–winning journalist Ross Gelbspan calls for an end to fossil-fuel subsidies and a stringent Fossil Fuel Efficiency standard that would rise five per cent a year. Both would be glacier-friendly and astute political goals. Gelbspan agrees that it's getting late in the day to avert "a cascade of major and destructive impacts," but the honest truth is that we don't know for sure. "We do not know where on the trajectory of disintegration we stand."

So here's my wishful forecast. I'd like to think that sometime soon, we will all be chattering about glaciers the way we breathlessly talked about 9/11. That politicians, aroused from a deep slumber like modern-day Rip Van Winkles, will excitedly champion the importance of glacial-fed rivers and belatedly acknowledge how they quench our thirst, make fish, irrigate farmland and keep us happy. That energy czars will stop pumping water down oil wells and instead pledge allegiance to glaciers. That our newspapers, after expressing their customary shock and dismay in editorials about the new threat to our national security, might finally pay more attention to climate change and our fossil fuel addictions.

But since none of that is likely to happen soon, here's my immediate plan. Tomorrow or the next day I am going to get in my car and cook up some more glacier-killing gases and drive to Num-Ti-Jah Lodge on Bow Lake along the Icefields Parkway. I will pack a lunch and bring along my boys. We will hike along cold water the colour of jade and maybe pause for a moment to think how dull every mountain lake will look without the contributions of glacier melt.

I will tell my sons that ice is the beginning of all things and that this is where Calgary's water comes from. We will take deep breaths and enjoy what the Vauxes called "the nerve restoring air." I will tell them about Jimmy Simpson, a soft-spoken remittance man and mountain guide, who, at the end of the 19th century, followed the Bow River to its origins. He was so smitten by the Bow Glacier and its lake that he built his home and what is now Num-Ti-Jah facing it. Simpson watched the Bow and other related glaciers melt so quickly between 1920 and 1950 that he predicted that Lake Louise would become a sinkhole early in the next century. He also thought that the Saskatchewan and Bow rivers would soon float no more than a good-sized shingle. Not long after the glacier disappeared from sight, old Jimmy died.

We will climb up hard moraines and enter a great rock amphitheatre. I will tell them that the Bow Glacier built this spot and once defended it like a gladiator. One of my boys will ask where the glacier is now and I will answer that it is hiding, just out of view, beyond the falls. For the Bow Glacier and all its relatives have packed up 25 per cent of their ice and are now leaving us. But I won't tell my boys that bit of news, just yet. Instead, we will enjoy the falls spilling over a cliff with a purity that is absolute.

We will find a rock and sit for a while. We will swat mosquitoes and I'm sure somebody will tell a fart joke. Slowly but surely the sound of mountain water, nature's original symphony, will drown us out. And I will recall the voice of Wallace Stegner, who said it is impossible to believe that one could be tired or thirsty in such a place.

And we will be refreshed. Then we will take our leave.

I will tell my boys to wave goodbye.

THE STORY
OF BEAR 99

CHRISTIE McLAREN

SEPTEMBER/OCTOBER 2005

AT 1:55 PM on June 5, 2005, Bear 99 stood on a path in the woods above Canmore, Alberta. Listening. Sniffing the wind.

So far, it had not been a peaceful day. After a week alone in the high and quiet places, the young male grizzly found himself back in the noisy place. This morning, he had been spooked by voices. A few minutes ago, someone had screamed at him. Next, he'd been sprayed with water. So the bear had moved uphill, into the forest. But now there were new sounds, in the distance. Movement, above him. People, coming towards him.

"Woo! *Bear.*" Jean McAllister stopped, and Maria Hawkins and Isabelle Dubé, each a stride apart, stopped behind her. Eighty feet ahead of them, a grizzly. The bear stepped forward, and paused. The women backed up. Bear 99 began walking towards them. Isabelle spotted a tree and started to climb. As the grizzly advanced, the others backed away, until they lost sight of Isabelle.

Bear 99 began to climb.

THE BILLBOARDS start 30 kilometres east of Canmore, the last town on the Trans-Canada Highway before you enter Banff National Park. From a ski hill in B.C.: "Forecast: 95 per cent chance of grizzlies." From the sight-seeing gondola at Lake Louise: "Home of the Grizzly Bear." And from a golf course in Canmore, the name says it all: SilverTip. To the average tourist heading towards a vacation in the Rocky Mountains, the mammoth pictures of grizzly bears hold out a tantalizing and slightly scary promise: where you're headed, a bear could be around every corner. On one hand, this is truer than most people realize. On the other, nothing could be further from the truth. The grizzly bear—*Ursus arctos horribilis*, Great Bear, emblem of the wilderness—is in trouble in Alberta.

Just how much trouble became clear this summer when the Eastern Slopes Grizzly Bear Project, the largest-ever grizzly study in Canada, released its findings. The grizzlies that live on the eastern slopes of the Rockies are undernourished, reproduce less frequently than other grizzlies in North America, are being pushed out of prime habitat by human developments and recreation, and are dying too often at the hands of human beings. The 11-year project examined the grizzly's fortunes across 40,000 square kilometres of the central Rockies ecosystem, including 11,400 square kilometres of the eastern slopes, from Bow Lake to the prairie. Its authors call for at least two key actions to help the species survive—reduce the number of deaths of adult females, and eliminate the conflicts between bears and people that almost always lead to the bear being destroyed.

Project chairman Steve Herrero says he would like to see the grizzly formally designated as "threatened" in Alberta, which would give the bear legal protection until the population can recover to a long-term sustainable level of at least 1,000 breeding-age adults. Currently, Alberta has about 700 adult grizzlies, compared with 10,000 to 17,000 next door in British Columbia. "If we want to keep grizzly bears," Herrero says, "now's the time to act."

THE GRIZZLY that would become known as Bear 99 sauntered into the public consciousness in Canmore when he showed up, as if out of nowhere, on the May long weekend. Just before 5 PM on Monday, May 23, Joe Robertson was stepping out of his house on Benchlands Terrace—a street perched on a thickly wooded ledge above the Trans-Canada Highway—when some passersby in a car told him there was a bear in his backyard. "Yeah, right," said Robertson, who had never seen a bear in town. When he went to investigate, Robertson saw "a black mass" 50 feet away, dropping down the slope at the end of his property into a deep, tree-choked gully separating two residential streets. From a sidewalk across the gully, excited onlookers followed the bear west, until it emerged from the undergrowth and headed across open, grassy slopes in the general direction of the forest.

Close to 5:30, what was later described as a "huge" male grizzly stepped out of the woods onto the SilverTip Golf Course. For the rest of the evening, the bear—which seemed unperturbed by nearby golfers—had complete command of the fifth fairway, eating grass, flipping over the occasional rock or log, and taking a dip in a water trap.

Provincial Fish and Wildlife officers watched the bear until dark. When he started moving upslope towards the forest, they set off noise-makers to urge him on his way. Around 10:30, he melted into the woods.

DESPITE A widespread reputation as bloodthirsty killers, grizzlies are primarily herbivorous, and the Alberta grizzly is more so than most. Its diet is about 80 per cent vegetarian, consisting mainly of grasses, roots, berries and insects. Unlike bears on the B.C. coast, the Alberta bears—which once roamed the prairie but were driven into the mountains by agriculture—don't have easy access to a rich source of protein such as salmon. In fact, if the west coast of North America is the Hilton of grizzly bear habitat, the eastern slopes of the Rockies are the Super-8 Motel. Half the mountain landscape consists of rock and ice that's inhospitable to bears, and the other half is fast filling up with development. The eastern slopes are colder, drier and less fertile than the western slopes of the B.C. Interior, offering fewer calories per acre. Meanwhile, grizzlies have poor digestive systems and need a lot of volume. The grizzlies in the eastern Rockies require twice as big a home range and have to cover more ground each day, just to fill their stomachs. "That's why bears here are small, skinny bears," says Mike Gibeau, a grizzly biologist who is the carnivore specialist for the mountain national parks. "We call them food-stressed."

And now, the three Rs of affluent mountain life—residences, resorts and recreation—are squeezing the bears into even more marginal habitat on the fringes of increasingly urbanized centres. Nowhere is this more acute than in the Bow Valley around Canmore, where grizzly bears "are hanging by a thread," says Jon Jorgenson, the province's wildlife biologist for the region.

FOR TWO days after the noisemakers were fired at him, Bear 99 kept out of sight. Everyone thought they'd seen the last of the golf-course grizzly, until Niki Davison heard twigs snapping in the forest on Wednesday, May 25.

Assuming the noise above her was a mountain biker, Davison, a young, soft-spoken redhead, didn't even look up from the orchids she was photographing. When she stood and saw a bear staring at her from 50 feet away, she grabbed her basset hound by the collar, stepped onto the narrow trail and, stooped over, slowly started to drag the dog away.

It was 7 PM. Davison's only thought was to make it out of the woods to the edge of town, about 200 yards away. But when she glanced back and realized the bear was following her, she stopped. The bear stopped. He had advanced about 45 feet. For 10 or 15 seconds, Bear 99 "just looked at me," she says. "He was totally interested in what I was doing." Then he turned and headed in the opposite direction, away from town.

Davison resumed walking, but soon, the bear was following her again. She forced herself to stop. Again, the bear stopped. "He was not aggressive," she says, "just very interested." But he was closing the gap; this time there was just 30 feet between them.

Again, she stayed still. Again, the bear lost interest and turned away. But when she continued hobbling with the dog, he turned and followed her once more. At that point, Davison says, "I realized it was going to get dangerous if I didn't stop." For the third time, she forced herself to halt. Bear 99 slowed down, stepped off the trail opposite her, and stopped.

Now they were about six feet apart. From her stooped position, "I felt like if I reached out, I could have touched his nose," says Davison. For the first time, she saw the bear's claws and realized with a shock that he was a grizzly. "That's when I started to sing and talk."

For two or three minutes, she sang softly and spoke calmly to Bear 99. It was a kind of prayer: "It's going to be alright, it's going to be okay."

Occasionally she darted a quick glance upward at his eyes. They were brown. She remembers thinking his fur was "fluffy." She could hear the bear breathing. "He was very calm." But Davison never felt safe. She kept a stranglehold on her dog, which by now was staring at the bear. She fought the instinct to run. "We just stood there. And we waited, and hoped."

Then, Bear 99 shifted his weight away from Davison, pivoted, slowly, towards an opening in the trees behind him, and padded away. She forced herself to wait 60 more seconds until he was completely out of sight. Then she picked up her dog and ran home in the opposite direction as fast as she could.

SID MARTY tells this story about a grizzly bear. One early spring day in a remote area of Banff National Park, the Alberta author and former national park warden spotted a grizzly on a faraway ridge above a long, snow-covered slope. The bear sat down on its rump, lifted its immense paws in the air, and—as if to say *wheee!*—slid, toboggan-style, all the way to the bottom. "And I knew," Marty once told me, "that I wanted to share the planet with a creature like that."

It's not something that would surprise Mike Gibeau, the parks' carnivore specialist. Grizzly bears are highly intelligent, and, like people, or dogs, he says, are all individuals. "There's a complete range of behaviours, right from Mary Poppins to Charles Manson." Even siblings can be radically different in temperament. Gibeau remembers three females from the Lake Louise area a few years ago. One was very comfortable around people, the second was "a complete recluse," and the third fell between the two extremes.

On the eastern slopes, grizzly cubs don't leave home for good until they are three or four years old, in late May or early June. Young, sub-adult males, like Bear 99, can be compared to teenagers on their own for the first time, Gibeau says. Some will try anything once, while others are afraid to make a misstep. Males in particular "are by their very nature curious and exploratory," adds Steve Herrero, and "often get into situations where they test their relationships with people." No wonder the first year of independence is one of the most dangerous times for the sub-adult male grizzly. With no guidance from his mother, he must venture into the world, find his own home range, get enough to eat and avoid being killed by an adult male.

HOW BEAR 99 spent the day on Thursday, May 26, is not known. But in the evening, Marc Lilley, general manager of the SilverTip Golf Course, got a call from a homeowner who had spotted the bear strolling once again down the fifth fairway. A golf tournament was just ending. When Lilley went to investigate, the bear was munching on dandelions on the sixth tee. For an hour, Lilley watched the grizzly from his truck, parked about 80 feet away. Unconcerned, 99 went on foraging. "He couldn't have cared less if I was there." When a new resident ran towards the bear to snap a photo, Lilley was terrified, but the bear seemed unfazed.

Even for Lilley, who grew up around bears in small-town B.C., it was a remarkable hour. He admits to being struck by Bear 99. "He was the most beautiful, perfectly shaped grizzly bear."

But 99's escapades were getting to be a bit much for Fish and Wildlife officers. In an effort to save the life of the bold young bear, they had already decided to relocate him away from people. A long-distance move was ruled out, for fear that he would encroach on the territory of an established adult male and be killed. Instead, Bear 99 would be moved into the wilderness 15 kilometres northwest of Canmore. The goal was to keep the grizzly within what was probably his own home range, but out of the portion that overlapped with SilverTip and the north slopes of Canmore.

On the golf course in the early morning of Friday, May 27, Bear 99 walked into the trap that, ironically, could have set him free.

Being captured, drugged and handled is traumatic for bears, and 99 was no different. Confined to a steel barrel, the wide-ranging grizzly was not very happy, Lilley says. He paced and pawed at the grille, but eventually grew quiet. Ninety minutes later, conservation officers transferred the trap to a pickup truck, and Bear 99 rode to a government warehouse on the edge of town. There, he was darted with a tranquilizer and removed from the trap.

As he lay on a stretcher, with a blindfold over his eyes, a handful of people stole some of the mystery from Bear 99. They measured his paws and limp body; they extracted a tooth; they drew blood, snipped hair and excised a small piece of tissue. These specimens would go to research. When they hung the stretcher from a scale, there was a slight surprise: the "huge" bear in fact weighed just 198 pounds. His fur made him seem, literally, larger than life. Around his neck went a hefty, $5,000 GPS collar with a VHF transmitter that would allow conservation officers to follow his movements two ways—by satellite and radio signal. An orange transmitter tag, bearing the number that gave him his name, was punched into his ear.

The plan was to relocate 99 that afternoon. But when biologists tuned into the collar's VHF frequency, there was no signal. The gear was malfunctioning and would need to be replaced. The bear would have to spend the night.

Jon Jorgenson, the province's biologist for Canmore-Kananaskis, says by the time everyone left, the bear was sitting quietly in the trap. He had water. The doors were locked and in the cool, dark warehouse, Jorgenson says, 99 slept.

IT IS a rare thing to be attacked by a bear, and rarer still to die in such an attack. According to one set of U.S. statistics, your lifetime odds of dying in an airplane crash or a lightning strike are one in 40,000. Your odds of being attacked by a bear are one in 410,000. The chance that a bear will kill you? One in 1.2 million.

But it happens. And for hikers, bikers or outdoor workers in bear country, a quick glance at nearly 40 years of Alberta bear-attack statistics is enlightening. From 1960 through 1998, bears killed 12 people in Alberta—fewer than one person every three years—and inflicted serious injuries on 30 others, according to a University of Calgary study.

Grizzlies, which caused twice as many serious and fatal injuries despite being outnumbered 39 to one by black bears, are clearly the more dangerous of the two species, but not necessarily because they are more aggressive. In fact, while 58 per cent of the attacks by black bears in Alberta were judged to be predatory (and a larger percentage of black bear attacks were fatal), only 18 per cent of the grizzly attacks were similarly rooted in the intent to kill. Two-thirds of the attacking grizzlies acted in self-defence, after being startled by people less than 160 feet away. The grizzly's greater power to destroy may have more to do with anatomy than motive: just one swipe of the Great Bear's long, sharp claws can rip a person wide open.

The overwhelming majority of the grizzly bears involved in attacks were adult females with cubs (90 per cent). Mama bears come by their fearsome reputations honestly—although they account for just 20 per cent of the grizzly population, they inflict more than half the injuries. Of the victims, the vast majority (90 per cent) were in groups of three or fewer, and three-quarters were male.

Although the number of injuries doubled from the 1960s to the 1990s, it's worth noting that Alberta's population also doubled, so the rate of attacks did not change. Since 1998, there have been a handful of maulings, but until June of 2005, Alberta had not had a bear-related fatality in seven years.

ON SATURDAY, May 28, Bear 99 was briefly re-tranquilized and fitted with a new collar programmed to trace his position via satellite every two hours. That afternoon, Niki Davison happened to see the bright white culvert trap dangling from a helicopter as it flew over her neighbourhood. *That's my bear,* she thought. Around 3 PM, 24 hours later than originally planned, 99 was released above tiny Stenton Lake, at South Ghost Pass, just east of the Banff park border.

The exact timing of his movements over the next seven days are unclear, but Bear 99 likely put his first 12 kilometres behind him that afternoon and evening, dropping from the wind-scoured pass below treeline, bushwhacking into Banff National Park, and finally reaching the steeply forested south shore of Lake Minnewanka. He didn't see a soul.

A sometimes gloomy place, Minnewanka stretches for 30 kilometres along a narrow valley, squeezed between mountain walls that soar 5,000 feet skyward and seem to plunge straight into the water. Even bears find it hard to navigate here without using a trail. On Sunday, May 29, Bear 99 crossed the lake near its eastern end and stepped onto the north shore.

To his right was the wilderness of the Ghost Lakes, the park's eastern terminus at Devil's Gap, and the foothills beyond. But Bear 99 turned left, onto the narrow lakeside trail heading west.

For the next 15 kilometres, the bear passed unseen by four campgrounds and a warden's cabin. It was likely Monday, May 30, when he reached the steep side trail to Aylmer Pass, which offered the promise of higher ground and a place to graze. For the next 24 hours, maybe more, the grizzly lingered between 5,500 and 7,000 feet, roaming across meadows populated by bighorn sheep.

IN CONTRAST to Minnewanka, the Bow River Valley is the ecological treasure of the eastern slopes. Wider and greener than the side valleys, it is the only significant east-west trough in a landscape of limestone peaks that march stolidly north and south. The long-term survival of the grizzly bear may depend upon the species' ability to use the valley to travel—for food and to disperse its genes—across the broader landscape, from the United States to the Yukon.

Ten years ago, Bear 99 would not have run into the problems that he did in the Bow Valley last spring. Until the early 1990s, Canmore remained a relatively small mountain town of 6,000, and bears and other wildlife could pass by the community unimpeded. But change was coming. In 1992, Alberta's Natural Resources Conservation Board—an environmental assessment body—gave the green light to the controversial Three Sisters housing, golf and commercial development proposed for the mountain slopes on the south side of the valley. In return, the developer was required to set aside sufficient land for wildlife-travel corridors. They were to be at least 1,150 feet wide and left as undisturbed as possible.

But in 1993, when a team of five prominent biologists was asked to identify where these and other corridors should be located, they "were in direct conflict with where all the development was going to be," says grizzly specialist Mike Gibeau, who was a member of the team. The corridors mapped out in 1994 were a compromise from the start, based on the land that was available, not the land that was most important.

Within a decade, Canmore's population virtually doubled as major residential and golf course developments—Three Sisters, the Peaks of Grassi, Eagle Terrace and SilverTip—gobbled up wide swaths of land identified as critical to wildlife. Meanwhile, new research showed that bears and carnivores needed much wider corridors. But today, many of Canmore's wildlife corridors are just 1,000 feet wide, on steep slopes above housing developments, riddled with trails and full of people.

For grizzlies to survive over time, 68 per cent of the fertile landscape must be linked, intact habitat, the Eastern Slopes grizzly project says. But in the Bow Valley, just 43 per cent of the land fits that description, and in Alberta's beloved Kananaskis Country, it's a mere 36 per cent. In some places, development has choked off all possibility of animal movement, says Gibeau, who argues that it's pointless to quibble about the width of corridors at this point. "We've built this place wall to wall, from one side of the valley to the other."

Meanwhile, the town continues to expand. Gibeau says he withdrew from the debate in 1997 out of frustration with the lack of understanding, or commitment to wildlife, on the part of local and provincial politicians. "I might as well have had those discussions with a wall. It was not making any difference whatsoever." Now, he fears it is too late to ensure that grizzlies have a future in the Bow Valley. "I'm pretty much resigned to the fact that in the long term, there'll be this big empty space around Canmore, with no grizzly bears."

IN THE rain-hushed backcountry near Aylmer Pass, Bear 99 headed back down the trail to resume his westward progress along the shore of Lake Minnewanka. Around June 1, near the lake's western terminus, he made an exploratory push into steep-walled Stewart Canyon, before abandoning the idea and crossing the creek near its mouth. Like a ghost, the bear then passed invisibly through some of the park's most popular destinations. Skirting the Minnewanka parking lot and the Devil's Gap tour-boat launch, he stepped onto the Cascade Valley trail, where he made another fateful choice. A turn north would have taken him deep into the Cascade wilderness. But 99 went south, towards civilization, emerging a few minutes later at the Upper Bankhead picnic area. From there, he shifted southeast, past Two Jack Lake and its campgrounds, crossing two roads and the Cascade River, eventually arriving on the lower benches of the Fairholme Range, above Johnson Lake. Since leaving Aylmer Pass, 99 had travelled about 20 kilometres. But it was poor weather for tourists. No one reported seeing a grizzly.

June 2 brought more chill rain. From the lower benches, Bear 99 made another detour from his mostly linear travels and climbed a thousand feet up the slopes of Mount Girouard. For the second time that week, the bear stayed put for close to a day and a half, browsing, foraging, maybe sleeping, in the meadows and forest above 5,000 feet.

IN HIS office at the SilverTip Golf Course, Marc Lilley points out the window at a bush laden with red, ripening buffalo berries. The irony is not lost on him. Here is the favourite summer food of the grizzly bear, just steps from his desk. It's one reason why Lilley's job at the 170-acre, 18-hole course gives new meaning to the company's marketing slogan: "Where Nature Plays Through." Not only does he have to keep golfers happy; often, he has to keep them safe from bears. Always, that means giving the bears the right-of-way.

SilverTip sees a lot of bears. Rated as one of the top courses in Canada for scenery, it sits smack in the middle of the wildlife corridor on the north side of the Trans-Canada Highway, with spectacular views across the Bow Valley. By July 18 this year, bears had wandered onto the links 35 times, a dramatic increase over 2004. All were black bears, save for 99. The vast majority are just passing through, Lilley says, and since SilverTip opened in 1998, the company has followed its bear-management plan and halted or diverted play numerous times to give a bear space. Closing the course entirely is a different matter. It takes at least half an hour, and "means money," Lilley says. On five occasions when a bear has lingered, the company, controlled by Calgary oil executive Guy Turcotte, has voluntarily shut down completely.

Golf courses are attractive to bears and are in fact good bear habitat, according to a report commissioned for the Alberta government in 2000, because they offer high-quality food in the form of lush, fertilized grass and other nitrogen-rich plants on the fringes of fairways. On the other hand, the report said, golf courses are hazardous for bears, because the odds are good a bear will have a run-in with a human and wind up dead. Ultimately, says Jon Jorgenson, the province's biologist in Canmore, "golf courses are probably not appropriate in an environment like this."

ON FRIDAY, June 3, the grizzly dropped once more to the lower benches of the Fairholme Range, at 4,700 feet. As if guided by an internal homing device, Bear 99 travelled almost due south for about eight kilometres, in the direction of the SilverTip Golf Course.

In Canmore, Isabelle Dubé, a 36-year-old teacher and competitive mountain biker, got in touch with biking partners Maria Hawkins and Jean McAllister. Isabelle and Maria had been teammates in the gruelling TransRockies Challenge mountain-bike race the summer before, placing third in their field. For a few weeks now, the three women had talked about getting out for fun, but it always seemed to be raining. This time, Isabelle and Maria made a date for one o'clock on Sunday. If it rains, they agreed, we'll just go for a run.

That night, high above the Trans-Canada Highway, Bear 99 found shelter against the threatening skies in the forest between Banff and Canmore. Behind trees and the folded landscape, his resting place was screened from the constant whine of transport trucks, a thousand feet below.

On Saturday, June 4, the bear woke early. At 5:30 AM, Fish and Wildlife officers picked up a signal from 99's radio collar near the hamlet of Harvie Heights. One week to the day since he'd been flown into the backcountry, the bear was back, just four kilometres from SilverTip. Using the forest as cover, he traversed the benches above Harvie Heights and slipped past Cross Zee Ranch and its riding stables. In the light morning drizzle, he navigated a gentle slope towards the highway and dropped into an overgrown gravel pit, a stone's throw from the Sheraton Hotel. As the day wore on and the rain began to fall in earnest, 99 hunkered down, eating dandelions and flipping over rocks in search of ants. From the roadside, District Fish and Wildlife officer Ron Wiebe kept his telemetry equipment trained on the grizzly. The bear didn't budge. That night, the skies opened up. On the edge of civilization, 99 slept.

IN THE days to follow, a lot of people said the Fish and Wildlife officers messed up, that they should have stopped Bear 99 before he got back to Canmore. But until his encounter with Isabelle Dubé, 99 exhibited no signs of aggression towards people, according to those who knew him best. Sometimes he had shown curiosity, but mostly he was "indifferent," says Jon Jorgenson. And because he was young, he was trainable. If 99 returned to the area, the plan was to "haze" him—using dogs, noisemakers and rubber bullets—out of the portions of his home range that overlapped with human development. Ultimately, explains Ron Wiebe, "you're trying to teach a bear a way to survive."

Did that decision cause a tragedy? No, says Mike Gibeau. The blame lies with the cascade of decisions over the past decade that deposited people into the same space as bears, wolves and cougars. "Then in 2005... there's a fatality, and everybody says, 'What's wrong with the Fish and Wildlife people?' Well, there's nothing wrong with the Fish and Wildlife people. Against all odds, they're still trying to keep bears here, to allow them to be here... These guys have got an absolutely impossible task."

Indeed. Wiebe and his two staff are responsible for keeping bears and people apart across a 4,000-square-kilometre chunk of Alberta's mountains and foothills. The area is home to about 130 black bears and 60 grizzlies. The Bow Valley portion has between 10 and 20 black bears and between five and seven grizzlies, but last year, more than half the black-bear problems—78—and a third of the grizzly problems—21—occurred in the valley. And despite Canmore's population explosion and the steady advance of golf courses and trail users, Wiebe's district hasn't had a staff increase in almost 20 years. That could change if Alberta approves a proposed provincial Grizzly Bear Recovery Plan. Biologists say the plan, which has been several years in the making, would go a long way towards helping the population recover and could mean more resources.

Wiebe allows that he "could always use more people in this corridor," but that federal agencies such as Parks Canada and the RCMP can be relied upon to help. Jorgenson is a tad less diplomatic. "We're frustrated," he admits, "because we are trying to do the best job we can for wildlife and public safety without having a lot of land to work with, or resources to work with. We don't have enough resources to do all this stuff." Up at the SilverTip Golf Course, Marc Lilley is blunt. "They're desperately underfunded and understaffed."

AROUND 11:30 AM on Sunday, June 5, Jim Stanton looked up from his work at the Cross Zee Ranch when one of his horses began kicking up a fuss. Across the yard was a grizzly bear, feeding on grass. Stanton went inside to tell his family, and when they stepped onto a balcony, full of chatter, Bear 99 glanced up and scampered off into the forest.

By one o'clock, when Maria Hawkins arrived at Isabelle Dubé's house across from the Summit Café, it was drizzling. Deciding that it was too wet to bike, the women ran uphill to Jean McAllister's house in Eagle Terrace. Around 1:10, the trio set off at a comfortable pace, straight uphill into the wildlife corridor, towards the popular Upper Benchlands Trail.

Instead of running to Harvie Heights, Isabelle and Jean suggested a shorter, one-hour workout that would take them a kilometre west of the SilverTip golf course and loop back on the lower Montane Traverse. Now on the upper trail, the women talked about summer plans. Passing in and out of the trees, the route offered panoramic views of the overcast Bow Valley as they moved farther west.

At about 1:30, a SilverTip employee heard a loud scream for help near the 18th hole. A terrified woman in her fifties was cowering behind a tree, 65 feet away from Bear 99. Contrary to some reports, Marc Lilley says, the grizzly did not behave in a menacing fashion. The woman—who later disappeared before anyone got her name—was enveloped in a cloud of perfume, and Bear 99 was sniffing the air. By the time two employees drove a truck to the scene, the young grizzly had lost interest and was heading in the opposite direction, down a service road. But when the woman made a sudden dash for the truck 200 feet away, the bear wheeled and bolted towards her, stopping 10 feet short of the truck after she'd vanished into the cab.

Bear 99 stood on his hind legs. As the truck backed away, he dropped down on all fours and turned in yet a different direction, towards the eighth tee and the wildlife corridor immediately above it. Concerned for the golfers on nearby fairways, one of the employees used a remote control in the truck to activate a wall of sprinklers on each side of the bear. The grizzly sped up, scrambled up a short hill and disappeared into the forest. He stepped onto the Montane Traverse and turned west. It was 1:40.

At 1:45, a couple of hundred feet above, Maria, Jean and Isabelle met a uniformed provincial parks employee on the upper trail. The women wondered if she was investigating a wildlife sighting. "Have you seen a bear?" Jean asked. "No," the woman replied. "Have you?" No, the runners said, and they continued on their way.

A few minutes later, about a kilometre west of the golf course, the trio began descending a twisty side trail through the trees. Near the bottom, as she rounded a curve, Jean stopped dead. "Woo! *Bear.*" Eighty feet below, Bear 99 stood on the lower trail, facing them. Maria, next in line, saw "a round head, and fur" radiating outward like a crown. Immediately, the women started backing up. Maria remembers someone saying: "Don't run. Stick together. Back up." Bear 99 took two steps forward, paused briefly and began walking up the gentle slope towards them. It wasn't more than half a minute, Maria thinks, when Isabelle, who had moved farther up the slope than the other two, hit on the idea of climbing a tree. She said: "Find a tree, you guys—climb a tree." Maria couldn't see one that she felt confident about climbing. She and Jean kept backing up, now past Isabelle. Now Bear 99 was rounding the corner. As Jean and Maria backed out of sight, Isabelle was starting up the tree.

Back on the upper trail, the women debated what to do. They could hear Isabelle yelling at the bear. In fear, Maria thought. Jean wanted to stay with Isabelle. Maria's mind was a tumult: *Stay or go? No bear spray; can't beat it with a stick. Which way to go? Where's the quickest place to get help? If she's in a tree, hopefully she's safe.* Maria looked at her watch. It was 2:06. Jean yelled: "We're going to get help!" They didn't hear an answer. Six minutes later, by Maria's watch, the women flew out of the woods onto the golf course and flagged down a group of golfers, who used cell phones to call for help.

Around 2:30, mountain biker Cameron Baty and two friends turned off the Upper Benchlands Trail and pointed their bikes downhill on the twisty trail. They braked at the sight of a grizzly, behind a big fallen log. Startled, Bear 99 ran away, putting 100 more feet between them before he turned back and started to move towards them. The bikers slowly

retreated, and Bear 99 stopped. Out of sight, the men turned and pedalled towards the golf course.

By the time two RCMP officers, two Fish and Wildlife officers and a
bear dog gathered on the golf course, it was approaching 2:45. Led by
Jean, they set off at a run for Isabelle's tree. The group of five met Baty
and his friends, who guided them back to the bear. From a distance, Jean
could see Isabelle's bright red shirt on the ground. Again, Bear 99 bolted.
Baty thinks he got about 100 feet.

To Maria, who was waiting at the golf course, it seemed like a long
time had passed when she heard the shot.

Later that afternoon, 13-year-old Leah Pengelly was walking the family retriever when a helicopter pounded into view under the low-hanging
clouds. It flew so near that Pengelly could see that the bear slung in the
net beneath it was a grizzly.

OVERNIGHT, BEAR 99 underwent a metamorphosis in the public imagination, from gentle giant to terrifying predator. On the morning of June
6, Isabelle Dubé's death was national news. Front-page headlines spoke
of the young mother being "mauled to death" by a "killer bear" in Alberta's first "fatal mauling" since 1998. Souvenir-seekers, in a bastardization
of ancient tradition, called government offices looking to buy claws and
teeth from the man-killer bear.

Meanwhile, in the back of a pickup, the bear that was hardly bigger
than a man completed his final journey, to Alberta's wildlife forensics
laboratory in Edmonton. The necropsy performed later that day found
"no indication of anything unusual" in the bear's condition. Bear 99 was a
normal male grizzly, three to four years old.

AS A human, it's almost impossible not to speculate about what Bear
99 was thinking or feeling before and during his encounter with Isabelle Dubé. Was he still traumatized by his capture and relocation? By
the screaming on the golf course a half-hour earlier? In Maria Hawkins's
view, the bear had been through too much that week. "I think it was
stressed and was fed up with people, and had seen enough people, thank
you very much."

Scientists are reluctant to indulge in this kind of thinking; there is no evidence to support it, Jon Jorgenson says. More likely, they say, Bear 99 was simply being a bear—that is, continually scanning his environment and making decisions from one moment to the next, as survival dictates. Bears are innately curious creatures, says Mike Gibeau, and "it's a very fine line, where curiosity melts into instinct." Fish and Wildlife spokesman Dave Ealey says they will react instinctively "to things that run away from them or have high-pitched voices... that might sound like an animal in distress." Anything that runs away from a bear "is potential prey."

ON THURSDAY, June 9, in a meeting with Isabelle's mother, her brothers, Jean McAllister and Maria Hawkins, Ron Wiebe explained what he knew of the circumstances of Isabelle's death.

Isabelle had climbed 51 feet up the tree. None of its lower branches were broken, but at 51 feet, a sturdier branch was freshly snapped. There was bear fur all the way up to 50 feet. Wiebe said they couldn't tell whether Isabelle had fallen from the tree or been pulled by the bear. Bear 99 had no broken bones or other signs of trauma; most likely, he climbed back down. Isabelle had some bite wounds on her body.

Maria says she was left with the impression that Isabelle was killed by the fall. "It was comforting to us to know that she had climbed amazingly high. That she had fought, she had done everything she could, and gone as high as possible." Before the meeting, she said, people imagined the worst. "Speaking to Wiebe and hearing the facts kind of took away that unknown. And you didn't have to imagine that she only got 10 feet up and was mauled horribly." Isabelle's peaked cap was found snagged in the tree at 36 feet. Maria said it was hard to watch when Wiebe pulled it out of his pocket and handed it to Isabelle's mother.

That evening, in the presence of Isabelle's husband and family members, one of Isabelle's brothers climbed the tree and placed in its branches a bouquet of yellow roses.

UP AND down the Bow Valley, wildlife biologists and land managers say the same thing: sooner or later, someone in Canmore was going to die in an encounter with a wild animal. "It was just a matter of time," says Jon Jorgenson, who echoes others when he says it could happen again, anytime, especially as the town continues to grow.

In July, Isabelle's family and friends wrote the Alberta government, proposing a central clearinghouse of wildlife information for trail users in the Bow Valley. The group wants a Web site and telephone number with significant wildlife sightings updated daily. Wildlife managers say such ideas are impractical, because animals are everywhere, and they move around too much. But Jean McAllister says it might prevent situations like that in her own neighbourhood this spring, when a cougar was frequenting a well-travelled gully across from the Summit Café. "People will still get killed," she says matter-of-factly. "What we're trying to do is reduce the risk."

In late June, after years of research and consultation, the Alberta government closed dozens of established trails in Canmore's wildlife corridors to humans, including the Upper Benchlands Trail. While some 200 kilometres of trails remain open, and new ones are being built elsewhere, many mountain bikers—and runners and hikers—cried foul. Jorgenson says those who love outdoor recreation "are being forced to bear the brunt of the development" in Canmore that has squeezed hikers, bikers and animals onto the same narrow strips of land. But he says wildlife managers have few options. "People can't have it all. Sacrifices have got to be made, if you want to live here."

ISABELLE DUBÉ's funeral in the ballroom of Canmore's Radisson Hotel on June 10 was a four-hour, standing-room-only celebration of her life, attended by more than 500 people. A religious service, personal tributes and a slide show set to music painted the dark-haired beauty as a kind of Superwoman: tough, strong, determined and stubborn; an ardent snowboarder, rock climber and mountain biker; a proud Francophone; a devoted mother; a fierce competitor; a passionate practitioner of *joie de vivre*; a great cook; an adrenalin junkie who always seemed high on life. "She did in 36 years what most people will never do in a lifetime," one friend told the crowd. Isabelle was laid to rest in the Canmore cemetery, under sunny skies, just down the road from her home.

THERE WAS no funeral for Bear 99. At the Edmonton lab, his skull and testes were severed from his body for research, and on Friday, June 10, or maybe the following Monday—no one is sure—the remains of his carcass, including his dark brown hide, were incinerated. A few days later, the ashes of Bear 99 were dumped in a city landfill site.

HAMMERING
AWAY AT ETERNITY

DANIEL WOOD

JANUARY/FEBRUARY 2002

AS THE BEAVER floatplane descends towards the sparsely forested muskeg, I try to compare the landscape below to the navigational chart the pilot has just handed me. But near treeline in the Northwest Territories, orientation isn't easy. The earth here is amphibious—half land and half water, a featureless expanse of black spruce and bogs that, based on appearances, seems to contain no past and no future. There is only the engine's guttural drone and the altimeter slowly unspooling.

The plane's compass is set for Lat. 65° 10′30″ N and Long. 115° 30′30″ W. I scan the ground. Low drumlins of granite, snaking eskers, tannin-filled ponds, amoeba-shaped lakes, a brown burn where a forest fire once passed... but the thing we're looking for is so obscure, it seems to have vanished amid the sub-arctic vastness. Somewhere below is a place I've been heading since I heard my brother was dying of leukemia and I began seeking a talisman to protect him from an unpleasant future. It's a place that those who know about want to visit because of its cosmologic importance. It is, in Biblical terms, the place God created on the Third Day. Recently discovered on a small unnamed island in an unnamed lake 300 kilometres north of Yellowknife, on a seemingly insignificant glacier-scoured outcrop of Canadian Shield, the Acasta Gneiss lies somewhere below. At 4.03 billion years, it dates to the beginning of time. It is the oldest rock on Earth. To hold a piece of it, as I'd planned to do for my brother, is to glimpse eternity. It would be the Alpha to his Omega. Brotherwise, it was—among limited options—the best I could do.

WHEN THE 17th-century Irish bishop James Ussher announced that the world began in 4004 BC—at sunset on Saturday, October 22, to be exact—no one laughed. His assessment, based on scrupulous counting of Biblical generations, was taken as gospel for centuries and shapes the view of fundamentalist Christians to this day. But the earth's longevity has undergone some serious re-evaluations since Ussher's calculation. Time has made a great leap backward in recent decades, even as I and other baby boomers have faced the relentless tick-tick-tocking of oncoming middle age. Oblivion beckons. Time becomes an expletive. I find my bathroom shelves, like those of millions of others, slowly filling with pills and ointments. I pursue my muse, eat more fish, whistle past the graveyard. Time's arrow is, I know, pointed at me. If I can't avoid the hit, can I find some place to stand that will provide a solid perspective on Beginnings and Ends?

The Beaver pilot is now looking for such a place, and, as he makes clear with a circling gesture, I'm of no help: I'm holding the map upside down.

"Know where we're going?" he asks me.

"No. Don't you?"

"Not really."

Over my shoulder I see Don Davis, a geophysicist from Toronto's Royal Ontario Museum, press his forehead to the window. *The pilot doesn't know where he's going?* All I know is this: we're north of Yellowknife, almost halfway to the Arctic Ocean, somewhere this side of worried.

The pilot notices my expression, then points at the map. "Little Crapeau Lake."

"*Crapeau?*"

He nods. "Yeh, *Crapeau.* The Acasta Gneiss. It's right near Little *Crapeau.*"

We exchange stupid grins.

I read the map: Grizzly Lake. Brown Water Lake. Black Lichen Lake. And just as my eyes hit Little Crapeau Lake, Davis calls out, "There it is." We all look to the left below: a peninsula on a small, muskeg-covered island with two back-to-back crescent beaches bracketing a tiny, silver shed.

The floatplane descends until its racing shadow meets its pontoons. With boots and gear held high and pant legs rolled, we wade ashore through icy water. In all likelihood, the pilot informs me, we are the only people to visit the site this year. Fresh tracks of a grizzly crater the sand. But there's no bear. The island's reception committee is, however, there in force. Within a few minutes, any exposed skin has worked its delective power on hundreds of mosquitoes and black flies that attack with a fury driven by the apparent year-long drought of human blood. It occurs to me that any hopes I'd had of thinking big metaphysical thoughts at the site of the Acasta Gneiss (pronounced "nice") will be circumscribed by the fact that I'm fresh prey. Bugs are everywhere. The air organic. I take little comfort from my NWT guidebook that reports there has never been a recorded death of a human by *exsanguination*—blood-sucking. I unroll my pant legs. Slap the residual black flies. And walk upon the beach. *I grow old... I grow old... I shall not wear the bottoms of my trousers rolled.*

Offshore to my right are a dozen islets whose jack pines are silhouetted against the low horizon. The arctic sky is as pale as tears. It is a quintessential Canadian Shield vista: sparse and elemental. Had Tom Thomson painted the scene, the trees' branches would be outlined in crimson. Ahead, the island's curving beach ends in a 130-foot bluff. Large glacial erratics, some the size of refrigerators, litter the highest reaches of this ridge. More boulders litter the shoreline below the cliff. To my left, a hundred or so derelict fuel barrels lie scattered in the tangle of dwarf willow and blueberry. It is there on this littoral that the little Geological Survey of Canada (GSC) aluminum silo sits—with spiked, bear-repelling covers over its portholes and a hand-painted wooden sign over its door. The sign reads: "ACASTA CITY HALL. Founded 4.0 Ga."

In geological nomenclature, Ga means *billion years ago*. Ahead of me—where the lower section of the bluff hits lake water and the smoke-grey gneiss becomes visibly banded with whites and pinks—is the exact place where earthly time begins. If shrines were built to eternity, this would be the Mother Church. I resist the temptation to hurry, bushwhacking slowly uphill to a ledge on the low ridgeline as the black flies rise to greet me. Davis, the affable 51-year-old geochronologist who has done the latest laboratory dating of these rocks, is already there, his smile testimony to the moment. He has never been to the site before. The two of us stand and look down at our feet. "The dream of all geologists," he says, toeing the rocks, "is to go back to the beginning." I nod and think of my brother David.

AS A boy, in the company of my brother, I chipped a few of my father's wood chisels trying to find fossils amid the granites of my New England home. I didn't understand—in fact, no one understood then—how rocks tend to lose their history under the combined effects of cataclysmic paleo-asteroid impacts, the recycling of subducting tectonic plates, the upheaval of mountains and their subsequent erosion, and the sheer duration of time. No one knew how to decode the cryptic evidence concealed in the atomic interstices of old, uranium-rich granites. No one knew the Earth's or the universe's age. I collected rocks then—and collect them still—for the pleasure of discovery: the fish-scale sheen of New Hampshire schist; an old beaked brachiopod disinterred from an Iowa road cut; a fern imprint from Nova Scotia. Rocks led me backward—to slobbering cavemen and erupting volcanoes and dinosaurs and whirling proto-solar systems, to things unimaginable and wonderfully grotesque. Had I the aptitude, I would have been a geologist. But math was my nemesis. The thing that stuck, however, was a fascination with Earth's ancient history, what writer John McPhee would call "Deep Time."

It is now known that the Earth and its planetary companions coalesced 4.5 billion years ago out of the inchoate dust and gas and fragmentary planetesimals that were swirling like Saturn's rings around the Sun. Under bombardment from space—including a massive asteroid hit that tore the Moon off the Earth—the early planet was often a place of fiery impacts and magma oceans. When the oceans cooled, they formed a scum of crustal granites that was, in turn, buried beneath the outflow of hundreds of thousands of erupting volcanoes. In geologic terms, this half-billion year period is called, in fact, the Hadean: it was *hell* on Earth. There is no geologic evidence of this today; the rocks are gone, lost forever to time. Earth's Hadean period has been deduced from what now exists—from a half-dozen examples of very ancient, datable granites found in places like Greenland, Antarctica, western Australia and, most importantly, the northwesternmost corner of the Canadian Shield near Great Bear Lake. Elsewhere, the old Shield rocks of central Canada were vulcanized and metamorphosed, eroded and buried, their origins now a confusing dog's breakfast of strata and transformations. But a few outcrops of ancient rock in the vicinity of Little Crapeau Lake have a presbyterian resilience, not dissimilar from that of Canada's founders. They are *obdurate*. They have survived virtually unchanged, in an almost incomprehensible bit of geologic luck, over four billion years of planetary turmoil. They were, scientists now know, the nucleus of the continent, formed deep within the Earth—the original basement rocks upon which all the newer rocks of North America once sat—until tectonic uplift and recent Ice Age glaciation revealed on the surface a tiny bit of Acasta Gneiss.

Which now lies directly under my feet.

I watch as the Beaver takes off to pick up two nearby Canadian geologists who have spent the past days mapping the surrounding land in an effort to determine the stratigraphic pattern of this region's rocks. The plane's drone subsides. I head uphill. Seated alone against a ridgetop boulder, where a cold wind disperses the insects, I put lunch to mouth and shove around, Sisyphus-like, a few obdurate boulders of my own.

A decade ago, I met the white-bearded, 76-year-old Hindu priest Swamiharmjyoti in his austere Kathmandhu lodgings, and he chanted to me in Sanskrit from the pages of his open *Ramayana*. The incense burning on his table dropped grey ashes that spun away into nothingness with the breezes from his window. Because I was in Nepal then to write about the extinction of rhinos and tigers, our conversation was often about time and change. The point he kept returning to—and the point I kept challenging—was that the lives of these endangered animals, like the lives of all sentient things, are really of little consequence. "Our bodies, our actions, will be joined like drops in a mighty ocean," he told me with a shrug of calm acceptance. "Everything goes. The plants, the trees, the animals, the humans. Nothing lasts. Look at the leaves out there. They're dancing." And the holy man wiggled his fingertips together in comic illustration. "Life's all a dance. You, me, everyone, every creature... *dancing*—in and out of time." He'd wagged his head in that meaningful side-to-side movement of South Asia that indicates acceptance. But not being a Hindu or a Buddhist, I knew that my Western, linear mind could not easily encompass the cyclical, Eastern Wheel of Life.

Can a member of the Boomer Now Generation find solace in timelessness and reincarnation? Can an old rock bring comfort? Does *anything* matter? As I sit on the ridgetop, I can feel the philosophic boulder slip from my grasp and begin its roll downhill towards existentialism. If I couldn't save my brother, how am I going to save myself? The wind subsides on the little island, the mosquitoes come back and I have something more tangible to fight with.

From my vantage point, the emptiness of the surrounding land only compounds my sense of detachment from mundane affairs. On the lichen-covered bedrock beneath me are striations and chattermarks and polished grooves inflicted on the gneiss by the movement of the two-kilometre-thick Pleistocene glaciers, now gone. After the glaciers departed 9,000 years ago, sabre-toothed tigers and woolly rhinos walked the land here. Gone, too. *Kaput*. Extinct. Joined in the mighty ocean of time. Over 7,000 years ago, paleo-indians, moving southward across the Canadian Shield, left the hearths of 105 campfires in the Acasta River Valley near here. They did not stay. In fact, in the surrounding region—a place with permafrost 165 feet deep and winter temperatures of −50°C—lives no one: no human, no habitation within 10,000 square kilometres. Today, the only people who even visit this region are a single Dene trapper and a few geologists, some searching for diamonds or mapping, and others— I've been told—participants in ongoing Bre-X-style gold-mining scams.

The discovery and the ensuing conflicts over the Acasta Gneiss make for one of those arctic tales that is a confection of northern absurdity and low drama. This is what happened. In 1983, GSC field scientist Janet King camped on the unnamed island in the unnamed lake and removed a few rock samples, believing they might be part of the original 2.5-billion-year-old core of the Canadian Shield. Four years later, alerted by King's initial interest, American geophysicist Sam Bowring removed some more rocks from the site and eventually shipped them to Australia for dating of the ultra-stable zircon crystals embedded in the gneiss. (The steady decay of uranium to lead within the crystals forms a precise isotopic clock.) Using a newly developed device called the Sensitive High-Resolution Ion Micro Probe, or SHRIMP, the Australian experts found—to the amazement of everyone—that the Acasta Gneiss zircons were 3.96 billion years old, over 200 million years older than anything previously dated elsewhere on Earth. (With my lifelong interest in old rocks, I still have a yellowing newspaper clipping, datelined October 6, 1989, that reports the discovery.)

Suddenly, around Yellowknife, the Acasta Gneiss was news. People wanted a chip off The Old Block. Bearded prospector Walt Humphries, then 42 and never a slacker when it comes to opportunity, chartered a ski-equipped plane seven weeks after the announcement, flew north from Yellowknife, landed in −35°C temperatures on the frozen lake, pounded four stakes through the two-foot-deep snow, and claimed the entire 82-hectare island as his mining property. Within the following year, he and two partners had dynamited and removed 8.5 tonnes of Acasta Gneiss from the lowest section of fallen boulders along the island's eastern cliff face.

Humphries gave pieces away as souvenirs and sold other chunks to rock collectors by mail order—200 grams for $19.95. He got it listed in the *Guinness Book of Records* and tried to interest others in Yellowknife in forming a company to market the Acasta Gneiss internationally. After all, he argued, someone had gotten rich selling Pet Rocks. But he wasn't prepared for the resistance of government bureaucrats and scientists, who'd been caught off-guard by Humphries' cheeky style. The local officials tried to shut him down. The place was a quarry, not a mine, they said. He'd filled out the wrong papers. Anyway, the place should be preserved. It's historic. Litigation was threatened. If the government had wanted to protect the site, Humphries countered, people should have acted. *They didn't act. I did. Until the government reimburses me for my investments, it's mine to mine.* This fight went on for a couple of years. Gradually,

Humphries lost interest in his project; it never turned a profit. The Acasta Gneiss became a liability. In his basement in Yellowknife, he has a box-ful of dusty mementos—small pieces of the Gneiss he'd glued onto little wooden plaques years ago—with labels that read: "The Oldest Known Rock in the World."

It was at this time—five years ago—I heard that, despite radiation and chemotherapy and a bone-marrow transplant, my brother was dying of leukemia. And I began thinking of what to say and what to do to help him face the abyss opening before him. I'd just finished writing a book on the triple intersection of nature, science and religion, and had, during my research, acquired from a geologist in Yellowknife a baseball-sized chunk of Acasta Gneiss. It is charcoal grey and banded in creamy stripes and, held in a certain light, sparkles with tiny zircon crystals. I've always liked the idea that when people die and the gases they've absorbed through breathing and eating are finally released, what remains—the charcoal-grey ashes for the urn—are the same 14 minerals from which all life is formed. Nothing more; nothing less. In time, the cycle of earth to ashes to dust becomes reversed as new life is reconfigured from the atoms that never die. In that way, we are—I realized—all related to the Acasta Gneiss. We are all descended from stardust. So, I took out my old Est-wing geology hammer, put the chunk of Gneiss on my concrete back step and swung at it. Sparks flew. My hammer bounced as if I'd struck steel. I swung a second time. The pointy adze-end of my hammer recoiled so fast, I nearly performed a do-it-yourself lobotomy on my forebrain. *Jeez,* I thought. *It's a fuckin' hard rock.* I swung again and again, until—amid mounting impatience and a shower of sparks—a golfball-sized piece flew off. I felt relieved, almost happy. It would be the talisman I'd give my brother... when the time came.

MY REFLECTIONS on the series of events that had brought me to this remote hilltop in the Northwest Territories are interrupted by the drone of the Beaver floatplane, returning to the island with its two new passengers. The first person to wade ashore is John Ketchum, a researcher at the Royal Ontario Museum's geochronology lab. He's here to collect a 220-pound piece of the Gneiss for display at the museum. The second is

Wouter Bleeker, a thoughtful GSC research geologist and one of Canada's leading experts on Precambrian rocks. For seven years, the 42-year-old Bleeker has traipsed—often alone—across the muskeg south of Great Bear Lake, collecting specimens, mapping the outcrops, revelling in the isolation—the silence—of his months in the wilderness. Herds of caribou pass. Clouds drift. Fish jump. And at this latitude, summer days linger past midnight. To ward off occasional grizzlies, he carries what he calls a "full metal jacket"—bear spray, bear bangers and a loaded shotgun. On daily 15- to 20-kilometre treks from his field camps, he reads below his feet the earliest history of the Earth. By learning about these rocks, he—like others in his field—is coming to a clearer understanding of how the Earth, the solar system and the universe were formed.

As the geologists and I hike upward from the beach to the low bluff, storm clouds are gathering to the northwest. The wind has turned, the mosquitoes have dispersed and Bleeker pauses to unfurl his maps and give his visitors a quick orientation. Here, he says, pointing to an aerial photo, is where we are, and here, he says, pointing at a well-annotated, transparent overlay, is the area's stratigraphy. A thin crescent of colour-coded green, drawn by Bleeker on the transparency and not much bigger than a fingernail paring, shows the location of the island's outcrop of Acasta Gneiss. The green appears a couple of more times to the immediate north and south, but—in total—the surface area of the world's oldest rock is probably no more than a few hectares. The history of early Earth currently balances on these insignificant slivers. From the low hilltop, I can see *all* the Acasta Gneiss.

Rain threatens, and the group hikes northeast, gradually descending through boot-sucking muskeg and stunted spruce towards the little lakeshore quarry that Humphries blasted, the exact site where the oldest rock was found. At water's edge, balancing on fallen boulders, we turn and examine the cliff face. Fireweed crowds the crevices. Grey and orange lichens, growing in blobby, protoplasmic shapes, cover the exposed vertical surfaces. The geologists smile and touch the rock as if it were braille and the contorted bands of feldspar and quartz running through the cliff were legible. *They can read the rock,* I think. *But I'm a journalist, a professional intruder. I don't know the language here.* I take out my geology hammer, stoop, and pound a boulder in hopes of removing a pocket-sized specimen for myself. But my hammer recoils amid sparks, just as it had years earlier. I feel slightly foolish. I've travelled 2,500 kilometres—three planes and two days north—to be here. I've got, as Robert Frost said, promises to keep. A friend is turning 60; he wants a piece. A writer from Winnipeg phones after hearing of my destination: could I bring back some for him? My younger brother e-mails to remind me that I've pledged him a piece, too. Swing, clang. Swing, clang. Didn't Leonard Cohen say there is a crack in everything? The rock resists my attack. I wonder if anyone behind my back is watching as I hammer without success. I feel like a man having an argument with God.

WHEN I got the phone call from my mother telling me that my brother David had abandoned all treatments and had decided to die, I could hear the urgency in her voice. *Come quick,* it had said. I checked flights to North Carolina and packed the little piece of Acasta Gneiss I'd broken off years earlier and began rehearsing what I knew would be hard to say. I imagined placing the rock in my brother's hand and telling him about its unspeakable age, its durability, its capacity to link those who hold it with things so fundamental that words fail and consolation seems almost irrelevant. I would promise him that it would go with him wherever he goes. I knew he would understand. But the next morning, I got a second call: my brother had suddenly died. I was—I realized at that moment—reconciled to his departure, but not to its abruptness.

He never got to hear the story of his talisman or receive its protection.

WITH MY frustration getting the better of my ambition at the Acasta Gneiss site, I holster my geology hammer and begin scavenging smaller hunks of quarry debris underfoot. However, in the lee of the cliff—out of the wind—the mosquitoes have found opportunity, too. They dance like a horde of petulant Greek Furies. They buzz. They bite. To them, I'm lunch. *You go to the Oracle and seek guidance and the Oracle is impenetrable, its secret protected by talismanic mosquitoes. So? So? Get used to it. That's life.* Yes, it seems about right. Free of any hope of having an epiphany, I turn my attention to practicalities: collecting some of the rocks that mark the beginning of time. Amid spitting rain, I hurriedly fill my daypack and jacket pockets—like some mumbling, gold-crazed, bandy-legged Yukon moiler who has just figured out his little patch of blasted muskeg is full of nuggets. The plane will be leaving soon. *Tempus fugit.*

To mediaeval Christians, time was divine. The calculations of its hours and holy days were the task of *computators*—time reckoners—who alone were permitted to understand God's celestial clockworks. Time was sacred, a matter for priests. In 1625, Bishop Ussher established that Earthwise, the world began with The Word—in 4004 BC. (In the Bible, in fact, the initial 11 verses of Genesis—all of 138 words—cover the first four billion years of the planet's actual geologic history.) Over the centuries since Ussher, time's duration has moved backward in exponential leaps. Darwin announced, just 140 years ago, that the Earth was 100 million years old, a suggestion that provoked ridicule from pulpits around the world. His successors allowed the Earth could be 200 million years old, maybe more. More apostasy; more damnation. With the discovery of datable fossils, time's priestly computators became 19th-century geologists. Then—with isotopes—20th-century geophysicists. Throughout the last 50 years, the Earth's beginnings have gradually disappeared into infinity—as hundreds of millions became billions—like the view down the wrong end of a telescope. The counting has, for the time-being at least, stopped at the Acasta Gneiss.

With pockets and backpacks bulging, the geologists and I return to the tethered floatplane. As the booty of those departing is hoisted into the fuselage, Bleeker and I have a few minutes to reflect. He is, by profession, skeptical of applying meanings to objects, he tells me. That's romantic. A rock's a rock. Even if it's ancient. New Age mysticism leaves him cold. But he allows that the age of the Acasta Gneiss *does* put things in perspective. "We're just a cosmic blip," he says of individuals and humanity. "We're just temporary residents of Earth. We're caretakers. If we do a good job, we may be around for a while. If we screw up…" And he shrugs.

The storm is moving in, and we take off into the buckshot of cold rain. Winter is descending across the Canadian Shield. The shoreline willows are turning jasmine. The plane banks south, and I catch a glimpse of the island below before it is erased in scudding clouds. Yes, I'd waited too long to give my brother his talisman. He never got to feel the tactile pressure of the rock. He never got to hold eternity. But I have the consolation that—within his urn now, along with the grey ashes—is the little piece of Acasta Gneiss that I'd meant to hand him. Together, they are travelling in time. And in my bulging jacket pockets as the plane climbs, are my *memento mori*, their isotopic clocks silently ticking out the duration of eternity. They are proof I tried to understand.

CONTRIBUTORS

MARK ANDERSON is an Ottawa-based freelance writer and part-time fishing guide. He contributes regularly to Canadian magazines, among them *explore, Outdoor Canada* and *National Post Business.*

LESLIE ANTHONY's "Confessions of a Herpetologist" was nominated for a 2003 National Magazine Award. He is currently writing a book about his adventures in the profession of herpetology.

IAN BROWN has won five Gold National Magazine Awards and two National Newspaper Awards. He is the author of *Man Overboard* and the editor of the recently published anthology, *What I Meant to Say: The Private Lives of Men.*

ROSS CROCKFORD is a freelance writer living on Vancouver Island and the author of *Victoria: The Unknown City.* "What Has Two Legs, 122 Teeth and Goes 80 Miles an Hour?" received a Silver National Magazine Award for 2002.

JILL FRAYNE lives on a bush property at the top of Algonquin Park in Ontario. Her travel memoir, *Starting Out in the Afternoon,* was published in 2003. "Into the Heart of Winter" was nominated for a 2003 National Magazine Award.

WAYNE GRADY is the author of nine books of nonfiction, including *Tree: A Life Story*, co-written with David Suzuki. Between 2001 and 2003, he wrote the "Biologic" column for *explore*; an updated collection of his columns has been published under the title *Bringing Back the Dodo*.

BRUCE GRIERSON, an award-winning magazine journalist based in Vancouver, writes mostly about eccentric human behaviour—a large subject. He is completing a book on mid-life reversals.

ADAM KILLICK is the author of *Racing the White Silence: On the Trail of the Yukon Quest*. "So This Is What It's Like to Sail through a Hurricane" won a Gold National Magazine Award for 2003.

JERRY KOBALENKO is a freelance writer and photographer and the author of *The Horizontal Everest: Extreme Journeys on Ellesmere Island*. "Gruelling, on a Summer Afternoon" was nominated for a 2002 National Magazine Award.

DAVID LEACH is an assistant professor in the Writing Department at the University of Victoria. "¿Por Favor, Señor, Dondé Esta el Singletrack?" received a National Magazine Award nomination for 2004.

JAKE MacDONALD is a freelance writer living in Winnipeg. He is the author of several books, including *With the Boys: Field Notes on Being a Guy*. "Some Funny Things Happened on the Way to the Caribou" was nominated for a 2001 National Magazine Award.

J.B. MacKINNON is a senior contributing editor with *explore*. Two of his pieces for the magazine, including "Behind the Grass Curtain," have won Gold National Magazine Awards for travel writing. His first book, *Dead Man in Paradise*, was published in 2005.

CHRISTIE McLAREN, formerly a reporter for the *Globe and Mail*, writes on a diverse range of topics but specializes in science, the environment and public policy. She lives in Canmore, Alberta.

CHARLES MONTGOMERY is the author of *The Last Heathen: Encounters with Ghosts and Ancestors in Melanesia*, winner of the 2005 Charles Taylor Prize for Literary Non-fiction. "Searching for Big Man Magik" received a Silver National Magazine award for 2004.

ANDREW NIKIFORUK is a Calgary-based journalist and author and the winner of seven National Magazine Awards and the 2002 Governor

General's Literary Award for Nonfiction for his book, *Saboteurs: Wiebo Ludwig's War Against Big Oil*. "The Big Melt" received a 2004 National Magazine Award nomination.

GEOFF POWTER, one of Canada's most experienced climbers, is the editor of the *Canadian Alpine Journal* and the president of the Canadian Himalayan Foundation. "The Happy, Tormented Life of a Mountain Legend" won a Gold National Magazine Award for 2002.

BRUCE RAMSAY is a writer living in Calgary. "Out of the Hole" was nominated for a 2002 National Magazine Award.

MIKE RANDOLPH is *explore*'s editor-at-large. He has received more than 20 National Magazine Award nominations.

MARK REYNOLDS is a Montreal-based writer and editor. "A Knight's Trail" was nominated for a 2003 National Magazine Award.

MARK SCHATZKER is a regular and award-winning contributor to *explore* who also writes for *Toro*, *Condé Nast Traveler* and *Slate*.

ALISA SMITH is a freelance writer living in Vancouver and a contributor to several major Canadian magazines. She spends part of each year at her remote cabin in northern British Columbia.

ANDREW STRUTHERS is a filmmaker and the author of two books, most recently *The Last Voyage of the Loch Ryan*. "The Mystery of the Monolith" won a Silver National Magazine Award for 2004.

DANIEL WOOD is the author of 15 books and has written for publications such as GEO, *Islands* and *Discovery*. He has received more than 30 awards for his writing, including both a Gold and a Silver National Magazine Award for "Hammering Away at Eternity."

DAVID ZIMMER is a freelance writer living near Huntsville, Ontario. "Don't Cry for Us, Argentina" was nominated for a 2004 National Magazine Award.